MODERN MARKETING RESEARCH

Prof. M. N. MISHRA
M.Com., Ph.D., D.Litt.

Head & Dean
Faculty of Commerce,
Banaras Hindu University,
Varanasi-221 005.

Himalaya Publishing House
ISO 9001:2015 CERTIFIED

First Edition : 1998
Reprint : 1999
Reprint : 2000, 2003, 2005, 2008, 2013
Reprint : 2015, 2021
Reprint : 2023

Published by : Mrs. Meena Pandey
for **HIMALAYA PUBLISHING HOUSE PVT. LTD.,**
"Ramdoot", Dr. Bhalerao Marg, Girgaon, Mumbai - 400 004.
Phone: 022-23860170/23863863, **Fax:** 022-23877178
E-mail: himpub@bharatmail.co.in; **Website:** www.himpub.com

Branch Offices :

New Delhi : "Pooja Apartments", 4-B, Murari Lal Street, Ansari Road, Darya Ganj, New Delhi - 110 002. Phone: 011-23270392, 23278631; Fax: 011-23256286

Nagpur : Kundanlal Chandak Industrial Estate, Ghat Road, Nagpur - 440 018. Phone: 0712-2738731, 2721216

Bengaluru : Plot No. 91-33, 2nd Main Road Seshadripuram, Behind Nataraja Theatre, Bengaluru - 560020.
Phone: 080-41138821, Mobile: 09379847017, 09379847005.

Hyderabad : No. 3-4-184, Lingampally, Besides Raghavendra Swamy Matham, Kachiguda, Hyderabad - 500 027. Phone: 040-27560041, 27550139

Chennai : No. 34/44, Motilal Street, T. Nagar, Chennai - 600 017. Mobile: 09380460419

Pune : First Floor, "Laksha" Apartment, No. 527, Mehunpura, Shaniwarpeth (Near Prabhat Theatre), Pune - 411 030.
Phone: 020-24496323, 24496333; Mobile: 09370579333

Cuttack : Plot No 5F-755/4, Sector-9, CDA Market Nagar, Cuttack - 753 014, Odisha. Mobile: 09338746007

Kolkata : 3, S.M. Bose Road, Near Gate No. 5, Agarpara Railway Station, North 24 Parganas, West Bengal - 700109. Mobile: 09674536325

Printed at : M/s Sri Sai Art Printer, Hyderabad. On behalf of HPH.

Dedicated to
My Highly Respected Father
SHRI PRATAP NARAYANJI MISHRA

PREFACE

Marketing Research has become an important tool of sound management. Marketing information based on marketing research has served the basic purpose of marketing management. Nowadays, no marketing management can succeed without the uses of marketing research. The executives, the researchers, the academicians and other interested persons are using the techniques of marketing research. Identification of the problems, research-design, determining the sources of data, designing the sample and collection of primary data, analysis and interpretation of data, preparing the research report and recommendations are important components of marketing research which are being used presently by all sound organisations.

The present book 'Modern Marketing Research' has been prepared considering the needs of executives, students and teachers in the areas of marketing management. The book consists of eighteen chapters devoted to the techniques of marketing research. Each chapter discusses the respective subjects in detail and in comprehensive manner. The book provides complete insights into and knowledge of the tools of marketing research. It has been designed to offer adequate materials to postgraduate and research students. The executives can frame the researches for solving the marketing problems. They can organise the researches effectively with application of the tools and techniques described in the book. The teachers can acquire all the teaching materials at a place in the present book. Some specialised topics are given for advanced research and analysts. The book may be used by consultants to solve the problems of marketing management. Suitable examples of Indian conditions are given at appropriate places.

I would appreciate comments and suggestions made by readers for the improvement of the book.

4, Brahmanand Nagar,
Extension I
Durgakund,
Varanasi-221 005.

M. N. MISHRA

CONTENTS

CHAPTER 1
INTRODUCTION TO MARKETING RESEARCH 1 — 21

1. Marketing Research Defined
2. Nature
3. Characteristics
4. Scope
5. Uses
6. Limitations

CHAPTER 2
ORGANISATION OF MARKETING RESEARCH 22 — 38

1. Form of Marketing Research Organisation
2. Factors Affecting Organisation
3. Scientific Method and Research Design
4. Types of Marketing Research

CHAPTER 3
MARKETING RESEARCH PROCESS 39 — 66

1. Identification of Problems
2. Research Design
3. Determining Sources of Information and Data
4. Sample Design
5. Analysis and Interpretation of Data
6. Research Report
7. Recommendation Follow up
8. Selecting Research Project
   (i) Cost and Value Method
   (ii) Decision Theory
   (iii) Decision Tree
   (iv) Bayesian Analysis

CHAPTER 4
RESEARCH DESIGN 67 — 91

1. Exploratory Research
   (i) Literature Search
   (ii) Experience Survey
   (iii) Case Study
2. Conclusive Research
   (i) Descriptive Research Design
   (ii) Experimental Research
3. Specific Experimental Designs

CHAPTER 5
DETERMINING SOURCES OF DATA 92 — 103

1. Sources of Data
   (i) Secondary Data
   (ii) Primary Data
2. Secondary Data
   (i) Internal
   (ii) External Data
3. Advantages of Secondary Data
4. Disadvantages of Secondary Data

CHAPTER 6
COLLECTION OF PRIMARY DATA 104 — 119

1. Primary Data Objectives
2. Types of Primary Data
3. Sources of Data
4. Methods of Data Collection
5. Media of Communication
6. Formulating the Plan of Primary Data Collection

CHAPTER 7
DATA COLLECTION FORMS 120 — 134

1. Questionnaire Defined
2. Functions of Questionnaire
3. Importance of Questionnaire
4. Assumption of Questionnaire
5. Steps for Preparing Questionnaire

CHAPTER 8
ATTITUDE MEASUREMENT 135 — 151

1. Components of Attitude
2. Determinants of Attitude State
3. Attitudes and Marketing
4. Attitude Measuring Methods

CHAPTER 9
SAMPLING PROCEDURES 152 — 169

1. Introduction
2. Sampling Process
3. Problems Associated with Sampling
4. Sampling Methods
   (i) Non-probability Methods
   (ii) Probability Methods

CHAPTER 10
SAMPLE SIZE 170 — 178

1. Determining Sample Size (Means)
2. Determining Sample Size (Proportions)
3. Stratified Sample Size
4. Sample Size in Non-probability
5. Other Determinants of Sample Size

CHAPTER 11
DATA COLLECTION AND FIELD FORCE 179 — 191

1. Task and Functions
2. Error Sources
   (i) Non-sampling errors
3. Sampling errors
4. Managing the Field Work

CHAPTER 12
PROCESSING OF DATA 192 — 203

1. Preparing Raw Data
2. Editing
3. Coding
4. Tabulation
5. Summary of Data

CHAPTER 13
DATA ANALYSIS: PRELIMINARY CONSIDERATIONS 204 — 218

1. Choice of Analysis Technique
2. Factors Deciding Appropriate Technique
3. Nature of Analysis and Interpretation
4. Summarising the Data
5. Overview of the Procedure

CHAPTER 14
TEST OF SIGNIFICANCE 219 — 268

1. Sampling Statistics
2. Difference between Sets of Data
3. General Hypotheses Testing Procedure
4. Non-parametric Statistics
5. Parametric Statistics

CHAPTER 15
ANALYSIS OF ASSOCIATIONS 269 — 292

1. Assumptions
2. Measuring Associations (Dependence)
3. Measuring Associations (Interdependence)

CHAPTER 16
ANALYSIS OF EXPERIMENTS 293 — 310

1. Randomised Experiments
2. Latin Square Design
3. Factorial Design
4. Analysis of Covariance

CHAPTER 17
PREPARATION OF RESEARCH REPORT 311 — 325

1. Role of Report
2. Types of Report
3. Content of Report
4. Principles of Report Preparation
5. Devices
6. Presentation and Communication
7. Follow-Through

CHAPTER 18
APPLICATION OF MARKETING RESEARCH IN INDIA 326 — 348

1. Introduction
2. Marketing Information System
3. Selected Applications
4. Marketing Research in India
5. Future of Marketing Research

CHAPTER 1

INTRODUCTION TO MARKETING RESEARCH

1. MARKETING RESEARCH DEFINED
2. NATURE
3. CHARACTERISTICS
4. SCOPE
5. USES AND LIMITATIONS
6. HISTORICAL DEVELOPMENT

INTRODUCTION TO MARKETING RESEARCH

The management decision process has become complex and requires an effective and foolproof management information system. This is specially true for a firm's marketing management because it is located at the interface between a firm and the customers of a firm. The production, finance and personnel activities are guided at the marketing situations and systems. The changing characters of markets, growing environmental impacts, emergence of consumerism, unknown competitions, volatility of international political relationships, changing production functions, and growing technology have given rise to the growing difficulties of making efficient marketing decisions. For sound marketing decisions, the management must be equipped with the latest information of the various variables as disclosed above. Marketing research has come to their rescue to provide the correct and latest information for arriving at sound marketing decisions. During the years of growing complexities, the management needs more and more rigorous marketing information to reduce the uncertainties involved in introducing new products and penetrating a new market. Marketing research has, today, become an important component of the marketing information system to manage all areas of management in general and to marketing management in particular.

1. Marketing Research Defined

To understand marketing research, the phrase should be understood separately. Marketing has been an important discipline of management whereby we manage the functions using marketing mix, i.e., product, price, promotion and distribution.

"Marketing, is defined, as the managerial process by which products are matched with markets and through which the consumer is enabled to use or enjoy the product."[1] Product includes services as well as physical goods. Marketing and production activities are inter-related. Matching products with markets is both a marketing and production problem. They are known as interdependent subsystems.

"Marketing is a social process by which individuals and groups obtain what they need and want through creating and exchanging products and value with others."[2] It is related with need, wants and demands, products, value and satisfaction, exchange and transactions. Marketing management is different from marketing. We are concerned with marketing management. "Marketing management is the analysis, planning, implementation and control of programmes designed to create, build and maintain beneficial exchanges and relationships with target markets for the purpose of achieving organisational objectives."[3] Managing marketing resources such as advertising, sales people and price-cut are the important scope of marketing management. The American Marketing Association defines marketing as "the performance of business activities that direct the flow of goods and services from producer to consumer or user." It reveals that the marketing management directs the flow of goods and services towards the consumers. It may, therefore, be called an ongoing or continuous process of defining, anticipating and creating customer needs and

1. Edward W. Cundiff, Richard R. Still and Norman A.P. Govoni: *Fundamentals of Modern Marketing,* Prentice Hall of India, 1985, p.5
2. Philip Kotler, *Marketing Management,* Prentice Hall of India, 1985, p. 4.
3. Philip Kotler, *Marketing Management,* Prentice Hall of India, 1985, p. 4.

wants and organising all the resources of the enterprise to satisfy customer demand. According to Hansen, "Marketing is the process of discovering and translating consumer needs and wants into product and service specification, creating demand for these products and services." Marketing management therefore, includes marketing mix, i.e., price, product, promotion and place to use the resources for the benefits of the firm or organisation.

Research

Research can be defined as "Logical and systematised application of the fundamentals of science to the general and overall questions of a study, and scientific techniques which provide precise tools, specific procedures and technical, rather than philosophical means for getting and ordering the data prior to their logical and manipulation."[4] Research seeks to find explanations to unexplained social phenomena to clarify doubtful and correct the misconceived facts of social life.

Research represents "a systematic method of exploring actual persons and groups, focused primarily on their experience within their social worlds, inclusive of social attitudes and values, the mode of analysis of these experiences which permit stating proposition in the form."[5] Thus the research can be defined as logical and systematised means or techniques to discover new facts or verify and test old facts, analyse their sequences, inter-relationship and casual explanations which were derived within an appropriate theoretical frame of reference, develop new scientific tools, concepts and theories which would facilitate reliable and valid study of human behaviour. The Encyclopedia of the social sciences has defined, "Social research is a systematic method of exploring, analysing and conceptualising social life in order to extend, correct or verify knowledge, whether that knowledge and in the construction of a theory or in the practice of an art." Marketing research is a social science research and can be defined as discussed above.

Marketing Research

"Marketing research is the systematic gathering, recording and analysing of data about marketing problems to facilitate decision making."[6] The marketing research is a tool of marketing information system which has become an important function of management. "Marketing research is the systematic design, collection, analysis and reporting of data and findings relevant to a specific marketing situation facing the company."[7] It shows that marketing research is required to solve specific problems, but it is more than that, since now it is considered a significant part of marketing information system which has been a continuous aspect of management. The American Marketing Association has defined marketing research as the "systematic gathering, recording and analysing of data about problems relating to the marketing of goods and services."[8] It emphasises on the systematic research rather than convenient research. The data are objectively and accurately gathered, recorded and analysed. There is no place for a pre-conceived view, "The systematic planning, gathering, recording, analysing and interpreting of data for application to specific

4. W.J. Goodes and Paul K. Hatt, *Methods in Social Research,* McGraw Hill Book Company, 1952, pp. 5-6.
5. Cohen and Nagel, *An Introduction to Logic and Scientific Method,* Harcourt Brace & Wood, 1934, p. 5.
6. Edward W. Cundiff, Richard, R. Still and Norman A.P. Govani, *Op. cit.,* p. 100.
7. Philip Kotler, *Marketing Management,* Prentice Hall of India, 1985, p. 194.
8. Gilbert A. Churchill, Jr., *Marketing Research,* The Dryden Press, Illionois, 1979, p. 7.

marketing decisions."[9] It is an improvement over the previous definition as it defines the scope of the research. The essential of marketing research is to provide information which will facilitate the identification of an opportunity or problem situation and to assist managers in arriving at the best possible decisions when such situations are encountered. It has become a constant source of solving all sorts of problems facing the management. "Marketing research is the systematic and objective research for an analysis of information relevant to the identification and solution of any problem in the field of marketing."[10] Marketing research in a broader term is the application of scientific method to marketing, i.e., the objective gathering and analysis of information. Marketing management needs essential information regarding products, prices, market conditions of demand and supply, consumer needs and desires, selling methods, physical flow of goods, competitive decisions, external marketing environment and other factors of marketing management. Marketing research has proved an essential tool to meet all the needs of marketing management. Marketing research therefore is the scientific and controlled process of gathering and analysis of marketing information to meet the needs of marketing management. It is a scientific study of a continuing basis of present and potential markets and of marketing operations. It is a science and an art consisting of systematic collection, recording and analysis of the facts and figures from the market in regard to the problem in marketing of goods and services. Glasser has defined it as, "Marketing research is the application of scientific methods to the study of the factors that affect buying decisions in a given market and the profitability of the business concerned."

Wentz defines it as, "Marketing research is the gathering and analysis of information to assist management in making marketing decisions. These decisions involve the manipulation of the firm's pricing, production, distribution and product variables."

Meaning

Marketing research is the collection, analysis and interpretation of facts and figures pertaining to marketing management. The management must exercise a prudent judgement in formulating courses of action based on the above research. Marketing research is the systematic, objective and exhaustive search for and the study of facts relevant to any problem in the field of marketing. Marketing research is considered all pervasive as its utility has been seen in all areas of management. It uses scientific method of gathering, recording, analysing and reporting of facts and figures relating to the flow of goods and services from producers to consumers. It has objectively to solve specific problems or to manage the day-to-day business of the firm. It is applied and related to the present and potential markets, marketing management and other areas of management. Market research does not implement decisions, but helps to take decisions on the basis of research findings. It is not restricted to given types of problems, but is extended to any phase of marketing activities. Marketing research provides intelligence, analysis and information of the marketing mix and its environments. It covers the entire management process and is not concentrated only on the market. The marketing mix e.g., price, product, promotion and distribution are internal factors which are the basis of marketing research. The environments, e.g., economic environment, competitive and technological environment, political and legal environment,

9. David, J. Luck, Hugh, G. Wales, Donald A. Taylor, Ronald Rubin, *Marketing Research*, Prentice Hall of India, 1982, p.6.

10. Paul E. Green and Donald E. Tull, *Research for Marketing Decisions*, 1966, p.2.

cultural and social environment are analysed in the objectivity of intended resources and objectives of firms to find out suitable measures and to manage firms effectively to get the objectives fulfilled.

2. NATURE OF MARKETING RESEARCH

The nature of marketing research is analysed in relation to its objectives.

Objectives: Marketing research as an integral part of the marketing information system is used in the decision-making process.

1. Planning: Marketing research is used for the formulation and evaluation of planning and its components.

2. Minimising Costs: The marketing costs, particularly, selling, advertising, and the promotion and distribution costs can be reduced with the help of marketing research. Research brings market closer to the consumers and reduces several costs of distribution.

3. Problems Solving: The main purpose of marketing research is to solve the problems relating to product, price, promotion, competition and distribution of goods and services. It finds alternative solutions for different problems.

4. Survival and Growth: Marketing research is used for the survival and growth of firms. It assesses competitive strength and policies, estimates potential buying power, a firm's share of the market, and provides suitable information for appropriate decisions. Growth is possible if initiatives are taken to expand markets for which market research is not essential. It helps development and introduction of new products.

5. Assess the Marketing: Marketing research finds out the actual position of marketing and the present trend of management. It assesses the present and probable volume of future sales.

6. Introduction of New Product: Before introducing a new product, the market research is used to find out suitable avenues and place of the new products. It reveals the various opportunities of new markets and reveals the methods to reach the markets.

7. Market-Orientation: The objective of marketing research is to enable the firms to produce the goods and services acceptable to the customers. It sees that the goods and services must reach the market easily, quickly, cheaply and profitably. The right course of action to approach and sustain the market is possible with suitable marketing research.

Marketing research is an integral part of the marketing information system. It is both a science and an art. It is a science because there is systematic application of the principles of research. It is an art because it tells us how to solve day-to-day and specific problems of management, particularly problems of marketing management. The nature of scientific research can be described in the following sentences.

1. Problem Formulation

Marketing research tries to solve problems of marketing management for which formulation of problems is very essential because well defined and formulated problems can be solved very easily and appropriately. Formulation of problems is the first step of marketing research. Unless the problem is well-defined, the cost of information gathering may well exceed the value of the findings. The problem formulation should be neither too broad nor too narrow. The problems may be operating and non-operating.

(i) Operating (Recurring) Problems: The operating or recurring problems may pertain to sales forecasting, sales expenses, sales volume, sales opportunities, sales field, share of market, salesman's performance and so on. Also to problems relating to product-quality, product-line, promotional methods, advertising effectiveness and pricing policies. These problems can be solved by routine types of marketing research.

(ii) Non-operating (Non-recurring) Problems: There may be specific types of marketing research to solve non-operating problems. There may be problems of changes of competitive forces, price changes, sales-policies, consumption pattern, product innovations, and distribution channels. Similarly problems pertaining to a new product or a change in product-lines may come under the non-operating problems for which specific market research is required for effective marketing management.

2. Collecting Marketing Information

The second nature of marketing research is the collection of marketing information. The marketing information may be pertaining to new ideas, fact-finding or testing of certain hypotheses. The data and information may be collected from the survey of individuals, case-study and secondary data

3. Selection of Respondents and Source of Data

Selection of respondents for collection of secondary data is another important nature of marketing research. The respondents are selected on the basis of the objectives of the research. The selected respondents are interviewed and information collected from them. The respondents may be customers, salesmen, wholesalers and retailers depending upon the nature and objectives of the research. The interview may be directive or semi-directive. The objectives of marketing research are influenced by the attitude and capacities of the interviewer. Data collection methods are rapidly changing under the impact of modern telecommunication and electronics.

4. Analysing the Information

In marketing research the analysis of information and data is essential to find out the required information. This is an essential nature of marketing research. The researcher tabulates the data and statistical techniques are used to analyse the data. The success of marketing management depends upon the ability of the marketing manager to evaluate the marketing information. He must be in a position to assess the nature of present and potential consumers, their needs and desires, their buying habits and preferences. The researcher applies advanced statistical techniques and models to discover new findings.

5. Interpretation

The interpretation of marketing information is a significant nature of marketing research. The marketing information is properly interpreted and analysed. The information collected will have to be edited, coded, tabulated and analysed to interpret the facts and figures of the market.

6. Conclusions

The findings of market research are presented in a systematic manner. The market research will be useful only when its reports or conclusions are known to the management.

The researcher has to draw out rational conclusions from the collected data. The logical and rational conclusions of the market research will be useful to the management.

7. Recommendations

Market research recommends some suitable measures to solve problems. It may suggest appropriate steps to be taken to avoid problems. Research is not only connected with the collection and analysis of data, it also predicts the results from a course of action and recommends a suitable course of action to attain the objectives of the management.

3. CHARACTERISTICS OF GOOD MARKETING RESEARCH

Having examined the major nature of marketing research, we highlight the characteristics of good marketing research.

1. Application of Scientific Methods

Marketing research will be useful and effective if scientific methods are applied for collection, analysis and interpretation of data. Mario Bunge has suggested eight steps of scientific methods in research: "(1) Ask well-formulated and likely fruitful questions, (2) Devise hypotheses both grounded and testable to answer the questions, (3) State assumptions, (4) Derive logical consequences of the assumptions, (5) Design techniques to test the assumptions, (6) Test the techniques for relevance and reliability, (7) Execute the tests and interpret their results, (8) Evaluate the truth claims of the assumption and of the techniques."[11] The scientific methods must be utilised for marketing research. It has some criteria to judge its validity on the basis of scientific activities. Freight has suggested five criteria for scientific activities: "Objectivity, reliability, definiteness and preciousness, coherence or systematic structure, comprehensiveness or scope of knowledge."[12]

2. Research Creating

The marketing research is limited not only to mere description of the facts and figures, but goes beyond that to explain the causes and consequences. It suggests some suitable measures to minimise the problems or to avoid the problems. It should create additional facts which have favourable consequences on the market. It develops innovative ways to solve the problems. It is predictive and can, with reasonable certainty, forecast what may occur in future in given circumstances. Market forecast has been a logical outcome of good market research. Correct assumptions with precise information and systematic analysis can predict rightly the various phenomena of the market.

3. Cost and Benefits

The cost of marketing research must not exceed the benefits derived from the use of the findings of marketing research. The cost benefits analysis of various types of marketing research will determine which type of research project should be used to conduct the research for the benefits of marketing management. The expected value of the research is evaluated in the context of the decision-making theory, and the degree of market research is decided accordingly. The value of information and costs uncertainty is balanced to find out good methods of marketing research. It will suggest adoption of a good research design and analytical techniques.

11. Mario Bunge, *Scientific Research,* Vol. 1, p. 8.
12. Herbert Feigl, *The Scientific Outlook, Naturalism and Humanism.* p. 11.

4. Use of Models and Data

Statistical methods are used to analyse the information. Good marketing research uses the statistical bank and model bank. The statistical bank is a collection of statistical procedures for extracting meaningful information from data "and the model bank is a collection of models that will help marketers develop better marketing decisions."[13] The application of models and data makes the marketing research fruitful and purposive research. Marketing management will succeed upon the application of the findings of such good marketing research.

5. Alternative Courses of Action

Sound marketing research finds out several alternative courses of action. The best course of action is applied in marketing management to attain the target. The validity of each course of action is evaluated before its application to marketing management. When a marketing manager chooses courses of action, he can rarely be certain of the consequences of each course of action. Good marketing research comes to his rescue and suggests the best course of action from the angle of the objectivity of the management.

6. Use of Specialist Services

Sound marketing research uses the services of research specialists. The specialists may be from within the business or from outside. The line management has neither sufficient time nor expertise to acquire marketing research. This is the reason, the management employs experts in the area of marketing research for its management decisions. The specialists will use scientific methods in all the areas of marketing management.

The specialists are in a position to study the selling techniques and eliminating the shortage of resources of money, material, market and men. They can suggest appropriate measures to exploit these resources at the optimum level for the benefit of the firm. There is need for constant and regular study of market potential, consumer needs and tastes, production and distribution functions, and promotion and price policy. This is done by specialists in marketing research. Inadequate and inaccurate research may lead to misleading conclusions which may mar the very objective of the marketing research. Researches in the areas of marketing are performance analysis, price analysis, advertising and sales promotion. Distribution strategies and product functions may require specialised knowledge and skills.

7. Precautions in Marketing Research

Sound marketing research makes use of some precautions to make the research findings as fruitful and relevant for market management decisions. The researcher avoids intruding his own bias and asking for irrelevant information. He has to apply different technical knowledge and expertise, spirit of research, relevant sample, right variables, required accuracy in collection, and analysis and interpretation of data. He has to avoid ascribing beliefs and emotions in the procedures, methods and techniques of marketing. The marketing research should be completed dispassionately. Non-committal or wild hunches, risk hypotheses and soft tests should be avoided in good marketing research.

---

13. Philip Kotler, *Marketing Management,* pp. 211-213.

4. SCOPE OF MARKETING RESEARCH

The need of marketing research is felt by marketing managements for different purposes which decide the scope of marketing research. "Marketing research is undertaken to guide managers in their analysis, planning, implementation and control of programmes to satisfy customer and organisational goals."[14] The core functions of management require research for them to be carried out by the specialists to increase efficiency of the management. The scope of marketing research management can be divided into (1) market measurement studies (2) marketing mix studies (3) studies of the competitive situation and (4) studies of uncontrollables.

1. Market Measurement

Market measurement research aims at obtaining information on potential demand and market performance.

(A) Demand Research: This tries to find out how much a particular product can be sold in a given market during a period of time. The research may pertain to the determination of the market potential, measurement of the market potential, short and long range forecasting, and export possibilities in the international market. These relate to market potential and sales potential. Market potential is the maximum possible sales opportunity open to all sellers during a given period of time. Sales potential is the maximum possible sales opportunity open to a specified seller during a given period of time. Thus, sales potential is the share of a particular company in the total market potential. Theoretically the total population may consist of the market potential, but it is only a segment of the population which can form the market potential. It is also known as the size of the market. The buyers' behaviour and attitude are also considered to decide the size of the market. The sales forecasting can help to decide the share of an enterprise in the total market. The sales forecasting is done by using certain techniques of forecasting. The market research will stimulate the taking of appropriate steps to increase the market share of the enterprise.

(B) Market Performance Research: The market performance research is conducted to measure the existing market. The market performance research is helpful in planning overall marketing strategy. It provides insights as to whether a potential market exists. It estimates probable market success. The marketer must have proper evaluation of his market. He may be under a wrong impression that he enjoys a wide market, whereas his share of the market may be limited to particular customers or in particular areas. The market performance research will reveal such misunderstanding and make the marketer aware of the possible decline of the market. The management may find ways and means to expand the existing market and may try to introduce a new product in the market based on the results of market performance. This research will also reveal which group of middlemen and what kind of articles may be promoted in a particular area or in specified time. Similarly he can decide dropping of certain products from specified areas and introducing them to other areas.

(C) Motivation Research: Motivation research studies the buyers' behaviour and attitude to expand the market in a particular place. It studies the psychological and sociological variables affecting buying behaviour. Therefore, psychologists and sociologists may be very useful persons to conduct this research. Such people may be appointed from

14. Gerald Zaltman and Phillip C. Burger, *Marketing Research,* The Dryden Press, Illinois, 1975, p. 8.

the institutions or from within the company. Such types of research are useful to motivate the customers towards the products of the company.

Similarly motivation research is also conducted with businessmen, middlemen, salesmen and other personnel involved in the expansion of the market. It can adequately stimulate the need for taking appropriate steps for removing the defects in their marketing efforts, or can identify opportunities for development. It provides the basis on which marketing efforts can be directed to secure the best possible market results.

2. Marketing Mix Researches

Marketing research can be conducted on every area of the marketing mix, e.g., products, price, promotion and distribution. The various factors, generally controllable, are appraised to reveal the degree of their effectiveness on the above marketing mix. It is frequently essential to appraise the effectiveness of all the promotional factors, sales methods and competition campaigns. Without formal studies, measures to avoid drawbacks may not be correctly and successfully applied to expand the share of the market. The impact of each and every controllable factors can be used by the marketing mix researches which are unfailing instruments to expand the market. They may be product research, price research, promotion research and distribution research.

(A) Product Research

Product research consists of conducting studies on new product acceptance and potential, testing of existing products, packaging research, improvement of present producting new uses for old products. Product research also considers the competitive position of the company's products, pretesting of a new product, customer preference, product elimination, costs and profits of new products and the name of the products.

(i) Product Line Research: This reveals what lines of products should be adopted, what new lines should be added and what existing lines should be dropped. The rapid advancement of technology has opened opportunities for new products, and improvements in the existing ones resulting in the expanded market of new and existing products.

There is a gap between the product line and market acceptability. The product line research will take the producer near to the customers' needs. When production is undertaken in different sizes and colours with various features, it is essential to know the profitability of each line of production, i.e., the size, colour, design, quality etc. The product line research is therefore known as production research. Adjustments in production on the basis of research findings help the enterprise in avoiding losses. The product inter-relationship can be better understood through research, and this assists the manufacturer in securing proper rationalisation. Too many kinds of products may or may not meet the varied needs of the consumers. The product line research of each kind will reveal their acceptability to the consumers. The assessment of demand of each line and follow up action of production will fetch the maximum market to the manufacturer. The cost of distribution, risk of accumulation of unwanted stocks and management of wide varieties can be avoided with the help of product line research. Appropriate changes in production technology has to be made to meet market needs. The product line research has played an increasingly important role in these changes.

The potential product lines are subjected to a screening process, and an unsavoury analysis to eliminate lines showing insufficient promise. In product line research, evaluation of various lines are made in reference to the time required for development, the projected patent position, the capital outlays required, estimates of manufacturing costs, facilities, skills needed, and evaluation of competitors and their products.

(ii) Product Marketing Research: The product marketing research determines consumer requirements to keep abreast of and channelise the product line. The new market, characteristics of existing markets and other market variables are screened and evaluated to find the consumers' requirements. The determination of product characteristics for new and existing products is an interrelated effort between marketing research and product line research. Marketing research is concerned with determining the market requirements for functional and technical changes. Product marketing research is used to design the product.

Consumers' reactions to the products are analysed under product marketing research. the scope of this research varies from a new product to an existing product.

The product must be sound while available in the market. A product technically sound but having only a small or even a non-existent market is not a good proposition. Therefore the market has to be explored before adopting a particular technique of production. Appropriate changes have to be made in the product-line according to the changes in the market which are revealed by the product marketing research.

(B) Price Research

The price research reveals the effective demand at various prices and the corresponding costs of supplying product. Supply-quantities, competitors' reaction at our price-strategies, dealers' behaviours, impact of price-changes on the market, production and distribution costs and prices research. Pricing and establishing of price policies are complicated problems which require a thorough probing of various factors. It is a complex problem which can be solved by specialists. Most of the uncertainties relating to pricing decisions can be reduced to a greater extent with price research. This research includes several forms of price analysis, but practically speaking, studies of price policies, discount structure in relation to the company's techniques and competitors' technique are the main forms of price research. Price research employs several techniques of research such as customer surveys, observational studies and dealer surveys.

(C) Promotion Research

Promotion research includes research pertaining to personal selling, advertising and publicity, sales promotion and public relations. It solves various questions such as what should be the total promotion budget, and how it should be allocated among products and among the various forms of promotion, e.g., advertising, personal selling etc. What specific product attributes and consumer benefits should be featured in promotion form? To what extent sales stimulants such as coupons, premiums, terms and conditions should be used? Which one or a combination of advertising media such as TV, radio, newspapers, magazines, charts etc. would be most suitable for the company? The existing promotion methods are properly assessed and the potential policies are pre-tested before their application to the market.

(i) Advertising Research: The advertising research can be broadly divided into four categories — Cost-benefit Research, Content Research, Media Research and Effectiveness Research.

(a) Advertising Cost-benefit Research: During this age of competition, advertising is becoming a tool with which to beat the competition. But, excessive cost incurred in advertising may not attain its objectives. Unless the cost-benefit research of the advertising is not undertaken the advertising cost may prove to be a wastage of resources. The company may be having its own advertising department or may avail of the services of professional advertisers. The marketing research pertaining to cost-benefit research may guide the company how far expenses should be incurred to desire the desired benefits from advertising. Cost accounts and other sales records have been the main sources of cost-benefit research of advertising.

(b) Advertising Constant Research: This seeks to find out suitable contents for appearing to the people. It has become an important function of communication management whereby suitable forms are decided to appeal to the audience. This research finds out the literary appeal suitable to the population to whom the advertisement is aimed at influencing. Recognition and recall tests, opinion and attitude rating, projective tests and variety of forms of experiments are used to decide suitable contents of advertisements. Content research uncovers new appeals and provides interesting and useful facts to be accepted by the people.

(c) Advertising Media Research: This decides the appropriate media to appeal to the right class of customers. Each media has separate pulling power with different sections of the community. They can be identified on the basis of income groups, sex, age, occupation, education etc. It guides the company in taking a creative approach. It decides how the advertising should be appropriated to newspapers, magazines, television, radio, direct mail advertising and other media.

(d) Advertising Effectiveness Research: Once advertising has been undertaken, it needs testing to determine its effectiveness, i.e., whether it has appealed to the people for whom it is projected or not. It is determined on the basis of reactions of the consumers. The effectiveness is examined in terms of the level of informing, level of persuasion and induced sales. It is an intriguing and challenging task. Experimental techniques of research have proved a useful technique for measuring advertising effectiveness.

(ii) Personal Selling Research: The method of personal selling through salesmen has become an important method of marketing promotion. Personal selling is a means of effective communication between the salesman and the customer. It has enough opportunities of flexibility to suit the requirements of the customers. Its success depends upon the effectiveness of the sales organisation. There is need for the selection, training and personal traits of the salesman. The personal selling research will decide the sales organisation, sales effectiveness, sales, territories, sales-quotas and sales compensation.

(D) Distribution Research

Distribution research reveals the distribution channels, costs of distribution, methods of distribution and the size of the inventory. Marketing research helps remove the gap between consumers and producers through retailers and wholesalers. It will reveal the precise areas of weakness of the flow of goods and services between consumers and producers. It also suggests modifications for getting better results. The distribution research fixes the sales-quota to be attained by the salesmen. It is fixed after realistic analysis of potential sales, demand and competitors' performance. The distribution research may be of two types: *(i)* Distribution channel Research and *(ii)* Location Research.

(i) Distribution Channel Research: The manufacturers have to select a proper channel of distribution of goods and services which may benefit them to the maximum extent and with the help of distribution channel research, it will be possible for them to decide the most suitable channel from the various channels available to them. An important segment of distribution channel research is distribution cost analysis. Studies of dealer costs and profits, store audits, dealer relations and the industry pattern of distribution are several other components of distribution channel research.

(ii) Location Research: Location research is required to determine the optimum location of distribution of products. It may range from local to national and international markets. Population, income, attitudes and desires toward a particular product are the factors to determine the location of distribution. The transportation costs and distribution logistics must also be studied to decide the location. Penetration into new locations and dropping of an old location may be the outcome of location research which studies the quantity of goods shipped, transportation cost per unit, costs of warehousing, times of delivery and service, using conditions of the political climate and other intangible considerations.

(E) Policy Research

Policy research helps decide marketing policy, premium policy and inventory policy. It provides necessary data and information to predict future market conditions and decide suitable policies in every area of marketing management. The economic, social and political atmosphere is assessed to decide appropriate policies to be adopted by the management.

(F) Method and Effect Research

This research includes sales methods related to advertising and selling emphasis, distribution costs, choice of advertising media, selection of distribution channel, sales performance tests, sales training method, advertising copy, advertising campaigns, media scheduling, brand research and image research. It places emphasis on all types of methods and efforts pertaining to product, promotion, prices and distribution. Methods and efforts relating to sales yield, market shares and sales effectiveness, and competitors' selling practices are also investigated under this research.

3. Competition Research

Competition research reveals the competitive position of the company as well as competitors' activities. It is of paramount importance to measure the share of the market owned by a company's product by assessing its own strength and weaknesses. Study of competitors' product improvement, measuring the impact of competitors' price changes and advertising campaigns will be helpful for the company to frame suitable policies and procedures to meet the challenges of the market. The company can conduct an intensive study of competitors' marketing practices and policies. The impact of competitors' actions on the company's marketing situation requires a thorough probe to take appropriate decisions by the management. Marketing management must have such intelligence to perform its task effectively.

4. Researches of Uncontrollable Factors

The researches of uncontrollable factors reveal the parameter within which the marketing management has to adopt various policies and procedures. Uncontrollable factors such as economic situations, political trends, demographic bases and social factors must be intensively studied to find out the workable premises to take appropriate market decisions. There are various publications which reveal adequate information pertaining to uncontrollable factors, such as the statistical abstract of India, and currency and finance reports. The Reserve Bank of India Bulletins and other private publications are important sources for supplying economic, demographic and other important information. The Statistical Substract of the United States, the Statistical Abstract of the United Nations and other international publications are rich sources of quantitative data on the uncontrollables factors. Marketing researchers use these data for their own company's marketing problems.

5. USES OF MARKETING RESEARCH

The uses of marketing can be discussed under the uses to business and industry and to the economy:

(A) Uses to Business and Industry

1. Decision-making Tool: Marketing research is useful for taking marketing management decisions. It provides necessary information and data in analysed and processed forms for making marketing decisions. With advanced technology, higher production functions and an increasing marketing complex, market research has become an indispensable tool for taking appropriate decisions. The hunches, guesswork, stipulation and other traditional methods of decision-making have been replaced by scientific research. Resorting to modern techniques of decision-making has become a dire necessity of today's management, otherwise, business will face hazardous consequences of unscientific decision.

2. Management Planning: Marketing research is used for management planning. It deals with marketing opportunities, i.e., those opportunities which are viable to be exploited by management. Thus, marketing management can assess the resources that will be useful for the business. Short and long-term planning can be effectively formulated with the help of marketing research. Assessment of uncontrollable factors such as economic purchasing power of consumers, political peace, legal limitations and other factors help decide appropriate planning for management. Management planning uses trend analysis, short-range forecasting and long-range forecasting, which are important components of marketing research. Research inputs are helpful to managers planning new market programme and existing market expansion.

3. Problem-solving: Starting from problem identification to formulation of alternative solutions, and evaluating the alternatives in every area of marketing management, is the problem-solving action of marketing research. Problem-solving marketing research focuses on the short-range and long-range decisions that must be taken with respect to the elements of the marketing mix, viz., product, price, place and promotion. It can help managements bring about prompt adjustment and innovations in the above areas of marketing management.

4. Control Technique: Marketing research is used as a control technique of marketing management to find out the weaknesses and shortcoming of the management decisions to reorient the planning and performance techniques. Control oriented marketing research helps management to isolate trouble spots and to keep abreast of current techniques. Market share, exploitation of potential markets, corporate image and new products are the major areas which require constant observation and control by management. When a plan is put into action, management must monitor its effectiveness. Marketing research measures the effectiveness of the marketing plans and performance.

5. Large-Scale Production: Marketing research helps large-scale production by providing suitable decisions to be undertaken by the producers to exploit the existing production resources to meet the growing markets. The resources of production and market potentials are properly assessed by marketing research. They provide the means and methods to match the production line with market opportunities. They help to explore, identify and locate markets to adopt intensive and extensive production techniques. They help management to bring about change in product design to catch up with the marketing needs.

6. Complex Market: The advancement of science and technology and the standard of living of consumers necessitate closer touch with the growing markets. The size and specialisation within the business unit and the intervention of numerous middlemen between the manufacturer and customers created a wide communication gap. The widening gap requires marketing research to fill up the communication gap between the consumer and the producer. The marketing intelligence systems from producer to consumers and back have required marketing research. Success is ensured only if the consumers' desires and preferences are adequately evaluated to meet their wants. The changes of markets are permanent features which must be assessed and foreseen for effective marketing activities. Marketing research enables management to anticipate and adapt to changes. It also reveals the new role of marketing new products, new demands, new competitors and new situations of the complex market. Marketing management copes with the new changes only with the use of marketing research. The marketing research suggests how to reach the consumers' minds, attracting their attention, the goods and services, creating desire and stimulating demand for the company's product. It helps in understanding the potential consumers, their habits, needs and desires, tastes and preferences. Thus, the solution of complex markets rest with marketing research.

7. Pattern of Consumption: The pattern of consumption is to be assessed by the marketing management. The study of buyers' behaviour, attitudes and capacity to purchase is very important in marketing research. The purchasing power of a consumer depends upon his disposable personal income. Thus, the total purchasing power of a country or geographical area can be assessed by the disposable income of the place. The consumption functions vary from place to place, time to time and person to person. The consumption pattern influences the market. The marketing research in turn reveals the consumption pattern. Availability of consumers' credit also influences the consumption pattern. The disposable income depends upon personal income, government control and structure of the marketing system. The marketing research reveals all these factors which influence the pattern of consumption.

8. Market Complex: The marketing activities are influenced by several internal and external environments. Internal environments include price, promotion, production and place (distribution), whereas the external environments include economic, sociological, political, legal and government motives. The external environments are also known as uncontrollable environments because the marketing management of any organisation cannot influence them but they must know these factors thoroughly and can assess their impacts on the marketing mix. The marketing research can reveal the influences of the uncontrollable factors on the marketing variables. A competent manager frames the marketing policies and programmes by considering the impact of uncontrollable factors on the markets. Changes in uncontrollables will influence the market widely. It will cause great reactions amongst the competitive marketers. An intelligent manager must foresee these changes and their impact on the marketing mix to decide appropriate marketing policies and progammes to attain the marketing objectives of the organisation. He can succeed in his mission only with the use of marketing research. The marketing research is competent enough to assess and analyse the reactions of a complex market. The action,interaction and reaction of marketing forces of one's own company and of other companies within the parameters of uncontrollables can be appropriately assessed with the help of marketing research.

9. Suitable Marketing Operations: Marketing operations decide production functions, and marketing operations can be better decided by the findings of marketing research. Marketing functions are concerned with the maximising of profit, and production functions have to minimise the cost of production. The blending of these two functions will give a higher margin to the company. Marketing research stimulates production research to cut back on cost. The production function can work properly within various variables with the help of marketing and production research. The marketing operation can succeed if the marketing research is used for penetrating new markets, expanding the existing markets, designing new products and other forms of marketing planning. The emergence of a buyers' market and increasing competition demand continuous need of marketing research to ensure maximum consumer satisfaction.

10. Pricing: In marketing management, pricing is not arbitrary for follow up action of competitors. It has to be judiciously fixed which is done effectively with the study of various marketing variables. The pricing objectives, market share, payment procedures, market demand, elasticity of demand, competitor's attitudes, price, volume relationship and changes in various market variables are studied by undertaking marketing research to frame suitable pricing policies. The pricing policies and their effects on the market can be assessed by the marketing research. There are various products which are not influenced by the pricing changes, they require value satisfaction to the consumers. Consumer behaviour has become an important segment of marketing research. The pricing policy should maintain a proper balance between profits and the cost of production and distribution. The maximising of profit may not be the sole objective of the company. Continuous growth of the market is taken as the ultimate objective for which skinning of the market, regaining cost, increasing the rate of return on investment, and increasing the market share have to be taken into account in determining pricing policies.

11. Marketing Strategy: Marketing management has to lay down appropriate marketing strategies to meet competition to pursue growth in the market and to attain organisational objectives. The market experiences several changes. Nothing is permanent except the change in a market. A manager, if he estimates the changes of the market variables in proper perspective, can formulate suitable marketing strategies, but it is not desirable to fix policies and strategies. They should be dynamic to achieve growth, maximum utilisation of resources, and meeting consumers' needs, interests and preferences. Formulation of marketing strategy requires a proper and deep study of product planning, channels of distribution, physical distribution, pricing, promotion of one's own company and also knowledge of these factors of competitors. The marketing research helps the formulation of marketing strategy.

12. Distribution: Marketing research helps the members of the channel of distribution to formulate suitable policies and programmes to solve their problems. This requires logistical planning. Between the manufacturer and consumers, retailers, wholesalers and agents are there to distribute the products at reasonable cost. The manufacturer has no direct control on the channel of distribution. A proper solution of the problems of distribution has to be worked out. Suitable distributors have to be selected to reach the customers at minimum cost and time. The margin of each distributor will have to be decided to fix the cost of distribution. Marketing research can help the manufacturer to decide the channel media and logistic planning to benefit the producer, distributors and ultimately the customers.

13. Sales Promotion: Marketing research can decide suitable media of sales promotion after a study of the various channels of promotion. The costs and benefits of advertising, personal selling and wide publicity should be studied to decide the most appropriate media of sales promotion. Advertising cost, the advertising agency, advertising effectiveness and advertising waste must be widely studied to formulate suitable advertising strategy and procedure. Marketing research has been of immense use to industry and business to solve their marketing problems, and also to avoid forthcoming problems of marketing management.

(B) Uses to Economy

Marketing research is useful to the economy as a whole as it helps further production, distribution, employment, increase per capita income, reduce recession and avoid crises.

1. Production: Suitable production functions are adopted to meet the market demand. In the absence of marketing research, production will be undertaken without knowing its ultimate result. It may exceed the market demand or may lag behind. It may not meet the consumers' needs, interest and willingness to purchase. The manufacturer may suffer considerably. But the use of market research frees the producer from all problems and cares. If the producer knows the market behaviour and quantum, he can produce suitable articles to meet the market requirements. His production will be directed in the right direction. He will benefit by his production and find an adequate market for his products. Once benefited by the appropriate production function, he will have the incentive to produce more goods and services. This will increase his re-employment capacity for investment. More investment, if suitably directed, will produce those goods and services which are required by the community. Thus, more production and more investment increase the total production of the country.

2. Distribution: The market researcher finds suitable channels of distribution. Those coming in the channel of distribution may get a reasonable margin for their services. Thus, the producers and distributors are benefited. The consumers' desires, interests and motives are better served by the marketing research. They can mutually agree to the terms and conditions. The misunderstanding between producers and distributors can be removed at the evidence of findings of marketing research. The producer reaches the final buyers through intermediate levels of distribution. He can plan the distribution logistics to benefit the distributors and the consumers.

3. Employment: The increased production, widespread distribution and promotion functions increase employment opportunities in the country. Increasing production requires more personnel; distribution needs more businessmen in the areas of wholesaling and retailing. Similarly, promotion functions employ additional persons to advertise for personal selling and other promotion functions. In a society where marketing research is commonly prevalent, the employment opportunities are bound to increase through diversified economic activities.

4. National Income: With the increase of production, distribution and marketing activities, the national income increases. The diversified economic activities act as an impetus to the growth of national income. The social and economic conditions improve as the producers and distributors apply more suitable information and data available from marketing research. Rising employment opportunities can increase national income. The marketing research helps increase employment opportunities. The increased national income helps to increase the per capita income, which increases the purchasing power of the consumers.

5. Reduce Recession: Recession occurs when the production exceeds the capacity of the market. The disequilibrium between production and the market can be avoided with the use of the findings of marketing research. In our modern age, the occurrence of a recession is minimised as many industrially advanced countries avail of research. Marketing research assesses the quantity of the market as well as the quality; also the design and attributes of the products required by present and potential consumers. Thus, the production function is able to meet the present and potential volume and pattern of demand, and can avoid a recession in the economy.

6. Avoid Crisis: Similar to recession, a crisis is also troublesome to people. The scarcity of production causes a crisis in the economy, and it is unable to meet the market demand. If the findings of market research are used, the disequilibrium between the market and production can be corrected. Adequate production can be made to meet the growing demands of the market. The market pattern can be foreseen and adequate changes in production function can be made to avoid any disequilibrium.

7. Non-Profit Organisations: The use of marketing research has not been extended to non-profit organisations to find out their clients and to pursue them in an effective manner to receive their support. "Also, marketing research techniques are increasingly found in non-business organisations, of which a conspicuous example is among political parties and candidates. Various social service organisations are now appearing among the clients of marketing research specialists, as are government agencies — notably for the recruiting of personnel for the armed forces."[15]

6. LIMITATIONS OF MARKETING RESEARCH

1. Not a Panacea: People have started thinking that marketing research provides solutions to all sorts of problems; but this is a misnomer. It cannot provide solutions to every business problem. It only offers accurate information which can be used to arrive at a suitable decision to reduce problems. The market research suffers from samples or statistical errors, but if these are eliminated the results obtained from market research may prove a very useful tool of management decision.

15. David J. Luck, Hugh G. Wales, Donald A. Taylor and Donald S. Rubin: *Marketing Research*, Prentice of India, 1982, p. 8.

2. Not an Exact Science: Marketing research deals with human behaviour and unlike the physical sciences does not examine controlled variables. There are various controllable and uncontrollable factors which influence market forces. Attempts are made to assess them scientifically and accurately, but these are very likely to arrive at wrong conclusions on account of the improper use of techniques of analysis and interpretations. It is a study of human psychology. The study of human behaviour precludes absolute mathematical accuracy and precision. It makes a valuable contribution to business management as the scientific methods of research are used in marketing research. Considering the limitations of the market, it can be used profusely for arriving at suitable decisions in management.

3. Limitation of Time: Marketing research can take a long time to carry out the research process. The report may be prepared after a long time when its utility may have been lost. There is a time limit. The collection of data, their analysis and interpretation will take sufficient time. The formulation of policies and procedures may also require considerable time. During the period of starting the research and implementation of the decision, the situations and assumptions of the research may have changed drastically and the decisions based on the research report may prove to be obsolete and may result in arriving at wrong conclusions. Considering the nature and limitations of marketing research, it is essential to complete the project within a reasonable time.

4. Erroneous Findings: The marketing research may arrive at erroneous findings on account of too complex problems of the markets. The complicated problems may not be comprehensively studied, and their respective impacts correctly assessed by the researchers on account of insufficient funds, time and techniques. If the research arrives at wrong conclusions, the management may be disappointed at the cost and time involved in conducting the marketing research. This disappointment comes from expecting too much from marketing research.

5. Not Exact Tool of Forecasting: The marketing research cannot be used as a foolproof tool of forecasting because there are a number of intervening factors between the findings of marketing research and the marketing complex. All the forces of the market may act, interact and react to give a complex state of marketing. The study of such a complex market is a difficult problem although new and sophisticated techniques are being used to study complex problems.

6. Inexperienced Research Staff: In many business organisations marketing research is not an internal function. It is borrowed. Some managements view marketing research as not an important job. Therefore they hire less able, less trained and less efficient personnel to discharge the marketing research. On the other hand, market research is a function of great expertise as it involves human psychology and social character. The researcher, the interviewer and the investigators must be well trained and adequately experienced to handle human behaviour for research purposes. If the research is well trained and highly motivated, it can perform marketing research to the expectation of the management.

7. Narrow Conception of Marketing Research: Marketing research is considered to be a plethora of management as it is only fact-finding research. The marketing research design sample, interview and reports are generally irrelevant to the management objectives. Research is not problem oriented. It involves too many techniques. It is slow, vague and of questionable validity. It depends too much on clinical evidence.

8. Marketing Research is Luxury: Marketing research is considered a luxury for the management as it involves high cost of operation. This is the reason why many companies do no adopt marketing research. They believe in management expertise rather than conducting costly researches. In this age of wide publicity and rapid flow of communication, marketing research is considered to be a luxury. But the research has definite advantages if properly conducted and used in proper perspective.

Historical Development

Informal marketing research is old. In 1380, Johann Fuggar left his native Swabian village of Graben to settle in Augsburg to engage in the international role of textile industry where he exchanged detailed letters on trade conditions and finances in the localities of their branches. They exchanged current knowledge of changing conditions of supply and demand of goods and funds. They were able to provide market data to each other to reinforce judgement on business problems. In 1720, David Defoe prepared careful inventories of the business and economic resources of England and Scotland. These publications continued for a long period because there was a great demand from the business community to arrive at business decisions. After the impact of the Industrial revolution, pressure for information on which to base marketing decisions increased considerably.

In the United States, N.W. Ayer and Son applied marketing research to marketing and advertising problems. In 1879, manufactures of agricultural machinery required a market survey for which they approached the Nicholas-Shepard company. Du Pont used the systematic analysis of salesman's cell reports which increased to 65 in 1962. In 1903, George H. Kerr organised a trade record bureau which became an important source of sales division. Du Pont had developed the Central Marketing Research Division to collect valuable information on markets. The development of market research techniques was inconsistent. There was no proper cohesiveness of the researches of various organisations. In 1900, H. Gole of the University of Minnesota used a mail questionnaire for the first time for the application of marketing research in the field of advertising. Marketing research made major advances after 1911 when J. George Fredrick devoted full time to his marketing research firm known as the Business Bourse. Later on the Bureau of Business Research of the Harvard Business School took over the job of marketing research when Seldon O. Martin published reports of the marketing research of 130 stores. In 1918, Northwestern University's School of Commerce instituted a Bureau of Business Research with Horace Secrist as its director. R. O. Eastman was the first man to use a postcard survey for his advertising company, Kellogg Company in 1911. Later he provided this service to the General Electric Company in 1917.

Charles Coolidge Parlin published "Sales Opportunities" giving information of the population density by areas and income groups. Parlin's office in Philadelphia was considered one of the leading marketing research organisations. In the United States, the first census of distribution was taken in 1929. Thereafter, a census of business was undertaken covering retailing, wholesaling, service industries and background materials of marketing research. C. S. Duncon's Commercial Research, J. George Frederick's Business Research and Statistics, Z. Clark Dickinson's Industrial and Commercial Research, and William J. Reilly's Marketing Investigations were some of the important publications on marketing research. In 1921, McGraw Hill published Market Analysis by Percival White. This was the first book on market research. In 1937, the American Marketing Association sponsored the publication of the Technique of Marketing Research.

Marketing research developed as a specialised function to obtain and to analyse information of market variables. It has now become a source of bridging the communication gap. Marketing information system or Marketing Intelligence Services have become the important areas of marketing researches.

Marketing Research in India

Marketing research in India is slowly developing, but very rarely are organisations adopting marketing research in India. Multinationals have resorted to marketing research in India. Hindustan Thompson Associates Limited have adopted marketing research in India since 1960. Urban Market Index and Rural Market Index are the basic sources of marketing research. Besides, there are various official and non-official sources of secondary data which are being used for marketing research. Apart from Hindustan Thompson's marketing research, there are several other marketing research associations in India. These associations are generally advertising companies. Government agencies and the Gazeteers of India undertake some important functions of marketing research in India.

❖ ❖ ❖

CHAPTER 2

ORGANISATION OF MARKETING RESEARCH

1. FORM OF ORGANISATION OF MARKETING RESEARCH
2. FACTORS AFFECTING ORGANISATION OF THE MARKETING RESEARCH
3. SCIENTIFIC METHOD AND RESEARCH DESIGN
4. TYPES OF MARKETING RESEARCH

ORGANISATION OF MARKETING RESEARCH

Marketing research is primarily concerned with marketing operations. It may be conducted by one department, some persons of the line organisation, or by appointing external agencies to conduct research for the company depending upon the needs and purposes of marketing research. There may not be a single form of organisation suitable to all types of business operations. The form of organisation of marketing research depends on various factors which will now be discussed.

1. FORM OF MARKETING RESEARCH ORGANISATION

The form of marketing research organisation can be both internal organisation and also external.

1. Internal Organisation

The form of marketing research organisation may be: (1) a one person operation and (2) one department.

1. One Person Operation: Small firms may not afford one full department of marketing research. They may appoint one or more persons to conduct marketing research and report to the firms to solve specific problems. They may report to the marketing executives or to the head of the company. In larger firms the market research reports are given to the head of the marketing department. With large research units, there may be different forms of internal organisation. The research may be different area-wise, i.e., product line, brand, line, market segment or geographical area. By marketing functions, such as field analysis, advertising research or product planning, and by research technique, e.g., sales analysis, mathematical and statistical analysis, field interviewing etc.

2. Marketing Research Department: For a larger firm, one independent marketing research department is established to conduct marketing research on a permanent basis. An experienced person is appointed to head the department. He should help other departments to solve their problems. He should also allow other departments to make full use of his findings and suggestions. There should be proper coordination between the line executives and the marketing research executives. The marketing research department may have full-time employees, i.e., executives, secretaries, assistants and others. The organisation structure and staffing of the department varies greatly. The marketing research department may be given other functions of the business operations along with the work of marketing research.

The marketing research department can function either on a centralised basis or a decentralised basis. The advantages of centralised organisation are greater coordination and control of corporate research activity, economy and greater utility to management. On the other hand the advantages of decentralised basis of marketing research department are valuable knowledge regarding markets, products, problems and other important information concerning markets. A mixed arrangement of decentralised and centralised functions is adopted to meet the various requirements of management.

2. External Organisation

Some independent or related agencies may conduct marketing research for the benefit of their clients or for themselves.

1. Advertising Agencies: Advertising agencies can conduct marketing research for their clients and for their own use. The researches are undertaken by them in the general areas of advertising, content of advertising and media studies. The market behaviour and its characteristics are also studied by the advertising agencies. Nowadays advertising agencies are in a better position to conduct image research, opinion research and market potential research. The advertising agencies have been the early users of marketing research, and have developed in a mature form today. N.W. Ayer & Son were the oldest advertising agencies to avail of marketing research.

2. Independent Marketing Research Agencies: The independent marketing research agencies have been conducting marketing research as professionals. Since the beginning of marketing research, independent agencies such as Duncan Commercial Research in 1919 and George J. Frederick's Business Research and Statistics in 1920 initiated marketing research. These agencies have been the specialised agencies. They themselves conduct marketing research, or help conduct marketing research by preparing questionnaires and providing trained interviewers to conduct surveys. These agencies conduct shop audit, perform listener, viewer and readership studies and prepare consumer panels, sales research and sales estimate research. They provide these services on a subscription or a prepayment basis. Many companies do not establish their own departments of marketing research, but rely on the expertise of the agencies. Some companies with research departments use the services of marketing research agencies as they provide special capabilities of marketing research.

3. Trade Associations: Trade associations have been conducting marketing research. They act both as collectors and collators of information regarding both industries and business. They benefit their members by supplying the results of marketing research. They provide marketing reports at lower costs to their members. This is an important fertile rendered to smaller firms; thus, the members who are unable to conduct marketing research can avail of the benefits of marketing research through the trade associations.

4. Manufacturers: Manufacturers of the same industry can perform marketing research for their benefit. They have to assess the marketing possibilities, marketing problems and effect of the marketing mix on their markets. The producers of consumer goods use marketing research to a greater extent than do the industrial goods producers. The producers of consumer goods have to assess and estimate the consumer behaviour, price behaviour, distribution channels, service motives, sales potentials and dealers' behaviour. The industrial equipment research is mainly undertaken by the manufacturers of industrial goods. They also conduct product research and new product research.

5. Retailers and Wholesalers: Retailers and wholesalers are also interested in marketing research for the expansion of their market and sales. Retailers have been predominantly concerned with shop location studies, special promotions, pricing, retail stores investigations and sales research and so on. Retailers are also in a position to assess precisely the needs of consumers' behaviour and attitudes towards a particular product. Wholesalers are interested in conducting marketing research of retailers' behaviour. They are interested to know the technique of controlling inventories, maximising sales deliveries and service research.

6. Government Agencies: Many government agencies, ministries and departments are collecting valuable information and data pertaining to the market. They collect some routine information of the market and market variables. Special studies of specific marketing problems are also collected from time to time. They have given some specific solutions to various problems. State and local governments have also contributed useful data for marketing research. The Central Government through its various census, surveys and committees provides suitable marketing information.

7. Universities and Institutions: Universities and institutions are also conducting useful researches in the areas of marketing research. Various departments such as those of commerce, management, economics, social sciences and psychology are actively engaged in marketing research. The researches are based on unbiased attitudes towards marketing research. The findings of these researches can be of immense utility to the business communities. Management institutes in India are conducting useful marketing researches.

8. Other Organisations: There are several private and autonomous government bodies which provide suitable and adequate data for marketing research. These organisations may be banks, insurance companies, transport companies, economic and business magazines. In India, the Reserve Bank of India, commerce, capital and other organisations are involved in assimilating information and data useful to marketing research.

2. FACTORS AFFECTING ORGANISATION OF MARKETING RESEARCH

Many factors influence the adoption of a particular organisation of marketing research. Sometimes, companies use their own staff mainly to design and guide the work of marketing research. They may interpret the findings of marketing research supplied by external agencies.

1. Product and Markets

The manufactures of industrial goods are not so much interested in marketing research as the consumers' goods producers are because the latter are much concerned with the consumers and their market segments. Their research contents are also different as they have different subject matters of study for different purposes.

2. Wholesalers and Retailers

The subject of marketing study for wholesalers are retailers' behaviour, distribution channels and relationship between wholesalers and retailers. On the other hand retailers are interested in examining consumer behaviour, price reaction and other kinds of marketing mix. The wholesalers may appoint on research department which the retailers may be greatly interested in such types of organisation. The research conducted by retailers involves forecasting, measurement of market potentials, determination of market characteristics, market share analysis, sales analysis and location analysis.

3. Relationship between a Company and Advertising Agencies

If the advertising agency is taking an active part in marketing research, the company will be free from many of the problems of marketing studies.

4. Nature of Product

The content of research and approach to marketing research vary with the different nature of the product. Market research is most prevalent among industrial and consumer manufacturing companies, while publishers and broadcasting corporations may not require marketing research to that extent. They may be interested only in the market coverage statistics to measure the size of the audience.

5. Nature of the Problems

The manufacturers and traders may need marketing research when they face certain problems. For executive functions, they rarely use marketing research. In Indian conditions, marketing research is mainly connected with the problems-oriented research. The fact finding and exploratory researches are rare. In foreign countries, too, the real growth in marketing research occurred when firms found they could no longer sell all they could produce. They had to gauge market needs and produce accordingly. Marketing became a dominant factor over product.

6. Attitude of Management

The marketing department has grown recently into a prominent department within the total spectrum of management. The attitude of the management towards marketing in general, and to marketing research in particular, influences the nature and size of marketing research. Increased sophistication of management and the data wrought by the computer require marketing research.

7. Costs and Benefits

Marketing research involves additional costs to management. In accordance with the benefits of marketing research, the research practices are adopted. Many of the small firms do not resort to marketing research because of the costs involved. A company must appraise the alternative costs and benefits associated with operating a lean internal department versus staffing specialists to handle specific types of research activities.

8. Availability of Market Information

Many companies do not adopt marketing research because abundant information and data are available pertaining to business and market conditions from the publications of banks and other financial institutions, public utilities, transport associations, autonomous bodies and private research organisations. Trade associations often collect and disseminate operating data gathered from members. Some small specialised marketing research firms provide useful market research.

9. Role of Marketing Management

The role of marketing management in a company decides the nature and form of the marketing research. In a big organisation with wide marketing activities, a separate marketing management department is opened to collect and collate the marketing information. In small marketing functions, the marketing research is not a very important function. If the marketing department is given the power of decision-making and managing whole areas of marketing functions, the marketing research may be resorted to and a separate marketing research department may be opened to have an efficient marketing intelligence system.

10. Reporting Level

The head of the marketing research department may report to the top executive or to the lower executives. If he reports to the general management directly, he has to perform more specialised and discrete jobs. In case he reports to a lower line executive, he will be consistently instrumental in getting its recommendations put into effect. In several cases, the researchers report to the chief marketing executive who is a specialised person. In such a case he has to be very cautious of specialised marketing activities. He must be in a position to analyse the marketing mix suitably.

3. SCIENTIFIC METHOD AND RESEARCH DESIGN

Every research design must have a scientific base to achieve the desired objectives. "A research design is the specification of methods and procedures for acquiring the information needed."[1] The method and procedures should be scientific. Therefore, we should understand the scientific methods and their application to marketing research before analysing the research design.

Scientific Methods

The basic traits of scientific methods are rationality and objectivity. "No method known to man can entirely eliminate uncertainty. But scientific method, more than any other procedure, can minimise those elements of uncertainty which result from lack of information. By so doing it reduces the danger of making a wrong choice between alternative courses of action."[2] When the marketing research uses the research techniques, they apply methods of science to the art of marketing research. For performing marketing research scientifically, we should know the main features of science.

Features of Science

1. Science establishes relationship between Cause and Effect

The cause and effect of a particular event is probed to establish the precise relationship between them. The relationship between reason and results help us understand the consequences of specific causes, and also to understand the causes of specific consequences or phenomena. The market-mix is examined in this light.

2. Facts Revealing

Science reveals and describes the facts. Facts are empirically tested to reveal their validity and reliability. Science clarifies theories. Marketing research analyses the facts of buyer behaviour and of others.

3. Explanation of Facts

Science reveals not only the existing facts but also creates new facts and new attitudes toward a particular product. New facts should be authentic. Therefore, they should be verified with experimentation. Marketing research reveals additional facts which have favourable consequences for the producer.

4. Analytical Explanation

Science explains new uses of a product in a systematic manner. Revealing new facts is not the end of science, but science goes beyond that to explain those factors in an

1. Paul E. Green and Donald S. Tull: *Research for Marketing Decisions,* Prentice Hall, New Jersey, 1966, p. 89.
2. Marie Jahoda, Morton Deutsch, and Stuart W. Cook: *Research Methods in Social Relations,* New York, Dryden Press, p. 28.

analytical manner. The research scientist examines the inter-relationship among the component parts of the buyer decision process. The original interest may influence the evaluation of the product. The original beliefs are analytically examined, and rational beliefs and interests are examined by the potential buyers' behaviour. The research scientists can analyse the whole decision process. These analyses are methodical and systematic.

5. Specialised Analysis

The analytical explanation is given by the specialised personnel in the field of marketing research. There are varied fields of marketing research and a person cannot be expert enough to analyse all the fields of research. Different research processes such as collection of data, field survey, laboratory experiments, census data, computerised analysis etc. are handled by different specialists in their areas of specialisation.

6. Clear and Precise Observation and Analysis

Scientific method adopts maximum clarity, unambiguous analysis, high precision and accuracy. The relevant criteria for delimiting marketing problems are clearly observed and precisely analysed. The errors of marketing research are minimised.

7. Verification

Science is verification. After thorough verification, a statement can be said to be a correct one. There are various scientific techniques of verification which are used in marketing research. The old theories are verified and new theories emerge. There are constant changing practices and no one theory can be stated as a permanent theory.

8. Explanatory and Predictive

The research scientists are able to describe certain phenomena in a predictive manner. They may state with reasonable certainty how a particular phenomenon occurs, and how it will occur in future. Correct assumptions and correct information may lead to true predictions. Science has the capacity to find correct assumptions and correct information.

Scientific Method

After understanding the various features of science, we can discuss scientific method. As is clear from the above analysis science is able to predict the unknown, so we try to use methods based on science to predict certain phenomena of the market. Scientific method prescribes a set of procedures for establishing and connecting general laws about events.

Features of Scientific Method

1. Objectivity: The research must be directed towards its objective. The cultural and personal bias in the scientific method is thus minimised. In marketing research bias cannot be totally eliminated as there are present social and human elements. Therefore, the scientific methods are directed towards minimisation of the bias, and maximisation of relevant information and analysis to get the objectives of research fulfilled.

2. Testibility: The scientific methods are amenable to empirical testing. "The quest for explanation in science ... is a quest for explanatory hypotheses that are generally testable ... the hypotheses sought must therefore be subject to the possibility of rejection, which will depend on the outcome of critical procedures, integral to the scientific quest, for determining what the actual facts are."[3] The findings of marketing research may be capable of replication by other social scientists. The findings must be communicable to the masses.

3. Reliability: The scientific method has the feature of reliability. The marketing researchers can depend upon the methods used for conducting the research. Poor information and good marketing research may lead to confusing consequences. Reliability is based on the fact that repetition of the same project will produce the same results. It has the essentialities of confirmation. Use of experimental and statistical tools make the findings more reliable.

4. Validity: The scientific methods are considered foolproof and have the validity to test various phenomena. Validity is the characteristic used to describe research which measures what it claims to measure. It is acceptability by the people. The scientific method must have the feature of validity, so that the findings derived from the use of the methods may stand to the criteria of correctness and acceptability in a given situation.

5. Definiteness: The Scientific method has the characteristics of definiteness. There is no confusion of the method to be used. The operational measure should be standardised. In marketing research however, it may not always be possible to have a standardised measure as it varies from context to context. There should be precise measurement of the facts and findings. The scientific methods have a certain precision in their application. However, in marketing, precision is not always possible.

6. Coherence: The information gathered should not be found in random relationships. It should be arranged in a logical manner. Relevant statements may develop hypotheses and relevant hypotheses may compose theories. The hypotheses may be tested by using scientific methods. The invalid hypotheses or conflicting statements get rejected by the use of such methods. The scientific methods are capable of establishing coherence between causes and consequences.

7. Comprehensiveness: The scientific methods provide comprehensive knowledge. A large number of theories applicable in relevant situations are assembled together to help market researchers in different situations. Application of scientific methods to marketing research has helped the researchers to arrive at correct consequences. Suitable suggestions and recommendations can be provided to the marketing management with the application of scientific methods.

The above methods are applied to marketing research, but there are certain difficulties in the application of scientific methods to marketing research. The researches in marketing areas tend to reduce their objectivity. They are also influenced by other factors. There is a lack of precision in marketing research. The reliability and validity may be influenced by different factors affecting the market and the marketing mix. There is a time lag that influences the findings, and their relevances to marketing problems may not be correct. The complexities of human actions and reactions do not make marketing research a very precise and comprehensive science. However, scientific methods are used to make marketing research more useful and which lead to relevant conclusions. The emphasis in marketing research is to use scientific methods.

---

3. Gerald Zaltman and Phillip C. Burger: *Marketing Research,* The Dryden Press, Illinois, 1975, p. 34.

4. TYPES OF MARKETING RESEARCH

Marketing research is now placed under the control of some staff executive to provide adequate information to the line management. In the days of specialisation, various types of marketing research are adopted. Each type of research is tailored to the individual needs of the management. There are five major types of marketing research with several sub-types.

1. Marketing Performance Research
   - *(i)* Market Potential Research
   - *(ii)* Consumer Research
   - *(iii)* Market Share Research
   - *(iv)* Sales Research
   - *(v)* Sales Forecasts and Estimate
   - *(vi)* Overseas Marketing Research
2. Product Research
   - *(i)* Product Line Research
   - *(ii)* Individual Product Research
   - *(iii)* New Product Research
   - *(iv)* Service Research
3. Promotion Research
   - *(i)* Advertising Research
   - *(ii)* Personal Selling Research
   - *(iii)* Brand Image Research
   - *(iv)* Readership Research
4. Distribution Research
   - *(i)* Distribution Channel Research
   - *(ii)* Dealer Surveys
   - *(iii)* Shop Audit
   - *(iv)* Retail Stores Investigation
   - *(v)* Location Research
5. Pricing Research

1. Marketing Performance Research

Marketing performance research provides information necessary for management to plan and control the performance of the marketing efforts. This research is primarily concerned with the identification of problems and their solutions. In this research a performance standard is fixed to gauge the marketing performance. There are certain goals of the performance which are to be achieved. It provides measurement of current performance and forecasting of future performance. After the performance, comparison of the performance with the standard is done to determine whether objectives of marketing management have been achieved or not. If the objectives have not been achieved, the causes of the short falls are diagnosed.

The establishing of marketing performance standard is not an easy and routine matter. It is decided by performance researches or realistic appraisal of the level. The realistic appraisal depends on sound data which are collected by applying scientific methods of collection of data. The collected data have to be scientifically analysed to compare the performance with the standard. Some of the widely used standards in the field of marketing management are the percentage of profit to sales, by product line, by geographic area, and by the distribution channel. The percentage of sales to total investment and percentage of cost production and cost of distribution is to total sales. These are concerned with the measurement of actual performance and the forecasting of future performance. Some of these data are available from internal records. However, determination of the market share is made by gathering data from outside sources. Important marketing performance researches are marketing potential research, consumer research, market share research, sales research, sales forecasts and estimate and overseas marketing research.

(i) Market Potential Research

Market potential research reveals the extent of a product or service that can be absorbed by the market during a period of time. It defines the market opportunity that exists during a particular time. Market potential is related to the sales forecast of a product of an industry. The potential of the marketability of the product can be estimated on several grounds. The potential may be assessed on the basis of territories, types of customers and also on the retailers' basis. The market potential is used to decide sales targets and sales quotas. The potential will help to establish sales territories when the potential of the product of the industry as a whole is determined, each firm may decide its share of the market. Not only the share of the potential, but also a device to achieve the target of the potential is revealed by the market potential research. This is not only the sales' forecasts of the industrial product, but also a revelation of the device to increase the sale to absorb the market potential. This research helps the management to availing the best available opportunities of sales.

(ii) Consumer Research

Consumer sovereignty is considered a modern marketing principle. It means that the producer has no right to intervene in the purchasing habits of consumers. They are free to spend their money in any manner they like. Therefore, it is essential to understand the consumers' behaviour to meet their requirements by providing suitable products and services. Thoroughly assessing the consumers' behaviour will help increase the sale of the firm. The planning and policy of marketing can be decided accordingly. The consumer research reveals the behaviour of the consumers in a constant market. It also reveals the behaviour of the consumers at the introduction of various marketing variables. The consumer behaviour includes not only purchasing habits and style, but it also reveals the housing, education, travel, media of publicity and interacting habits of the consumers and their families. Study of consumers behaviour is essential to reveal the environment in which the marketer can operate to achieve the maximum target of the market.

(iii) Market Share Research

The market share is decided on the basis of the market potential. It constitutes the ratio of a company's sales to the industry's potential sale. The performance standard is established after forecast of the sale is decided. After establishing the standard, the performance is measured accordingly. The level of the performance or the standard can be determined after making thorough analysis of product capabilities, prices and the marketing programmes of the company on the one hand, and the market potential on the other. The potential capabilities of the company can be estimated on the bases of market variables, market designs, advertising policies, product function, pricing policies and the distribution channel.

(iv) Sales Research

Sales research involves measurement of sales, sales potentials, cost of product lines, different market segments, sales territory, salesmen's attitude, salesmen's share, sales analysis, sales control research and market analysis. Sales analysis is conducted by firms to assess the amount of sales from time to time. The sales analysis is used to mean actual analysis of sales performance. Sales analysis is based on sales analysis by customers. The distribution cost of sales is compared with the amount of sales. The potential of the sale is assessed by the number and worth of prospective customers. Sales forecasting and salesmen's efforts are known as the field of sales research. Statistical methods and survey methods are used for sales forecasting.

(v) Sales Forecasts and Sales Estimate

Sales forecasts and sales estimate are other forms of marketing performance research. Sales forecasts are estimates of sales in units and volume for a given period of time. The sales forecasts may be short range forecasts and long range forecasts. Short range forecasts are related to one year's sale, and long range forecasts to a longer period. The forecasts can be broken area-wise, product-wise, dealer-wise and so on. The consumer-surveys can reveal the factual bases for increasing sales. The short range sales forecast are an important tool of management in marketing areas. The long range forecasts are useful for planning, programming and controlling the sale-performance. The sales forecast may be useful for setting territorial quotas and sales-efforts. Production planning and scheduling and other activities can be mobilised as per sales forecasts.

(vi) Overseas Marketing Research

Overseas marketing research is concerned with research in international markets. The information is collected from various overseas agencies. Field experiments are relied upon for analysing overseas marketing. Cost and efficiency are considered important factors for deciding a particular source of information. Local language, culture, terminology and traditions are adopted for conducting overseas marketing research. Desk research is considered an important design of overseas marketing research as field research involves excessive cost of collection of data. The respondents in a field sample may be unwilling to answer the questions and various other problems may arise in overseas field research. While analysing the collected data, various precautions are essential. The meaning of terms, the consumers' attitude toward the product, the interviewing situation and such factors may distort research findings. To cope with the various problems in overseas marketing research, the researcher must possess a high degree of cultural understanding, creative talent in adopting research findings, and a sceptical attitude in handling both primary and secondary data.

2. Product Research

It is the task of product marketing research to determine consumer requirements and to keep abreast of product technical research. It is the development of a product line which meets the needs of certain groups of consumers. The main feature of new product policy is the identification of those product opportunities which can provide maximum sale and the greatest return on investment. Product research involves overall product strategy based on market needs, industry structure and corporate resources. It also involves a flow of new product ideas from a variety of sources and procedures to screen product ideas, procedures for final screening product specifications with regard to optimum product and product testing and examination of the marketing. Researchers use tests as a way of determining whether potential customers have understood the idea behind the product. The main feature of test marketing is the test of a new product marketing plan by introducing it on a miniature basis. The commercialisation includes the product life cycle, package testing, promotion and demonstration. The product research decision is really the result of a collection of decisions. Product research may include product line research, individual product research, new product research and service research.

(i) Product Line Research

Product line research decides the lines of product to be added or the lines of product to be terminated, and the lines on which the product should be offered in the market. Rapid technological advancements have added various opportunities for many new lines of production to enhance the marketability of a product. The increasing competition, cost of manufacturing and cost of entering new markets required thorough product line research to maximise the market share of the company. The product line research concentrates mainly on the procedure of new lines of product to be added rather than dropping the old lines of product. Product line research means a continuing activity that may be identified as separate and consecutive. It discovers potential new lines that may meet the objectives of the company. It is a screening process for eliminating insufficient lines of a product. The sources of a particular line depend upon the thorough business evaluation and cursory analysis of the lines of a product. Almost all companies resort to product line research, i.e., formal or informal analysis. The informal and guess estimate may not prove successful in some cases; but formal and scientific research may certainly be helpful in adopting a particular line of research.

(ii) Individual Product Research

The individual product research is related to what products will constitute each line, and what characteristics each product should have to meet the market requirements. Research can be conducted on new product ideas, and screening of those products for use in potential product lines. It is a joint and interrelated effort between marketing research and technical research. The marketing research is concerned with determining the market requirements for production purposes, acceptable price, and range of the product. Technical research is related to the responsibility of designing the product to meet the market requirements.

The products are tested in a laboratory for their qualities, but are examined in the market for their saleability and to eliminate the undesirable characteristics of the product. Therefore, product tests are conducted to determine the product characteristics. These tests are conducted under actual use or market conditions.

(iii) New Product Research

Product research is conducted to find out a new product line or a new product in a particular line. When a new product in a particular line is to be added or dropped, new product research is conducted. The new product research may include the marketing product life, required inputs, future planning and financial appraisal. The marketability of the new product is decided before launching other functions of the new product research. the product is examined to find out whether any new feature can be added to the product. The performance characteristics and limitations of the product are examined. The product distribution channel, competitive products and other factors are decided to find out new product research.

The product life cycles are also estimated to find out new product. The raw materials and resources are decided to make the product at the lowest cost. Estimates for capital and plant requirements are made and the price decisions are taken accordingly. The effect of a new product on a company's growth, the effect on competitors, and plans, policies and the future of customers are analysed to find out new products. The financial appraisal of the new product is also made to find out the financial exigency of the new product. All these analyses are made thoroughly under new product research.

(iv) Service Research

Similar to product research, service research may be conducted by those concerns which provide services to the consumers, although there are some specific characteristics of the services for which the research will be different from the product research. The services are intangible, heterogeneous, and perishable. The services cannot be separated from those persons who are offering them. Therefore, the qualities and attitudes of those offering the services decide its market. In some cases the inherent virtues of the services will have to be propagated to the clients. The services are perishable and cannot be stored. Therefore, the offers of services cannot be bargained much on price front. Owing to these reasons, the services make fluctuating demands. The benefits of the services will have to be explained first before introducing them to the customers. Different marketing strategies will have to be adopted for different kinds of services, which may be intangible benefits with independent services, intangible activities with tangible goods, and intangible activities with tangible goods along with independent services. Therefore, the service research will have to be adapted accordingly, to expand the market and retain the existing market if it cannot be expanded according to the nature of the services and competitive situations of the market.

3. Promotion Research

Promotion research is mainly concerned with the expansion-stimuli of the market. Advertising research, personal selling research, brand image research and readership research are included under promotion research.

(1) Advertising Research

Advertising research can constitute advertising content research, advertising media research and advertising effectiveness research.

(a) Advertising Content Research

This research decides the contents of advertising so that it can most effectively communicate the product and services. The creativeness and skills of the advertisement are the basic factors that create the appeal. Constant research uncovers new appeals and provides useful facts about the way in which people perceive products. It also provides alternative appeals and copy. Various tests and experiments are exercised to select effective content, appeal and copy. These may be consumer jury tests, rating scales, portfolio tests, psychological tests, laboratory testing, enquiries simulated tests, recognition and recall tests. Consumer jury tests are based on the rating given to an advertisement by a group of consumers. The usual procedure is to ask a relatively small group of consumers who represent potential buyers of the product to rate alternative pieces of copy. Two methods are used in the consumer jury tests. They may be in order of merit whereby the respondents are asked to decide which of a group of advertising is the test, which is the next best and so on. The second method is the paired comparison method whereby the respondents are asked to state their preference for each advertisement relative to every other advertisement. Recall tests reflect the advertiser's ability to register the sponsor's name and to deliver a meaningful message to the consumer. Under recognition tests, qualified readers of a given issue of a magazine are asked to point out what they have read about the content research and usefulness of the subjects of promotion.

(b) Media Research

This research decides the optimum proportions of the advertising media, e.g., allocation to newspapers, magazines, television, radio, outdoor and other advertising media. Data obtained by audience measurement techniques, data on relative costs and the data obtained from supporting studies of the general uses in content research are employed in media evaluation and appropriation studies. Media analysts need information on the duplication between magazines. A media buyer is also interested in the ability of a given medium to generate the number of persons who will see the advertisement. The media audience is measured by the coincidental method, i.e., the respondent is called and asked whether anyone in the home is listening to the radio or viewing television. The interviewing is done shortly after the particular period is over after roster recall. A list of roster is used to aid respondents in remembering what programmes were listened to or viewed by the audience. Media models, the diary method and an audiometer may be used for assessing the media audiences.

(c) Advertising Effectiveness Research

The researchers may be interested to know the effectiveness of different contents and media of the advertisement. The ultimate objective of advertising is to increase the present volume of sales. The effectiveness may be measured in terms of capital expenditure, also in terms of the level of informing, the level of persuasion and the level of induced sales. There are many techniques employed to measure the effectiveness of advertising. Before and after measurements of experimental variables, and after experiments techniques are useful research techniques for measuring advertising effectiveness. As mentioned in the media research, several test techniques may be useful. The advertiser will have to specify what part of the process is intended to influence the consumer. To acquire an understanding of why, how and when a customer purchases will require an important test technique of advertising effectiveness research.

(ii) Personal Selling Research

Personal selling is a means of communicating a sales message through direct sale, i.e., by the salesman. It provides maximum opportunities for interaction between the salesman and the customers. Direct communication from the seller to customers provides adequate opportunities of flexibility in communication to influence the customers. Similarly, the seller has the opportunity to get a feedback from the customers. The attitudes and capabilities of the salesmen influence considerably the sales volume. The personal selling research helps increase the effectiveness of personal selling and removes the drawbacks and bottlenecks of personal selling.

Personal selling research is related to the areas of sales organisation and sales effectiveness. The sales organisation research has traditionally been concentrated in the establishment of sales, territories, allocation of the personal selling effort, preparation of the sales budget and other activities pertaining to the sales organisation. Sales effectiveness research consists of analysing the time involved in sales, determining ratios of sales made, the cost of sales, customer audit to salesmen's performance and establishing sales targets and quotas.

(iii) Brand Image Research

Marketing researches cluster around the researches of customers' attitudes towards products and services. The study of attitudes may lead to changes in the total marketing strategy and policy. The producer tries to develop a sound image of his product. How to develop a good image is subject to image research. When the producer tries to establish a brand of the product, he undergoes brand image research to find out a suitable image of the brand of the product. The brand image research may include topography, colour, package, design, etc. The image is featured in creating stimulating and maintaining demand. The brand image may have contrary effect or positive effect. Research should be undertaken to discover how the brand image may have a positive effect on the sales. The consumers associate a particular brand or trade name with consistent quality and repeated satisfaction. The consumers associate a particular brand or trade name with consistant quality and repeated satisfaction. The consumer preference for products of a particular brand can create a lasting market. This is well known as brand loyalty, which is the allegiance demonstrated by buyers towards one brand persistently over a period of time. If customers have developed loyalty towards a particular brand or product, it may exceed the sales of competitors. Therefore, the research has to create brand preference and brand loyalty. An image with high quality may compete satisfactorily in the market. Brand loyalty has several advantages. Therefore, the researcher has to find out ways and means of establishing a brand image. During the initial period of the product the advertising and introductory price offer may succeed in getting people to try the product. Repeated sales at a uniform quality and price along with the accepted image of the brand can establish brand loyalty. A sample survey of those persons who have used the product only once and have not resorted to repeated purchase may be undertaken to find out the basic reasons for not purchasing the product again. Instead of branding an individual product, a group or family of products may be branded to demonstrate a specific quality of the product.

(iv) Readership Research

Recognition test is recognised as readership research. This research involves selection of qualified readers of a given advertisement or form of sales promotion. Readers are asked about the design of the product, the product image, advertisement and other forms of sales promotion. Pretest-protest studies are useful in this kind of research. A small sample of readers is selected at frequent intervals to observe their attitudes towards the product.

Studies of print, media and copy research are included under readership research. Studies of attitudes of readers may be useful to frame suitable advertising and promotional strategies.

4. Distribution Research

Distribution research refers to the study of the physical flow of goods from the manufacturers to the final consumers. Goods may be distributed through different channels, e.g., the manufacturer, wholesalers, retailers and consumers. The main objects of distribution research are distribution channel research, retail stores investigation, dealer survey and location research.

(i) Distribution Channel Research

The distribution channel may be direct or indirect. Direct distribution means selling goods by the manufacturers to the final consumers by mail or through chain stores or depots. Middlemen between manufacturer and consumers are involved in the case of indirect distribution. There may be different channels open to the manufacturer to resort to the distribution of a product. These channels have their respective costs and benefits. Once a channel is accepted, it is very difficult to change it. Therefore, a careful selection of the channel must be made. It is possible with the help of distribution channel research, whereby costs, benefits, effectiveness and performance prospects are analysed to adopt suitable channels of distribution. Distribution costs, including opportunity costs, are more important factors than production costs. In many cases, the distribution costs are higher than the production costs. If the distribution cost is minimised, the product can get a stimulus in the market. The distribution cost constitutes a special study which examines the verified costs of distribution to find out their importance and possibilities of reduction of cost. Apart from the distribution cost, there are various factors to be studied before selecting the channel and appraising the existing channel. There may be the nature of the product, size of the market, availability of surplus capital, expansion of production capacity and degree of competition.

(ii) Dealer Surveys

This involves the research of the attitude and behaviour of distributors or dealers. The performance of a particular dealer is also evaluated in this research, whereby stock levels, stock condition, the size of the order and the selling effort of the dealer are studied. The salesmen are also required to examine the marketing activities of the dealers relating to examine the marketing activities of the dealers relating to the products. Ineffective and non-productive dealers are stopped supplies unless they improve their sales performance.

The dealer's performance can be evaluated by establishing some standards depending on the previous sale and work-norm. The dealer research can reveal how to establish good relations between the manufacturer and the dealers. There may be various ways of stimulating dealers, to make them more effective. Supply of advertising materials, house magazines and organising meetings may be useful methods of developing congenial relations. The periodic study of dealers' attitude, their selling methods and policies, level of stock, level of sales and their effectiveness are essential to evaluate the dealers' performance.

(iii) Shop Audit

A manufacturer can gather adequate information and data about his product's sale from shops. Some sample shops are selected, and information pertaining to his sales volume can be obtained from them. This will also reveal the trend of his sale. The causes of the trend can be revealed by the shops. They can also provide suitable and sufficient information pertaining to competitors' products sale. The manufacturer can improve the situation and increase his market. Thus, this research provides factual survey and not opinion. It is an easy and simple method of knowing the market position of his own product and competitors' product. But, it will not reveal the taste, attitude and desires of the consumers for which a consumer survey is essential. Effectiveness of advertising, price policy, brand image and other promotional policies can be measured easily by a shop audit.

(iv) Retail Stores Investigation

The retail stores investigations may involve investigations relating to customers and to goods and services. It will reveal how many are local customers, what are their trends of shopping and problems of sales. The retailers for investigation are selected at random. If the investigator wants classified information, stratified samples are selected. The retailers may receive enquiries about the problems of sales, the size and style of the sale, new lines of sales, competitors' attitude and sales, the effectiveness of publicity and advertisements, and customers' attitude towards the product of the manufacturer.

(v) Location Research

In the present age of international marketing, when the market is being expanded from a local market to national and even to an international market, the importance of location research has increased. This research facilitates determination of the physical facilities at a particular place. the population, education, income and infrastructure facilities are important elements to determine the potential market. Population movement, the trend in national income as well as disposable income, decentralisation of production activity, development of more rapid and improved forms of transportation, all these have increased the market potential. The location research will help decide the trend of demand of the product at a particular place. Quantities of goods moving from one place to another, cost of transport per unit, cost of warehousing, time and place of delivery, and the total amount of production are evaluated to meet the requirements of the market at a particular place. The external factors such as the socio-political environments, labour supply, and geographical conditions are also studied in the location research.

5. Pricing Research

Pricing research reveals the quantity demanded at various levels of prices. It finds out the bahaviour of the competitors, the market share, dealers' attitude, production and marketing costs and other relevant factors. Factors affecting determination of prices are examined thoroughly. The extent of competition, nature of the market and products, elasticity of demand, return on investment, channel of distribution and Government control are the various factors that affect determination of prices. Skimming the pricing, penetration pricing, profit maximisation policy, and several other pricing policies are adopted to procure the maximum market share. Pricing policy is one of four marketing mixes, i.e., production, promotion, pricing and distribution. It is a very complicated variable. Continuous research is required to fix the price accurately to tap the maximum share of the market. Pricing research involves prediction of the quantity demanded at various prices, prediction of competitors' behaviour, and prediction of external and other variables.

❖ ❖ ❖

CHAPTER 3

MARKETING RESEARCH PROCESS

1. IDENTIFICATION OF PROBLEMS
2. RESEARCH DESIGN
3. DETERMINING SOURCES OF DATA
   (i) SECONDARY DATA AND
   (ii) PRIMARY DATA
4. DESIGNING THE SAMPLE
5. ANALYSIS AND INTERPRETATION OF DATA
6. RESEARCH REPORT
7. RECOMMENDATION FOLLOW UP
8. SELECTING RESEARCH PROJECT

MARKETING RESEARCH PROCESS

The marketing research process involves identification of problems, research design, collection of data, analysis of data and interpretation of data for reporting the conclusions to solve specific problems. All research problems require their own special emphases and approaches. Since every marketing research problem is unique in some ways, the research process is typically tailored. However, there are some basic steps to be followed in each marketing research process. Each research process must be carefully planned, effectively coordinated and integrated. There are seven research steps involved in almost all types of marketing research.

(1) Identification of problems; (2) Research design; (3) Determining sources of data; (4) Sample design and collection of data; (5) Analysis and Interpretation of data; (6) Research Report and (7) Recommendation follow up.

1. IDENTIFICATION OF PROBLEMS

The more valuable role marketing research can perform is helping to identify the problem to be solved. When the problem is carefully and precisely defined, the research can provide a pertinent solution. Part of problem identification includes specifying the objectives of the research to be undertaken. "A marketing problem can be thought of as a situation which is perceived by the marketing organisation as a source of dissatisfaction for its members and for which preferable alternatives are considered possible. No problem exists until someone asserts that it does, although the particular difficulties of opportunities may have existed for some time. A problem exists when the decision maker faces uncertainty regarding which action is to be adopted in the situation. If there is only one action or no action at all, or there is certainty about the outcomes of the alternatives, there is no problem.[1] Thus there is a problem when there are *(i)* opportunities whose exploitation the decision maker has not yet determined how to solve, or *(ii)* difficulties that are manifest or anticipated. Opportunity oriented study clarifies the situation and enables the problem to be well formulated. Alternatively, one kind of research seeks solutions that might be considered. As mentioned earlier, the ultimate objective of problem identification is setting objectives for decision-oriented research. Thus, there may be six steps in problem identification:

1. Discovering problems
2. Problem formulation
3. Identifying the decision
4. Exploration for an alternative
5. Operational definition of the decision
6. Setting objectives for decision oriented research

1. Discovering Problems

Problems may be related to unexploited opportunities and difficulties. Management must have some early warning system to detect problems, so that adequate solutions can

1. Gevald Zaltman, Philip C. Burger: *Marketing Research,* The Dryden Press, Illinois, 1975, p. 84.

be provided to the problems, and opportunities known as positive potentials can be made profitable to the enterprise if capitalised upon by the management. The competitors may try to exploit the opportunities. Therefore, the management must be sufficiently alert and active to exploit the opportunities before the competitors so. The difficulties known as negative or counter productive consequences should be avoided in advance.

Internal and external data may be useful to find out opportunities and difficulties. The researcher can attempt to have "fall out" of data that suggests or pinpoints the existence of the problems. Information about the firm, its products, industry, the market, competitors, advertising and the general environment may be useful to discover the problems.

2. Problem Formulation

After discovering the problems, there is need of well defined formulation of problems in a soluble form. The problems cannot be solved unless they are framed in a suitable form. The premises of the problems should be correctly formulated so that their solutions can be found out easily. The problem formulation consists of the determination of sets of area and scope of the problems, i.e., regarding opportunities and difficulties.

Problem formulation requires good communication between the decision-maker and the marketing researcher. The researcher must know the problems of the decision-maker. This means that he should formulate problems in right perspective so that he can suggest suitable solutions. He is like a doctor who can properly diagnose the problems of the patient who suggests suitable medicine for him. If he is unable to diagnose the problem and goes behind the symptoms of the disease, he cannot suggest suitable solutions to solve the problems. Problem-formulation is just like diagnosis of the disease. If the problem is correctly diagnosed, the researcher can prescribe suitable measures to solve the problem. It is rightly said that "a problem well defined is half-solved." The urgency of the problems require quick relief solutions. Trivial problems should receive quick decisions.

In case of unknown and substantial risk, opportunity oriented research may be launched. This requires the correct definition of the problem, an understanding of its environments and problem recognition. The internal and external environments should be properly evaluated to estimate their influence on the problems and their solutions. Some kind of pilot survey may be useful for correct problem-formulation. The opportunity oriented research may enable the right problems to be determined. The decision-oriented research shows that the problem is very serious. There is need for the delineation of the problem.

3. Identifying the Decision

The researcher provides adequate information to the decision-maker. When the decision-maker is uncertain about the state of the environment the researcher will reduce the uncertainty. The research results are readily accepted when they are consistent with the decision the individual wants to make. When the research results conflict with the decision-maker's original position, the results are questioned at best and, at worst, discarded as being inaccurate. The researcher has to find out suggestions before determining the decision-maker's objectives.

The decision-maker or the executive has the major responsibility for making decisions. The researcher must know the purpose of the decision-maker to enable him to provide suitable information for solving the problems. He must know the environment within which the executive is working. It will inform the researcher a great deal about the resources, strength and weaknesses. Thus, the researcher can facilitate the establishment of realistic courses of action.

4. Exploration for Alternative Courses of Action

A course of action is a specification of some behavioural sequence such as the adoption of a new product design, or the introduction of a new advertising message and so on. A decision to stipulate a programme of action becomes a commitment, made in the present, for future behaviour. Courses of action may range in complexity from a single act to be implemented immediately, to a large set of related actions. The time interval of the courses of action is very important. Error may increase in course of time. The alternative courses of action are well planned: they should be neither over-planned nor under-planned. The costs of each course of action are stipulated before launching the action. The courses of action should be spelled out in greater degree depending upon the problem. The courses of action are known as decision rules. This course of action may be called the contingency plan as its implementation depends upon some unknown event at the time of stipulation. The courses of action are largely decided by the exploratory research. It is one way of learning more about a problem or opportunities, as well as searching out and identifying alternative courses of action.

The researcher has to explore the alternative courses of action as well as to evaluate the consequences of alternative courses of action. He has to assess the outcome of alternative courses of action. The cost, accuracy, and relevance of the courses of action are decided upon to be accepted as a specific course of action with possible outcomes of the action, and accepting it for solving a given problem. The researcher has to be certain about the various factors which influence at the decision's outcome. He has to evolve each and every course of action with their respective possible outcomes. The outcomes in turn depend upon the environmental factors. Therefore, the alternative courses of action are decided upon in the context of the related environment. Thus, in the problem identification, elaborate sets of actions, nature of actions, possible outcomes of the actions and pay-off figures are determined.

The choice of which variables are to be considered as alternative states of nature, and which are to be treated as fixed, will depend upon the uncertainties associated with each class of variables and the decision-maker's conceptual ability to deal with a number of interrelated variables. Thus, the choice of alternative courses of action, state of nature and consequences of variables depend upon the conceptualisation of the problem. Considering the problem's structure, these variables should be evaluated and alternative courses of action may be decided upon. This will reveal the suitable decision-process to be adopted in marketing research.

5. Operational Definition of the Decision

Alternative courses are the possible solutions to the problem. It is therefore desirable to frame as many alternatives as possible during the problem — the formulation stage and stated in the form of research hypotheses. "A hypothesis is an assertion about the state of nature and from a practical standpoint, implies a possible course of action with a prediction of the outcome if the course of action is followed. The prediction, thus, becomes an assertion about a state of nature frequently stated in terms of the objective to be accompanished."[2] When the alternative courses of action are few, the research may not be required and observation or description may be sufficient to solve the problems. Similarly, where the decisions are of a routine type with low risk, more certainty and minor opportunities, no extensive effort would be needed to explore alternatives and resort to any research design. The relevant alternative courses of action should be closely related to the objectives. It should determine which variables affect the solution to the problem, which of the variables are critical to the solution of the problem and which of the variables are controllable.

If an exploratory study of alternatives is to be conducted, a number of hypotheses should be formulated. Suitable statistics from specialists and consumers should be collected. For getting the operational definition of the decision, alternative oriented research can be highly profitable in establishing additional hypotheses for deciding actions. Good hypotheses must not be overlooked. The most suitable alternative of action or operational decision should be properly defined. There should be a definite conception much earlier in the development of the decision before the research is originated to find out plausible alternative solutions. The decisions must be put in writing to make them more authentic and to avoid confusion. The decision-maker can select suitable decisions from them. The researcher will provide a platform for decision-making. He does not take the decision, but provides various approaches for making decisions. He is not responsible for the decision method but is interested in defining the process of decision-making. The research design and interpretation of findings are used for operational definition of the decision. Thus, depending upon the nature of the decision, the research design can be formulated and problems can be properly identified. The operational definition of a decision includes the goal of the decision, the hypotheses to be considered, the pay off or criteria on which the determination is judged, and constraints to the solutions.

6. Setting Objectives

The last step in identification of problems is setting objectives of the marketing research. When the problems have been explored and various relationships between problems and alternative decisions have been established, it becomes essential to frame the ultimate and operational objectives of the marketing research. the objective is decided considering costs and techniques of research. The more important objectives are those that describe the required data for the decision needs.

The ultimate objectives and operational objectives are the bases of the problem solution objective. The operational objectives are part of the organisational or ultimate objectives. The operational objectives are concerned with the research problems. They are attainable and can be reached with the existing knowledge and technology. What constitutes sound test market procedure depends to a considerable extent on the objectives of the research. The objectives of marketing research may be several depending upon the opportunities available and difficulties faced by the management. All the components of the marketing mix may have several objectives of marketing research.

---

2. Paul, E. Green and Donald, S. Tull: *Research for Marketing Decisions,* Prentice Hall, Inc., New Jersey, 1966, p. 50.

2. RESEARCH DESIGN

A research design is a master plan or model for the conduct of formal investigation and survey. It is the specification of methods and procedures for acquiring the information needed for solving the problem. It decides sources of information and methods for gathering data. A questionnaire and other forms are tested to use for collection of data. Sample design is to be selected. Good research design insures that the information obtained is relevant to the research questions and that it was collected by objective. Since research design is simply the framework or plan for a study, it should be used as a guide in collecting and analysing data. It is the blueprint that is followed in completing the research study. It is like the blueprint of a house devised by an architect.

Research can be conducted without detailed blueprint. But the research findings will differ widely from the purpose of the research. The result may be interesting but will not answer the basic problem. The research without design will cost more because it will collect and analyse irrelevant information and data, too. The research design will direct the researcher to collect and analyse data with a view to fulfil the objectives of the research. The research design ensures that the research study will be relevant to the problem and will employ economical procedures and right research methods for conducting the study. One should not confuse the research design that it is a solution. It is merely a guide to conducting research.

The research design is classified for purpose of the investigation. It may be exploratory, descriptive and experimental. Exploratory research design has the main purposes of identification of problems, precise formulation of problems, identification of relevant variables and formulation of hypotheses. The major emphasis of this design is to discover ideas and insights. It generates possible explanations of the problem.

The descriptive study is typically concerned with determining the frequency with which something occurs or the relationship between the two variables. It is guided with the initial hypotheses. It describes the number, distribution, socio-economic characteristics, market share, sales by territory, size or model of product, characteristics of promotional policy and pricing policy etc. The experimental design is concerned with determining the cause and effect relationship. The relationship between cause and effect is studied under this research design. There may be associative variation, sequence of events and study of causal factors. Each of these types is appropriate to specific kinds of problems.

3. DETERMINING SOURCES OF INFORMATION AND DATA

After determining the problem and research design, the next step is to collect adequate information and data for research purposes. The sources of information depend upon the purpose and design of research. If insufficient information is known about the problem, exploratory research is needed. For exploratory research, flexible data collection strategy is required. Published data and interviews may be useful sources of data for the purpose. On the other hand, if the problem is precisely and unambiguously formulated, descriptive and experimental research design may be useful. For that the sources of data must be specific. They may be published data or primary data. These are varied sources of information and data; but in marketing research, they are broadly divided into *(i)* secondary data and *(ii)* primary data. Secondary data are those data which have been compiled already before conducting this research. They have their different purposes. They are already brought before the public in the form of published or unpublished data. Primary data may be described as those data that have been observed and recorded by the researcher for the first time. These data are collected from the field for the specific purpose of the research.

Secondary data may be internal as well as external. Internal data are collected from the company's records. The data are adapted to suit the requirements of the marketing research. External data are collected outside the company. These data may be formal or informal. Formal data are available on a regularly scheduled basis such as monthly, quarterly or annually. Informal data are available on a non-recurring basis. Secondary data should be used considering suitability of the secondary data to the problem, the organisation collecting the data, the purpose of the secondary data, methods used for collecting data and other relevant information pertaining to data.

Primary data are collected by the researcher for his specific research of the problem. Often, the information needed to solve the problem cannot be found in internal or external data. The researcher then resort to the source of collecting primary data because these are original data suitable for the problem. Before collecting primary data, it should be assured that no secondary data are available. If the data are available rapidly and at low cost, there is no sense in spending time money and effort for collecting primary data. Knowledge of secondary data can be useful for developing hypotheses which can be tested by analysing the primary data. The secondary data can be used for opportunity-oriented research, alternative-oriented research and decision-oriented research. Specific questionnaires are prepared to collect primary data. The questionnaire can be prepared at the existing knowledge of secondary data. The structured or unstructured form of the questionnaire can be prepared to collect primary data.

4. SAMPLE DESIGN

Sample design is an important aspect in marketing research. The study of the universe or population related to the problem is not always feasible. It involves exessive cost, time and effort. Therefore an alternative method is to take sample of the universe and study the units of the sample. Thus, the findings of the sample will constitute representative findings of the universe. The amount of work is always limited by shortage of time and resources. The management has a time limitation in which a decision has to be made. Similarly, the cost of gathering information is a compelling consideration in favour of sampling. A full enumeration of any large universe would to be too costly. The accuracy of the information may not be justifiably enhanced by analysing the whole universe. The non-sampling errors are very high in universe study. Therefore, full coverage of the universe neither desirable nor feasible. The universe study is time consuming, so the findings derived after long study will be obsolete, and may not serve the purpose of the study. The sample study is very useful because the information collected is representative of the market or area and is gathered at a low cost and takes less time and effort. The sampling is an essential factor in marketing research because it is representative of the population with which the management is concerned. Sufficient accuracy in the sample to provide stable results and using research resources as efficiently as possible are the main characteristics of the sample study. It would be grossly inefficient to lavish too much time or money on either *(i)* data that arrive too late for perceptive analysis and application to the problem which has little value of *(ii)* obsolescence and perishability of the data.

The sample design involves the sampling frame, sampling selection process and the size of the sample. The sample frame requires identification of the universe from which the sample is to be selected. The sampling selection process requires that the form of the sample be specified. It may be a probability sample or a non-probability sample. A probability sample may be routine stratified cluster sampling, similarly a non-probability sample may be convenient quota sampling and judgement sampling. The research problem, precision and confidence degree are to be taken into account while deciding the sample size. The sampling errors and non-sampling errors are balanced properly to find out the appropriate size of the sample. Sample design is useful for deciding collection of primary as well as secondary data, but it is also of great use in the collection of primary data from the field.

5. ANALYSIS AND INTERPRETATION OF DATA

After the collection of data, the next task of the research process is the analysis and interpretation of data. The questionnaire form is processed and edited to make sure that all questions are answered. The resulting data should be logical and consistent. After editing, the data are tabulated and analysed. Data analysis includes the statistical tests which may be editing, coding, tabulation and interpretation. Coding is the assignment of numerals to the observations so that data can be analysed, whereas tabulation refers to the classification and cross-classification of the observed data and information. The above analysis, i.e., coding, editing and tabulation functions are common to all types of research. The statistical tests are applied to some such researches where data are complex and causal relations are to be established.

Statistical tests are useful to describe the data at hand, test hypotheses and make predictions or estimates. Descriptive analysis is used to reduce the data at hand to a smaller set of numbers or summary measures which represent the relevant information. The summary measures of population or universe are called parameters and summary measures of statistics are called statistics. The difference between parameters and statistics are known as ampling error. The measure of confidence and sampling error decide the size of the sample.

6. PREPARATION OF RESEARCH REPORT

The research report is the statement submitted to the management by the researcher and summarises the research results and conclusions. The research report is the summary of findings of research. Unless the report is prepared, the research is not concluded. It becomes the standard to judge the performance of the research process. Therefore, the research report should be clear and accurate. The conclusions drawn on the basis of the analysis and interpretation are translated into major recommendations. These recommendations are the main components of the research report. Completeness, accuracy, clarity and conciseness are the main criteria to have a good research report. A research report must contain the title, table of contents, synopsis, introduction, research methodology, findings, limitations, conclusions, recommendations, appendix and bibliography. There may be different types of research report, e.g., basic report, reports for publication, technical reports, reports for executives and so on.

7. RECOMMENDATION FOLLOW UP

Research follow up is essential for the validity of marketing research. The validity appropriateness, acceptability and control are the essential factors of recommendation follow up. Control requires some check on various aspects such as time, cost, quality of work and so on. The marketing researcher should audit its performance validity, meaning the correctness of various aspects of the research process. Errors should be prevented to the greatest possible extent. The appropriateness is also a factor for following through the findings. The findings should be derived as per the objective. The findings should be acceptable to the executives. The researcher should take into account all these factors during the research process.

8. SELECTING RESEARCH PROJECT

While formulating problems of research, it becomes essential to decide the research project suitable for the research problems. In identification of the problems, the decision whether research will or will not be employed becomes pertinent. A large number of questions arise in the minds of the marketing manager to decide whether research will be useful or not. What will be the cost of the research? What are the various alternatives to the problems and their solutions? What will be the degree of accuracy of research and several other uncertainties? Answers to these questions refer to a selection of a particular research project. In brief, the formulation of specific research projects, or proposing and approving research projects, or the strategy of marketing research depends on the following theories.

1. Cost and value methods
2. Decision-theory
3. Decision-trees
4. Baynesian Analysis

These methods are discussed in the light of selection of a specific research project.

1. Cost and Value Method

The decision whether a research-project should be conducted or not depends upon the cost and value of the research project. Research is a cost-incurring activity whose function is to provide information for decision-making. Thus, it carries some of its value. The cost and value of a research project are considered for taking a decision for adopting the particular research project. The problem formulation and research design are viewed in this light. How much information can be acquired in terms of the number and length of marketing research are compared with the costs of conducting research. It decides what the probable costs are in terms of money, people, time and effort of the project. Also, what value or benefits or profits will probably result from it.

The researcher must be in a position to predict both the costs and the nature of findings before planning for the research project. The decision maker and the researcher are in a position to decide at the very outset whether they ought to proceed with the project; sometimes, the planning of the research is pretested before the proposal of the research project is made and approved by the management.

Steps in Proposing and Accepting a Research Project

There are six steps in proposing and approving a research project. They are specification of the plan of the project, determining the costs and values, preparing a proposal evaluating costs and values, deciding the approval of the project and scheduling the proposed work.

1. Specification of the Plan

The proposal of the research project is a formal statement including the statement of the problem and its background, and the objectives, methodology and requirements in concise form. It omits many details which are constituted in the working papers. They contain more detail, spelling out all the work to be done in the research. The proposal of the research project is specifically planned. All the researchers must keep records of planning which include the project title, problems, data objectives, design of the study, secondary data to be used, sampling methods, sampling size, communication method, questionnaire, data analysis plan, interpretation of data, presentation of findings, and estimates of cost involved at every stage. The plans are reviewed at every stage of the research process and may be modified keeping in mind the objectives of the research. Moreover, cost must be controlled at every stage.

2. Determining the Costs and Values

The next step in formulation of the project is to decide the costs to be involved in the research project, and also to stipulate the values or benefits of the research project. This is called cost/benefits or cost/value analysis. It is to decide whether a particular research project should be undertaken or not. Ratio analysis will decide which project should be pursued, and what will be the return on the investment of the research project. The costs of a research project can be estimated well in advance of a project and can be estimated well in advance of conducting the project, but the benefits can hardly be evaluated because the values or benefits are too intangible to quantify and to serve as a solid basis of measurement with the costs. However, attempts are made to quantify the values or benefits of a research project by applying various qualitative data and values. Forecasting of the expected profit to be earned is through the findings' contribution to arrive at a decision. The payoff that can result from favourable experimental results can be given a definite calculation. The project must be decision-oriented to measure the pay off. It is ascribable to the research, and to the incremental gain, because the decision is more profitable than a profit without adopting research findings.

When a project is to be conducted by outside research, the cost of the project can be easily estimated and forecast. The costs of marketing research may be calculated by a certain formula whereby costs are estimated at every stage. The time and effort are also converted in the cost of research. The fixed and overhead costs are specifically calculated. The contingency cost is also added to meet the variation in costs.

3. Preparing a Proposal

The purpose, the method of achieving the purpose, funds and the time required for the smooth conduct of the research project are the various factors which are recorded in the proposal of a research project. The research proposal should not be confused with the research plan which is the detailed description of the proposal. The research proposal is a concise statement of the research to be conducted. This proposal may be submitted to the clients or to the internal management.

The research proposal helps achieve organisational discipline, provides a means for determining priority among projects and tends to assure that a right decision has been taken at a right time. A research proposal includes a statement of the problem and objective of the study, the methodology and requirements of the funds and the required time.

4. Evaluating Costs and Values

With the given costs of the research project, the values are evaluated. On the reverse side the costs are also evaluated to find out the extent of the possibility of minimising the costs. The evaluation of the costs and values is a basis for accepting a proposal. It would serve as a rationale for urging approval. The evaluation may be cursory and quick, but for a big proposal, we may use several other methods. An institution is a method for evaluating the costs and values of a research project. It is based on the "gut feeling" about the risks associated with the problem of the proposed study and possibility of minimisation of the problems with the useful findings of the study. It may increase the depth of knowledge of the decision-maker. However, there is no basis for recording the views. The researcher cannot compare his views and there is no proof of correctness. So it is not being extensively used.

There is need of explicit and conscious judgement. The evaluation should follow systematic procedures. The variables which have a bearing on the decision are stated, analysed and concluded. The evaluation can be recorded on paper and may be compared with others' proposals. The decision theory is being commonly used to evaluate the costs and values of a research project. It reduces the decision-maker's uncertainties and also various contingencies. The decisions can be assessed properly because they can be expressed quantitatively. The decision theory is discussed in detail in a later section of the present chapter.

5. Approval of the Project

The research project can be accepted after evaluation of the benefits or value of the project. Some decision, theories are adopted to accept the project. The project is approved by experts after due consideration of various values of the project. Certain procedures are laid down for proper conduct of the research. There would be different levels of research project. Small research projects involve low cost and high research projects may require more funds. The higher executive may decide on a costlier project to be undertaken by the internal research or research agency. The funds of the research project can be allocated by the marketing research unit. The projects may be assigned annual budgets and a yearly review of the project is undertaken meeting of the executives. The project may be managed on a centralised or decentralised basis while deciding various proposals, while ranking is done. Those ranked near the cut off point should undertake a close examination to consider special situations. It would be better to conduct them on a less expensive scale rather than eliminate them. The executive concerned examines the proposed study. The higher level executives interact themselves to decide a particular research project. The executive may elect to make, i.e., rely on his own information or buy, i.e., utilise the marketing research resources on some particular problems. Marketing research may be used to generate information on the consequences of courses of action already made, new courses of action and the likelihood of various possible outcomes under these alternative courses of action.

6. Scheduling the Projects

The marketing research sets up schedules of the projects approved to help assure that each project can feasibly be completed by the decision-makers' deadline, to make sure that the personnel will be available to know the time of starting a project and to monitor progress. Schedules are a vital part of a research plan. It is a survey time-table whereby periods are assigned for each function of the research project. The time involved for planning, protesting, field survey, data processing, analysis and presentation of reports is decided when scheduling the projects. Such a well-known scheduling and controlling method is the critical path method (CPM) and with this program is related the important technique of evaluation known as program evaluation and review technique. The critical path method (CPM) along with the program evaluation and review technique (PERT) provides more precise planning and evaluation. A resource summary may be used to evaluate the needs of personnel, funds and facilities.

2. Decision Theory

The decision theory decides whether a proposed research project is justified. There are several decisions to be taken by the executives who are known as decision-makers. The basic decision whether or not the decision-maker should take a particular action, results in whether a proposed study would reduce the basic decision's risks. The decision theory involves the following three stages:

1. Situation Analysis
2. Prior Analysis
3. Posterior Analysis

We shall discuss them in the following paragraphs.

1. Situation Analysis

Problems arise in some situations in which the decision-maker has to evaluate whether to take a proper decision. He decides whether a proposed course of action should be adopted in a particular situation or not. The decisions have been preceded by identification of problems, optional solutions and reduction to a few decision. They require predictions of the actions. Prediction involves uncertainty or risk because the present situations or environments may not have been properly assessed, and the future environment may change considerably from the present one. So, the prediction made considering the present environment may not be constant in the future. Therefore, when the risks or uncertainties are large, there is need for a more systematic decision method. The decision-maker uses his intuition based on the state of his knowledge to predict certain phenomena and course of action. If he takes the decision in a logical and systematic manner along with "by gut feeling", his decision will be very useful. The probability theory has been useful in such situations. In the given situation the decision-maker must know the best course of action to take bearing in mind certainty, risk, and the outcome of the course of action.

2. Prior Analysis

The decision whether a research project should be conducted requires comparison of the value of the decision without research, to the anticipated value of the decision assuming research were to be conducted. If the anticipated value of the research is higher, the research project is expected; but if the cost of the research is higher than its potential contribution to management decisions, then the research project is rejected. The criterion whereby to judge in this case is expected value. It has been used in company the potential value of the decision with research to the potential value without research. Expected value is a weighted average of the various consequences in the pay off table. The weights are the probabilities assigned to each state of nature. Expected value is calculated for each alternative course of action and the expected values are compared. The alternative offering the highest expected value would be the most suitable choice. This expected value is also known as probable value. The probable value without research is stipulated on the basis of the probability theory in several states of nature.

3. Posterior Analysis

This analysis deals with which act should be chosen after the receipt of new information. The benefits of information are precisely evaluated. This provides the maximum background for the decision-making process. The posterior analysis, after analysing the available data, may decide whether to accept the said research project or reject the project. The decision-maker can adopt a critical value below which the results will not be accepted. It may be profit or sale of a fixed amount. It is not zero profit at break-even point. If the decision results in a fall in sales or a profit below the critical value, the decision is rejected. So, in a research project, if the value of the research project falls below the minimum or critical value, the research project is rejected. But if it gives a higher value than that of the critical value, the research project is accepted.

The researcher can propose an experiment that would test the price policy's outcome in some selected areas. Suppose five experiments are undertaken and five results are recorded. Some of these results will be considered unfavourable and may be rejected, because they have been found to be below critical value. The probable result of each test is calculated. The conditional probabilities may be assigned to each result, and posterior probabilities are calculated for each function. Thus, the research projects above critical value are selected for research purposes.

4. Preposterior Analysis

While selecting a particular research project, the benefits or decision pay off through the research is then considered. So should the decision-maker use the present information available to obtain additional information for the decision. The expected value of the optimal act after the research considering the cost thereof are compared. "How much benefit or decision pay off is gained through the results of the proposed research, and are the benefits sufficiently in excess of its costs?" The research will try to determine the greatest possible increase in expected value. If the research information predicted perfectly the state nature, i.e., the level of product demand, it can determine the expected value of the optimal act. The executive can price the product accordingly. For example, if the research indicated that the demand for the product may be light, the executive may choose the skimming price. On the contrary, if the research indicates that the demand for the product will be moderate, the intermediate price will be optimal, and if the product demand is likely to be heavy, the penetration price would be accepted. The gain associated with each alternative price is stipulated by the probability that the individual will be told a given state of nature. The best estimates of these probabilities are the probabilities assigned to each state of nature since the individual is not given a choice as to which state of nature will result but is only told in advance which one will happen. Once the executive is told this, one can proceed with certainty in the choice of alternatives.

Expected value under certainty (EVC) is found by multiplying the probability with the optimal act given with the particular state of nature. Suppose, the probability of the decision maker is given in a particular state of nature A_1, A_2 and A_3. The value associated with the optimal act given the particular state of nature may be S_1, S_2 and S_3 respectively. Suppose A_1 = 100 A_2 = 100 and A_3 = 80; and S_1 = 0.6, S_2 = 0.3 and S_3 = 0.1. The expected value under certainty will be

$$V(C) = (0.6 \times 100) + (0.3 \times 100) + (.1 \times 80) = \text{Rs. } 97$$

On the other hand the expected value under uncertainty (EV) is nothing more than a weighted average of the various consequences in the pay off table where the weights are the probabilities assigned to each of the possible states of nature. For example,

$$EV = (0.6 \times 100) + (0.3 \times 50) + (0.1 \times -50) = \text{Rs. } 70$$

So, the expected value of perfect information EV(PI) is the difference between the expected value under certainty (EV) (C) and the expected value of the optimal act under uncertainly (EV). For example:

$$\begin{aligned} EV\ (PI) &= EV(C) - EV \\ &= \text{Rs. } 98 - \text{Rs. } 70 \\ &= \text{Rs. } 28 \end{aligned}$$

Thus Rs. 27 is the net benefit that can be obtained with perfect information. If the research project costs more than Rs. 27, it should not be undertaken and the pricing decision should be made without price-research.

The executive can purchase the findings of pricing research in this case if the purchase cost is not more than the benefits. He will make the pricing decision under that condition. There is another alternative left to him that he can resort to test marketing to predict eventual product demand at different prices. There is one hazard in test marketing that the result cannot be used with certainty. Sometimes, the product may be sold poorly in test marketing but have wide market at national level and vice versa. The usefulness of test marketing depends upon the success experienced in test marketing in previous years.

The managerial decisions should be changed as per the findings of the research. If the managerial decision will be the same regardless of the research findings, the research should not be conducted regardless of its cost. When the utilities of research findings are conveyed to the executive, decisions may be changed accordingly. In the preposterior analysis, the possible research results are simply anticipated and the prior probabilities are revised systematically employing Bayes' rule. The posterior probabilities depend on both the test market results and the initial assessment of the prior probabilities. Two people given the same test market may arrive at different final probabilities for the states of nature. Different people may arrive at different conclusions on the basis of the same evidence. The decision-makers, sometimes, do not care about the research findings because they depend upon their experience and pre-notion of the same happenings. Their prior probabilities are such that the research is not required to warrant any significant change. In such cases the research will be wasted.

Research may be needed to revise the prior probabilities, i.e., the possible anticipated research results. It requires the optimal decision to be determined for each potential research outcome. For this purpose, calculation of the value of the research is made on the basis of the optimal decision for each possible research result. The expected value of each alternative pricing strategy is calculated for each sample result. If the test market is unsuccessful, the skim pricing will be optimal because it offers the highest expected return.

On the other hand, if the test market is moderately or highly successful, the intermediate pricing strategy may be optimal. The prior probability of heavy product demand may be initially so low that heavy demand will not become the dominant state of nature regardless of the test market results. The projections on the basis of a possible test market result can be used in conjunction with the optimal acts to determine the potential value of the proposed research. The expected value of the test-marketing procedure is found by weighting each expected value of the optimal act given each research result, by the probability of receiving that expected value. The research should continue as long as it costs less than the increment in expected value with the research.

Limitations of Decision Theory

The decision theory is not free from defects. There is no ready-made solution for all the problems. The researcher must be aware of the very objections of the decision theory and sensitivities to problems of coping with them. Executives should be acquainted with the methods and benefits of the decision theory. They should know how to use its techniques. They should be free from prior notions that the time and effort required for application of the decision theory are unprofitable. They should not consider it rigorous and abstruse. The decision theory should be applied with precaution.

It has been observed that the decision theory has not gained favour with executives because they are not well aware of the precautions and sophisticated techniques of the decision theory. Recently, professional executives have started entering the business world. Since they are quick to learning the decision theory, they have acquired the benefits of this theory. People in management use mostly intention and structured decisions and are hesitant in applying the decision theory. If they are told about the benefits of the decision theory, they may make frequent use of the theory. However, the subjectivity of the decision theory cannot be denied in the context of the prediction of probability. The decision theory cannot precisely describe the set of outcomes or pay offs. The exploration for alternatives may be even less structured and the pay offs less identifiable in advance. There may be no crisp decision or pay off that may be projected for the research. The decision theory can be used suitably in decision-oriented research; but it is unlikely to be used in opportunity-oriented and alternative-oriented research.

Benefits of Decision Theory

The decision theory has been applied in many marketing decisions. There is enough opportunity for using this theory. It is beneficial in a sharper decision-making situation that reveals more starkly the structure of the problem and the nature of the variables. This theory reveals the extent of expected downside risks and upside opportunities. It may increase the decision-maker's expectations as the decision is likely to be enhanced by the more explicit recognition of the variables, and of the probable effects of a number of forces concerned with them. This theory helps in judging which projects ought to be undertaken and which to be refused. It is also helpful in the formulation of the decision and in making predictions. The executives can talk freely at the researcher's decisions and expectations. The decision-maker will be in a position to decide the size of the potential market, income potentials, the amount of time taken for the investment, fixed costs and total costs. Also competitive and market dynamics, the extent of a company's experience in a given market, and the product and decision-maker's extent of knowledge.

3. Decision Trees

The alternative approach to deciding the research project is the decision tree, which is simply a decision flow diagram in which the problem is structured in chronological order. The decision tree consists of *(i)* decision forks, *(ii)* outcome forks, *(iii)* probabilities associated with each outcome and *(iv)* rewards or penalties associated with each outcome.

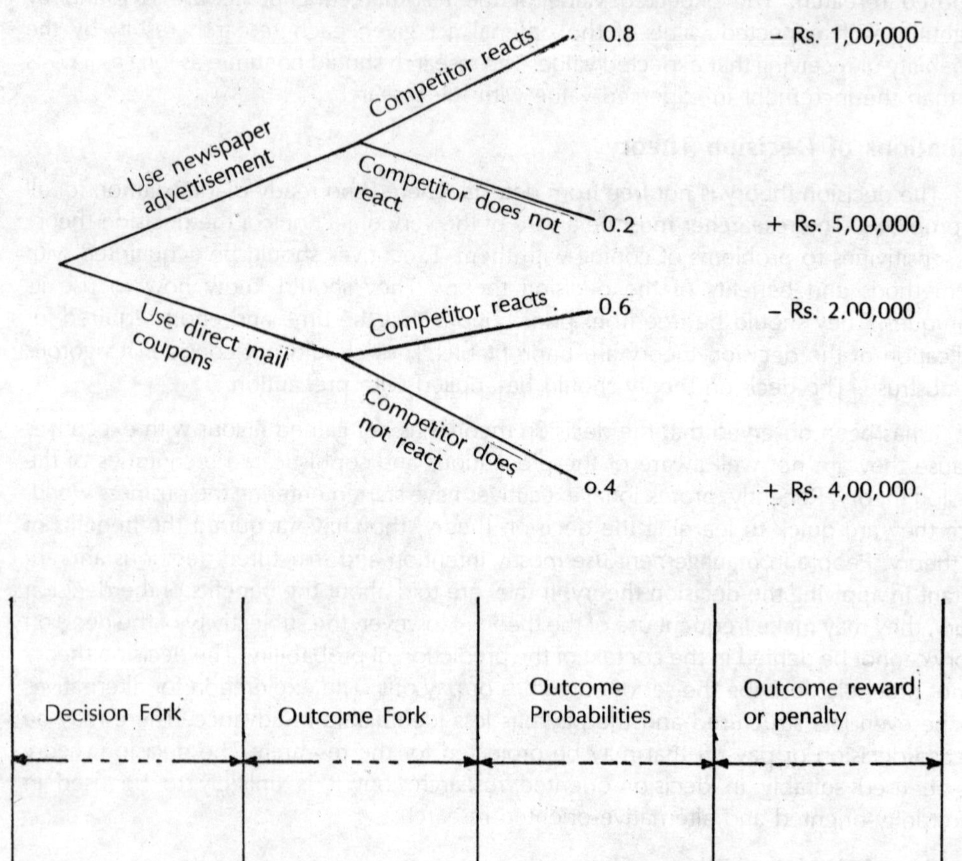

Fig. 3.1 Decision Tree for Promotion of Decision

Figure 3.1, shows a decision fork which represents all of the alternative courses of action being considered, viz., use of newspaper advertisements or use of direct mail coupons. To the right of the decision fork are the outcome forks, i.e., branches of the decision fork which reveal all the possible outcomes that might occur if the decision is made. For example, if a newspaper advertisement is inserted a competitor may or may not react. The competitor may react to the extent of 80 per cent, i.e., 0.8 probability is assigned to competition. So, the probability of competitors not reacting is estimated at 0.2. Consequently, a loss of Rs. 100000 and a profit of Rs. 500,000, may be assigned respectively to the probabilities of competition and non-competition. As similar method of reasoning may be associated with the use of direct mail coupons. The figure reveals a larger probability of no competing response and a smaller profit for the direct mail coupon branch. The fourth stage is the outcome reward or penalty which reveals the total outcome of a decision.

Evaluation of Alternatives: The marketing manager has to evaluate the alternatives attached to the decision tree. This is done by calculating an "expected value" for each alternative. An expected value consists of two components — the reward or penalty associated with an event and the probability that the event will occur. In the above diagram the expected value can be calculated by selecting one of the decision alternative branches. The expected value of each outcome may be arrived at by multiplying the outcome probability by the outcome reward or penalty. By doing this for each outcome and summarising, one can calculate the expected value of each decision alternative. The expected value of using a newspaper advertisement is:

(.8) (–Rs.100,000) + (0.2) (Rs. 500,000) = Rs. 20,000.

In the same way, the expected value of using direct mail coupons is —

(.6(–Rs.200,000) + (.4) (Rs. 4,00,000) = Rs. 40,000.

The expected value is calculated on the information currently available pertaining to possible outcomes, outcome probabilities and outcome rewards or penalties.

Determining the Need and Time or Research

A decision tree analysis can be helpful in determining the need and the time of research. It can successfully test an alternative decision. For example, before the introduction of a new product, there can be three alternatives *(i)* introduce the product nationally, *(ii)* test the product in one market and *(iii)* do not introduce the product.

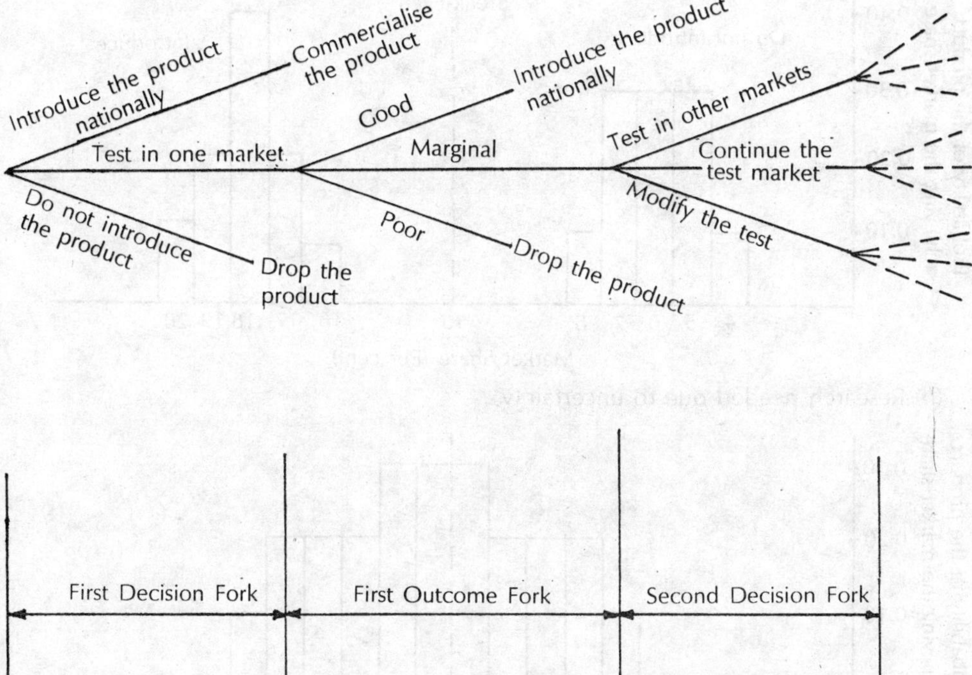

Fig. 3.2 A Decision Tree Diagram for Evaluating the Need for Research

From diagram 3.2, it is clear that there are several alternative methods of introducing a new product. If the management is confident that the product will be a success, they may choose the first alternative. If they are confident that the product will not be a success, they may choose the third alternative. In either case, there is an uncertainty about the consequences of these decisions. If the management is uncertain about the profitability of introducing the product in either case, they may choose to undertake a test of one market. There may be three possible test market outcomes — good, marginal and poor. If the outcome is considered good, the management may take the decision of introducing the product nationally. A poor outcome may result in a decision to drop the new product. In either case, the research or test market will have to be undertaken to arrive at a decision. If the outcome is expected to be marginal, the research may not lead to sufficient reduction of uncertainty to permit the management to decide either to introduce the product or to drop it. The decision fork may involve the alternatives of testing in other markets, continuing the present test market or modifying the test market. The decision fork indicates that additional research may be undertaken — and may continue to be undertaken until the new information adequately reduces the management's uncertainty.

Graphic Presentation of Uncertainty and Research

The decision to undertake a research project or not to undertake a research project can be understood by graphic presentation. For example, the product will be profitable if it gains more than 10 per cent of the market share. The choice of any alternative would be based on the estimate of the market share of the product

(a) Adequate certainty, no research needed prior to decision.

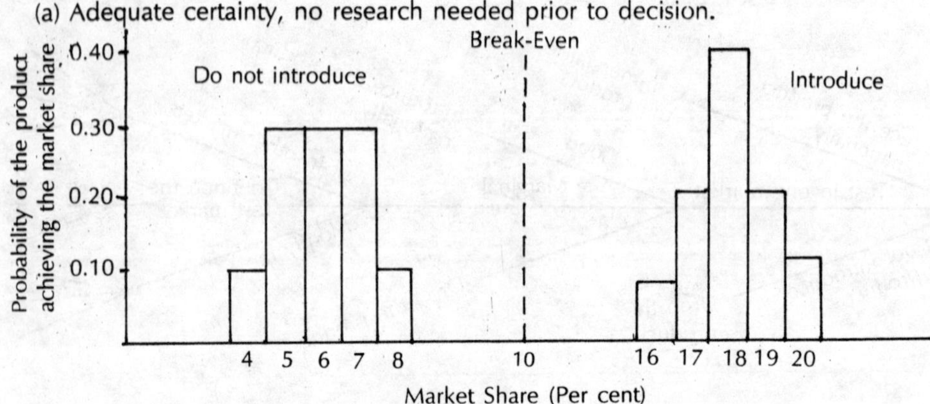

(b) Research needed due to uncertainty.

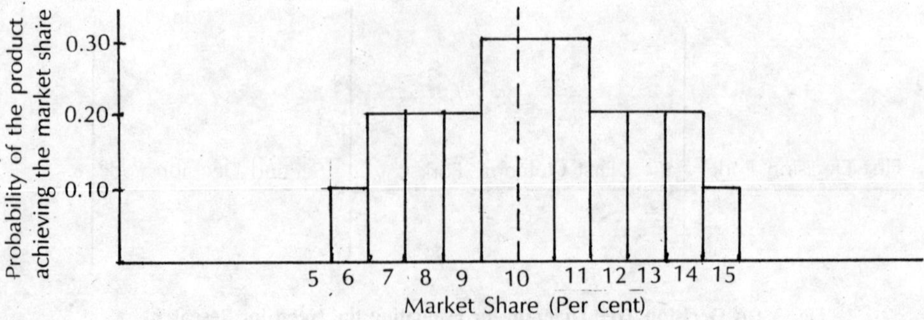

Fig. 3.3 Uncertainty and Research

The marketing manager will have to estimate the probability of the market share of the product. It may be a 10 per cent market share, 11 per cent market share and so on. Suppose the marketing manager has estimated that there is a 0.10 probability that the new product will attain a 10 per cent market share, a 0.20 probability that it will attain a 17 per cent market share, a 0.40 probability that it will attain an 18 per cent market share and so on. These may reveal the uncertainty of the market share which may range from 16 per cent to 20 per cent. The manager may feel the certainty of the market share above 16 per cent which is much larger than the break-even market share of 10 per cent. In such certainty, the marketing manager may need to undertake marketing research. The manager may estimate that there is a 0.05 probability that the new product will attain a 4 per cent market share, 0.30 probability that it will attain a 5 per cent market share, 0.30 probability that it will attain a 6 per cent market share and so on. It shows some uncertainty in the 4-8 per cent range but also reveals certainty that the product will not reach the level of 10 per cent break-even market share. If managers do feel certain that the product will attain no more than a 4-8 per cent market share, they need not do any research prior to deciding not to introduce the product.

There may be another type of probability of distribution which is shown in Figure 3.3 (b). The marketing manager may attain a market share as low as 6 per cent and as high as 15 per cent or in probabilities between these two. The manager is not very sure of any of the market shares as all have approximately the same probability. The manager is uncertain whether he will incur loss or profit. He may prefer to conduct research because the research will reduce the marketing managers' uncertainty to a level where he may decide either to introduce or drop the product. A large degree of uncertainty fosters the decision to conduct research, as it helps to decide whether to drop the new product idea, to introduce it nationally or to continue testing the market.

Decision Tree Analysis to Determine the Need for research

The decision tree analysis is helpful in deciding the need for research. For example, the analysis pertaining to price changes can be discussed in six major alternative courses:

1. Adopt the new price policy nationally as soon as possible.
2. Stay with the present price policy until a major competitor converts and then decide what action to take.
3. Convert one of the company's markets to the new price policy, test market and then decide.
4. Same as 3 above, except meet all needed market now.
5. Undertake two months of consumer research and then decide.
6. Same as 5 above, but meet all needed market now.

The decision tree for this situation involves six alternatives at the first decision fork, followed by six different outcome forks. It reflects the two major questions *(i)* what action would the company's competitors take, and *(ii)* what effect would the new price policy have on the consumer's evaluation of the company's image. There may be three possible first order consequences if their decision was an immediate introduction of a new price policy, viz., (1) no reaction, major competition does not convert branch B_1, (2) major competitor follows conversion to the new price policy — branch B_2, and (3) independent conversion by major competitor — branch B_3. Each of these first order consequences would be followed by decisions from the rest of the industry — branches C_1 to C_6.

The marketing manager can estimate the probabilities associated with the occurrence of each possible type of reaction by the major competitor. There may be 0.05 probability that the competitor would not convert, 0.15 probability that the competitor would follow the company's action and 0.80 probability that the competitor would convert independently of action taken by the company.

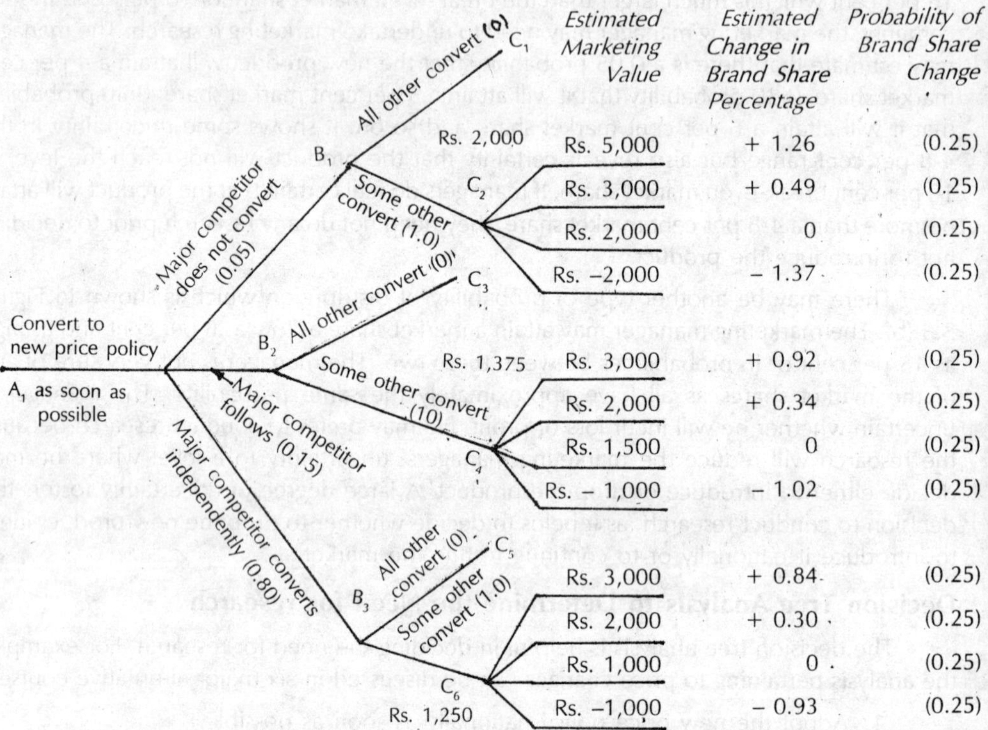

Fig. 3.4 Expected Values of Decision to Convert to New Price Policy (in thousand Rs.)

There may be certainty (1.0) that some others in the industry would convert price policy — C_2, C_4 and C_6 and a certainty (0.0) that all others would not convert — C_1, C_3 and C_5. For each branch (C) of the tree, changes in the company's market share should be estimated. Each of four possible market share changes was given 0.25 probability of occurring, i.e., each of the four was considered to have equal probability of occurring. With this portion of the decision tree completed, it is possible to calculate the expected associated with alternative A1 — the immediate nation-wide introduction of the new price policy. Similarly, the expected value of each C branch can be calculated.

C_2 = Rs. 5,000 + 3,000 + 2,000 – 2,000 = 8,000 × .25 = Rs. 2,000

C_4 = Rs. 3,000 + 2,000 + 1,500 – 1,000 = 5,500 × .25 = Rs. 1,375

C_6 = Rs. 3,000 + 2,000 + 1,000 – 1,000 = 5,000 × .25 = Rs. 1,250

Thus, the value of B branch can also be calculated:

$B_1 = C_1 + C_2 = 0 + 2{,}000 = \text{Rs. } 2{,}000$

$B_2 = C_3 + C_4 = 0 + 1{,}375 = \text{Rs. } 1{,}375$

$B_3 = C_5 + C_6 = 0 + 1{,}250 = \text{Rs. } 1{,}250$

Thus assigning probabilities to each branc!. we get the value of A_1, i.e., value at the conversion to the new price policy.

$$\begin{aligned} A_1 &= B_1 \times p + B_2 \times p + B_3 \times p \\ &= 2{,}000 \times .05 + 1{,}375 \times .15 + 1{,}250 \times .80 \\ &= \text{Rs. } 1{,}306 \\ &= \text{Rs. } 13{,}06{,}000. \end{aligned}$$

Thus, there may be various alternatives of the new price policy. It should be noted here that these values are estimated, i.e., the monetary values associated with different market shares, and the probabilities assigned to the various outcomes such as the competitor's reactions and the resulting market shares. If the estimate is based on the best information, the management need not undertake any research. On the other hand, if the management is unable to decide the uncertainty about the accuracy of the estimate, it may need research.

4. Bayesian Analysis

Bayesian analysis is a sophicated analysis to determine whether research should be undertaken or not. The basis of Bayesian analysis depends upon various alternatives of a problem or opportunity.

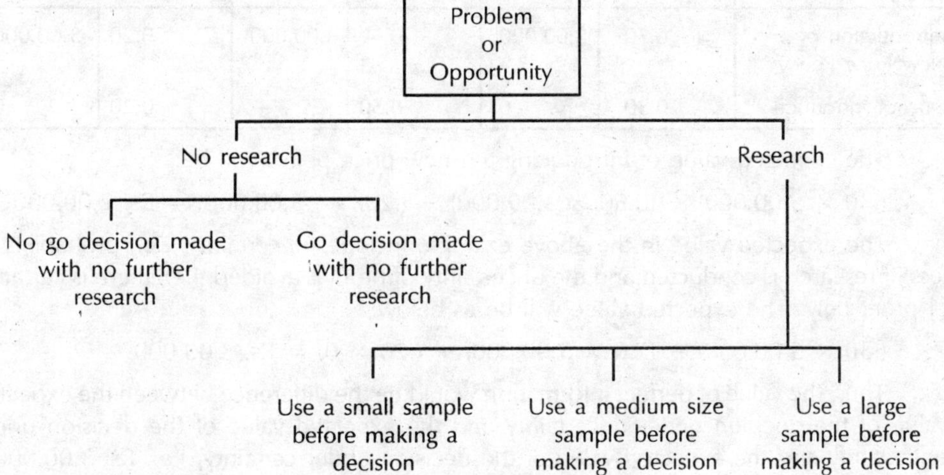

Fig. 3.5 Framework of Beyesian Analysis

As discussed in the previous section, there may be a number of possibilities of a problem apart from the decision arrived at without further research. In the above figure there are three alternatives of research, viz., use a small sample, use a medium size sample and use a large sample. The management will have to decide to what extent research has to be undertaken because research involves additional cost. He has to compare the additional cost and additional value of the information derived from the research. The value of information may be calculated with the probability. Suppose the value of success of a new price policy is 0.80, then the value of failure will be 0.20. In this case if the probable profit is Rs. 20,000, there may not be any research. But the uncertainty may always be there whether to earn profit or not. The value of perfect information is possible only at the research that will reveal the value of success and avoid lack of success. The profit at 0.80 probability may be expected to be Rs. 4,00,000 as the failure is avoided. the expected value is almost perfect value. Therefore, research is conducted in this case. But, it does not tell how much should be spent on a specific research project. For the purpose, the Bayesian analysis is useful.

The market share of the firm has a great impact upon the profit. If the market is highly receptive to the new price-policy, it will achieve a market share of more than 5 per cent and the profit may amount to Rs. 5,00,000. If the price policy is only average by receptive, the market share may range between 1 to 5 per cent and the profit may go upto Rs. 3,00,000. On the contrary a poor market share, i.e., less than one per cent may result in a loss of Rs. 4,00,000. the probability related to each share may be estimated at 0.30, 0.50 and 0.20 respectively for a 5 per cent share, one to 5 per cent share and less than one per cent share. The pay off figures containing the above information are given in the following table.

Table 3.1

Pay off from introduction of new price policy

	State I (S_1)		State II(S_2)		State III (S_3)	
Alternative decisions	Probability	Profit	Probability	Profit	Probability	Profit
Introduction of New Price Policy	0.30	5,00,000	0.50	3,00,000	0.20	–5,00,000
Do not introduce	0.30	0	0.50	—	0.20	0

The expected value of introducing the new price policy will be:

(.30 × 5,00,000) + (0.50 × 3,00,000) + (.20) × –5,00,000) = Rs. 2,00,000

The expected value in the above example includes uncertainty, i.e., probability of loss. If research is conducted and the uncertainty of profit is avoided, i.e., there is certainty of profit only. The expected value will be as below:

(.30 × 5,00,000) + (.50 × 3,00,000) + (.20 × 0) = Rs. 3,00,000

Thus, the value of perfect information would be the difference between the expected value of the decision under uncertainty and the expected value of the decision under uncertainty and the expected value of the decision under certainty, i.e., Rs. 3,00,000 – Rs. 2,00,000 = Rs. 1,00,000. So, no research could be undertaken if the research costs more than Rs. 1,00,000.

The Bayesian analysis provides several alternatives for solving the problems. There may be several samples to test the suitability of the alternative of the problem, e.g., project 1, project 2 and project 3. The Bayesian analysis pertaining to project 1 may be divided into seven steps.

1. Establishing prior probabilities.
2. Determining conditional probabilities for different outcomes.
3. Calculating joint probabilities.
4. Estimating the occurrence of research outcomes (marginal probabilities).
5. Calculating posterior probabilities.
6. Developing a decision tree for research project.
7. Calculating the expected value of decision-making after research project.

Now, we discuss each step in a lucid manner.

1. Establishing Prior Probabilities

Prior probabilities are the expected values which are assigned to each state of nature. In the above example of finding values of a new price policy we have expected the probable values, 0.3, 0.5 and 0.2 respectively for 5 per cent of the share, 1-5 per cent of the share and less than one per cent share of the market. These are known as prior probabilities because these exist prior to obtaining additional information. They are based on the manager's experience, past research, recollections and other pertinent inputs. These are expected to be present in the real world. An experienced manager can estimate relatively real probabilities. Before deciding to embark upon the research project, the manager will decide how much the probabilities can be changed as per information available after research. If the probability after research shows several variations, there may be no or less use of research. It may be possible because the research may not always be completely accurate. The most accurate research gives results corresponding to the real world. There may be four different types of probabilities which are attached to the research project: conditional probability, joint probability, marginal probability and posterior probability.

2. Determining Conditional Probabilities for Different Test Outcomes

If the research project is undertaken about the impact of the new price policy, it may show different shares of the market, e.g., a market share more than 5 per cent, a market share between 1-5 per cent and a market share of less than 1 per cent. These are the different outcomes of the new price which are revealed by the small research project.

If the new price policy is introduced and the market share is greater than 5 per cent (S_1 exists), what is the probability that the research outcome will show a market share of less than 1 per cent, i.e., what is the probability that the research outcome E_1 will result? Similarly, if S_1 exists, what is the probability that research outcome E_2 will result or that research outcome E_3 will result? These are conditional probabilities, and they are shown in the first row of S_1. Similarly, conditional probabilities of S_2 and S_3 are also indicated.

Table 3.2
Conditional Probabilities

	Possible Research Outcomes		
If state of nature is	E_1 *(Below 1 per cent market share)*	E_2 *(1-5 per cent market share)*	E_3 *(Over 5 per cent market share)*
S_1 (Over 5 per cent share)	0.15	0.30	0.55
S_2 (1-5 per cent share)	0.30	0.50	0.20
S_3 (below 1 per cent share)	0.70	0.20	0.10

The sum of probability for each state of nature will be 1.0, i.e., one of three outcomes will certainly occur. But the probabilities are that each market share does not equal one because it is not certain that any one of the state of nature under each market share will occur. The above table shows that there are 0.55 probabilities that the new price policy will fetch more than 5 per cent share, 0.50 probabilities that these will be between a 1 to 5 per cent share and 0.70 probabilities that these will be less than 1 per cent of the market share. The second step in the Bayesian analysis reveals that the manager and the researcher estimate the conditional probability that research outcome E_j (i=1,2,3) will occur if the true state of nature is S_i (i=1,2,3). These probabilities must be estimated for all combinations of E_j and S_1.

3. Calculating Joint Probabilities

If the management is certain about any one of the three states of nature, research would not be required and the decision to introduce or not to introduce the new price policy could be made with certainty. But the management is uncertain to what extent the new price can achieve the market share. Therefore, there is a need to conduct new research.

If, additional information is available, then the next question is how likely it is that the state of nature S_1 (or S_2 or S_3) actually exists. The management may recognise that the research results can easily differ from the actual state of nature. The management, quite apart from the findings of research, may have confidence in its own judgement of the market. If the management has confidence that its judgement is similar to that of the findings of the research it may rely on its judgement. The conflict between its judgement and the research findings provides a base for it to improve the judgement. It likes to continue the new research information with its prior judgement. Joint probability is obtained by combining conditional probability of the state of nature with the prior probability of the specified state of nature. The joint probability is that a given state of nature exists, and that the test market research will provide a given result, say E_1, E_2 or E_3. The management has estimated the probabilities of the existence of each of the three states of nature, i.e., S_1, S_2, S_3 at 0.30, 0.50 and 0.20 respectively.

Table 3.3

Joint Probabilities for combinations of given States of Nature and Given Research Outcomes

State of Nature	Possible Research Outcomes						
	(a) Probability of S_1 being true state	*(b) Probability of E_1 research outcome if given S exists*	*(c) Joint probability of E_1 and S_1*	*(d) Probability of E_2 research outcome if given S exists*	*(e) Joint Probability of E_2 and S_1 (a×d)*	*(f) Probability of E_3 research outcome if given S exists*	*(g) Joint probability of E_3 and S_1 (a×f)*
S_1	0.30	0.15	0.0450	0.30	0.0900	0.55	0.1650
S_2	0.50	0.30	0.1500	0.50	0.2500	0.20	0.1000
S_3	0.20	0.70	0.1400	0.20	0.0400	0.10	0.0200
Total	1.00		0.3350		0.3800		0.2850

The conditional probabilities that outcome E_j will occur, given that S_i is the true state of nature are given in the columns (b), (d) and (f). The joint probability that state of nature S_1 is the true state of nature and the research, outcome W_1 will occur, is given in the column (c), i.e., column (a) × column (b) of the above table. In case of S_1, the joint probability in research outcomes E_1 is calculated as 0.0450. It shows the probability according to the management's best judgement based on the true state of nature S_1 and research outcome E1. It is the joint probability of the prior judgement of management and of the research outcome. Similarly, the joint probabilities of the true state of nature, or prior judgement of the management and of the research outcome under E_2, i.e., 1–5 per cent share and E_3 i.e., below 1 per cent share are given in the column (e) and (g) of Table 3.3.

4. Estimating the Marginal Probabilities of Research Outcomes

The probability that a particular research outcome will take place is known as the marginal probability of the research outcome. The joint probabilities as calculated in the previous step are used to estimate the probability that a particular research outcome, i.e., E_1 will occur. The marginal probability of each research outcome is calculated by summing up the joint probabilities associated with the research. The marginal probabilities of the joint probabilities of E_1 is 0.045 + 0.150 + 0.140 = 0.335 are as given in the total of column (c). Similarly, the marginal probability of research outcome of E_2 is 0.380 and of E_3 is 0.285 which are shown at the total column of (c) and (g) of Table 3.3. It shows the best judgement of the management based on the management's prior probabilities, and the estimated probabilities as per the research outcomes of different states. If the small sample research project is undertaken, the probabilities of research outcomes E_1, E_2 and E_3 occurring are 0.335, 0.380 and 0.285 respectively.

5. Calculating Posterior Probabilities

The posterior probability is the revised prior probability. The probability is called posterior probability because the management's prior probability (judgement) gets modified after receiving new information from the research.

The management had estimated prior probabilities of the impact on the increase of sales under the new price policy in case of more than a 5 per cent share of the market (S_1), a 1-5 per cent share of the market (S_2) and less than one per cent share of the market as 0.3, 0.5 and 0.2 respectively. These prior probabilities are modified by the management as per the information available at research project no.1.

The joint probabilities after the research outcome under E_1 (below 1 per cent market share), E_2 (between 1 to 5 per cent market share) and E_3 (above 5 per cent market share) have also been calculated as 0.335, 0.380 and 0.285 respectively in the above situations. The posterior probabilities of E_1 can be calculated on the basis of the total of S_1, S_2 and S_3. The posterior probabilities of E_1 will be 0.045 × .335 = .19 under the state of nature of S_1, 0.1500/0.235 = .64 under the state of S_2 and 0.1400/.350 = .60 under the state of nature of S_3. Similarly the posterior probabilities under research outcome under E_2 and E_3 under different market shares are given in (c) and (d) column of Table 3.4.

Table 3.4
Posterior Probabilities

States of nature (a)	*Possible Research Outcomes* E_1 *(b)*	E_2 *(c)*	E_3 *(d)*
S_1	0.0450/0.3350 =0.130	0.0900/0.3800 = 0.24	0.1650/0.2850 = 0.58
S_2	0.1500/0.3350 = 0.450	0.2500/0.3800 = 0.66	0.1000/0.2850 = 0.35
S_3	0.1400/0.3350 = 0.420	0.0400/0.3800 = 0.10	0.0200/0.2850 = 0.07
Total	= 1.00	= 1.00	= 1.00

6. Developing a Decision Tree for Research Project No. 1

The Baynesian analysis from step 1 to step 5 has been devoted to estimate marginal probabilities and posterior probabilities. These can also be discussed with the help of a decision tree.

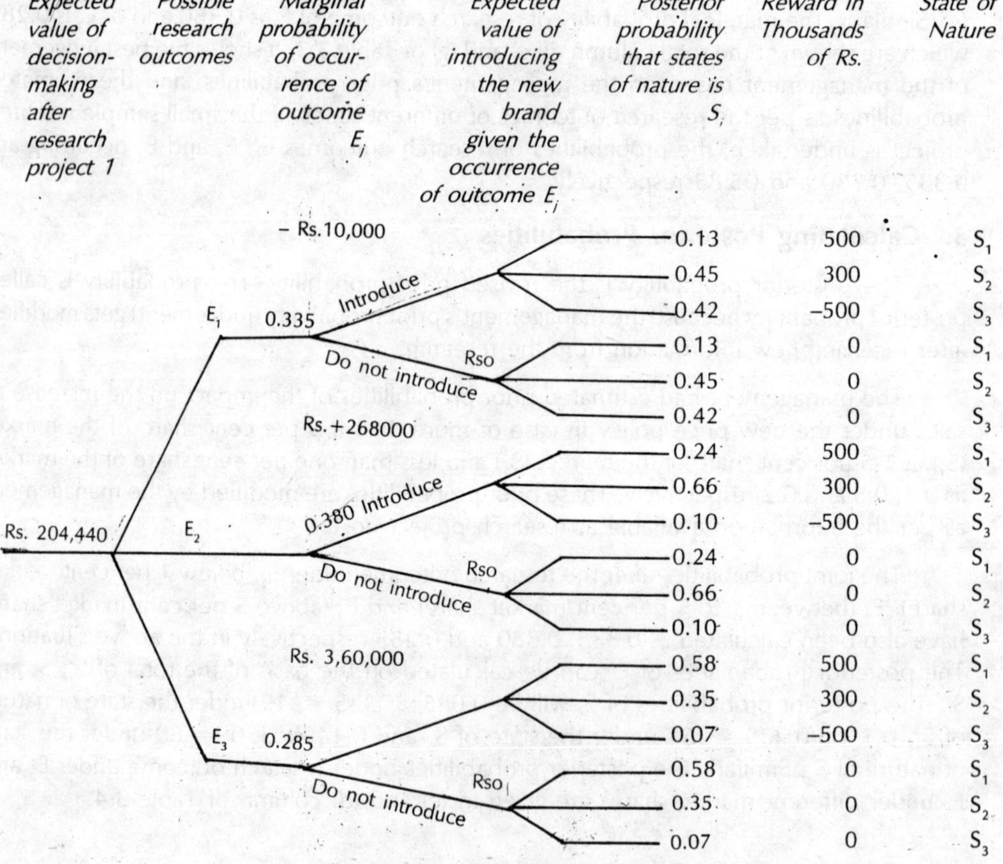

Fig. 3.6 Decision Tree Analysis

The expected value based on the posterior probabilities comes to a loss of Rs. 10,000 in E_1 (whether the market share is less than one per cent.) If the new price policy is introduced, the posterior probabilities based on the research information and prior judgement of the management would be 0.13, 0.45 and 0.42 in the state of nature of S_1, S_2 and S_3 respectively. Calculating the reward of each state of nature and respecting posterior probabilities, the expected values in each case come to Rs. 65,000, Rs. 135 and Rs. 210 respectively. Thus, the total expected value of E introducing the new price policy comes to Rs. 10,000. If the new price policy is not introduced there is no reward. Therefore, the expected value of not introducing a new price policy becomes zero, and the total expected value in the E_1 case becomes a loss of Rs. 10,000. Similarly, the expected values of E_2 and E_3 are also calculated with the posterior probabilities and rewards of each state of nature in the respective research outcome. The expected value of E_2 comes to Rs. 268,000 and of E_3 comes to Rs. 3,60,000.

7. Calculating the Expected Value of Decision-making after Research

The next step is to calculate the value of the information which will be generated by the research project. From the decision tree, it is clear that the expected values of research information will be Rs. 26,800 if research outcome E_2 occurs and Rs. 3,60,000 if research outcome E_3 occurs. If research outcome E_1 occurs, the management would incur a loss as the expected value of introducing the new price policy would be negative, i.e., Rs. 10,000. Therefore, the management would not introduce a new price policy. Each research outcome has its respective marginal probability of occurrence, i.e., 0.335 in E_1, 0.380 in E_2 and 0.225 in E_3. Multiplying the expected value and marginal probability each research outcome comes to:

= (0.335) (Rs. 0) + (0.380) (Rs. 2,68,000) + (0.285) (Rs. 3,60,000)

= 0 + Rs. 1,01,840 + Rs. 1,02,600

= Rs. 2,04,440.

The expected value of introducing the new price policy without conducting research has been calculated as Rs. 2,00,000 in the initial discussion of Bayesian analysis. Therefore, additional value expected by the research information comes to merely Rs. 204,440 – Rs. 2,00,000 = Rs. 4,440. The management would not be willing to get research conducted if the cost of research is Rs. 4,440.

Calculating the Expected Value of Decision-Making Projects 2 and 3

In the beginning of the Baynesian analysis, three research projects have been given as various alternatives of decision-making. We have discussed the small size research project 1 whereby it has been decided that the expected value without conducting research was Rs. 2,00,000, and the expected value after getting information from the research project would be Rs. 2,04,440. Thus, the additional value from the research has been Rs. 4,440. If the research project 1 costs less than Rs. 4,440, research of a small size would be undertaken by the management.

The analyses of research project 2 and research project 3 involve the same stages of analysis as discussed above. The only changes will be in the assigned conditional probabilities, i.e., the probabilities of the various research results which will occur if given states of nature exist in the medium sized sample and the large sample. The medium sized sample will give results closer to the true state of nature than the medium size sample. In the large sample research project, the management would assign a higher probability to the occurrence of research outcome E_3 if the true state of nature was S_1 than that of the small research project. Similarly higher probability is assigned to the probability of research outcome E_2 in the large sample study if the true state of nature was S_2.

On the basis of analysis stages of research project 1, the management would calculate the additional value of research project 2 and research project 3, to decide whether a particular research project will be undertaken in the light of their respective costs of conducting the research. The Bayesian analysis is an explicit and comprehensive tool of deciding the research project.

❖ ❖ ❖

CHAPTER 4

RESEARCH DESIGN

1. **EXPLORATORY RESEARCH-DESIGN**
   1. **LITERATURE RESEARCH**
   2. **EXPERIENCE SURVEY**
   3. **CASE STUDY**
2. **CONCLUSIVE RESEARCH**
   1. **DESCRIPTIVE RESEARCH**
      - **(i) LONGITUDINAL STUDY**
      - **(ii) CROSS-SECTIONAL STUDY**
   2. **EXPERIMENTAL RESEARCH**
      - **(i) LABORATORY EXPERIMENTS**
      - **(ii) FIELD EXPERIMENTS**
3. **SPECIFIC EXPERIMENTAL DESIGN**
   1. **PRE-EXPERIMENTAL DESIGNS**
   2. **TRUE EXPERIMENTAL DESIGNS**
   3. **QUASI-EXPERIMENTAL DESIGNS**
   4. **STATISTICAL EXPERIMENTAL DESIGNS**

RESEARCH DESIGN

A research project conducted scientifically has a specific framework of research from the problems identification to the presentation of the researc report. This framework of conducting research is known as the research design. "A research design is simply the framework or plan for a study that is used a guide in collecting and analysing the data. It is the blueprint that is followed in completing a study."[1] Research can be conducted without a research design but it may not solve the problems. The basic objective of research cannot be attained without proper research design. The cost and energy involved may also be high in such cases. The research design specifies the methods and procedures for acquiring the information needed. It is the overall operational pattern or framework of the project that stipulates what information is to be collected from which sources and by what procedures. If it is a good research design, it can collect the data economically and by objectives. There may not be a single, standard and correct method of research. There may be different types of research design to suit different purposes of research.

Types of Research Design

The marketing research designs are classified on the basis of the fundamental objective of the research. They may be exploratory or conclusive.

1. Exploratory Research
   - (a) Search of Secondary data or Literature search
   - (b) Survey of knowledgeable persons or experience survey
   - (c) Case Study.
2. Conclusive Research
   - (a) Descriptive Research
     - (i) Longitudinal Study
     - (ii) Cross-sectional Study
   - (b) Experimentation.

1. EXPLORATORY RESEARCH-DESIGN

Exploratory research design seeks to discover new relationships between several facts. It discovers ideas and insights. The marketing researcher is involved in investigating an area in which no sufficient knowledge is available and no clear hypotheses have been developed about the problem. The major purpose of the exploratory research design is the clear identification of problems segregating from irrelevant variables and alternatives. The broad and vague problems are broken in smaller and more precise statements. These statements may take the forms of hypotheses. "In effect, a hypothesis is a statement which specifies how two or more measurable variables are related."[2] Hypotheses are usually drawn from ideas developed or from previous studies. Exploratory study is the initial stage of marketing research as it is in a developing stage. Each study adds a little more to the existing knowledge about the marketing-mix. Thus each study adds a new hypothesis in marketing research.

1. Gilbert A. Churchill, *Marketing Research,* The Dryden Press, Illionois, 1979, p. 46.
2. Fred N. Kerlinger, *Foundations of Behavioural Research,* 1973, p. 18.

Exploratory research reveals the most likely explanations of various problems of the marketing mix. It can explore various hypotheses in each mix of the market, viz., product, price, promotion and distribution. The exploratory study may be used to clarify concepts and the causes of problems. It generates information about the practical possibilities of research. It is used to increase the analysts familiarity with the problem.

It is also useful to test the applicability of a new policy, for formulating problems, developing hypotheses, establishing priority of further research, gathering practical problems of carrying out research and clarifying concepts. It is dynamic and changes with new ideas and concepts. Keeping the objectives as a leading factor for exploratory research is essential to solve the problems in right earnest.

The objective of an exploratory study is to find new ideas of relationships; no formal design can be set up. Ingenuity, judgement and flexibility play a part in designing the exploratory research. The researcher goes on discovering new ideas until he finds a better idea towards which he can turn his research activities. Formal design is conspicuous, the imagination of the researcher is the key factor to design the research process forms. Notwithstanding the flexibility, some formal exploratory designs may be observed. They are:

1. Literature Search
2. Experience Survey
3. Case Study

These have their respective merits and demerits and can be suited to different situations. We discuss them in the following paragraphs.

1. Literature Research

The quickest and most economical way is to find possible hypotheses from the available literature. The past researches may be suitable sources of information to develop new hypotheses. The findings of marketing research are generally published in trade and professional journals which can be fruitful sources of information. Such research-findings are available in company or public libraries. Various forms of literatures such as conceptual literature, trade literature, published statistics and socio-psychological literature are available in these libraries. The researcher can search them for his research-purposes.

A specific problem can be solved by searching the available literature. Why sales have declined can be answered by analysing published data and other related literature. The problem may be confied to one firm or it may be common to all firms in an industry or to all types of industries. The firms' share in the market can be assessed accordingly. In such types of research, the major emphasis is on the discovery of ideas and tentative explanations of the phenomenon. An advertising company in the USA had concluded from the exploratory research, i.e., examining of available literature that sales increased on account of advertising. Therefore, a particular company adopted advertising practices and sales increased considerably. The survey of literature may provide such types of new hypotheses which may be useful in marketing management. Electronic data processing has made it easy to store a large quantity of data and information which can fruitfully be utilised for marketing management. Many businesses have computerised data banks covering the literature on various aspects of marketing variables.

2. Experience Survey

Experience survey indicates the use of reservoir of knowledge and experience possed by those familiar with the specific subject to be investigated. All persons who have information of market-variables are potential sources of information. These pesons are known as the focus group who supply suitable information to the researcher. It may be structured in the form of a formal questionnaire to be acquired from the focus group. This design is to be acquired from the focus group. This design is to look for competent, articulate individuals and discuss with them the problem.

The knowledgeable persons may be housewives, retailers and others who can furnish suitable information to the researcher. Similarly, top executives of the company, the sales manager and product manager may be a good source of information. Experience survey obtains insight into the relationships between variables. Those persons who have competence or experience in the areas are approached and not those persons who have no knowledge of the problems. The emphasis in exploratory resarch is on developing tentative explanations. It is important here, to give respondents the greatest possible freedom of response.

The main use of experience survey is that it provides a quick summary of the main issues. Interaction among members of the group brings out variations at many points. It tends to bring about relaxed and natural discussion.

3. Case Study

A detailed case analysis of selected organisations or individuals may be helpful in gaining information and new ideas about the marketing mix. It involves the intensive study of selected cases of the phenomenon. This method includes the examination of existing records, by observing the occurrence of the phenomenon. The researcher seeks explanations of the hypotheses and does not test the explanations. Attempts are made to find new information of existing as well as new cases. The attitude and integrative powers of the researcher are key factors in a case study. A particular case is examined in entities with intensity. The unique features of each case selected are sufficiently inquired into. All aspects of the cases are investigated. An inquiry is also made to sales representatives about their experience with the cases. For example, to study the productivity of the sales force, the researcher may make inquiries two or three of the best salesmen and also two or three of the worst salesmen. New hypotheses are developed from the above studies.

The findings of a case study are always suggestive rather than conclusive since the examination is being conducted after the fact basis, and it is not possible to manipulate the variables. The interpretation of the results should be made taking into consideration the relevancy and relationship of variables because they are subject to error. Despite the shortcomings, the case study displays sharp contrasts or striking features which can be useful in marketing management.

2. CONCLUSIVE RESEARCH

Conclusive research provides information which helps the executive make a rational decision. The marketing executive has to arrive at a suitable decision from the various alternative decisions. The various alternative conclusions and selecting the most suitable conclusion may be done by descriptive research design or experimental research design.

In descriptive research design, only a partial situation is clarified, but in the case of experimental research design, a precise alternative is selected. Therefore, the experimentation is considered an important conclusive research design. First we discuss descriptive research design.

1. Descriptive Research Design

Much of the marketing research is concerned with the description of the marketing mix. Market performance research, market potential study, market share study, product research, promotion research, distribution research, pricing research and competition research are based on the descriptive research design. These studies often describe the relationship between two or more variables. The relationship between the variables may be used for prediction purposes. Descriptive design can be a sound basis for making predictions pertaining to specific marketing problems, although it does not explain the nature of the relationship involved.

Many descriptive designs may aim to collect data without having any clear objective of the use of the data. Such types of descriptive studies are actually more exploratory than they are conclusive. To be specific, the descriptive design must aim to collect data with a definite purpose. "What makes facts practical and valuable is the glue of explanation and understanding, the framework of theory, the tie-rod of conjective. Only when facts can be fleshed to a skeletal theory do they become meaningful in the solution of problems."[3] Thus, the data if explained and described can be useful in marketing research. The data must rest on some specific hypotheses. The conjectival statement may be there in designing the research method. Descriptive studies are rigid and conclusive.

Difference between Exploratory Design and Descriptive Design

Descriptive design in contrast to exploratory design is marked by the prior formulation of specific research problems. Descriptive design clearly defines what it is that the researcher wants to measure and to set up appropriate and specific means for measuring it. The exploratory research reveals substantial amount of research problem which can be used as a basis of descriptive research. Whereas an exploratory design is characterised by its flexibility, descriptive studies can be considered rigid. Descriptive research requires a clear specification of the who, what, when, where, why and how the research is to be done. Formal design is required to insure that the description covers all phases. Precise statement of the problem indicates what information is required. The descriptive research, then designs specific methods for selecting sources of information and for collecting data from these sources. Descriptive study provides a sound basis for prediction but does not show a direct cause and effect relationship, i.e., the purpose of causal research or experimental research. Thus, exploratory research designs the problems, descriptive research provides the base for prediction, and experimental research establishes cause and effect relationship to provide suitable models of solutions of the problems.

While designing the descriptive research, some cases are essential to insure complete description of the situation, to insure minimum bias in collection of data, to reduce the error and minimise the cost of research. Since the purpose of the descriptive study is to provide answers to specific questions more care should be exercised against the possibility of systematic errors than is the case with the exploratory research.

---

3. Robert Ferber, Donald F. Blanlserty and Sidney Hollander Jr. *Marketing Research,* Ronald Press Co., New York, 1964, p. 153.

There are two types of descriptive research design: (1) Longitudinal method and (2) Cross sectional method.

1. Longitudinal Method: Case methods are not widely used in descriptive research design. They have been more of an exploratory nature than that of a descriptive nature. However in the descriptive study, the case method is in the descriptive study; case method is intensively used to find out solutions to problems. These are also known as panel studies. A panel is simply a fixed sample of individuals or some other entities from whom repeated measurements are taken. The main feature of longitudinal study is that there are repetitive measurements of the same events at different points of time. Changes that take place during the intervals of time are recorded for purposes of analysis. The performance analysis can be suitable to this design. The effects of some factors indicate useful hypotheses. This type of research is helpful to the problems in which interrelationships of a number of factors are involved, and in which it is difficult to understand the individual factors without considering their relationship with each other. The similarities at a particular point of time and dissimilarities at other points are compared to find out suitable conclusions about the variables of the market. Thus, the longitudinal analysis may reveal common features, uncommon features and specific features of the panels selected for study. The longitudinal study may be of two types — *(i)* True panel and *(ii)* Omnibus panel.

(i) True Panel: The true panel relies on repeated measurements of the same variables. For example, a consumer panel may be selected whereby each family may be examined at different points of time to examine their behaviour. Similar characteristics of all the members of the panel are looked into to arrive suitable conclusions. Panel-members are constantly contacted for getting periodical information of size of the market, brand share, brand loyalty, frequency of purchase, influence of price, impact of a new brand and impact of advertising or distribution strategy.

(ii) Omnibus Panel: In an omnibus panel, a sample of members is selected and maintained, but the information collected from the members varies. A a particular point attitudes towards new products and at another point the advertising impact or pricing impact may be asked. The sample of members of the panel must be representative to the population while the subsample may be drawn randomly.

The true panel measures the same entities over time. It is just a study of time series. The turnover table may be prepared for the true panel. But in the case of the onibus panel, there may be different attirbutes and features of the mambers of the panel to be examined. The true panel mainly reveals similarities, while the omnibus panel concentrates on dissimilarities of the variables.

Advantages of Panel Study

The panel study may be analytical and so the findings will be useful for the marketing management. The study can reveal the impact of changes in individual behaviour, advertising changes, price changes and so on. The changes in the variables can be vividly identified. Accurate classification is made under this study to arrive at classified findings of a particular phenomenon. Since events and experiences are forgotten more readily, the panel study may be useful to record the various changes, attitude beliefs or persons' self-esteem. The researcher can interact with the respondents who may belong to distinct personalities and different social roles. The researcher and the respondents develop a good rapport because of continuous contact. The respondents rely on the researcher and provide him with most confidential information. Thus, more accurate data are obtained in the longitudinal research design. It describes a real event or situation. Correct inferences are derived from a study of the entire situation and event.

Disadvantages

The respondents may reveal only appealing information to the researcher. They may not be representative if the panels are selected without considering the representation. The respondents may ignore the questionnaire. Sometimes, attempts are made to select quota samples to create a representative panel in respect of age, occupation, education etc. The researcher cannot force individuals to participate in the interview. Certain individuals may not, though included in the panels, participate in the research process. This is the reason the respondents are offered some premiums or allowances to participate in the interview. Many members of the panel may quit the panel leaving the panel to become unrepresentative; mail panels suffer relatively greater losses.

In a panel study, informal methods are generally used as it is difficult to develop formal methods of observation. So the results may be more subjective than objective. Since formal statistical procedures are not used, the results may be subjective rather than objective. Since formal statistical procedures are not used, the results may be according to the affects of the intuition of the researcher.

2. Cross-Sectional Design

The cross-sectional design is termed as field study since the repetitive nature of inquiry is not present in this case. It seeks a comparison between various groups, and in differing characteristics of these groups. The size of sample covered is much greater than in a longitudinal study, to have ample opportunities of study of varied features of research. For example actual purchase behaviour may be related to demographic characteristics, e.g., age, occupation, sex, dominance, self-actuation and sociability of revealing distinctive features of each segment of the variables. The cross-sectional study selects the sample of members from the population at a particular point of time, and provides a snapshot of the variables of interest during that time. Unlike the longitudinal research, it does not study the panel at different intervals, but it studies only at a particular point of time.

The objective of cross-sectional study is to establish categories in such a way that classification in one category implies classification in one or more of the other categories. Statistical methods are used to analyse cross-sectional data. Since panels involve more cases or members, merely comparing individual cases by analogy will not serve the purpose of study. There is need for the use of averages, percentage, measures of dispersion and more statistical procedures. The cross-sectional study and representative sample is essential, which is undertaken by application of statistical methods. The representative data are also analysed with the application of statistical methods. There are two types of cross-sectional design *(i)* Field study and *(ii)* Field survey.

(i) Field Study: It has greater depth of the study. It is less concerned with the representation and is more concerned with the in-depth study of a few typical situations. The emphasis in a field study is on the inter-relationship of a number of factors. When a number of factors are not comparable, it is essential to use a field study. The main advantages of a field study lie in the realism, strength of variables and heuristic quality. This study gives a realistic view of the phenomenon as it involves a study of the real facts. No attempt is made to manipulate a controlled variable. The influences of variables are possibly recorded. The study designs a system of classification and cross classification. The objective is to establish categories such that classification in one category implies classification in one or more of the other categories. The intensive study of a few cases may give new hypotheses. The descriptive study in this case tries to explain certain statements.

The field study is only the posterior study. It has no control on the respondents or on the field. There are many factors to influence the variables and it becomes difficult to segregate the related factors from the composite impact. There is no precision with which to measure the validity of the field.

(ii) Field Survey: The field survey relies on the survey functions. The survey attempts to be representative of some known universe. The basic difference between field study and field survey is the greater scope of the survey and the greater depth of the study. The emphasis in a survey is on the generation of summary statistics such as average and percentage. In the field study, more sophisticated statistical tools such as coefficient of co-relation and regression are used to establish the inter-relationship between the variables. The greatest value in cross sectional study is not analysis of one factor, but analysis of several variables at the same time. This study is useful to indicate possible relationship but it cannot prove cause and effect relationships. The large sample is the main feature of the field survey. Sub-samples may be selected to have a clearer idea of the survey. Unlike the field study, the field survey does not use sophisticated tools of statistics. The field survey attempts to be a representation of some known universe. Therefore, greater care is exercised in selecting sample members by using statistical methods, i.e., probability sampling.

The field survey is prone to sample error. A large number of sample members are selected to minimise the sample error. The hypotheses can be observed in cross-sectional study and survey method is considered an important method to have extensive study of the variables. The survey method is an extensive study and is not much concerned with the intensive study as the field study may be. The average study under the survey method is not realistic because the average does not exist. It is expensive in terms of time and money. In survey research, much time is taken from problem identification to the design of the sample, collecting the data, editing, coding and tabulating the data. At the time of interpretation of the findings, enough time has lapsed and the presentation of findings will be outdated. It requires a good deal of technical skill in designing the survey and in the interpretation of findings. Therefore, the sample survey is a time, money and energy consuming design. However, it is becoming very common in marketing research to observe various situations and problems.

As compared to exploratory and panel researches, it provides more accurate findings. The tendency in the said research design is to jump to general conclusions from a few cases which may or may not be typical of the universe; but a properly selected sample survey is apt to be typical of the universe. The generalisation of this design can be more reliable than that of other methods as discussed above although it does not prove a cause and effect relationship. Some such shortcomings can be removed by the application of field study. This design can imply cause and effect on cross-classification when several cross classifications are used, the analysis becomes complex. This method will not prove them in the way the experimental design can prove.

2. Experimental Design

Experimental Design is effective in measuring the cause and effect relationships unlike the descriptive design where cross classification is made to identify the effect of the causal factor. Measurements of cause and effect by cross-classification is not scientific, but experiments are organised to make the research design a relatively unambiguous interpretation. Experimentation is given more exhaustive treatment in marketing research on account of its inherent attributes. It is a rational and ideal design for marketing research. It reveals the conclusions which remain almost observed. The degree of extraneous analysis tends to be substantially reduced in experimental designs and causal relationship is established. In experimental design, the actual trial of a proposed course of action or hypotheses are so conducted that their effects can be measured objectively and may be distinguished from the effects of extraneous variables.

In an experiment, a test group whereby a hypothesis is tested to solve the problem is selected, and injection of a particular factor to the test group will reveal the impact of the particular injection (cause) as the other group is left without the cause. The cause and effect relationship implies a probablistic relationship. The experimental design can obtain more conclusive evidence of the cause and effect relationship between two variables, although scientific design establishes the relationship between more than two variables.

This design has the ability to set up a situation for the express purpose of observing and recording accurately the effect on one variable, when another is deliberately changed to prove or disprove the hypotheses.

Features of Experimental Design: There are two groups — *(i)* test group, and *(ii)* control group in experimental design. In the test group the experiment is done, i.e., the variables are allowed to change, according to the result of the cause. The consequences of the cause are noted which are then compared with the control group where variables are not changed and no experiment or cause is incurred. The extraneous variables are held constant in the control group. Attempts are made to examine the test group and control group under the same situation. But in marketing research, they confront the vagaries and dynamics of human behaviour. So, attempts are made to wave deliberate manipulation or control of extraneous variables. The nature of variables under test are specified and deliberate treatment is applied. The results, or payoff, ensuing from its application can be identified and measured in the given problem. The extraneous variables are identified to exclude their effects from the effects of the treatment.

Advantages — Internal and External Validity

The experimental design has the advantages of internal and external validity. Internal validity means that no other plausible cause of the observed results should exist. Before and after experimental treatment, the experimental variables are unchanged and the effects can be assigned to the treatment. But there may be influences of attitudes and knowledge of the researchers. The internal validity exists only when such non-experimental treatments and their effects are there in the experimental design. This design involves caring to minimise human judgements, and whenever separate groups are used for different treatments or controls, they are identical in all pertinent characteristics. In experimental design, the researchers are successful in eliminating the effects of other factors which may observe or confound the relationship of the variables under this study. Other factors are held constant and the effects are due to the manipulation of the experimental variable or treatment.

The experimental design has external validity, too. External validity demonstrates that the conclusion drawn from one experiment can be valid in the experiment, or it has worldwide acceptability. This is a reliability of predication that can be expected to occur in other situations too. Similarly, it can be said that the experimental design has the virtue of generalisation to other populations and situations. The internal validity and external validity cannot go together. Internal validity requirements may be invalid externally and vice versa. If the treatment is made under field experiments where the test group is representative, the external validity will exist under the controlled extraneous variables.

Extraneous Variables: In experimental research design, the extraneous variables are identified and controlled while the research process is being operated. This design rules out extraneous factors to the extent possible. The extraneous variables are history, maturation, testing, instrument variation, statistical regression, selection bias and experimental mortality.

History: History refers to the specific events which are external to the experiment, but occuring at the same time may affect the variables. For example, to study the influence of price out, 20 per cent price is off. The sales per week are observed to note the impact of the price, but production, meanwhile declined because of shortage of raw material, and sales therefore could not increase. Thus, we cannot conclude that price-cut has affected a decline in sales because a history of external events has occurred during the period of experiment. We cannot control the event but we can identify the event as well as the results of the event in some situations. But in many circumstances, we cannot conclude the impact of history, because there may be various complex variables to abrupt the experiment. The longer the time period between two measurements, the greater the danger that history may confound the result. There is little chance that the impacts of history can be controlled. The only possibility is to recognise their impact on the effects of the experiment.

Maturation: Maturation is like history with the only difference that it occurs gradually and is less evident. It refers to gradual change over time. The results of maturation occur mainly on account of the passage of time. They can mildly effect test results. Between, before and after measurements, some biological and psychological changes may take place with the passage of time. Such changes are called maturation. The maturation effects have been observed in those experiments where elaborate contravances of an artificial nature and willing cooperation of the test members are required over a significant period of time. Maturation refers to the fact that people get older, become tired and become hungry. Change in attitude, change in consumer behaviour and such other changes occur that are not due to any change in marketing strategies.

Testing: The process of experimentation may also affect the observed result. The testing effects may be of two types: the main testing effect and the interacting testing effect. The respondents may not understand the purpose of an interview and can respond differently. If the pattern of testing differs, the results may also vary. But the influence of tests may not be observed clearly. In many situations, the main testing effect may manifest itself in the respondents' desire. For example, the respondents reply to later questions parallel to the replies to similar early questions. This means that their responses to the latter part of the questionnaire are not made independently but are conditioned to their responses to the early questions. The main testing effect may also be reactive as there are very few things in marketing research that can be measured. The very fact that a person is reporting his attitudes to someone else may also change that person's attitudes.

There are also interacting testing effects. It means that a prior measurement affects the test unit's response to the experimental variable. Persons who are asked about a particular concern become excessively aware of the concern and may not provide a response similar to common population. The interacting testing effects should be minimised to have unbiased results of behaviour. The main effect manifests itself not in the relationship but in the interacting testing effects; the process of measurement results in some change in the test unit's reaction to the experimental stimulus. The main testing effect usually exerts its greatest impact on the internal validity of an experiment, whereas the interactive testing effect most typically affects the external validity of the conclusion. These testing effects will have to be identified and are excluded from the main findings of the result.

Instrument Variation: Instrument variation is another factor which may cause variations in the before and after measurements. The techniques of the measurements may vary in two measurements. Thus, it refers to any and all changes in the measuring instruments that might account for differences in measurements. The change may be on account of change in the instrument itself or on account of variation in application of the instrument where there are several interviewers. Thus, it is difficult to ensure that all the interviewers will ask the same questions with the same voice-inflections, with the same rapport and with the same probes. There may be differences in response because each interviewer handles the interview differently. Similarly, the same interviewer cannot handle the respondents. Thus, differences are bound to be there in the reported score owing to different methods of handling the respondents. When the measurement techniques or the instruments themselves are being modified as the interview goes on, the difference between these changes should be identified and an attempt should be made to make uniform the interview. The interviewer becomes better acquainted with the test subjects as time passes. The last interview would be apt to elicit somewhat different information than would have been made on the first interview. The researcher, therefore, must be aware of such changes and their impact on the results.

Statistical Regression: This type of extraneous variables is related to the tendency of extreme cases. They may have been specifically selected because of their extreme positions. People of extreme behaviour may be selected to study the average behaviour in extreme circumstances. Such types of studies are called statistical regression. There are some variations in behaviour, attitudes, knowledge and other human factors. In extreme cases, the variation will be very wide. So statistical regression is observed in such a phenomenon, the identification of which may render the results authentic.

Selection Bias: Selection bias may arise when the group selected is partially informed of the questions and demonstration. This may arise from the way in which test units are selected and assigned in the experiment, and there is no way of clarifying that groups of text units were equivalent prior to administering the test. In certain demonstrations, viz., TV broadcast, one group may be aware of the demonstration and another group may not be or even see the show. Their understanding of a particular declaration, therefore, may be biased. Thus, there is no way to find out any fallacy in the argument of such groups who are exposed or unexposed. It should be understood here that the exposure groups, before demonstration, were equal. There may be a bias in a particular advertisement according to the acceptability of the audience. To avoid the fallacy of a select bias, randomisation is preferred. Cross sectional or group matching techniques may be observed to ignore the select-bias.

Experimental Mortality: This refers to the loss of test units during the course of experimental design. Replacing other units at the place of the loss units may not make the test group representative. It has become a noticeable source of bias in the before and after experiments because there is a loss of test units between the time of before and after measurements. It is a fallacy to ignore the loss-units when the experimental and control groups are different. In the experimental design when the experimental group has to perform certain tasks during a period of time, mortality may become relatively heavy among the experimental group. In the course of the experiment, several control respondents dropped out of the panel. There is no easy way of knowing if the attitudinal result would have been different if they had stayed in. The main difficulty with experimental mortality is not that they have indeed operated, but rather whether or not they have operated and affected or not affected the variables.

The experimental design may be a laboratory experiment and a field experiment.

1. Laboratory Experiments

In marketing research, the laboratory experiment has been used in the U.S.A., for the first time. Like physical science, marketing research can use laboratory design whereby some variables are put as controllables and others are left to vary. The respondents are selected from a particular area, and they are treated as laboratory units to which certain actions are administered and their results are noted down to compare with the controllable units. "A laboratory experiment may be defined as one in which the investigator creates a situation with the exact conditions he wants to have and in which he controls some and manipulates other variables. He is then able to observe and measure the effect of the manipulation of the independent variables on the dependent variables in a situation in which the operation of other relevant factors is held to a minimum."[4] In laboratory experiments, test members are brought to a particular place and exposed to an experimental variable. For example a place of shopping is selected to inquire into the purchase volume at different prices. The purchase volume at each price is recorded to find out the impacts of price changes. Similarly, at that place, a different purchase volume will be recorded at the influence of various doses of advertisements.

Thus the impact of each type of advertisement can be recorded to find out the efficiency of a particular advertisement.

The main feature of the laboratory experiment is that the behaviours of consumers are recorded at a particular place at the different intervals of time on different treatments of market variables. The extraneous factors are considered to be constant and, if any factor is there, the impacts of those factors are identified and are attempted to be excluded from the main findings. Since all the other factors, except the experimental variables are kept at constant watch and considered to be constant; the impact of each experiment can be recorded at different points of time of the experiments. Price and brand researches are important in laboratory experiments. There may be a paired preference experiment which requires each member to make preference choices among all possible pairs of brands in a single merchandise. Each member is also asked to indicate how much the price of the preferred brand can be increased to switch to another brand.

4. Leon Festinger: *Research Methods in the Behavioural Science*, p. 137.

The laboratory experiment typically possesses the advantages of greater internal validity as the respondents can be controlled and manipulated. The laboratory experiment does not depict accurately the real world environment.

2. Field Experiments

In field experiments, the experimental variables or test factors are taken to the fields, i.e., at different places. In field experiments, the study is undertaken at different places in conditions of real environments. "A field experiment is a research study in a realistic situation in which one or more independent variables are manipulated by the experimenter under as carefully controlled conditions as the situation will permit."[5] The field experiments are more of the representative type than the confined one. It is conducted in a natural setting than that created in a laboratory setting. The laboratory experiment consists of a set of simulated shopping trips, whereas the field experiments consist of several places of observation. In the experimental places, the variables are varied to observe these influences. In field experiments, no attempt is made to set up conditions. The situation is accepted as such and the manipulation of the experimental variables is done in a natural environment. On the other hand, the laboratory experiment is contrived.

The field experiments are more significant and consistent. They depict real life and are representative of the population. They do not believe that the extraneous variables are constant but recognise the differences.

They attempt to affect differences or measure their influence on ultimate findings. They have more external validity and general acceptability.

3. SPECIFIC EXPERIMENTAL DESIGN

The researcher may use some specific experimental design for his research purposes. There are several experimental designs and each of them has distinctive advantages. The researcher has a hypothesis that if an experimental variable (for example, advertising self display, training) is applied to an experimental unit (for example, a group of consumers, a store, some sales representatives), it will have an effect which can be measured (for example, the number remembering the brand name, units sold, calls made). The purpose of the plan or design is to measure the results of exposed experimental units to the experimental variable in controlled conditions.

There may be four types of specific experimental design — Pre-experimental Designs, True Experimental Design, Quasi Experimental Designs and Statistical Experimental Design.

1. Pre-experimental Designs

The pre-experimental design is that design in which the researcher has little control over the time and experimental units to experimental stimuli and also on the experimental measurements. This design is almost close to exploratory and descriptive designs, and is better than these designs in the sense of causal study. Pre-experimental design may be:

(i) The one short case study.
(ii) One group pretest post test design.
(iii) Statistic group comparison.
(iv) Post test only design.

5. Fred N. Kerlinger: *Foundations of Behavioural Research,* p. 401.

(i) The one-short case study: In one-short case study, a single group of test units is exposed to only one experimental variable. Its response can be observed only once. The group is self selected or is selected arbitrarily by the researcher ignoring randomisation. The study is merely a matter of convenience. The sample may be selected at the convenience of the researcher. The study of a magazine may reveal the impact of advertisements to a certain product. The result (0) may be the affect of an experimental variables or stimuli (x). This study does not study the impacts of other variables.

There is little study of the hypothesized causal relationships because it provides too little control over the extraneous variables. The controlled units and controlled variables are absent in this study. However, a causal comparison gives some understanding between the cause and effect of a particular phenomenon. It can establish hypotheses for a test but does not test the hypotheses.

(ii) The one group pretest-post test design: This is an addition of pretest to the above one-short case study. The result before the application of test (0_1) is compared with the result after application of test (0_2) in relation to stimuli or an experimental variable (x). Thus it can be noted as below:

$$0_1 \times 0_2$$

In this study, a convenient sample is selected to observe the impacts of a stimuli (x) before (01) and after (02) test application. For example, a convenience sample of designated respondents are interviewed for sale before price-cut and after price-cut. The difference between before and after price-cut will be the impact of price-cut. Thus,

$$d = 0_2 - 0_1$$

is the impact of price-cut. The other variables of the marketing strategies can be examined to find out their impacts on the objectives of marketing-research.

This study suffers from the extraneous variables because their effects may multiply the conclusion. For example in the above example, there may be a host of other factors apart from the experimental variable occuring simultaneously with the experiments that caused the increase in sale. Because of a change of consumers' status, there may have been more purchases irrespective of the price policy. There may be a change of history and maturation during the period of experiments. The main testing effects, i.e., those responding parallel to the first interview (0_1), in the second interview (0_2), may also distort the main conclusions. The statistical regression i.e., the effect of extreme cases and experimental mortality, i.e., the loss of units, may affect the result either positively or negatively. Apart from these extraneous variables, the one-group pre-test post-test design suffers from the convenience sample which may not be representative of the universe and external validity may not be present.

(iii) The static group comparison: In this design there are two groups *(i)* group administered test and *(ii)* group not administered test. Both the groups are selected at convenience and not at random. It may be stated:

Experimental Group (EG) : 0_1

Controlled Group (CG) : 0_2

The group members who are aware of advertising are selected for study purposes. They are known as the experimental group. On the contrary, those members who have not seen the advertisement may be called the controlled group. The attitudes of each group towards the experiment variable are recorded to find out the effectiveness of the experiment (advertisement). The difference (d) between the results of the experimental group (0_1) and controlled group (0_2) will show the effect of the market variable. Thus:

$$d = 0_1 - 0_2$$

Technically, the above difference (d) is a variation of attitudes between those members who have seen the advertisement and those who have not seen the advertisement. It refers, implicitly, to the impact of the advertisement. This study suffers from the extraneous variables, e.g., select bias and main testing effects. Those members who have a favourable attitude towards a product may pay more attention to the advertisement than those who have an adverse attitude towards the product. Thus, the select bias may be present there, and the main conclusions may be confusing. Similarly, the main testing effects may cause the conclusion to be a biased one. This design may not be representive as the sample is a convenient one.

(iv) Post-test only design: Another design of a general type is the post-test only design. It is not experimental in the true sense. It consists of measuring the dependent variable after and only after, the experimental members have been exposed to the experimental variable. It assumes that every experiment gives change before and after treatment. The researcher may be interested in knowing the relative difference between the two groups after the proposed treatment. The post-test only design runs the hazard that Group A and Group B were different before the test in significant aspects. The interpretation of the design is based on the assumptions that controlled and experimental groups are identical and that after test there is some change in the experimental group. But there is no true identification of the two groups. There may be unrepresentation of the results because they are not selected on a random basis. Under this design, the before measurement is implicitly estimated on the basis of vague past experience which is an inferior assumption as compared to pretest-posttest design.

2. True Experimental Design

The experimental design is concerned with the randomised factor. Unlike the pre-experimental design, it is unconcerned with the convenient sample. It tries to make the sample as much representative as possible. The researcher, under an experimental design, can assign treatment at random to randomly selected test units. He can control the time and the experimental units, and also the time and methods of experimental measurements. The random assignment and the random sample have the advantages of representativeness of universe. The true experimental design may be:

1. Pretest-Posttest with control group design.
2. Four-Group six study design.
3. Post-test with control group design.

1. Pretest-Posttest with control group design: This experimental design was developed to permit measurement of the effect of experimental variables. The randomisation is there, so we can assign randomisation with test units. The experimental group and the control group are selected in such a way that they are similar, i.e., they are interchangeable for test purposes. The control group and the experimental group are measured at the same time before and after introducing controlled variables. Using the randomisation to the design, we can express the design in the following diagram, where R denotes representation.

	Before measurement	After measurement
Experimental Group (R)	X_1	X_2
Control Group (R)	Y_1	Y_2

The difference between the after and before measurement of the control group is due to extraneous or uncontrollable variables, i.e.

$$d_0 = (Y_2 - Y_1) = \text{Uncontrollable variable} = UV$$

The difference between the "after" and "before" measurements in the experimental group is the result of the experimental variable plus the same extraneous or uncontrollable variables which affect the control group.

$$d_1 = (X_2 - X_1) = \text{Uncontrollable variables plus Experimental variable} = UV + EV$$

So, the impacts of the experimental variable can be measured as

$$d_1 - d_0 = (X_2 - X_1) - (Y_2 - Y_1) = UV + EV - UV$$

$$d_1 - d_0 = EV = (X_2 - X_1) - (Y_2 - Y_1)$$

The effect of the experimental variable can be determined by subtracting the difference in the two measurements of the control group from the difference in the two measurements of the experimental group. The experimental group in studying the impact of advertising will be those who are exposed to advertising, and the control group will not be exposed to advertising. The experiment in this case may be the introduction of advertising. The control group is a group of consumers similar to the experimental (group, except for not being exposed to the experimental) variable. The experimental group should include a wide range of the population to make the study representative. If the study is limited to one group or area, it will not have external validity. The researcher cannot arbitrarily assign test units to the experimental and control groups. He has to select the sample randomly.

This design has been considered an ideal design for marketing research. It provides generalised conclusions. This design excludes the effects of extraneous variables, e.g., history, maturation, pretesting and measurement variability. In this design selection bias is a confounding factor. However, selection bias may be eliminated by the random assignment of individuals to groups. The experimental mortality can be minimised by replacing another member to the groups. There may be test interactive effects of the conclusions of this design. Their results can be classified into two groups *(i)* results due to the experimental stimulus and *(ii)* results due to the interactive testing effect. The first impact can be minimised if these facts are kept at constant watch and not made aware of the experimental variables. The interaction effect similarly can be reduced by expert interviewing techniques.

2. Four-group Six-study Design: The four-group six-study is useful to avoid the interactive testing effect which cannot be eliminated in pretest-posttest design. In situations where it is doubtful that the units are subject to the pretest measurements and can influence the members sufficiently to distort the posttest observations, the four group-six study may be designed. In many research problems, the prior measurements are of such a nature that the test units are not sensitised to the experiment, and the interacting testing effects, i.e., interactory between the respondent and the questioning process are present if they are informed of the experiment variables. The four-group six-study is designed therefore to overcome these problems. The design can be explained as below:

	Before measurement	*Experiment Administered*	*After measurement*
Experimental Group-I:			
(R) or EG I: (R)	x_1	Yes	x_2
Controlled Group I:			
(R) or CG I: (R)	y_1	No	y_2
EG II: (R)	No	Yes	x_3
CG II: (R)	No	No	y_3

In the four group-six study design two groups are selected. The first group is just like "before-after" with the control group whereby two groups, one experimental group and second group are observed. In additional to "before-after with the control group", one experimental group without pre-information of the experiment and control group are added. These groups are not measured before the experimental variable. The experimental variables are introduced in the two experimental groups, and all four groups are measured after the administered experiment. All the four groups are preselected on a random basis, i.e., all the members have equivalent chances of being selected. It can be assumed that the two "before" measurements are approximately equal, i.e., $x_1 = y_1$. So, the other two groups would have shown similar measurements, the average of x_1 and y_1 is, therefore, taken to be the "before" measure of experimental group 2 and control group 2. If the "before" measurements had no effect on the variable units being studied, the two experimental groups will give the same "after" studied, measurements, as the two control groups. If the experimental variable had any influence, the results of the two experimental groups will vary significantly from the results of the two control groups. On the other hand, if the "before" measurement does influence the test units directly, and also interacts with the experimental variable, each of four groups will give a different "after" measurement.

This design can easily net out the impacts of the extraneous variables or uncontrollable variables (UV). As pointed out in the pretest-posttest control group design, there will be an interacting testing affect. But that effect is easily weeded out because there is no prior measurement to sensitise the respondents, i.e., the experimental group II has not given the information of the experimental variable, there, one question may arise how to calculate the effect of the experimental variable. The answer to this question is to have an average measurement of first experimental and first controlled groups, i.e., $1/2\ (x_1 + y_1)$ because the four groups were equal except for sampling variations. While taking the design for research purposes a large sample is taken which is divided into four equal parts (in subjects or units), e.g., experimental group I with pretest measurement, experimental group II without pre-test measurement or pre-information of the experiment, and controlled group I and controlled group II having pretest knowledge and not having pretest knowledge, respectively. The impact of uncontrollable variable or extraneous variable (UV) will be the difference (d_0) of observation of controlled group I after measurement, and controlled group I before measurement (y_1). Thus,

$$d_0 = (y_2 - y_1) = (UV)$$

The impact of uncontrollable variable or extraneous variable (UV) plus experimental variable (EV), and interacting testing effect (I) will be the difference (d_1) of the findings of experimental group I after measurement (x_2) and experimental group I before measurement (x_1).

$$d_1 = (x_2 - x_1) = (UV) + (EV) + I$$

The impact of uncontrollable variable (UV) in no pretest information will be the difference (d_2) of the observation of controlled group II after measurement, and the average of observation of experimental group I and controlled group I before measurement, i.e., $1/2\ (x_1+y_1)$.

$$d_2 = [y_3 - 1/2\ (x_1 + y_1)] = UV$$

The impact of uncontrollable (UV) in no pretest information, and the experimental variable will be the difference (d_3) of observation of experimental group II after measurement (x_3), and the average of observation of experimental group I and control group I before measurement, i.e., $1/2\ (x_1+y_1)$

$$d_3 = [x_3 - 1/2(x_1 + y_1)] = UV + EV$$

Thus, the impact of the experimental stimulus will be

$$EV = (UV + EV) - (UV)$$
$$= [(x_3 - 1/2(x_1 + y_1)] - [y_3 - 1/2(x_1 + y_1)]$$

The impact of the interacting test effect will be

$$I = (UV + EV + I) - (UV + EV)$$
$$= (x_2 - x_1) - [x_3 - 1/2\ (x_1 + y_1)]$$

Thus the real experimental variable's effect can easily be calculated by deducting the impact of uncontrollable variables and of interacting testing effects from the difference of after measurement, and before measurement of the experimental group I. The uncontrollable variables' effect is taken from controlled group I

$$EV = [(x_2 - x_1) - (UV + I)]$$

The four-group six-study design has become a conceptual ideal. In practice, this design is not very popular owing to excessive time, energy and money involved in this design. This design requires a wider coverage of a sample to be studied in four equal parts. If the group is small, it will not have the advantage of randomisation. The Law of large numbers and probability methods are two important bases of this design.

3. Post-test with control group design: The "four group six study design" has concentrated greatly on group II of experiment and control. Group I is taken to measure the impact of "before measurement." The interacting test effects are measured in the first group. Regardless of the interacting test effects, the results of the second group are equal to the results of the first group. Therefore to get the result only of the experimental variable, the second group may be sufficient and there is no need of study of group I.

We know that the impact of experimental variable (EV) in the previous diagram is:

$$EV = (EV + UV) - (UV) \text{ of the second group}$$
$$= [x_3 - 1/2\ (x_1 + y_1)] - [y_3 - 1/2(x_1 + y_1)$$
$$= x_3 - y_3 \text{ as } 1/2\ (x_1 + y_1) \text{ is common in both the groups.}$$

Thus, we can calculate the impact of the experimental variable only with the help of $x_3 - y_3$, i.e., study of group II including the experimental group after measurement, and control group after measurement. Therefore only "after measurement or post test with control group design" constitutes a logical measurement. Thus, the following is sufficient

	Before measurement	*Experimental variable*	*After measurement*
Experimental Group or EG : R	No	Yes	x_1
Control Group or CG : R	No	No	y_1

Here we do not introduce the measurement instrument to the experimental group to avoid the interacting test effects. Thus, the researcher can select a random sample of large members of the population, one half of them would be randomly assigned to the experimental group and the other half would form the control group. Neither group will be pre-informed of the measurement-instruments. The experimental group will be send the questionnaire, and after a lapse of time, both groups would be measured for their knowledge and functions. The experimental variable's impact would be measured by the difference between the experimental group and the control group. It should be kept in mind that no "before" measurement is made in either of the groups. In the above diagram, the effect of the experimental variable is determined by computing the difference between the two after measurements, i.e., $x_1 - y_1$. Thus, the impact of pretest is avoided in this group.

This design is much simpler to administer and less expensive, besides it has all the advantages of the "four group-six study" design. The impacts of uncontrollable variables or of extraneous variables, i.e., extraneous errors can be eliminated in this experiment. Since the extraneous factors affect both groups, their impact is eliminated by experimental groups and of controlled groups. The interactive testing effect is eliminated because there is no pretest.

This design is not free from drawbacks. This design is very sensitive to problems of selection bias and experimental mortality. Since there is no pretest, one cannot compare this with the pretest attitude. Similarly, the number of persons dropping out of both the groups can cause an impact of experimental mortality, and the ultimate findings may not be free from distortion. The pretest-posttest design permits an analysis of the process of change which is not possible in the case of posttest design.

3. Quasi-Experimental Designs

The quasi-experimental design is less vigorous, less specific and informal. It is advantageous over the experimental design because it is less difficult, less costly and less time consuming. In true experimental design, the researcher has control over the respondents who are exposed to the experimental stimulus. But in the quasi-experimental design, the researcher has no control over the time and exposure units and cannot be assigned to the experimental stimuli or to the randomly assigned test. The quasi-experimental design may be

1. Static group comparison.
2. Historical design such a regression and time series.
3. Simulation.

1. Static group comparison design: When it is not possible to determine ahead of time who has received the variable or treatment, the static group comparison design proves useful. This is also known as ex-post-facto design. This design differs from the posttest design in the sense that ex-post groups are selected before introduction of experiments whereas posttest groups are selected after the experiment variable is introduced.

In the static group comparison, the respondents are studied in several sections as per the objectives of the marketing research. For example, to study the impact of an advertisement the sample can be divided into four groups, depending on the purpose to assess the actual purchase of the product and exposure to the product. Thus, the respondents can be divided into four groups: *(i)* Exposure-purchase group, *(ii)* no exposure-purchase group, *(iii)* exposure-no purchase group and *(iv)* no exposure-no purchase group. Their impacts are compared by preparing a matrix table such as:

	Number exposed	*Number not exposed*
Number purchased	60	36
Number did not purchase	46	58

Total number of sample member = 200.

The impact of the advertisement may be 24(60 – 36). Thus, the impact of the advertisement on the purchase was 24/200 = 12 per cent. In this case, in terms of true experimental design, the exposed-purchase group is known as the test group or experimental group, and the not exposed purchase group is the controlled group. It looks like true experimental design. But there is one significant difference. In true experimental design, the test and control groups are randomly selected and are homogeneous. But in this case, the controlled group and test group may be different. Therefore, the result may be attributed to some other variables other than the exposed variable, i.e., advertising in this case. This design requires a large number of units. If the selection bias affect is removed, it will be equal to posttest only with control group design. The test groups have received influence in an entirely natural way. The ex-post-facto design is a cross-classification and is not experimental in the true sense. It is not descriptive in the true sense as the test group is studied after the test is introduced. The group is divided on equal characteristics.

2. Historical Designs: Many designs are historical in the sense that they depend on historical data. The data are collected on the behaviour of one or more variables. The historical designs differ from the experimental designs because the historical designs are not current tests staged by the researcher with any control group, the data are obtained from secondary sources and not obtained by the researcher from the field, and the researcher has to analyse whatever is available to him rather than deciding the precision and objectivity of data. They may be

(a) Regression Analysis.

(b) Time-series experiment.

(a) Regression Analysis: This is similar to a static group comparison and can be referred to as a concomitant variation. The difference between exposure-purchase group and non-exposure purchase group reveals the impact of exposure. This difference or variation is statistically analysed in this design. It reveals the associative relationship between one or more variables. The effects of these relationships are also analysed. The causal impacts of the independent variables on the dependent variables are also examined on this basis, the dependent variables are projected and anticipated changes are revealed. For example, the volume of sales per year as per unit introduction of advertisement can be observed for ten years, and then the statistical tool of regression analysis is applied to measure the impact of the advertisement on sales. This is mere expectation. One cannot say that the increase in sales is caused merely by the advertisement. There may be various factors influencing sales. The correlation and regression analysis may be spurious. This analysis undoubtedly reveals the trend of the impact of the exposure, i.e., independent variable, here it is the advertisement amount and units on dependent variable, i.e., sale in the above example. The trend can be a useful factor for forecasting purposes. The validity of this analysis depends on the validity of data and coverage of sample of the collected data.

(b) Time-series experiment: The trend analysis can be calculated on time-series analysis with five yearly or more averages. Unlike the regression analysis this excludes seasonal variation, cyclical variation and irregular events. Adjustments are made for each of the three variations and the magnitude of the variations can be determined to find out the impact of the test variable on the trend. Except the above, several marketing variables can influence the trend, which cannot be revealed by the trend analyses of the time-series, i.e., by using five yearly averages.

The time series experiment is considered the important quasi-experimental design, whereby the trend of the impact of the test variable can be estimated by using moving average technique. To exclude the impacts of the variables other than the test one, several panels composing different units may be selected for study. Their inter-comparison will reveal the impact of the test-variable. The relationship can be established and pave the base for forecasting the dependent variable.

3. Simulation: Simulation is a new technique and is an imitation of a real world situation. Simulation is simpler than the real world. It provides information from an imitation of this situation. There may be an hypothesized course of action. After experience with alternative courses of action and the collection of actual data, it may be possible to develop a model depicting the functional relationship between the independent and dependent variables. When the cost, time and problems with field experimentation preclude the source of information for particular operational situation, it becomes desirable to construct a model of the operational situation and experiment with it. This manipulation is called simulation. With such a model, a researcher can manipulate the magnitude of the variable. The relationships are depicted on a mathematical function. They build simulations of the inter-related variables and use the simulation to solve the problems.

The model can be tested under widely varying simulated conditions of attitude, desire and performance. Conceptuals are constructed and manipulated to obtain information on the impacts of mixed combinations of the variables. Simulation in marketing uses a variety of procedures such as Monte Carlo techniques, operational gaming, experimental gaming and heuristic programming.

4. Statistical Experimental Design

The descriptive research design has not established causal relationship. The experimental design may need control over some groups. One tries to keep aside the impacts of extraneous factors to arrive at correct conclusions of the researcher. These needs and advantages can be achieved by using a statistical experimental design. The techniques using statistics may solve various problems of marketing research. The statistical experimental design provides a most useful tool for analysing he results of experiments. For example a pretest-posttest design may be statistically interpreted to provide general inferences of the findings. The statistical empirical designs, may be:

1. Completely Randomised Design.
2. Randomised Block Design.
3. Latin Square Design.
4. Factorial Design.

1. Completely Randomised Design: The main feature of this design is that the experimental treatments are assigned to the test units completely at random. No prior precaution is needed to some extraneous variables before the assignments are randomly made. For example to study the various effects of different price levels, e.g., three price levels, all the retailers in the city will be divided into three categories at three price levels. The total sales of each retailer of a particular price level are recorded and the effects of the price level are observed. Similarly, the analysis of a product may require categorisation of the retailers according to the nature of the products. The effectiveness of each product, can be assessed accordingly.

2. Randomised Block Design: The randomised block design requires that the test units be divided into blocks. The classification is made using some external treatments. There will be as many test-units per block as there are treatments. This design is useful when the population is very large. In the above example, three price treatments would require three test units per block. The extraneous influence can be studied by categorising the blocks into three classes. The first group or block will consist of the three largest retailers. Similarly, three medium retailers will be included under the medium size block, and the three smallest retailers will be included under the smallest block. It is to be noted here, that in each block three or more retailers may be included depending on the size of the population or universe. Whatever may be the number of retailers in a block, there must be the same number in all the blocks, i.e., in a large block, medium block and small block. Each retailer in a block would be assigned two or more treatment conditions. Thus, each group or block is representative of large, medium or small stores. Similarly, representation of each type of retailers may be analysed by classification of retailers into specific types. For example, drugstores may be included in the drug-stores block, general stores in the general store block and, similarly, stationary stores may be included under the stationary stores block. Similarly, each block may be divided into new or old goods. Thus, all these divisions are made on a random basis.

3. Latin Squares Design: This design suggests that this test will form a square because there will be as many test units as treatments. This design is used to control important extraneous influence. It is assumed that each treatment occurs once with each store on a block. There are several stores in a block. There must be as many blocks as there are treatments. It may be three, four and so on. Three blocks, three treatments, four blocks, four treatments and so on. This is the reason, why it is called a square design. For example to study price treatment at different times, the latin square design will be:

Prices Blocks	Price Treatment Spring	Summer	Autumn	Winter
A	x_1	x_2	x_3	x_4
B	y_1	y_2	y_3	y_4
C	z_1	z_2	z_3	z_4
D	o_1	o_2	o_3	o_4

Thus, the price treatment will reveal the impact of prices at different times and stores. Consequently one can conclude the price effect on sales. There are some special features of this design *(i)* each treatment is applied once in each store of a block *(ii)* each store is tested once in each time and *(iii)* the order of testing runs both ways, i.e., 1 to 2 and 2 to 1 during an equal number of times. Thus, the extraneous factors' impact affecting them are minimised. The varying store characteristics and sequence in which the treatments appear are concealed.

This design measures the error resulting from two non-interacting variables, i.e., the difference in test stores, and the difference in time on the results, as well as the effect of the treatment on the results. The statistical interpretation is a complex one because a treatment is observed in case of several stores at several points of time. The variances of vertical effects, the variances of horizontal effects and the variances of treatment have to be calculated. These can be analysed by adopting several methods.

The sum of the vertical column may be used to determine the vertical dimension or the "column effect." Similarly, the sum of horizontal column may be used to assess the horizontal dimension or "row effect." The treatments' total effect can be determined by analysing the impact of the treatment on the sale. A degree of freedom may be applied to correct the row, column and treatment effects.

4. Factorial Design: The factorial experiment design allows the researcher to test two or more variables at the same time. It determines whether the variables interact to produce an observed response, or whether the variables operate independently to produce the response. The factorial experiment is used when there are three or more experimental variables. It is applied when the design is completely randomised, or is a randomised block or Latin Square. The main feature of this design is that the impact of various variables can be examined. It involves some complex computations. We can calculate the interaction of the variables on each other, which requires variance analysis and notching out the main effects of each experimental variable. Standard deviation and mean squares are calculated to find out the impacts of variables. Thus, this design determines not only the main effects of each of the variables, but also measures the interaction effects of the variables. For example, the use of coffee may be preferred with a high content of sugar and high flavour. To test these contents, various doses of sugar may be introduced and the number of consumers purchasing them may be recorded to find out their consequences.

Flavour intensity	*Sugar-content* *1*	*2*	*3*	*4*
1	5	6	7	6.5
2	9	10	11	10.5
3	13	14	15	14.5
4	9.5	10.5	11.5	12

The above example reveals that the third degree of sugar content and third degree of flavour are preferred. The fourth degree of sugar content and the fourth degree of flavour are not preferred. The degree of study depends upon the thoroughness of study required and the cost involved in the study. In the above example only two variables are tested and more than two variables are included to test their influences upon the sale.

Use of Experimentation

The experimental design is more useful than other designs. It has been used to examine the sales effectiveness of almost every variable of the marketing mix. It can be employed to measure the sales effectiveness of a new promotion policy, the responsiveness of the consumers to a new product design or product quality. It can also examine the market share at every price level and the sales potential of new products. Similarly, it can be used for any variable of test-marketing. It can also be used for examining various variables at a time.

The exploratory and descriptive designs are not useful in establishing the existence of causal relationships. Exploratories are less of a problem-solving than finding new facts. The experimental design does establish causal relationship and forecasts certain events. The experimental and control groups are set up in such a way that it is reasonable to assume they did not differ in terms of the response variable before exposure to the experimental variable. The researcher measures the test units.

Problems in Marketing Experimentation

The advantages of experiments in determining the cause and effect or relationships are many. They can predict some events. The causal relationships can be established and models can be developed. Apart from the advantages of experimentation, there are several problems of experimentation.

1. Lack of Theory: Experimentation lacks theories to use the research design. The marketing research has been primarily descriptive and extensive information is now available in the area of marketing. But there is no adequate and proper theory or hypothesis to test them and to find out the real relationship between marketing variables. This is now gradually developing with the expansion of research facilities, and there is much scope of development of research theories in marketing areas.

2. Cost of Experimentation: Experimental research is costlier. At least two groups are required to test the hypotheses, i.e., the experimental group and the control group. The data are collected twice in many cases. A large number of sample-members is collected. Thus, it is expensive enough to control a wide variety of data. The processing of data is also very costly. Therefore, the experimentation is used only when the benefits of the research are more than that of the cost involved in the experimentation. Test marketing requires tremendous resources; it would be wasted if the test failed.

3. Time: A longer time is involved in experimentation. At least one year is the permitted minimum period of research. The researcher may continue for a longer period. The long period may involve additional problems of control and competitive reaction. The history and maturation effects may influence the ultimate decision. The conclusions derived after a long period may become obsolete to suit the current marketing decisions.

4. Other Problems: There are several test problems relating to collection of data and their interpretation. The survey and sample to be selected appropriately pose another difficult decision. The cooperation of respondents poses another problem while collecting the data. This research design may not be useful in cases where secrecy is required to compete in the market, because field research will reveal the purpose of research, and the competitors will adopt competitive methods to beat the market.

The selection of a particular research design depends upon the objectives of the research and the cost, time and problems involved in the research. There may be opportunity-oriented research, alternative-oriented research and decision-oriented research. The descriptive studies are useful in opportunity-oriented research and alternative-oriented research. For testing hypotheses or decision-oriented research, the experimental design may be useful provided the cost and time are within the limits of the marketing management. The external validities and internal validity are also considered in the decision-oriented research. Thus five considerations, i.e., time, internal validity, external validity, cost and security are emphasised while deciding a particular research design.

❖ ❖ ❖

CHAPTER 5

DETERMINING SOURCES OF DATA

1. SOURCES OF DATA —
   (i) SECONDARY DATA
   (ii) PRIMARY DATA
2. SECONDARY DATA —
   (i) INTERNAL DATA
   (ii) EXTERNAL DATA
3. ADVANTAGES OF SECONDARY DATA
4. DISADVANTAGES OF SECONDARY DATA

DETERMINING SOURCES OF DATA

1. SOURCES OF DATA

All market research requires a vast reservoir of information. There may be different types of information and data. Some of the information may be published, while some is unpublished; some is complete and some is incomplete, and some is reliable data and some is biased. Some information may be available without charge, and some may require nominal expenditure. The costs and values of particular information may decide the selection of a particular research project. The research may require general or specific data. The researcher must be well aware of the techniques of obtaining general data as well as specific data. It is necessary for the researcher to know the kind of information which is usually employed in marketing research work, and the types of sources from which it is generally collected. The specific problem can be solved after collecting specific information and data. The researcher has to collect more specific information from specific sources of marketing data for solving specific problems of the market. The research problem decides the nature of the sources of the data. They may be secondary data and primary data.

1. Secondary Data

"Secondary data are statistics not gathered for the immediate study at hand but for some other purposes."[1]

They may be described as those data that have been compiled by some agency other than the user.

2. Primary Data

"Primary data may be described as those data that have been observed and recorded by the researchers for the first time to their knowledge."[2]

These data are originated by the researcher for the purpose of the investigation at hand. The secondary data have some advantages and disadvantages which are discussed at the end of this chapter. If the data are available that can be secured rapidly and at low cost, there is no sense in spending time and effort to acquire primary data. Primary data are collected generally by experienced personnel. The knowledge of secondary data are essential for planning the collection of primary data. Therefore, we discuss the secondary data in this chapter.

The cost of collection of secondary data is less than that of primary data. The secondary data are adapted to suit the requirements of the research project. Secondary data do not mean more accurate data. They refer to the source rather than to the accuracy or importance of the data.

2. SECONDARY DATA

There can be a number of ways by which secondary data can be classified. One of the most useful is by source which suggests the classification of internal and external data. Internal data refer to data that are part of the company's records for which the research

1. Gilbert A. Churchill, Jr.: *Marketing Research,* The Dryden Press, 1970, p. 128.
2. David J. Luck & Others: *Marketing Research,* Prentice Hall of India, 1982, p. 74.

is being conducted. Internal data are those found within the organisation for whom the research is being undertaken. External data refer to those which are collected by the researchers outside the company for which the research is being conducted. They are obtained from outside sources.

1. Internal Secondary Data

"Data that originate within the firm for which the research is being conducted are internal data. If they were collected for some other purposes, they are internal secondary data."[3] They may be adapted for the marketing research purposes. They may be formal data and informal data. Formal data are available on a regularly scheduled basis, such as monthly, quarterly or annually in a form that allows comparisons through time. Informal data report basic marketing knowledge and are available on a non-recurring basis. The internal secondary data reveal many research problems. It is useful for evaluating past marketing strategy or assessing the firm's competitive position in the industry. Sales and cost data are used for planning purposes. The internal secondary data are available readily at a lower cost. The internal sales data are useful to analyse the company's sales performance. The cost data are used for determination of the profitability. The accounting data are classified on the basis of managerial units, e.g., areas, customers, product, classes etc. For marketing research, the marketing cost is separated from the production cost so that the marketing cost can be compared. There may be so many other internal secondary data such as price-lists, customer correspondence and service records.

Internal secondary data are not systematically collected. They are not readily available to be used in the original form for research purposes. Therefore, they should be adapted for marketing purposes. If these data are properly collected, they can provide a continuous source of relevant data and information. A large number of internal secondary data depend upon the company's operating procedures and systematic recording of the data and information. Sales analysis and invoicing are considered important sources of internal secondary data.

1. Sales Analysis: Sales analysis is an important tool of marketing research. It is the first step in the marketing research programme and acts as a basis for the development of further marketing research. It reveals the current operating problems in the marketing area where the scope for marketing research can be adequately explored. In smaller organisations, sales analysis is an important source of marketing information. It provides a major share of the factors for marketing research. The sales figure can be converted into suitable information for advanced research. Sales analysis is the least expensive. It makes many important and productive contributions to marketing research objectives. It does not require a high level of technical skill and experience. External analysis from the angle of consumers and retailers may add to the advantage of the sales analysis.

Steps in Sales Analysis: In sales analysis, the following steps are observed:

(a) Territorial Analysis: Sales data per territory or region are classified and are put in comparable form to have a bird's eye view of the total sale. Sales vary from region to region and time to time. The causes of such variations can be revealed by investigation and survey of retailers of the region.

3. Gilbert A. Churchill, Jr., *Marketing Research,* The Dryden Press, 1979, p. 132.

(b) Customer Analysis: Sales data according to different nature of customers are classified and compared. They provide the useful purpose of understanding the nature of customers and their behaviours to the sale.

(c) Product Analysis: Sales data product-wise can be a significant source of marketing research. The sales may vary from product to product. Understanding of their behaviour will be useful for framing product policy.

(d) Time Analysis: Sales data classified as per different segments of time, viz., monthly, six-monthly and yearly may be useful source of analysis of sales.

2. Invoice Analysis: Company invoices have been provided a very useful source of information. A copy of an invoice is preserved and information from it may be punched, tabulated, processed and summarised to provide suitable information to the researcher. The invoice data may be classified according to customer, nature of product, region and area. The invoice record may be of immense use provided it has been used with precaution and scientifically. Sales may be changed as per territory, extra-ordinary transactions, change in the base period, new product introduction and so on. In normal cases, the invoice-lists which are preserved systematically for a long period can provide significant information about the sales-record in a particular area. A sudden decline in sales in the area may reveal some problems which influence the sales adversely. Territorial sales may be useful owing the expansion or restriction of sales in a particular area. A sudden distortion in the normal figure of sales may be due to extraordinary sales or an extraordinary decline in sales for which significant reasons are revealed. The sales may be influenced by different reasons place to place and product to product. The tabulator of information must be very careful about the information and its use. Sales may decline if a large customer shifts to another seller. The knowledge of such customer will provide a controlling factor for protecting a decline in sales. Knowledge of sales of different products may provide suitable guidelines for product policies, whether sales of different sizes of a given product should continue or be combined into a single product, and whether products of an unlike nature may be combined into a heterogeneous total.

2. External Secondary Data

The second form of secondary data are external sources which are generally published and are available in different forms and from different sources. Although external secondary data may be obtained from different sources, some of the sources are given here.

1. Libraries.
2. Literature.
3. Periodicals.
4. Census and Registration Data.
5. Trade Associations.
6. Government Departments.
7. Private Sources.
8. Commercial Data.
9. Financial Data.
10. International Organisations.
11. References and Bibliographies.

12. Volumes of Statistics.
13. Advertising.
14. Other Sources.

1. Libraries

Researchers first attend libraries to find out relevant data pertaining to research. They provide many sources where suitable data may be obtained. Public libraries, and college and University libraries contain a large amount of business information which provides sources of other data. Many Libraries have specialised sections of collections of suitable research findings and published materials. Books and literature which are too costly to be purchased by individuals can be purchased by these libraries. Recently the Government of India has inspired business-management teaching whereby adequate and relevant libraries are maintained. Management books, theses, management journals and other publications can be consulted in these libraries. Management institutes, research institutes, banks, insurance companies, public utility companies and manufacturing units have maintained adequate libraries. Libraries have provided to be very useful sources of secondary data, and also guides for the preparation and collection of primary data.

2. Literature

A great amount of secondary data are available from literature, particularly literature on marketing subjects. With the development of marketing researches in different countries, new and interesting facts are coming into the picture which are available in various publications. Consultations of this literature may provide proper guidance pertaining to publication which can be used from time to time. National and international publications are available in several forms. The researchers try to obtain some of these publications for their research purposes. Bibliographic indices of various books, publications and dissertations, Central and State Government publications are very good sources of secondary data.

3. Periodicals

Business periodicals published fortnightly, monthly, quarterly, semi annually and annually are often consulted by the marketing executives and researchers to plan and design their marketing research. Also to use the available data for research purposes and to verify the conclusions derived from the marketing research, specially of field research. Periodical economic abstracts on economics, finance, trade, transport, industry, labour and management are being prepared by the Government as well as by the non-government agencies. Journals of the Marketing Association, Management Association, Research Agencies, Advertising Agencies and other related periodicals are becoming very common in India and abroad. Sometimes, house magazines prove a very useful source of marketing research. Periodical publications of the Ministry of Information and Broadcasting have been used by the management personnel to find out the economic and commercial progress of the country. They are guides to understanding the market potentials of the country as a whole, and also specific problems and potentials of some regions.

4. Census and Registration Data

Census and registration data have become very comprehensive sources of marketing research. Previously, these concentrated only one population census, but it now extends to a census of agriculture, cattle, trade, transport and industry; mining and manufacturing industries; banking and finance. These data are the major sources for a sales forecasting, development of market problems and potentials, and in deciding the market share and other purposes of marketing research. The data revealed by census and registration are the basic and fruitful statistical sources. The census given in the following paragraphs are being used in some form or other by the market researchers.

(i) Census of Population: A census of the population is conducted at the beginning of every decade in India, viz., the census of 1901, 1911, and so on. The last census of the population was carried out in India in 1991. In Western countries, the census is conducted at the end of the decade, i.e., 1900, 1910 and so on. The census of the population reveals many interesting characteristics of the population. Population by state, city, metropolitan area and rural areas are revealed by the census. Characteristics of the population such as age, sex, race, mother tongue, citizenship, education, families and their composition, employment status, place of work, main occupation and subsidiary occupations are revealed both area-wise and region-wise. Similarly a census of housing is also conducted by the Government wherein information pertaining to the year of a building equipment, water-source, fuel used, rent paid, value of the house and ethnic characteristics of the locality are mentioned.

(ii) Census of Agriculture: The census of agriculture is of recent origin. It has been commonly undertaken in western countries. The census includes information and data pertaining to the number of farms, size, acreage value, farm expenditure, crops and value added, facilities and equipment, cattle and their uses. The National Sample Survey is an important agricultural data collection agency. The Ministry of Agriculture conducts some sample surveys to find out the problems and potentials of agriculture in some selected areas of the country.

(iii) Census of Cattle: In India, sample surveys have been conducted to find out the number of animals such as goats, sheep, milch animals. They have revealed the possibilities of market expansions of industrial products related to cattle, e.g., milk-meat, leather and so on. Sample surveys are the basis for enumerating the number of animals in the country and also in different parts of the country.

(iv) Census of Trade: The census of retail trade, wholesale trade and selected service industries has yielded statistics pertaining to total sales, number of employees and number of establishment for each type of business. The census may be conducted state-wise and area-wise. The import and export registered with the Ministry of Commerce has become a very good source of data for foreign trade.

(v) Census of Transport: The census of transport is conducted periodically. This has been undertaken by the Ministry of Transport to find out the existing transport facilities and also possibilities for the future expansion of the business.

(vi) Census of Industry: The census of industry, mining and manufacturing is conducted from time to time. The sample surveys of industry, mining and manufacturing have become very good source for deciding the level of industries, mining and manufacturing in India. Sometimes, these surveys have been used to evaluate the total volume and value of commodities transferred and mined in India. The census of industry is also conducted to find out the number and size of establishment, ownership, man-hours, and sales by customer and class. Also inventories, selected costs, book value of fixed assets, capital expenditure and investment, energy used, value added by manufacture, and quantity and value of materials consumed.

(vii) Census of Banking and Finance: The Reserve Bank of India has prepared detailed statistics on various performances of banking and the positions of financial institutions. The financial and banking positions decide the potentials of market expansion.

Registration Data

Registration data are the outcome of legal requirements of the submission of final accounts and reports to the Registrar of Companies and to the ministry concerned for securing licences and other requirements. These data are compiled and tabulated by the ministry and are publicity available. Data pertaining to trade, industry and business are available from the Ministry of Commerce. Similarly the Ministry of Transport and Communication provides data pertaining to transport and communication. The Ministry of Railways publishes monthly journals and reports which are based on the data available within the railways and adjoining environments. Similarly, almost all the ministries or the Government of India as well as the Reserve Bank of India have been publishing comprehensive and suitable data and information pertaining to different fields of the economy.

Apart from the government agencies and departments, there are several non-official and official agencies which are registering data pertaining to demographic features such as deaths, births, marriages, education, and the business and economic conditions of the people in a particular area. Tax payment, tax incentives, prices, income, export performance trade associations, automobile registration and licences, unemployment and employment provided by the employment exchanges etc. are the various important data and information available from the registration of data. People are required to submit their data and information to the registrar concerned. The marketing researchers have to process these data and compare them with other data to avoid any shortcomings and errors because the data of registration are generally biased according to the attitude and motives of the reporting persons.

5. Trade Associations

Trade associations may be an excellent source of data pertaining to an industry. The trade association of one industry may exchange data with the trade association of another industry, and within one industry a firm may exchange data with another firm with the help of the trade association of the industry. These data and information are basic and relevant because they are not published, and may not be available in a library. There are a large number of trade associations. These are combined associations known as chambers of commerce or chambers of business or chambers of industry, or all of them. They are formed at city, district, state, country and international level. These associations collect data from their members and also from other business houses. They attend to various enquiries of the members. Marketing associations have been providing suitable information to their members.

6. Government Departments

Different government departments have different data which are not available in libraries. But these data are very useful for understanding various aspects of the economy.

The researchers can utilise them for the purposes of their researchers. Information and data pertaining to agriculture, industry, trade, transport, banking and finance can be obtained from the respective ministries of the Government of India.

7. Private Sources

Private sources include varied sources available in the form of books, monographs, bulletins, journals, commercial reports and so on. They are priced and publicly circulated. Some of the sources include extensive original research, and some summarize the research findings of other persons. Many of them are statements of facts and opinions. Elaborate discussions are given there. These sources of data and information are based on the financial statements of business and industrial organisations, trade associations, universities and colleges. Some individuals and institutions are engaged in compiling several important data and information related to marketing and financial aspects of important business and industrial organisations. The All India Management Association, the Indian Marketing Association, Commerce Ltd., Capital, the Economic Times and Financial Express etc. are important private institutions which supply suitable information and data to the public in the form of journals, books and newspapers. Sometimes, they conduct research and the research findings are suitably priced.

8. Commercial Data

There are several institutions and companies which purchase and sell marketing information and data. Some of the companies are solely engaged in marketing research. They collect information and data directly from field surveys. Some such companies collect and process the secondary data and supply them to their subscribers. The purpose of collection of data have been general; but they can be suitably adapted to the specific problems of individual firms. In the United States, several important organisations are well known throughout the world for such kinds of activities. Neilson Retail Index is one such organisation. It provides continuous sales data on foods, tobacco, confectionery, pharmaceuticals, cosmetics, proprietary drugs, beverages, toiletries and other products. Neilson obtains these data every 60 days by auditing inventories and sales of 1,600 carefully selected stores located in different parts of the world. The subscribers of the information of Neilson Retail Index can obtain information of total sales of the product class, sales of the client's own brands and sales of competitive organisations.

This index includes retailer inventory and stock run, sale prices, gross margin, advertising and so on. Similarly, SAMI (Selling Areas — Marketing Inc.) provides comprehensive marketing information to manufacturers. These data and information include the movement of products to retail food stores from the warehouses of wholesalers. There have also been many other commercial research services which have been providing marketing information and data to their clients and also to interested parties.

9. Financial Data

The financial data of reputed concerns are available in several magazines, newspapers, journals and in summary of statistics. The Directorate of Income Tax publishes information pertaining to taxes and income ranges. Such information and data are useful to forecast the market potential of a particular product. Private institutions such as the Economic Times of India, Commerce Private Ltd. etc. are publishing assets and investment-wise data of several large companies. The market researchers are indirectly benefited by such data and information. The financial ratios of the companies published in such publications may provide guidelines to meet the requirements of competitors.

10. International Organisations

International Organisations such as the International Monetary Fund, the World Bank, the United Nations Organisation, the Asian Bank, the African Bank, Foreign embassies etc. publish several useful statistics which can be used by researchers. The statistics may relate to the population problem, trade, institutions, culture, agriculture, regional festivals, superstitions, education, consumption, transportation, forestry, manufacturing and so on. There are several other publications such as the World Almanac, Thomas Register etc. which publish much useful information for marketing researchers. The Statistical Abstracts of the United States have been widely used for the purposes of marketing researches.

11. References and Bibliography

In every publication, the researcher can find references and a bibliography which can be very good sources of information of marketing research. The researcher can consult them for further information and data. An encyclopedia may also be consulted for acquiring further information. Past researches may also provide clues for finding more sources of information of marketing research. All these sources can be consulted at a given place in libraries where various references, bibliographies and encyclopedias are kept in systematic order.

12. Volume of Statistics

There are several private and public organisations which prepare a summary of statistics. In India, the Indian Statistical Institute publishes the Statistical Abstract. Commerce Pvt. Ltd., the Times of India Ltd. and the Financial Express compile Directories of different subjects. The Government of India publishes the Economic Survey of India wherein statistics relating to every field of economic activities are compiled in a suitable form. Various ministries of the Government of India and of state government publish statistics relating to their respective ministries which can be suitably adapted for the purpose of marketing research.

13. Advertising Agencies

Advertising agencies have proved to be very useful sources of marketing research. Recently, a large number of agencies have come into the findings of the advertising researches for their clients. Advertising agencies sometimes, publish reviews, resumes and tests of marketing researches. The consumers' behaviour, consumption pattern and demographic features are generally revealed by these agencies.

14. Other Sources

There are several other sources of marketing researches. Individuals conduct their own researches which may be purchased by other institutions. Marketing Associations, Management Associations and individual business houses have been conducting marketing researches for other researches. There are a large number of research organisations in foreign countries which are selling their research findings to organisations requiring to know the outcome of their researches.

3. ADVANTAGES OF SECONDARY DATA

The use of secondary data has certain advantages over the primary data. They give cost and time economies. The researcher simply has to go to a library, locate the appropriate sources of data and collect them from these sources. It saves time and money by avoiding field work and preparing a questionnaire. The primary data collection requires selection and training of the field staff, sample selection, interviewing and filling the questionnaire and processing the data. This work may involve months and years. Moreover, preparation of the questionnaire, selection, training and recruitment of the staff involve additional cost. These expenses are not required to be incurred in the case of secondary data, as they had already been incurred while collecting and preparing the secondary data. The users of secondary data may sometimes be required to pay a very nominal fee for the use of the data.

The secondary data can be obtained quickly. Sometimes, data that are not available from a primary source may be available from secondary data. Government publications, census results, registration and the economic, social and political set up of the country are available in important journals and publications of the ministries of the Government. Therefore, it is suggested not to bypass the secondary data, but to use it unless it is exhausted, and then proceed to collect primary data for verification and further extension of the available information and data.

4. DISADVANTAGES OF SECONDARY DATA

Secondary data suffer from non-suitability for the present research and inaccuracy of the data. Since the secondary data are collected for purposes other than for the existing research, it is rarely possible for them to fit the present problems and accurately interpret the existing situations.

1. Non-suitability

Secondary data do not satisfy the immediate needs of the present data because they are compiled for other purposes. They may be of little use, or of no use, unless they are adapted to suit the present requirements. There are three bases of difference: *(i)* measurement unit, *(ii)* class definitions and *(iii)* publication-lag.

Units of measurement are common deficiencies of secondary data. For example, consumer income may be measured by individual, family, household, tax return and spending units. The present study may require measurement by an individual, but the secondary data may be available by a family. So the use of secondary data requires approximation of the measurement which may not be a correct measurement of the secondary data for purposes of the existing research.

Similarly, the class boundaries given in the secondary data may be quite different from the needed class intervals. Suppose, frequencies of income are given with class interval 0-999; 1000-1999 and 2000-2999, whereas the required class interval may be 0-249, 250-749, 750-999 and so on. Efforts have been made to have a uniform class interval; but it has not been established yet, therefore, the secondary data must be used with precaution.

The secondary data suffer from a time lag. The latest secondary data may not be available because their collection and computation take time. They become obsolete. Their utility diminishes with time. Marketing decisions require current data rather than historical information and statistics. The socio-economic statistics are generally old, they may thus be used with precaution in marketing research.

2. Inaccuracy

The secondary data may suffer from various inaccuracies and errors for collection, analysis and presentation of data. So use of the data will not be free from these inaccuracies and errors. These data would have to be modified before applying them to the existing research. The source, the purpose of publication and evidence of quality are taken into consideration while using the secondary data.

The secondary data may be obtained from the primary source or the secondary source. The primary source represents correct and reliable data. The secondary source may involve several errors and omissions and their intention to collect may be somewhat different. The primary source describes the process of collection and analysis. It reproduces significant footnotes, textual comments on which the primary sources had been based. It discovers the facts.

The purpose of publication, if not known, can lead to wrong conclusions. The inclusion of new information may not be possible. Publication errors may continue unless they are verified with facts. Data published to promote sales, to advance the interests of business and to carry on any propaganda may not serve the original purpose of the research.

The third criterion whereby to judge the accuracy of data is evidence of quality. The status of a particular organisation reflects the quality of data. In India, reports and publications of the Indian Statistical Institute and of the Reserve Bank of india are considered more authentic than that of any government and private publications because these institutions have no sufficient staff and organisation to procure primary data. Sometimes they are biased keeping the purposes of their presentation. The researchers must be aware of the sampling plan, questionnaire, method of observation, experience of field staff and collection and processing methods of secondary data before using them for their research purposes.

Adaptation of Secondary Data

The secondary data have been considered as insignificant by many of the researchers. But they are very useful sources of marketing research if adapted to the needs of the existing marketing research. There is need in scrutinising the existing secondary data. The objectives and the features of the original data are to be examined. Methods of collection and classification of data must also be studied.

1. Scrutiny of Data

It must be kept in mind that the person using secondary data is using the data of others, whose objectives may be dissimilar to the previous users. Therefore, the secondary data must be scrutinised bearing in mind the research objective. The nature of the collected data must be well specified and known to the researcher because the original data collectors may have some ulterior motives and may be prejudiced towards its interpretation to "prove something." They have had quite different purposes from the present study. The original secondary data may be obsolete and may serve the purpose of the present study after being thoroughly scrutinised.

2. Objectives of the Original Study

The purposes of the secondary data may have been different from the purposes of the existing research. The data must pertain to the present study. The units of measurement, the period of time, the universe of interest and relevance of data must be similar in both the studies. The researcher must be aware of all the situations and objectives of the original study, otherwise he will be misled by the original data.

3. Persons who Collected and Published Data

The researcher should know who has collected and published the data. He has to see to the long-term satisfaction of his clients. He has to appraise the capabilities and motivation of the individuals responsible for the data collection and publication. Independent researchers may produce accurate reports and may be relied upon for the present study. The reputation, experience and degree of independence of the persons collecting and publishing data influence the report. It is pertinent to note that information so collected must be handled with care to present a correct and true picture of the existing research.

4. Methods Employed

If proper methods are employed to collect the original data, the use of secondary data may be relevant to the present study. Unless we know the methods of data collection, selecting the sample and area of coverage, we cannot properly interpret and analyse the data for our purpose. Therefore, it is essential to know the methods employed for the collection, interpretation and analysis of data. Caution should be exercised to reveal the weakness of the method employed. The sample selected, the objectives of the data, the questionnaire employed, and the field workers' experience should be known before analysing and processing the data.

5. Classification and Presentation

The classification and grouping of original data have different purposes and segments. Sometimes, it is not possible to group them for the present study. Attempts should be made to group them to the present requirements. The government publications have shown standard classification and grouping of the data. Several Sources can cross examine the data and find out good data from the data available. The time liners of the data should be known before their use.

❖ ❖ ❖

CHAPTER 6

COLLECTION OF PRIMARY DATA

1. **PRIMARY DATA OBJECTIVES**
2. **TYPES OF PRIMARY DATA**
3. **SOURCES OF DATA**
4. **METHODS OF DATA COLLECTION**
5. **MEDIA OF COMMUNICATION**
6. **FORMULATING THE PLAN OF PRIMARY DATA COLLECTION**

COLLECTION OF PRIMARY DATA

Research problem of general nature can be solved to a greater extent with the use of secondary data. But when research is undertaken on significant and complex problems, primary data are needed. There are six steps involved in the collection of primary data.

1. Primary Data Objectives.
2. Types of Primary Data.
3. Sources of Data.
4. Methods of Data Collection.
5. Media of Communication.
6. Formulation of the Plan of Primary Data Collection.

The primary data collection has to adopt the above steps to obtain appropriate and correct information and data for the marketing research.

1. PRIMARY DATA OBJECTIVES

The objectives of primary data are formulated on the basis of research objectives. Objectives set the guidelines and directions of research planning. Formulating the objectives offers the best feasible means of solution. The research study should yield measurements related to the research objectives as the measurements will provide directions for a decision. The findings of the research should be capable of being utilised for the better performance of the organisation. The cost-benefits analysis should be made for determining the objectives of the primary data collection.

The objectives should be precise, attainable and economic so that the findings may be accurate, reliable, valid and useful. Good measurements are reliable and valid. Reliability means avoidance of chance of error. Validity refers to purposive data. Competent researchers are aware of inaccurate and invalid data and they try to avoid them. Data objectives are relevant and immediate objectives of the research process. They are concrete and workable. The present situations are appraised to frame future objectives. The type of data needed, sources of data and methods of data collection are decided on the basis of established objectives.

2. TYPES OF PRIMARY DATA

There are a number of primary data which can be gathered and collected from primary sources. Some of them may be relevant to a particular study. Therefore the data collection planning is divergent from the objectives of data collection to the convergence of the types of primary data and so on. While selecting the types of primary data to be collected, the nature and function of the data have to be decided.

(1) Data classified by their nature: The nature of data may be classified according to various categories: Facts, knowledge, opinions, intentions, motivation and behaviour.

(a) Facts: Facts refer to actuality but they not necessarily be material. The measurable facts can be measured precisely and definitely. The descriptive facts relating to people may be demographic and sociological. These characteristics represent the attributes of people, e.g., age, sex, income and level of education. The sociological data are related to how people are organised in and related to society. Facts are considered ideal types of data because of a high degree of measurement reliability. Facts-data do not reveal causation; but they are essential because of their factual description.

(b) Knowledge: Knowledge refers to what people know. Potential buyers' knowledge and awareness of products or brands are important data of marketing research. The respondents, awareness and knowledge are evaluated to get sufficient data for marketing research. The awareness of the product, product features, prices of the product, product manufacturing etc. are some of the examples of knowledge and awareness data of marketing research. Similarly knowledge about brands, advertisements, retail stores and prices can be obtained by marketing research.

(c) Opinions: Opinions are people's perceptions. What people think or what is in their minds are called opinions. Their perceptions may or may not be true. Thus, they may be well defined as attitudes. These are products of mental sets and may be referred to as images. Since opinions affect the behaviour and attitude of people, they should be appraised properly. Some authors have differentiated opinions from attitudes. Attitudes refer to respondents' views or feelings towards some phenomenon, while opinions are verbal expressions of attitudes. But for research purposes, they are treated alike. Attitudes are considered the forerunners of behaviour. So, the researchers are interested in persons' attitudes toward the product and their overall attitudes towards quality, price and brand.

(d) Intentions: Intentions are acts that are in the minds of people. These are expectations of behaviour, or intentions to indulge in particular marketing behaviour. These are individuals' anticipated or planned future behaviour, which are of great value to the marketing researchers. Intentions include a definite intention to buy, a probable intention to buy, a definite intention not to buy and undecided intentions. The marketing researchers try to find out the correlation between anticipated and actual behaviours.

(e) Motivation: Motivation is how to steer and direct people's actions. It is known as the inner state of mind that energizes activities and moves or directs the behaviour of people. If the researcher can understand the motives behind a person's behaviour, he can find out ways to influence his future behaviour. It is a need, a want, an urge, an impulse that influences or channels the behaviour of a person. Their relevation by marketing research will help executives to take appropriate decisions.

(i) Behaviour: Behaviour is the outcome of various instincts as discussed above. It is a physical activity and involves one or more actions. It involves a description of the activity. The marketing researcher tries to study the behaviour of the people and place it in a systematic form to reveal the future demand of the product. The present and past behaviours are considered the base for the prediction of future behaviour.

(ii) Data according to Function: Data are also classified according to their functions. While planning data, the researchers anticipate the future analysis and synthesis according to their function. They try to avoid redundant data and collect necessary data. Data according to function may be causal, payoff, descriptive and classification.

(a) Causal Data: Causal data reveal the cause and effect relationship. One hypothesis is measure in terms of effects. Data required to measure the hypothesis are termed causal data. Such types of causal data are required in the marketing mix. They are used for experimental purpose in all the fields of marketing variables. They reveal certain phenomenal observations. The coefficient of correlation regression and other sophisticated statistical tools are based on causal data. The researchers treat them as very useful data for their research purposes because several relevant conclusions can be drawn on the basis of the data. In experimental design, the causal variables or data are measured.

(b) Payoff Data: The payoff are resultant data. They are the outcome of certain causal data, i.e., results of certain phenomenon. The causal variables are measured in terms of payoff or effects. This means that payoff data are required to measure the causal variables.

(c) Descriptive Data: There is need of such types of data which may describe the situation, statement and facts. Even in the case of experimental data, one variable requires to be controlled for which descriptive data are used. In such cases, a description of the samples is needed when drawing conclusions. Descriptive data have no payoff data but draw conclusions by inferring from descriptive data. Descriptive data used in an historical design provide the base for conclusions.

(d) Classification Data: In sophistication experimental design the compound data have been classified to arrive at simple analysis and conclusions. The classification data, i.e., the data classified in relevant categories are conceivable and may be easily described. The classification data in complex and multiple groups, i.e., more than one causal variable or rotation of treatments in sub-groups have functional utility. The sample survey also provides classification data, e.g., according to age, sex, income, location etc.

3. SOURCES OF DATA

Primary data may be obtained from the sources of groups of individuals, institutions or specific respondents. In any case the individual is involved. Therefore, the individual is the basic source of primary data. Since individual may be of several types, the sources of primary data may be several, depending upon the nature and kind of individuals. The selection of a particular source depends upon the purpose of the marketing research. For industrial houses, the sources of marketing research would be the business houses which are clients of the industrial houses. But for the business houses, the consumers would be the sources of marketing research. Thus, the sources of the data of marketing research are decided upon by the objectives of the research. A pilot survey is conducted to decide the possible respondents.

4. METHODS OF DATA COLLECTION

After deciding the source of the data, the next step is to decide the methods of obtaining data from a particular source. The methods of obtaining data are adopted in accordance with the objectives and nature of the research methodology. There are two main methods of obtaining data: *(i)* observation and *(ii)* communication.

1. Observation

Observation is used to obtain information on the current and past behaviour of people. One can record and measure some descriptive facts through perceiving situations or actions. Observation includes human means of perception and recording. It may also be non-human or mechanical. Human or manual observation involves the use of personal observers who see or hear the phenomena specified. Examining of inventory and other material facts are the examples of manual observation. Instead of asking such questions as what brand of television set the consumer uses, the best and simplest procedure may be to look at the set. Mechanical observation may be undertaken by machine usually electronic. Tape recording and photography may be used for mechanical observation. The A.C. Nielson company uses a special device to observe television sets.

The observation method has been preferred from the cost and accuracy points of view because respondents may not reveal true and fair information of the facts; but the observations of the facts may reveal the correct picture of the phenomenon. With objectivity in reporting, observation tends to have an advantage in reliability. But care must be exercised to avoid the observer's errors. The observation method may be classified into the categories of the audit, recording devices and people watching.

1. The Audit: The audits are performed on distribution and on consumers. Each store in the sample is audited to obtain information on purchases, inventories, sales, special promotions, and prices of each brand of each product. The acquired data are compiled, analysed and reported to the clients, i.e., the marketing management which is interested to evaluate market performance and the effectiveness of marketing changes. Thus, the audit observation can provide information pertaining to the market size, market share, market pattern, seasonal purchasing pattern and effectiveness of various marketing strategies. The manufacturers perform the audit observation through their salesmen. They collect comprehensive information on inventories and prices. Consumers' audit is conducted by the field force to take an audit of inventories of their brands, quantities and package size.

2. Recording Devices: A number of electronic devices have been used to record the facts and information. These devices may be used in laboratory type investigations and natural setting behaviour. By-camera and a psycho-galvanometer are used for laboratory studies. Pretesting of advertising has been the main example of laboratory studies. Eye-cameras are designed to record eye-movements in relation to the specific location of material. Significant analysis can be made of the pattern in which the advertisement is "read" through the use of the photographic record provided by the eye-camera. It reveals the portions of the copy actually read, and has drawn the attention of people. Similarly, a psychogalvanometer is used for measuring the responses made by people to the advertisement. The electrical resistence in the palm of the respondents is recorded by this device and can measure the stimulation aroused by the advertisement. There may be some other devices to measure the behaviour under laboratory conditions. An audiometer is another device for recording respondent behaviour under normal conditions. The audiometer is installed in the television set of the selected respondents.

3. People Watching: Direct observation of the respondents has been a common method of collecting information. The shopping behaviour is studied by direct observation. The researchers rely upon the salesmen who observe displays, availability of goods, brands, and the quantity purchased, number and location of the sales force and cash registers. The salesmen can assess the possibility of sales and the expansion of business. They can observe the location of banks, retail stores, and the entire shopping centre.

2. Communication

The second method of data-collection is through communication. The interviewer may use different methods of communication, but he has to select only those media and techniques of communication which are most suitable in the particular situation. While using different media of communication, suitable techniques are selected for obtaining information from the respondents.

5. MEDIA OF COMMUNICATION

Communications have been important media for obtaining information from respondents. They may seek data that have already been recorded or may create new information from the answers of the respondents. The questionnaire is used as format structured communication. Questionnaires are used when communication by mail is required. They are also used when consistent and appropriate information is required. Unstructured questionnaires are used with interview proceedings in motivation research, group interviews and other thought provoking researches. Panels may also be appointed to collected information. Personal interviews, telephone interviews, mail interviews and panel interviews are discussed.

1. Personal Interview

A personal interview is face to face communication with the respondent. The interviewer gets in touch with the respondent, asks the questions, and records the answers obtained. It is the interviewer's responsibility to record the answers either during the interview or after the interview. The interview may be conducted at any place, but it is appropriate to meet the respondent at his place of work or at his resident. The main purpose of this consideration is that the answer must be recorded clearly and correctly. The personal interview may be either structured or unstructured. In a structured interview the formal questionnaire has been formulated and the questions are asked in pre-arranged order. There may be other classifications of a personal interview on the basis of approaching the questions. It may be either direct of indirect. In the case of indirect questions, the main questions are intentionally disguised. Thus, there may be four types of personal interview: (1) structured and direct interviews, (2) unstructured and direct interviews, (3) structured and indirect interviews and (4) unstructured and indirect interviews. Indirect interviews are of recent origin and have been used for in depth information and motivation research.

(i) Structured Direct Interviews

The usual type of interview is the structured direct interview. A formal questionnaire consisting of nondisguised questions are used for this interview. The main purpose is to get the facts. A formal list of questions is prepared and questions are asked in sequence. No other questions except from the questionnaire are sought from the respondents. Answers are limited to a list of alternatives from which the respondents have to select the best answer. This method has some definite advantages. The structured interview provides more reliable results, i.e., if the research project is repeated in the same manner similar results will be obtained. Different methods of phrasing a question and obtaining different answers have been reduced to a few questions and a few answers. Since the questionnaires are formulated in advance all the required information is sought an orderly and systematic fashion. The exact wording of the questions are worked out in such a way as fully to reduce the possibility of misunderstandings and biased answers. A pretest is made on the questionnaire to discover any problems in the wording and ordering of the questions. The same questions are asked in the same order to provide maximum control of the interviewing process. This demands less ability in the interviewing and lower cost per capita. Editing, tabulating, analysis and interpretation become standardised.

The main problems with the structured direct interview are related to the framing of questions and getting unbiased and complete answers. The greater reliability of structuring the questionnaire sometimes ignores its validity as it prevents the interviewer to ask for more information. The misleading, evasive and inaccurate information may not be cross examined by the interviewer as he has to rely upon the structured questionnaire. This type of interview is, therefore, restricted to the collection of factual information or opinions.

(ii) Unstructured and Direct Interview

The structured questions provide limited answers. Sometimes they give only two alternatives, i.e., yes or no, whereas the marketing management may desire to know the reasons for the facts and the phenomena. Direct questions in this case rarely elicit useful answers, diagnose the problems or find motive behind the responses. To overcome these difficulties, marketing researchers have adapted psychoanalysis. Instead of approaching the respondents with a fixed list of questions, the interviewer is given the freedom to talk openly about the subject. The interviewer is given only general instructions about the type of information desired. The purpose of the interview is clear, but the response to the question is open ended. For example, the interviewer may ask, "How do you feel about the success of the colour T.V. in your city?" Here the question is constant; but the interviewer is free to talk openly on the subject. The interview becomes totally instructed. The respondent's reply, and the interviewer's probe questions as also the respondent's successive answers provide a comprehensive statement of the question. The interviewer puts the respondents at ease and encourages them to express any ideas on the subject. The interviewer encourages the respondents at every stage to explain the point, to explain the fact so that the interviewer can receive the respondent's surface reasons for the marketing decisions and find the underlying and basic motives.

Unstructured direct interviews are used in exploratory researches. These interviews are considered useful for obtaining a clearer understanding of the problem and the areas to be investigated. The respondents can explain certain problems in adopting particular marketing decisions. They may sometimes suggest important measures to overcome the problems and reduce the difficulties. A pilot interview with the use of the unstructured and direct method may be useful for framing questions of final interviews. This type of interview is also useful for obtaining information on motives. The interviewer is in a position to derive a more accurate picture of the respondent's statements. However, skilled probing of the respondents requires an experienced interviewer. This interview provides detailed and comprehensive responses. If some idea of interest is expressed during the interview, the interviewer may ask for more information by probing. For example, the interviewer may state, "You are precisely correct, what is your opinion about the decision?" This stimulates the respondents for further discussion. When the statements are used to establish motives, the unstructured direct interview is known as "In-Depth Interview." The probing continues until the interviewer feels that he has obtained full information considering time limitations, problem requirements and willingness of the respondents to cooperate with the interviewing process.

The unstructured interview is free from the restrictions of the structured or formal questions. The in-depth interviews provide more information. Ideas and feelings which are not normally disclosed are brought out by this kind of interview. The interviewer is free to adjust each interview to the given situation and to the respondent's personality. Thus, this form of interview is in a better position to obtain clear and in-depth ideas.

The in-depth interview causes several problems. The in-depth interview requires highly skilled interviewers who are hard to find and also expensive. The interviewer's judgement affect the response. In-depth interviews often take a long time to complete. There will be variation in the results of the interviews because responses vary from interviewer to interviewer, and also on account of a difference in administering the questionnaire and application of the interviewing technique. Since there is a possibility of variation in results, it is difficult to compare results. Averages and percentages cannot be computed with validity. The attitude and inclination of the interviewer may also influence the results. The length of the interview may also create difficulties in securing the respondents' cooperation. This type of interview involves a higher cost. Analysis and interpretation may also be subjective, and may not provide standard and comparable results. The unstructured and direct interview can only be as effective in obtaining complete, objective and unbiased information as the interviewer is skilled in formulating and asking questions. This type of interview is best suited to exploratory research.

(iii) Structured and Indirect Interview

The structured and indirect interview has become a technique of unbiased research because the biases of the interviewer and of the interpreter are avoided. It has advantages over all the structured interviews and probes of the respondents. Instead of direct interviews, the respondents are asked the questions indirectly. It is supported on the ground that the respondents' knowledge, perception and memory are conditioned by their attitudes. When the direct question fails to get an answer, the interviewer can depend upon indirect questions. Greater knowledge reflects the strength and direction of the attitude of the respondents. When the respondents do know the answers to the questions, they guess them according to their attitude. The in-depth interview has the disadvantages of non-comparability, but structured and indirect interview has all the advantages of the in-depth interview and none of the disadvantages of the in-depth interview. Since the respondents influence the answers according to their beliefs, attitudes and interests, indirect questions are essential to avoid them. The purpose of an interview is to know the respondents rather than what they feel. Since the questions are structured, their answers can be properly coded and tabulated.

(iv) Unstructured and Indirect Interview

It has been found that the researchers face varied problems owing to the unwillingness of the respondents to reveal all the information. They are sometimes unaware of the subjects. The unstructured and direct interview may give biased reports. Structured questions do not provide an ample opportunity to express their willingness, attitudes and interests. Therefore, clinical psychologists have developed disguised method of gathering information and data. The respondents cannot know the object of the study and may not be biased in their answers. The more unstructured and indirect a stimulus, the more a subject can and will project his needs, motivations, emotions and attitudes.

The unstructured and indirect interview is very well-known as a projective technique. In this technique, all individuals in describing a situation interpret the situation to a degree. Various projective techniques are used, but the most common methods are word association, sentence completion and story telling. In word association, a series of words is read out one at a time to the respondent who has to select the first word from several words. The test words are dispersed throughout the list and are intermixed with some neutral words to conceal the purpose. Sentence completion requires respondents to complete partial sentences. In story telling, respondents are shown pictures or given descriptions and asked to tell a story about them. Details of word association, sentence completion and story telling are given under the next section, motivation research.

The projective technique, i.e., the unstructured and indirect interview has the advantages of depth interviews. Interpretation is very subjective. Cost, time and difficulty in securing competent field workers are also the main problems of the projective technique. The problems of editing, coding and tabulation of replies and suggestions are present there. The projective technique is more suited for exploratory research.

2. Telephone Interview

The telephone interview is used when the information to be collected is limited. The telephone interview is used in lieu of personal interviews. It is most frequently used when the information has to be collected quickly and inexpensively. However, it is not as versatile as personal interview as it is difficult to handle over the telephone information needed probes. The telephone interview is suitable for inquiring about information just released or telecast by radio or television. The respondents may be asked whether they watch the particular programme regularly. What are their views about the programme? The indirect and unstructured questions are not suitable for the telephone interview.

The telephone interview produces more noncommittal answers than definite choices. People do not like to reveal personal matters over the telephone. The quality of the telephone interview is better than that of the personal interview because the interviewing process can be better controlled and supervised. The interviewer can concentrate on a few questions and surveys. In the United States, the wide area telephone service (WATS) as offered by the Bell system has been widely used. It has become important media of telephone surveys. Using WATS, the interviewers can make a sizable survey quickly and economically. WATS has made it feasible for research organisations to employ full time interviewing staff. Recently, it has developed a computer system from which the interviewer reads. Responses are recorded by use of a keyboard similar to that of a typewriter which places the answers directly into a computer.

The telephone interview has the advantages of speed and economy. It is easier to obtain the cooperation of people over the telephone than in a personal interview. It is specially useful for executives who cannot spare time for interviews. It is faster than other methods. Replies can be recorded without embarrassment to the respondents. It can be used more effectively in conjunction with personal interviews. The interview can be conducted in the evening when many respondents are relaxing after their work. Telephone interviews are by far the fastest of the three media of communication. More interviews can be used to shorten the time required to complete the interview. Man hours and administrative problems become less in the case of telephone interviews.

The telephone interview has several limitations. Only a limited amount of information can be obtained. The respondents have their own attitudes, interests and ambitions; so their replies are biased accordingly. There is no control over the interview-technique. Moreover, telephone interviewing suffers from bad lines, cut offs and other problems. The telephone interview cannot be a useful method of interviewing in the Indian context where a very small number of respondents have telephone facilities.

3. Mail Interview

The mail interview places a great deal of importance on the construction of the questionnaire, because there is no interviewer in mail surveys to ask questions and record answers. It cannot be used to conduct an unstructured study. Personal and telephone interviews are more flexible in the sense that they can be stopped or altered at any point whereas the researcher has no control on the interview once the questionnaire is mailed. The mailing questionnaire is accompanied with a covering letter instructing the respondent how to complete the questionnaire and return the questionnaire to the researcher. The respondents complete the questionnaire at their own leisure and mail the replies to the researcher. This kind of interview requires that the questionnaire has to be even more carefully compiled, structured and pre-tested than the personal interview questionnaire. The respondents must be convinced about the importance of the research, and their interests should be kept at a higher level. The covering letter should weigh the significance of the respondents and the reason for selecting their names for the survey. There are various sources from which to select the names of respondents such as institutions, colleges, universities, offices, the telephone directory etc.

Information Obtained

The questionnaire used for the mail interview should be neither too long nor too short. It is reckoned that a questionnaire longer than six pages may not be useful for a mail interview. But the number of questions and not the number of pages is the important factor for deciding the appropriate size of the questionnaire. Pretesting and experiments will reveal the number of questions required for a mail interview supplied directly by respondents instead of through an intermediary or enumerator.

Return of Mail Questionnaire

Experience reveal that the mail questionnaire is not answered in its entirety in every case. It may be to the extent of 50 per cent to 80 per cent of the questionnaire. Sometimes, the questionnaire set to the respondents does not reach them. The interviewer will have to take into account all these shortcomings. The respondents have developed the habit of not returning the questionnaire. In such cases, they require motivation, direct incentives, mechanical and perceptual devices.

(a) General Motivation: General motivation refers to motivation concerning all sorts of respondents who have different interests. This is achieved by making the questionnaire as interesting as possible. All researchers try to make the questionnaire attractive by printing on good paper and leaving sufficient space for replies. Paper of various colours may serve the purpose. There must be a feeling of personal connection between the respondents and the researchers. This may be achieved through cover letters sent with the questionnaires and by having the questionnaire signed with a specific request.

(b) Direct Incentives: A cash award or premium incentives may be provided for completion of the questionnaire. It has been observed that the larger the incentive, the larger the response to the mail questionnaire. Trading stamps, ball-point pens, pencils and a pocket of coffee may serve as suitable direct incentives for replying to the mailed questions.

(c) Mechanical and Perceptual Devices: Contact with the respondents before sending the questionnaire, informing them about the objectives of the research and requesting cooperation tend to increase the reply of the mail interview. Registered letters receive greater response than unregistered letters. Return envelopes result in a larger response. It is also necessary to have a follow up campaign for those who do not reply to the first mailing.

Control of Sample

The mail survey requires a mailing list which may be prepared from telephone directories, tax lists, business directories, departmental stores and so on. It has to be properly selected to get a representation of the population. Control of sample refers to the researcher's ability to direct the inquiry to a designated respondent, and to secure the cooperation desired from that respondent.

The direction of the inquiry is guided by the sampling structure, i.e., the list of population elements from which the sample will be drawn. Therefore, the interviewer should select only such persons who are representative of the purpose of the survey. For example, a telephone directory may prove only limited representation because all the representative members do not have telephones. More than one mailing list may serve the purpose of sampling. The quality of these lists determines the sampling bias. If the list is good enough, the bias can be small. If there is an accurately applicable and readily available list of population units, the mail questionnaire allows a representative sample. The personal interview affords sampling control in directing the questionnaire to specific sample units. In the mail interview area sampling procedures are employed in order to have sampling control.

There is need of information control because the amount and accuracy of the information may vary with the various methods of data collection. The mail questionnaire is not useful for extensive probes. There is also a danger of sequence bias. If the questions are ambiguous, there does not exist any opportunity for clarification in the case of a mail questionnaire. There is little variations in the administration of the mail questionnaire. There is small cost of administration.

4. Panel Interview

A panel interview may be composed of either individuals or corporate units. It is a convenient method of obtaining information about the continuing behaviour of a group or panel of respondents. The very nature of the panel interview is that the group comprising the panel-member is interviewed on the same or similar topics at regular intervals over a reasonable period of time. Since the data are obtained for a fixed panel or group over a successive period, the basis is provided for determining trends and changes over a length of time. The panel interview is not greatly different from setting up any other type of sampling operation. Either the random or quota methods may be used for sampling purposes. Experience has shown that a steady flow of interesting inquiries helped occasionally by free product trials have stimulated cooperation from the members of the panels.

The consumer purchase panel has been considered the important panel interview. It furnishes information at regular intervals on the continuing purchases of the products. The type of the product, weight or quantity of units, brand, number of units, kind of package or container, price, special promotion store etc. are the various kinds of information collected under the consumer purchase panel. The consumer panel is one way of measuring public opinion without the intervention of the interviewers. There are different uses or the consumer panels. The members of the panel are usually housewives. They are provided with a diary whereby they are required to write down every day what they actually buy. They are also requested to note their opinions about the programmes viewed on television and heard over the radio. Similarly, there may be different panel interviews.

The panel interviews have distinct advantages since changes in the level of sales may be analysed directly without the problem of determining changes in inventory levels. Trends and shifts in market composition, a continuing analysis of the brand position, the trend of sales by package or container types, the relative importance of types of retail outlets, trends in competitive pricing and special promotions and their effects and the effects of the manufacturer's own price and promotional changes can be analysed and interpreted easily with the use of the panel interview. The weaknesses and difficulties revealed may be corrected by the panel interview.

Panel interviews have certain limitations and disadvantages. It requires the cooperation of members of the panel which may or may not be obtained. The sample of families to comprise a consumer purchase panel may be chosen randomly, but the panel has experienced a high refusal rate. Willingness to cooperate in the panel interview may indicate certain characteristics in members which may not be representative. In the case of dropouts from time to time, it is difficult to ensure their replacements having similar characteristics. The constant interviewing may lead to conditioned and biased responses. Panel members may behave in a typical manner as a result of being part of the panel. They acquire a feeling of price and recognition and thus behave unlike the general public. Despite the limitations, if the panel is administered carefully, the resulting data are important additions to the information required for arriving marketing decisions.

Relative Merits of Principal Methods of Data Collection

Personal Interview	*Mail*	*Telephone*
1. It is a more flexible means of data collection.	1. Its coverage is wider and more representative.	1. It is representative and wider in coverage amongst the respondents having telephone facilities.
2. The identity of the respondents can be known and more information can be obtained.	2. No field staff is required.	2. No field staff is required. It is convenient to handle at comfort.
3. Non-response is usually very low.	3. Cost per questionnaire is relatively low.	3. Cost per questionnaire is low.
4. Sample control is possible.	4. Respondents feel free to express their motives and desires.	4. Respondents control is easier.
5. Products, advertisement cartoons can be demonstrated to the respondents.	5. No interviewer bias is possible.	5. It is a quick way of obtaining data and information.
6. Observation methods can be applied. Respondents' reactions can be analysed.	6. Respondents can answer at leisure and have time to think.	6. Non response is very low.
7. Results are more accurate due to interview control.	7. Certain segments of population can be reached very easily.	7. Call backs are simple and economical.

8. Misunderstanding and misinterpretation can be quickly avoided and amended.	8. Questions are more standardised and relevant.	8. High income groups and senior executives can be approached very easily.
9. It is best suited to collect a large amount of complex data.	9. Confidential and sensitive data can be easily obtained.	9. Access to remote area is possible.

Relative Demerits of Principal Methods of Data Collection

Personal Interview	*Mail*	*Telephone*
1. It is most expensive of all methods.	1. Bias cannot be determined.	1. Period of interview is too short to provoke to get full information.
2. Supervision and control on interview are very essential.	2. Control over reply and question is not possible.	2. Confusing and ambiguous responses may be there.
3. There is danger of interviewers' bias as well as respondents' bias.	3. Interpretation of omission is very difficult.	3. Thematic Apperceptions test is not possible.
4. Busy persons are difficult to approach.	4. Cost per return may be high if non-response is very large.	4. Non-telephone owners cannot be approached.
5. Large sample cannot be completed with limited period.	5. Complex questions requiring explanation may be left unanswered.	5. It is unsuitable for large sample and impracticable for in-depth and wide interview.
6. It requires trained and experienced interviewers.	6. Probe questions cannot be replied. Replies are ambiguous and unrelated.	6. It is unsuitable for complex interview.
7. Timing of interviews may cause resentment amongst the respondents.	7. Ambiguity in omission of replies may cause analysis to be very difficult.	7. Antagonism to the technique is caused by repetition.
	8. It is difficult to amend wrong answers and omissions.	
	9. It is slowest of all techniques.	
	10. Control on response is difficult.	
	11. Validity of sample may be doubtful because of heavy non-response.	

MOTIVATION RESEARCH

Marketing research is no longer confined to a formalised means of obtaining information from people. Where it is not amenable to exploration a projective technique is required. A project technique was originally developed by clinical psychologists and has been adapted for use in marketing research. It is now, very well-known as motivation research. But it does not mean that this technique is inapplicable to non-motivation research. Motivation research is applied to discover research. Motivation research is applied to find out the motives of the respondents which could not be revealed by ordinary research techniques. There are many important motives and reasons which are not disclosed by the consumers because a truthful description could damage their ego and recognition. Some consumers do not know the correct and suitable answers to the questions. Motives are of paramount importance in consumer behaviour. The main thrust in such techniques has been that of concealing the subject of inquiry by using an indirect stimulus and presenting it in a very provocative form. Many of these techniques employ the principle of projection, i.e., the subject is given a non-personal, ambiguous situation and is asked to describe it. The description will be influenced by the respondents' needs, motives and values. Thus, the researcher can understand their inner motives and can find out the truth of the questions. The projection technique or motivation research may involve several techniques such as word association, sentence completion, story telling, third person technique, thematic apperception tests, depth interview and other techniques.

1. Word Association

Under this technique, test words are dispersed throughout the test and are intermixed with some neutral words to conceal the objective of the study. The respondents are asked to select one of these words. The responses are judged by three angles: (1) by the frequency with which any word is given as response, by the amount of time that elapses before a response, and by the number of respondents who do not respond at all. There may be some common responses which may reveal a pattern of interest, motivation and drives. The association of words may be classified as favourable-unfavourable, pleasant-unpleasant etc. The amount of time that elapses before a response is given to a test word is carefully evaluated. Respondents who hesitate to respond are known as emotionally involved in the interview. The pattern of response will reveal the respondents' feeling and attitude towards the subject.

2. Sentence Completion

The sentence completion test requires that the respondents should complete the sentence according to the first thoughts that come to their mind. The responses are noted down verbatim and analysed later on. Some selected responses may be illustrated to direct the respondents to complete the sentences. The ways in which sentences are completed will indicate the motive and interests of the respondents. The respondents are provided a stimulus over word-association projective methods. There should be enough direction to evoke some association; but they should be careful not to convey the purpose of the study. Skill is required to develop a good sentence completion. This has become a common technique of motivation research.

3. Story Telling

The story telling technique depends upon the pictorial materials such as photographs, drawings and cartoons. Some of the pictures are of ordinary events and others are of unusual events. Some of the pictures are clearly represented and others are relatively observed. The respondents' interpretation of the picture reveal their personalities. They may be categorised as impulsive, intellectual, creative or unimaginative. The story telling was used for the first time to reveal the use of Nescafe instant coffee. Each housewife was asked to read the shopping lists and describe them. On the basis of the description, the housewives were classified into the categories of lazy, thrifty, spendthrift, planned and good wives.

4. Third Person Techniques

The simplest method of obtaining information through indirect questioning is to ask for the view of a third person, e.g., neighbour, associates and others. This facilitates the respondents project their own views and attitudes without being involved in ego and image damage because they answer in the name of other persons. For example one may ask, "Are you afraid of inflation?" The respondents may not reply correctly although they are afraid of inflation because of position and prestige consciousness. The questions may be correctly answered if the question is "Are your neighbours afraid of inflation?" This technique should be used carefully because the respondents may not wish to be involved in the replies of others.

5. Thematic Apperception Test (TAT)

The thematic refers to the theme of the study which may be cited in the form of an example, picture, cartoon etc. Apperception means perceptual interpretation of the theme.

So, the Thematic Apperception Test involves perceptual interpretation of the subject of the study. The theme or subject matter may be given in an ambiguous manner and the respondents may be asked to describe the theme. The most common form of thematic perception is in the form of cartoon. The respondents are shown cartoons in random order and are asked to describe the cartoons. The researcher may interpret the description on an impassionate basis, classifying all the respondents in some systematic order.

6. The Depth Interview

The depth interview is used to discover underlying motives and desires. It requires great skill and considerable time. This is also known as a qualitative interview. It has been adapted from clinical psychology, sociology and cultural anthropology. In motivation research, the depth interview varies with the level of use where "depth" has a lower level than that of psychology. It may consist of either direct or indirect questions or some combinations of the these two. The direct open questions may follow the indirect question. The interviewer can explore and probe the underlying motivations of the respondents by following leads and cues provided by them, phrasing questions to continue the flow and pattern of the conversation. The depth interview was used for the first time by the Institute for Motivation Research.

7. Other Techniques

Other techniques may include play, psychodrama and graphology. The general underlying principle is that the person will project his own psychological interpretation of the situation.

6. FORMULATING THE PLAN OF PRIMARY DATA COLLECTION

The planning for collection of primary data is formulated in consonance of the research objective, design and methodology. The plan should meet data objectives with accuracy, efficiency and economy. There may be single planning for all the stages of research; yet planning for collection of primary data has its distinctive advantages. The planning is prepared as per a specific situation purpose and directive process. The planning may involve data objective, data type, data source, method of obtaining data and communication media. Each of the components is dispelled in detail to direct the data collection. Apart from all these aspects, the design of the questionnaire, or forms of data collection and determining the proper size of the sample are also important features of planning the data collection. Proposing and approving a plan involves the same technique of analysis as has been discussed in the chapter on planning the research. Cost-benefits analysis, decision roles, evaluation of the plans and approval of the plans have their specific role in formulation of the plan of collection of primary data.

Preparation of the questionnaire, measurement, sampling design, data collection and the field force are important aspects of planning of primary data collection which are discussed in detail in the following chapters.

❖ ❖ ❖

CHAPTER 7

DATA COLLECTION FORMS

1. QUESTIONNAIRE DEFINED
2. FUNCTIONS OF QUESTIONNAIRE
3. IMPORTANCE OF QUESTIONNAIRE
4. ASSUMPTIONS OF QUESTIONNAIRE
5. STEPS FOR PREPARING QUESTIONNAIRE

DATA COLLECTION FORMS

Marketing research calls for data collection or information gathering. There are several methods of data collection which have been discussed in the previous chapter. Data collection requires certain forms or documents which may be used for storage of data and analysis purpose. The questionnaire is the ubiquitous form for data collection. The questionnaire, i.e., the data collection form is a universal form of data collection. It is the very foundation of data collection methods, e.g., the personal interview, mail survey, and the telephone and panel interview. Whatever methods are used, there is need for a standardised form of data collection which is very well-known as the questionnaire.

1. QUESTIONNAIRE DEFINED

The questionnaire is a standardised form for recording answers on the basis of set questions. The recording of answers may be undertaken either by the interviewer or by the respondents as the methods of data collection require. "The term questionnaire usually refers to a self-administered process whereby the respondent himself reads the question and records his answers without the assistance of an interviewer."[1] This is a narrow definition of a questionnaire. It is not only for self recording, but may also be used in a personal interview, depending upon the methods of communication discussed in the previous chapter, when the form and type of questionnaire will vary. In this definition, the self-administered questionnaire is related to a highly structured and more standardised form than those of a personal interview. But "questionnaire" is more useful than the unstructured questionnaire used for a personal interview. The questionnaire may differ according to the purpose and made of data collection. The main thrust of a questionnaire is that it is a schedule of questions. It is not static and fixed in a wider sense. It may be recorded, rephrased or rearranged according to the judgement of the interviewer. The level of standardisation of a questionnaire may vary from structured to partially structured and also unstructured form of questions. Different respondents may interpret the standardised questions differently, but the basic theme and purpose of data collection should be preserved by them. The interviewer encourages the respondents to give full information. The questionnaire is a useful method of data collection as it provides standardised methods of data analysis. Standardised procedure helps achieve speed and accuracy in recording data.

2. FUNCTIONS OF QUESTIONNAIRE

The main function of a questionnaire is to obtain specified quantitative and qualitative information with accuracy and completeness. It gives the respondent clear comprehension of the questions and interview and identifies the needs to be recorded and verified. It induces the respondent to cooperate with the information collection procedure. It provides instructions to the respondents to record the answers. It facilitates interviewers to record the information and data successfully. It is designed in such a way as to fulfill the requirements of the data collection purpose of the marketing research. An appropriate questionnaire discourages biases, confusions, suspicion and inconvenience.

1. Gerald Zaltman and Phillip C. Burger: *Marketing Research:* The Dryden Press, 1975, p. 251.

3. IMPORTANCE OF QUESTIONNAIRE

The standardised form of questions known as the questionnaire is helpful for getting the desired data with speed and accuracy. If the questionnaires are not prepared, the interviewer may ask different questions differently from the respondents resulting in wide variable data, thus making it difficult to analyse and interpret. But the questionnaire removes all the problems. It is a list of questions to be asked from the respondents. Each question is worded exactly as it is to be asked in sequence.

Since the questionnaires are prepared after a thorough test and pretest, there is no chance of some important questions being omitted. Some consider the preparation of a questionnaire an easy task; but it is a difficult process. Slight variations in question wording may bring about considerable changes in the answers and results. Standardised answers may be recorded with the standardised form of questions. There is no chance of any questions and information being omitted. Incorrect, unambiguous and irrelevant questions may be easily avoided. Different types of questionnaires serve various purposes of marketing research. The questionnaire provides valid and reliable information.

4. ASSUMPTIONS OF QUESTIONNAIRE DESIGN

While the questionnaire is being prepared, it is assumed that the respondents will cooperate to answer the questions. Sometimes, some respondents may not wish to reveal information of personal desires and interests. In such cases, the questionnaire should be framed in an effective manner, i.e., a project technique should be used. It is also assumed that the respondents may not be fully aware of the information or may have forgotten the information. The questionnaire has to provoke the respondents in such cases. The behaviours and desires of the respondents may be influenced by psychological and social desires, or economic and political status. Therefore, while the questionnaire is being prepared it must incorporate these sentiments. Some feelings and emotions may repress the respondents. The questions may be framed accordingly.

The questionnaire assumes that the respondents will accede to the requests of the interviewer. If the request is not made, the respondents will not reveal the information. The questionnaire may motivate the respondents to the answers to some difficult questions. The type of information and data depend upon the nature of the questionnaire. It is thus assumed that the information and data will vary according to the technique of interviewing. The responses reveal the psychological and social realities of the respondents. The interviewer should discount the impacts of the social and psychological behaviour of the respondents to arrive at the correct information for the marketing research.

5. STEPS FOR PREPARING QUESTIONNAIRE

Construction of the questionnaire is much more of an art than mere knowledge. Even to date, no principle or procedure has been developed that will produce a good questionnaire for all purposes. Certain questionnaires will be suitable for some purposes while others may be suitable for other purposes. The construction of the questionnaire results from experience and acquired knowledge. Since human experience and elements are involved in the interview, there is need of a good questionnaire; otherwise the objectives of the data collection may be defeated. In many questionnaire preparations, the following steps are involved.

1. Information required.
2. Types of use of questionnaire.
3. Question contents.
4. Form of response.
5. Number and sequence of questions.
6. Pretest of the questions.
7. Revision and final draft of questionnaire.

The interviewer has to decide cautiously on the above subjects.

1. Information Required

Questionnaires are prepared to meet research objectives and to motivate the respondents to cooperate with the survey. Therefore a specific statement of the information required for research purposes is prepared and put in operation to motivate the respondents. The specific characteristics of the information are decided upon for the proposed analysis and objectives. The objectives of the research have been discussed already. The objectives are useful to decide specific hypotheses and the value of the information. Hypotheses guide the preparation of the questionnaire as they reveal the information required for the marketing research. Moreover, dummy tables are prepared to investigate the hypotheses and the information required to test the hypotheses. They will also decide the type of questions and form of responses. The dummy tables are examined and re-examined to arrive at workable hypotheses which will help decide the information and preparation of the questionnaire. The time, cost and effort may also be decided by the proposed questionnaire. While preparing the questionnaire new hypotheses maybe launched, and may require testing with the additional information. There may be some ideas about the hypotheses which may be interesting but may not be relevant to the objectives of the research. Therefore, such hypotheses are not taken into account for preparation of the questionnaire. If the researcher can identify the variables needed for research, the information required to establish the relationship can be projected easily while deciding the information required. Not only are the research objectives taken as a guide, but the methods of analysis, tabulation and interpretation are also taken into consideration. Planning ahead for quantitative requirements will avoid much confusion later. Not only can the researcher save time and money, but can avoid resistance from the respondents. The proposed sample units are also considered to decide the information. The methods of collecting data are also evaluated to find out suitable methods of data collection and the information required by the method.

2. Types of Use of Questionnaire

After deciding the information required for the research, the next step is to decide the method of using the questionnaire or administering the questionnaire. The questionnaire can be used by personal interview, mail, telephone or all of them. The choice of these alternatives is determined by the type of information required and by the kind of respondents. The methods and sequence of asking questions determine the type of questionnaire, i.e., the structure of the questionnaire. Deciding the structure of the questionnaire depends upon the use of the interviewing techniques and administration of the questionnaire. For example, a telephone interview precludes a pictorial image. Similarly, a mail interview does not require an unstructured and indirect questionnaire. The type of data and information to be collected has an important bearing on the questionnaire. All the methods of formulating a questionnaire would not be attractive because of cost and other considerations. In the case of attitude measurement a telephone interview would not be suitable. Similarly, an open ended questionnaire will not result in comprehensive answers in case of a mail interview.

3. Individual Question Content

After deciding the information required and structure of the questionnaire, the next important factor to be decided is content of the individual question. But there are some additional factors which are to be considered before deciding the content of an individual question such as "Is the question necessary?" "Are several questions needed instead of one?" "Do respondents have the necessary information?" "Will respondents provide the information?"

Is the question necessary? It is commonly accepted that no question should be included in a questionnaire unless it is necessary. Recently however, it has been realised that interesting questions may be included in the questionnaire to arouse interest amongst the respondents although they are not important from a research point of view. Uninteresting and irrelevant questions should be avoided because they will involve cost and effort. The respondents will also resist answering questions which are irrelevant and long. The objectives of the research are also taken into account to decide whether a question is necessary or not. Whether the question will add something to the research objective or not. If it will add something the question is essential. If it does not add to the objective of the research it should be eliminated because it is unnecessary.

Are several questions needed instead of one? If more than one element is involved in a question, the answer becomes ambiguous. Sometimes, one question may require several answers. The expected answers to a question and the sequence of the question are considered essential for deciding the framing of questions. Where several answers may be obtained relating to one question, it is better to break the question into several questions to obtain the several alternative answers of the question in classified ways.

Do respondents have the necessary information? The researcher should examine the issue whether the respondents have the information required. This is also to evaluate whether the respondents will be able to give a reliable answer, and the collection of data will not involve a great deal of time and effort. The respondents should understand the questions properly. Many respondents do not understand the questions because they are confused and cannot reply properly. The respondents should be asked only those questions which are known to them. The following points are considered under this heading.

(a) Does the question called for give the correct answer?

(b) Is the point of the question within the respondents' experience?

(c) Will the respondents have to do a great deal of work to answer the question?

(d) Does the question asked deal with opinions on matters unfamiliar to the respondents?

(e) Can the respondents remember the information?

(a) Does the question called for give the correct answer? The researcher has to confirm whether the respondents can reply correctly to the questions put to them. He has to evaluate whether the answers to be received are meaningful for the research objectives. Therefore, the researcher has to frame the questions very cautiously.

(b) Is the point of the question within the respondents' experience? The questionnaire should be framed considering the experience, statics and requirements of the respondents. if the questions are beyond the knowledge and experience of the respondents, they may either not respond or respond incorrectly. If the researcher asked about the use of a particular detergent from the respondents who had not used the detergent, the answers will be partial and non-representative. If the researcher in unaware of the respondents' experience, he may ask about that directly from the respondents.

(c) Will the respondents have to do a great deal of work to answer the question? If the questions are such that the respondents will have to collect and compare various statistics from several sources, the respondents many not wish to do that much work and may give incorrect or biased replies. Therefore, it should be confirmed while preparing the questionnaire that the answers can be given without much exertion and calculation. Where calculation is involved in answering the questions, the respondents will guess rather than calculate the statistics. If calculation is insisted upon, or some additional labour is required, the respondents will be irritated and may not wish to cooperate with the researcher. Thus, such questions should be avoided.

(d) Does the question asked deal with opinions on matters unfamiliar to the respondents? The opinion-questions should be framed with precaution because the answers may not be given properly. The respondents may be unaware of the subject matter of the opinions. So they may reply properly or reply with prejudice.

(e) Can the respondents remember the information? The respondents may not be in a position to remember all the information required. They should be given some clues for recollecting the information. Where memory is involved, the researcher must be cautious not to over-estimate the accuracy of response. The respondents may not remember the information because of a long time lapse, improper stimulation and giving less importance to the event. Therefore the researcher should confine himself to asking those questions which can be easily remembered and answered accurately.

Will respondents give the information? The researcher must know that the respondents may not wish to give all answers. They may not respond because they are unable to phrase their answers or they do not want to answer. There may be some questions which may hurt the feelings of the respondents. The researcher should be careful to frame such questions which may motivate the respondents. It should be borne in mind that the respondent have no particular interest in the accuracy of the responses. They may hesitate to answer such questions which relate to their social status, religious belief, family life and political beliefs. Questions on such matters must be framed cautiously. They are developed with the wording of "other people's belief" or "with indication of third persons." The questions should be made as innocuous as possible by concealing the question of the subject matter, and stating that the behaviour or attitude is not unusual before asking the specific questions. A ballot box may be provided to the respondents to answer confidentially.

4. Form of Questions and Responses

The researcher has to decide the form of questions and responses. The question may be direct or indirect, open ended or fixed, alternative or dichotomous.

Direct Questions

Direct questions are explicitly asked for the information desired. It is also related to the way the response is interpreted. The direct question assumes that the respondents possess the information. It is readily accessible to them. The researcher must make sure that the direct questions do not hurt the feelings of the respondents and that they are willing to reveal the information. No stigma should be attached to any answer they might give. A series of direct questions may be used to ease the respondents to the subject area.

Indirect Questions

Indirect questions have been used successfully to acquire the information desired. But, too distantly posed indirect questions may not be effective in revealing the correct and relevant data. While framing indirect questions, it is essential to ask questions closer to the research objectives. Indirect questions are those questions the responses to which are used to indicate or suggest information other than the actual facts. Under such questions, the respondents and the interviewer do not share a common language for dealing with a concept, a person's ego, prestige or emotional attitude and undesirable or socially unacceptable aspects of a personality. A generalised third person approach is adopted to reveal all these facts. Some theories or approach about which the respondents are unaware may be used in indirect questions. Questions relating to personality are asked under this approach. For example, a large number of questions on the buying patterns of consumers are asked to indicate the tendency of the respondent. There may be other forms of indirect questions such as the use of pictures, stories or other ambiguous stimuli. Motivation research as discussed in the previous chapter is also used for obtaining such information which may not be otherwise directly supplied.

Open Ended Questions

Open ended questions provide freedom to respondents to express their views and interests. The interviewer does not suggest any alternative answer. These questions are called free answer questions because they do not provide any explicit choice of alternatives. The respondents are free to answer within their own frame of reference. Open ended questions are employed as openers. The researcher proceeds from the general to the specific in framing questions. The open ended questions are used to probe for additional information. For example, "What brand of detergent do you use? Why?" Here the number of brands as perceived is silent. He may state any brand as an answer and thus provide a further probe to ask the next question. Open questions include questions and probes. More extensive information can be structured. If the question is left wide open, almost every respondent will be able to give some answer. The questions acquaint the respondents with the subject of the survey, get general attitudes for interpretation of results and open the way for more specific questions. Open questions influence the answers obtained less than the alternative questions. The multiple choice questions influence the answers obtained, but the open questions do not suffer from this weakness.

The open questions are useful for exploratory research. On the basis of the research findings multiple questions may be framed for further research. Where the objective of the research work is to determine the respondents' level of information, the intensity of their feelings, and the structure and basis of their attitudes, the open ended questions may be highly effective because they can elicit the information in their own language and individualistic flavour. The specific points, comments and explanations which are included in the answers are useful for the interpretation and final results of the survey.

Open ended questions have their limitations. The questions may not be systematic and organised because the respondents did not have prior considerations and guidelines. They may simply answer "no" because it is easier than thinking about the point. In case of a mail questionnaire, open ended questions require a high level of literacy and a greater amount of energy and motivation. The analysis and interpretation of open ended response questions may be very difficult because a large number of varied questions do not provide grounds for suitable comparison and tabulation. Coding of the answer is suggested to ease the problem. Another main shortcoming of open-ended questions is the possibility of the interviewer's bias. The interviewer may vary the recording of the answers given by the respondents. If he records the response verbatim, the respondents may lose interest in responding to the questions. The interviewer interprets the replies he receives from the respondents at a later stage when the interview is over. Thus, the response becomes a mixture of the interviewer and the respondents. Persons belonging to higher strata reveal more points of open ended questions as compared to those of lower strata. Open questions are more costly because of the added time required to record answers, to edit, classify and tabulate. Conclusively, it can be stated that open questions are superior to structured questions where the study of attitudes is involved.

Fixed Alternative Questions

Fixed alternative questions are also known as closed questions or fixed alternative response in which the respondents are given a limited number of alternative responses from which they have to choose the best answer. "Other" alternatives given in the response may allow the respondents to explain their own answers. The fixed alternative questions may be put in several forms. The fixed alternative questions may be dichotomous having only two stated alternatives. A typical response alternative which has a yes or no, true or false type of two opposite alternatives and multiple choice questions. The alternative answers must be mutually exclusive and should represent the appropriate range of possible replies. Check lists and rating scales are also important examples of multiple choice questions.

Fixed alternative questions can be posed quickly and require little effort on the part of the respondents. The standardised form of the responses makes coding and analysis relatively easier. But, the disadvantages of the fixed alternative questions are that the standardised responses eliminate the spontaneity and expressiveness of the respondents. The alternative responses given in the questionnaire may not be known to the respondents. A slight misunderstanding of the alternative questions may lead to wrong conclusions and interpretation. The fixed alternative questions are appropriate where the respondents have substantial information about the responses.

Dichotomous Questions

The dichotomous questions are those which offer the respondents a choice between only two stated alternatives. The responses are reduced only to two simplest forms. The questions provide exclusive answers. Much more common alternatives are yes or no. Such questions are suitable for simple factual questions. The responses can be classified in two classes: one in a positive way and the second in a negative way. There may be sometimes a third category of no answer or neutral answer. The dichotomous questions are quick and easy for the field worker to handle. The analysis and interpretation also becomes simple. The respondents and the interviewer cannot display any bias in the answers.

The dichotomous questions do not reveal the feelings and inner motives of the respondents. Sometimes they may answer wrong questions because they do not actually follow the questions given only in two alternative forms. Instead of two alternative answers, there may be many alternatives which are not given in the dichotomous questions. The answers are not always representative because responses are confined only to two alternatives.

Multidichotomous Questions

The multidichotomous questions or multiple choice questions are those questions which have fixed alternative answers. The respondents are required to select one or more answers. This type of questionnaire is called the "Cafeteria" questionnaire and is suitable for expressing opinions and motives. The respondents are allowed to select one or more answers. For example, there may be several reasons for using a particular brand of soap, which are specified in the questionnaire. The respondents are required to select one or more answers from them. The multidichotomous questions do not permit individuals to elaborate their true position, but requires that they condense their complex attitude in one or two answers. Such types of questionnaire may be elaborated by increasing the number of alternative answers. A good deal of prior research is essential to have multiple choice questions. While designing this type of questionnaire, the researcher should keep in mind that people have a limited memory and data-processing capabilities. It has been observed that the sequence of answers affects the response. Therefore, the order of responses should be changed from question to question. The multidichotomous questions may pose some difficulties. The words used in the responses may be understood differently by the respondents. Since the responses are not easily quantified, the tabulation and analysis become difficult. In some cases, responses are classified in various classes. Use of statistical tools may not always be useful in such cases. Apart from the difficulties, the multidichotomous questions are better than those of the open ended questions because of the simplicity and the speed in answering the former questions.

Banking Questions

Banking questions are opinion questions. The respondents are asked to rank the answers given in the questionnaire. While framing the questionnaire, the researcher should see whether the responses are comprehensive of all possible answers and are within the purview of the respondents' experience. The importance of the facts can easily be evaluated by this method. It may be cumbersome and time consuming if not properly framed. The respondents should be told the method of answering the questions.

Checklist

A checklist is a form of questionnaire in which the respondents are required to check one or more of the responses those that are listed in the questionnaire. For example, the researcher may ask which brand of soap do the respondents use? They have to answer the question by selecting one of the various brands given in the question-responses. It is a simple method of fact finding research. The items are listed in a few words needed to describe them.. There should be a random sequence or degrees of some attribute. This facilitate tabulation and analysis, but care should be exercised to list all categories of possible answers. "Other" answer may also be given, and space should be provided to list the other answer most suitable to the respondent.

Scales

Another type of alternative question is to employ a scale to response. For example, "How often do you use the talcum face powder?" The question can be answered from among the following alternatives:

Never	Occasionally	Sometimes	Often

The advantage of this method is that the descriptors can be presented at the top of the page, and a number of possible responses can be listed along the left margin. The respondent may be instructed to select the responses. It has become a popular type of format in which the respondents are given a range of categories in which to express their opinions. The qualitative information can be presented in a quantitative form. It provides enough ground for comparative judgements, of motivation attitudes and behaviour of the respondents.

Scaling techniques are being used in marketing research to arrive at an appropriate decision. There are several scaling techniques. A few of them, e.g., semantic differential, Likert Scale and Stapel Scale are discussed here in brief. A detailed discussion of scaling techniques has been given in the next chapter on Attitude measurement.

1. Semantic Differential: The original semantic differential scale consisted of a great many bipolar adjectives which were employed to secure people's reactions to the adjectives. The respondents are asked to express their feelings about whatever is being evaluated by recording their responses on the scale of adjectives. For example, "Do you like smoking Filter cigarettes?"

Polar X Strong	Extremely 1	Quite 2	Slightly 3	Neither 4	Slightly 5	Quite 6	Extr. 7	Polar Y mild
		X				Y		

The respondents can select any one of the scales. The interviewer can easily tabulate and analyse the result. The bipolar scale developed in multiple forms later on. The example of several scale positions is given below:

	Very	Somewhat	Neither	Somewhat	Very	
Exciting	—	—	—	—	—	Dull
Boring	—	—	—	—	—	Interesting
Like	—	—	—	—	—	Do not like.

The scale is prepared keeping a favourable scale on both sides. Such type of scale is self-administered. The middle point is put for the respondents who have no opinion. The neutral scale or neither scale may be omitted to avoid the respondents' bias because they may not like to consider the question, and may easily select the neutral scale or neither scale. Therefore extremely, quite, slight, slight, quite, and extremely may be put on the scale for evaluating each bipolar adjective.

2. Likert Scale: In the Likert Scale, the apposite scale is avoided. Instead of two adjectives on a scale only one scale is used. The respondent, a six number scale may be stated as below:

	Strongly Agree	Generally Agree	Moderately Agree	Moderately Disagree	Generally Disag.	Strongly Disag.
Brand						
Quality						

It has the advantage of easyness because the respondents can think of only one adjective on the scale, and there is no problem of finding the exactly opposite adjective.

3. Stapel Scale: Stapel scale is a modification of the semantic differential scale. It differs from the latter scale in the sense that the adjectives are tested separately instead of simultaneous bipolar base. It points on the scale number which may range upto 10 instead of 7. Respondents are asked to rate each of the numbers described for the adjective. The respondents can select a plus number for words they like. The more accurately they think, the larger the plus number upto +5. Similarly, if the respondents do not wish to do so, they may select a minus number. They can rate the disliking to the extent of -5.

The advantage of the Stapel Scale is that there is no need of developing a bipolar adjective. It is easier to construct the scale avoiding the search for exact antonyms.

Deciding the Wording of Questions

In the preceding sections, we have discussed the type and content of questions/ responses. In this sections we shall discuss the wording of questions. Language is an important tool of communication. One may consider it easy; but selecting words and phrasing for questions is a very difficult process. Some important issues of wording of questions are discussed in this section.

Define the Issue

The questions to be framed should be evaluated properly to find out whether they refer to the main objective or not. The meaning, place, time, form, reason and methods of question must be known to the respondents in proper perspective of the objectives of the marketing research. Who, where, when, what, why and how are the leading questions to understand the issue of the subject. These words may be a measuring rod of the proper question. There should not be wrong assumptions. The researcher must ask what does the question mean? It is not language and vocabulary of a high order but they should be shared by the researcher and the respondents. The researcher should conform to the level of understanding of the respondents.

Subjective or Objective Questions

Many questions may be used in subjective or objective form. For example, do you think the Uptron TV is better than the Oscar? Is the Uptron a better TV than the Oscar? The first question is subjective as it is phrased in terms of an individual's feelings. The second question stresses that the respondent should think more in terms of the general thinking of people. We observe that the subjective questions give a more reliable answer as they evaluate the personal feelings of the respondents.

Positive or Negative Statement

The questions can be stated in a positive or negative way. The questionnaire can be framed partially in a negative way and partially in a positive way. The issues may be presented either in a positive way or in a negative way observing the consequences of each of them. There may be variation in either of the statements of the questions. There may be inclusion of negative and positive forms of the statement in the question to avoid the variation caused by either the negative or positive form. For example: Do you think the price level should be decreased or increased to expand the sale of the commodity? While framing the questions, the researcher should be aware of the consequences of the form and wording of the question to avoid any biased answer.

Keep Meaning Clear

The problem is not only to use familiar words and phrases but also to use them in such a way that the number of possible meanings should be reduced to one. Unfortunately, it is not easy to find a word projecting one meaning only. There may be several meanings attached to a word and also complex meanings when used in different sentences if a word is used frequently. Therefore, it is advisable to avoid phrases and expressions of typical meanings. When words have several meanings, the respondents can misinterpret the question. Such usage may create an embarrasing situation. Double meanings can be avoided by providing a clue to the question. It is very well said, "Words can have double meanings, but questions themselves can be double barreled. If the respondents are asked: "Do you agree or disagree with the statement", they may be confused whether to agree or disagree.

Avoid Ambiguous Questions

Ambiguous questions are those questions which are not properly understood by the respondents. Unlike double or multimeanings, the question itself is not followed by the respondents. The intent of the question is not known to make one think. The subject of the query may also be ambiguous. The ambiguous question also relates to projecting different meanings for different people. Thus comparable replies cannot be obtained. Therefore questions should be framed in such a manner and in such suitable words that their meanings properly and accurately understood.

Continuity

The flow of a question is a very important point of a questionnaire. The questions should be linked together. The thought process should lead smoothly step by step. Those demanding the least introspection or memory should precede the difficult questions. The respondents' experience should be evaluated before using the questionnaire. The interviewer should qualify the respondents for the interview. The interview should continue without waiting for the answers to all the questions. The personal data should be separated from the main data. The personal data should be handled with caution because many respondents will feel reluctant to answer them. The basic information relating to the subject of study should be asked before all questions. The respondents may divulge the personal data at the end when they become aware of the purpose of the study and have developed rapport with the interviewer.

Avoid Leading Questions

When the question suggests its answer, it is called a leading question. For example, "Don't think that Phillips radio is a good one?" The question indicates that the radio is good and the answer should be "yes." Leading questions may motivate the respondents to answer but the answers may be biased because the questions are not neutral. The marketing researcher should try to avoid biases pertaining leading questions. So far as possible neutral questions may be asked to get a correct picture of the survey. There may be misleading questions owing to biased thinking. For example, "Would you not prefer "Kinetic Freez?" This indicates that the respondents should like "Kinetic Freez." The questionnaire, therefore, should avoid all misleading questions.

Avoid Loaded Questions

Loaded questions contain loaded words or phrases. Such questions indicate an emotional feeling attached to particular words or concepts in the questions. The respondents may react to the words or phrases used in the questions. If a certain brand or design is specified, the respondents may not wish to answer those questions in a positive way, or may ignore the questions. The respondents may react in terms of their own images and experiences. The responses may be influenced by the predisposition of most people to accept the point. The prestige of the respondents, ego-threatening and embarrasing questions should be avoided in the questionnaire. The loaded questions create bias.

5. Number and Sequence of Questions

The number of questions dealing with a particular subject depends upon the objective of marketing research. The researcher should know that the order of questions and the number of questions are crucial for the successful conduct of the survey. Neither too many questions nor too few questions will serve the purpose of the interview. If the purpose of the interview requires recall or willingness of the usefulness, multiple questions may be used to repeat the general questions in a different form, structure and context. The cross questions reveal the true picture of the subject. The inner motives and feelings of the respondents can be revealed by such questions.

Question sequence is important. Usually the questionnaire may contain two types of information — basic information and classification information. Basic information includes the subject of the study, also the intentions or attitudes of the respondents. Classification information includes detailed information of the phenomenon of interest. Demographic and socio-economic characteristics of respondents are recorded under this group. It is generally understood that a proper questionnaire includes basic information first and classification information subsequently. The basic information is more crucial for study. The researcher should not ask personal questions before getting to know the heat of the study. Therefore it is better to place the classification information at the end. Personal data asking for information relating to income, education, size of family etc., are placed at the end of the questionnaire. The respondents can answer the questions with the same facility because these questions are very easy.

The basic information questions require a special setting of sequences. Difficult questions should not come at the beginning. The questionnaire must begin with easy and simple questions. If difficult questions are asked at the beginning, the respondents may feel diffident and slighted. Similarly, the early questions should not be sensitive. The opening questions should be so designed as to secure the respondents' cooperation and willingness. The sensitive questions should be relegated to and intermixed with the non-sensitive questions. Embarrassing questions may be interspersed with other questions. Easy questions and the frame or reference facilitate the logical flow of information. While framing different questions, the length and time of questions must be taken into account, so that the questions are not unnecessarily long, thus involving more time to answer them.

The respondents should be placed in such a situation by the sequence of questions that they may take an interest in answering the new questions. The process of exploration should be introduced gradually. Thoughtful sequence of questions helps the recall of information. The basic principle is to start with the general questions and to come to the specific questions later on. Initial specific questions may contaminate later answers. So, general questions should precede the specific questions. The questionnaire should have a logical flow from questions to questions to avoid respondents' confusions and frustration. George Gallop has developed five types of question-sequence.

1. Awareness of the particular topic.
2. Spontaneous attitudes are asked next by free-answer.
3. Specific attitudes are then covered by fixed alternative questions.
4. Fixed alternative questions are followed by free-answer probes.
5. Questions designed to ascertain the intensity of feelings.

In brief the questionnaire-sequence should be framed in such a way that the opening questions win the respondents' interest, difficult questions are placed in the middle of the questionnaire, succeeding questions are put after evaluating the influence of the previous questions, and questions are arranged in the logical order. Special care should be exercised for the mail questionnaire. It is not possible to take advantages of sequence position in the same way as in personal interviews. Questions put at the end to avoid bias may be read by the respondents at the opening of the questionnaire. But so far as possible the bias of the respondents should be avoided. The opening questions must catch the interest of the respondents.

Deciding on Layout and Reproduction

The layout and reproduction of the questionnaire influence the success of the interview. While planning the layout and reproduction, three important points are considered. They are *(i)* securing acceptance of the questionnaire, *(ii)* making it easy to control the questionnaire and *(iii)* making it easy to handle the questionnaire.

(i) Accepting of the questionnaire: The physical appearance of the questionnaire influences the interest and attitude of the respondents. If the questionnaire is prepared on rough paper, typed unimpressively and designed poorly it may not attract the respondents to read and answer the questions. On the other hand, a questionnaire typed or printed on good quality paper may attract the respondents to read it. The respondents may be requested not to disclose their identities. The researchers, sometimes, to avoid any bias, may avoid the use of their company's name.

(ii) Ease to control: The questionnaire should be numbered serially to make it possible to control the questionnaire in the operation. It will make it easy to edit and tabulate the answers. All questions must be accounted and evaluated properly. Numbered questions are easy to follow and simple to operate throughout the survey time, and analyse thereafter.

(iii) Ease of handling: The reproduction of a questionnaire may influence the fieldwork and analysis. It is essential that a large number of questions must not be put in a short space. If the questionnaire is crowded, it makes a bad appearance. This may cause errors in collection of data and tabulation as it is hard to read the answers. Too large a questionnaire cannot be handled properly. Questions should be laid out and reproduced in an easy way for the field worker to follow the sequence.

6. Pretest of the Questionnaire

The questionnaire should be pretested before its presentation at the interview. Although the researcher has reviewed the drafted questionnaire meticulously on all points of good design, it is likely to contain some errors. Therefore, pretesting the questionnaire is essential. Before its final presentation the questionnaire must be examined under the similar sample of the study. When the pretesting of the questionnaire is over, certain unworkable questions are detected. The questionnaire is presented, the interview is conducted and the possible answers are recorded. The process of interviewing is closely watched. During the pretest interview, some questions may create confusion, while some questions may induce resistance. Such difficult and unwanted questions should be removed before preparation of the final interview. The pretesting will reveal the scope and place for the modification of the questionnaire. The problems relating to the mode of the interview may also be revealed by pretesting the questionnaire. The relative problems connected with the personal interview, mail questionnaire and telephone interview are disclosed by such testing. The responses and results of the pretest interview may be useful for revealing the problems, of tabulation and analysis. The responses may be coded for the purpose of analysis. The preparation of a dummy table may be useful for pretesting of the tabulation and interpretation. The possible difficulties which may arise during the final interview and tabulation can be revealed by such pretesting. The trial tabulation will reveal that all the data collected will be put to use and that necessary data may be collected by revision of the questions.

7. Revision and Final Draft

After pretesting the questionnaire, the revision of the draft can reveal the point of effective utilisation of the questionnaire in the final interview. The process of correcting the first draft should be undertaken by the experienced researcher. The wording of the questionnaire, the number and sequence of the questions, the technique of administering the questionnaire and all other elements of the field-survey should be properly revised and redrafted after the pretesting and re-examination of the questionnaire. The researchers should be aware that the first draft will not provide a usable questionnaire. Revision and re-examination will remove all confusing, ambiguous and loaded questions. The innocuous questions may create more problems. So they are removed at the time of revision. Revision and re-examination will remove serious shortcomings and put the questionnaire in a workable order. Effective pretesting will guide the useful revision of the questionnaire. The revised questionnaire will remove uneasiness, confusion and the resistance of the respondents. The problems of the interview are removed. Some irrelevant and unwanted questions are deleted from the questionnaire, and other important and useful questions may be added to the questionnaire.

❖ ❖ ❖

CHAPTER 8

ATTITUDE MEASUREMENT

1. COMPONENTS OF ATTITUDE
2. DETERMINANTS OF ATTITUDE STATE
3. ATTITUDES AND MARKETING
4. ATTITUDES MEASURING METHODS

ATTITUDE MEASUREMENT

Attitude is one of the most pervasive motions in marketing. It plays a pivotal role in the major aspects of consumer behaviour. The main reason attitude plays this role, is influence behaviour. Purchase decisions are based solely upon attitude. Attitude represents a predisposition to respond to an object and not actual behaviour toward the object. It is also known as directional quality. It connotes a preference regarding the outcomes involving the object, evaluations of the object and feelings for the object. It represents a person's ideas, convictions and liking with regard to a specific object or idea. The underlying ideas behind the definitions of the attitude are an automatic approach to the object and fact. There is consistency in the thinking on account of the attitude of the persons. The attitudes are revealed by certain stimuli, viz., situation, social objects, social issues, social group and other objects of the attitude.

1. COMPONENTS OF ATTITUDE

Attitudes have three components — cognitive, affective and behavioural.

Cognitive: The cognitive component of an attitude is sometimes called the belief component. It sub-assumes certain beliefs of the persons towards an object. This component can be expressed as "I believe, I think, or I know" and so on. The idea of centrality is the main feature of the cognitive component. Those beliefs which deal with the individual and for which there are unanimous social supports are central to the cognitive component of an attitude. There may be beliefs less central, peripheral which are inconsequential. It is around ego-involvement that the cognitive system is organised. This is more difficult to change than peripheral beliefs.

Affective: The affective component of attitude refers towards liking and disliking of the object. It is the emotional component that indicates the feelings of the object. In this case, the emphasis is on the individual as compared to the cognitive component of attitude which lays emphasis on the object rather than on the individual. Attitude can be affective and normative. Affecting attitude involves emotion or feeling while normative attitude involve correct behaviour to the object of the attitude. The affective attitude is the way a person feels about an attitude object. It is the outcome of the previous association of the object with pleasant or unpleasant experiences. These affects are also known as positive and negative affects. The normative attitude consists of seeking or avoiding contact.

Behavioural: The behavioural component is the action tendency. It is predisposition of action. It refers to the individual's most likely course of action. It is closely related to norms of behaviour. The relationship between attitude and behaviour may not be direct. Prof. H.C. Triandis pointed out, "Attitudes involve what people think about, feel about and how they would like to behave toward an attitude object. Behaviour is not only determined by what people like to do but also by what they think they should do, i.e., social norms, by what they have done, e.g., habits and by the expected consequences of the behaviour."

2. DETERMINANTS OF ATTITUDE STATE

Attitudes are not static. They are formed and changed constantly. Attitudes are altered by the following five factors:

1. Information and feelings gathered in the past related to want satisfying experiences.
2. Information and feelings gathered in the past unrelated to want satisfying experiences.
3. Group affiliations, particularly the individual's perception of the beliefs, norms of others.
4. Attitudes toward related objects in the relevant attitude.
5. The individual's personality.

Thus, attitude changes may be brought about by different want satisfaction experiences, exposure to new information, changes in group membership, changes in attitude to related attitude objects and changes in personality.

3. ATTITUDES AND MARKETING

Attitudes play a central role in marketing and marketing research. There are three areas in which attitudes are used in marketing: *(i)* in the modelling of consumer behaviour, *(ii)* as an aid to identifying and reaching specific market segments and *(iii)* to determine probable customer response to new or existing products, services or companies. The researchers use attitude as an important explanatory variable in creating models of behaviour. The manufacturer can know the attitudes of both present dealers and prospective dealers with attitude research. Attitude study helps both manufacturers and dealers to change their marketing strategies. The executives are also interested to know and measure the attitudes of consumers for effective formulation of policies.

The disposition to act is affected by attitudes, i.e., belief and feeling. The consumers may behave positively and negatively. The importance of attitude can be realised by the fact that any buyer behaviour model cannot be constructed with making explicit reference to attitudes. A firm's attitude towards technological innovation would be related to the time of adoption. Researches on attitudes are conducted in order to determine consumer response to some attitude object. Attitude research is frequently used to evaluate the attitude profile of the ideal product, brands and advertising. The policies and strategies may be changed to suit the consumers' attitudes. It should be accepted here that attitudes are constantly changing and any policy to suit a particular attitude may, therefore, not last long. There are other factors which influence the overt behaviour of consumers. However, attitude research or measurements are essentially undertaken to formulate effective marketing policies and strategies.

4. ATTITUDE MEASURING METHODS

As discussed in the previous section, measurement of attitudes is essential for the marketing policies and strategies. Measurement methods of attitudes are discussed in this section. Under attitude measurement, it is necessary to define measurement and review the types of scales used for measurement.

The Formal Properties of Measurement

Measurement consists of rules for assigning numbers and objects in such a way as to represent quantities of attributes.[1]

1. Jum, C. Nunnally: *Psychometric Theory,* New York, McGraw Hill, 1978, p.3.

This definition is very useful to understand the features of the measurement of attitudes. It reveals that the measurement is of attributes, i.e., attributes of an object. It is not the measurement of persons but the attributes and qualifications related to them. For example, attributes measure persons' income, social class, education, behaviour, attitudes, feeling, convictions, biases, inclinations, declinations and so on. This definition also refers to assigning a number or quantities to the attributes. But it does not reveal how quantities are assigned to the attributes. Attitudes are composed of several ingredients, e.g., beliefs, emotional feelings, interests, thinking etc. Attitudes are complex and not fully understood. The attitude measurement cannot claim that the measurement has a high degree of accuracy.

It must be understood properly that measurement is a scaling of attitude. It is a generally accepted scale, but there is a possibility of some inherent drawbacks; even then, the scaling is used with precision. No one is entirely sure what an attitude is, and there is no clear point from which to begin the measuring process. The problem has nothing to do with the determining of the properties of measurement; we should determine the properties of the attribute itself to measure them. Measurement consists of pieces of information that have application in many different places and times.

The theory of signs or the field of semiotic have been related with measurement. Semiotics have three fields of investigation: *(i)* Syntactics, *(ii)* Semantics and *(iii)* Pragmatics. Syntactics deal with the relationship among signs. Mathematics and logic deal primarily with the syntactical aspects of propositions. The rules of mathematics may not be proved by logic; such as $2 + 2 = 4$. No one can prove why this rule is constant. Thus, there may not necessarily be a direct relationship between the signs and real world designates. Basic terms are generally left undefined. The abstract mathematician is interested in consistency, independence and sufficiency of the postulates. Testing of the tradition attributes requires symbols to objects and the establishment of their inter-relationships.

The semantics deal with the relationship between signs and objects. Semantical statements are never proved or disproved absolutely unlike syntactical truth or falsity. The truth of assertions about the real world can be stated in a probable way. Hypothesis can be developed. Models of the real world require language to express relevant properties. The language will express the semantical entities, i.e., hypotheses corresponding to syntactical entities, i.e., theorems. It is an attempt to give meaning to abstract system.

Any theory may be syntactically and semantically complete but may not be useful to the decision-maker. For this pragmatics are required, whereby the relationship between signs and the users of signs are established. The judgements are based on various theories.

Types of Scales

Measurements possess a natural zero and a constant unit of measurement in day-to-day life. But in the social sciences, the researcher must frequently settle for less informative scales. In the marketing field, a scale does not possess the properties associated with most physical measures. The attributes can be measured by nominal scales, ordinal scales, interval scales and radio scales.

1. Nominal Scales

In this case, the numbers serve as labels or tags for identifying objects, properties or events. One of the simplest properties of a nominal scale is identity. For example, males are coded "1" and females "2." There is nothing implied by the numerals other than identification of the sex of the person. Here no. 2 for females does not mean that they are superior or inferior. The numerals can be reversible without losing their significance because the only property conveyed by the number is identity. If we assign no.2 to males and no.1 to females, they may be recognised by their respective numbers. A nominal scale is symbolic of a telephone number whereby only one number is assigned to one subscriber. Football players are assigned a specific number for purposes of identity. For example, player X will be given no.1 and he will be recognised as no.1. But this does not mean that he is a very superior player. This number has nothing to do with the qualities and merits of the object. We should be careful that no two or more players receive the same number. Arithmetical operations performed on the numbers have no meaning with respect to the real world objects. Where more than one telephone number is used by a subscriber, the numbers are characterised as a class of entities.

A prefix and suffix number may be used for distinguishing the class. The notion of equality is known as equivalence, reflexive, symmetric and transitive classes. Reflexive class refers to all entities in the class whereby each entity is equal to itself. Symmetric class indicates any two entities in the class, e.g., x = y, y = z. Transitive class refers to any three entities in the class not necessarily distinct, e.g., x = y, y = z and z = x. The objects may differ in income, but they retain their individual tags. In nominal classes, we use for the most rudimentary operations.

We may make various contingency tests but the usual statistical operations, viz., calculation of means, standard deviations etc. are not permissible. With a nominal scale the only permissible operation in counting the Mode is the only legitimate measure of central tendency. We may say only more or the maximum number of an object.

2. Ordinal Scales

Ordinal scales are ranking scales. They are orders of numbers. These scales require the ability to distinguish between elements according to a single direction. In this scale we can say that two is greater than one and three is greater than two. The numbers 1,2,3,4 and so on are in order. The larger the number, the greater the property. The difference between one order and the second is the same as the difference between the second order and third order. An ordinal scale possesses all the information of a cardinal scale,i.e., identity and equivalence. Moreover, it has some additional features. The relative standing of two persons is equivalent. If one first, denotes 1 and second denotes 2, and in other classifications one shows 10, the second and third will show 20 and 30 and so on. The class-interval is always equal. The difference in class-interval does not reveal the difference in frequencies. In other words, the assignment would still indicate the class-interval of the two points. The ordinal scale allows any monotonic positive transformation of the assigned numerals. The difference in numerals is void of meaning other than the order. The attitude should possess the ordinal property for allowing ordinal scaling.

The application of statistical tools to the ordinal scale is limited to mode, median, quartile, percentile and other statistics dealing with order entities.

3. Interval Scales

An interval scale possesses a consistent unit of measurement. The zero point of the scale is arbitrary. The common example is the interval scale of Fahrenheit and Centigrade to measure temperature. An arbitrary zero is assigned to each scale and equal temperature differences are found by scaling equal volumes of expansion in the liquid used in the thermometer. The interval scales permit inferences to be made about the differences between the entities, e.g., temperature in this case, but they are not a multiple of another. The difference between scales of Fahrenheit and Centigrade is not proportionate although their respective scales are proportionate. For example 50° centigrade is twice of 25° centigrade. Similarly 40° Fahrenheit is twice of 20° Fahrenheit. But it does not mean that they are equally representative.

The interval scale shows that we cannot compare the absolute magnitude of numbers. Interval scales are unique upto positive linear transformation, i.e., $y = a + bx$ where b # 0. Interval scales can be transformed from one to another by means of a positive linear transformation. The differences between interval scale values can be expressed in terms of multiples of one another. The interval scale can be useful for the arithmetic mean, standard deviation, correlation coefficient and so on. But geometric mean and coefficient of variation would be misleading if applied to the data derived from the interval scale.

4. Ratio Scales

Ratio scales represent the elite among scales. All arithmetic operations are permissible on ratio scale measurements. These scales possess a unique zero point and are found in the physical sciences, e.g., measuring of length, weight etc. One can move from one scale to another by applying an appropriate multiplicative constant. A ratio scale contains all the information, e.g., class, equity, order, quality of differences and so on. With ratio scales, we can compare intervals, rank objects and others. Ratio scales do not allow addition of an arbitrary constant. Only proportionate transformation is possible. All the relationships are preserved whether the comparison is made in higher or lower scales. Usually all the statistical tools can be used for the analysis of the data derived from ratio scales.

The above four scales are not exhaustive. New scales are being suggested as a result of the latest researches.

Measurement of Psychological Attributes

Powerful scales have been developed to measure the attributes. The characteristics of psychological attributes determine the measurements. The characteristic and its qualities set the upper limit for the assignment of numerals to objects. The researcher must know something about the attribute itself before assigning numbers to it. For example, ordinal scale should be used for the attributes that are ordinal in nature. A nominal scale may be useful for the attribute. The procedure used in constructing the scale also determines the types of scale. More powerful scales allow stronger comparisons and conclusions. For example, a ratio scale cannot properly measure attributes belonging to nominal, ordinal and interval scales. The researcher, therefore, should know the properties of the attributes of the object. Therefore, before applying the measurement, the researcher must know the basic nature of the attribute and the measurement procedure. He should be very careful in conceptualising the construction of the measurement.

The marketing researchers view the stimuli of marketing from various attributes. The responses may involve several preferences. The procedures of collecting data may be paired comparisons, ranking methods, scoring procedure, rating scale and so on. The marketing researcher may utilise the responses for decision-making purposes. In many of the decision-making processes, consumers' perceptions, motivation, attitudes, beliefs etc. are evaluated and are done by psychological scaling techniques. The researcher has to transform data on preferences, interest, attitude and belief into the possible effects on product sales under alternative courses of action. Attitudinal data must be translated into relevant policy-making purposes.

Attitude Scaling Procedures

Attitude measurement has been viewed differently by different authors. Torgerson classified the scaling procedures into judgement approach and responses approach; judgement approach assumes some attributes in advance. The stimuli are defined with acuteness. The subject responds to a stimulus where the attribute continuum is not defined in the case of a response approach. The subject is asked to choose the statement which concurs better with his own attitude. In this case interest centres on both intersubject differences and stimuli differences. The nature of response, properties of scale, physical versus psychological stimuli, form of response and experimental procedures are kept in consideration while measuring the attributes of the object.

There are other ways to measure the attitude. They may be self-reports, observation of overt behaviour, indirect techniques, performance of the objective, physiological reactions and multiple measures. The self-report has been a more common approach because in this case the respondents are asked directly their beliefs or feelings toward an object. A large number of scales have been developed. The observation of behaviour assumes that behaviour is conditioned by attitudes and feelings. An artificial situation is created to evaluate the behaviour of individuals. The indirect techniques of attitude measurement use an unstructured and disguised questionnaire. This has been discussed in the previous chapter under questionnaire. An objective task believes that a specific assigned task depends upon the person's attitude. The individual's physiological responses provide an indication of the intensity of his feelings. Multiple measures are used to evaluate the attitude.

The Judgement Approach

The judgement approach assumes that subjects can be treated homogeneously and that only the stimuli are scaled. The judgement method may be classified into quantitative judgement and variable judgement. Usually, the quantitative judgement approach and variability judgement approach have no major differences in regard to ordering the stimuli, but the approaches differ with regard to the method for obtaining a unit of measurement.

In the quantitative judgement approach, the respondents are asked to make direct estimates of the relationships among the stimuli. Different scales may be constructed to measure the attributes. The researchers have to develop an interval scale or ratio scale. For example to determine the effectiveness of a detergent soap, the scale of 7 equal intervals may be constructed.

The variability judgement methods require fewer demands on the subject. The development of interval scale and ratio scale requires certain assumptions. The respondents are asked to select several subjects in order of preference. For example, they may be required to select five effective detergent soaps in order to preference. The central idea underlying the variability judgements is that the less variable the preferences are, e.g., stimulus A versus stimulus B, the greater the difference in scale values between them. Thurstone's law of comparative judgement is useful technique of measurement.

Thurstone's law of Comparative Judgement

The Thurstone procedure involves deriving an interval scale from comparative judgements of the brands 'A' and 'B.' In this case 'A' is the better brand than 'B.' Therefore the scale of A is longer than B and so on. Such types of attributes are analysed in the comparative judgement. The attributes judged may be quantitative or qualitative. The procedure would fall into the variability judgement. Scale values are estimated from the data in which single individuals make a repeated series of comparative judgements for each possible pair. The scale between one scale to the other scale is not uniform. For example, scales A and B have a longer distance than B and C scales. Similarly B and C scales are longer to C and D scales and so on. This law provides a means for developing interval scale values from comparative ratios. This test can work effectively backward. It states the process by which respondents react differently to a set of stimuli. Since the same individual reacts differently at different times to the same stimuli, a model discriminatory process which represents the process occurring most often is postulated. The distance between two points of scale as represented by the model discriminatory process for any two stimuli represents the degree of separation to be present on the individual's psychological scale. This distance or difference is called discriminal difference which is assumed to be normally distributed.

Thus, the Law of Comparative Judgement as expressed by Thurstone can be described as below:

$$S_1 - S_2 = Z_{12} \sqrt{\sigma_1^2 + \sigma_2^2 - 2p\,\sigma 1 \sigma 2}$$

where

$S_1 - S_2$ = A linear distance on the psychological scale between stimulus 1 and stimulus 2.

Z_{12} = Sigma value of observed proportion in which stimulus 1 is preferred to stimulus 2.

$\sigma 1^2, \sigma 2^2$ = Discriminatory dispersions of stimuli 1 and 2, respectively.

p = Coefficient of correlation for the discriminatory deviations in each of the stimulus 1 versus stimulus 2 judgements.

If the discriminatory dispersions are equal and the correlation between the discriminal deviations of the same judgement is zero, i.e., $\sigma^1{}_2 = \sigma^2{}_2$, the law can be expressed as below:

$$S_1 - S_2 = Z_{12}\sqrt{2}$$

The comparative judgement can be illustrated by one example. Suppose 100 housewives are selected to give an opinion on a particular brand of washing soap. If there are five brands of soap, each brand is preferred to other brands as illustrated in the following table:

Preference of Brand X (Top) to Brand Y (Side)

in percentage

Side \ Top	*A*	*B*	*C*	*D*	*E*
A	—	80	70	25	35
B	20	—	30	10	15
C	30	70	—	20	30
D	80	90	80	—	60
E	70	85	75	40	—

The table shows that 80 per cent of the respondents preferred brand B to brand A, 70 per cent of the respondents preferred brand C to brand A and so on. With the use of Z values and scale values the brand preference can be given as below:

$$B > C > A > E > D$$

	Brand B	Brand C	Brand A	Brand E	Brand D	
1.50	1.25 1.00 .75	.50 .25	0 –.25	–.50 –.75	-1.00	–1.25

The difference between one scale and another can be computed from Thurstone's law of comparative judgement. It may permit the marketing researcher to develop interval scales from the frequency of preference for one stimulus over another, and can thus assign quantitative motion to the preference.

The judgement approach suffers from certain drawbacks. When individuals are asked to mark the point on an attitude scale, they may not make an accurate judgement. It is possible that they may not make an uniform judgement. Therefore indirect approaches to the problem have been developed. A series of statements related to the attitude is developed, and individuals are asked to indicate agreement or disagreement with them. On the basis of the responses, a score is determined to measure the attitude, which is well-known as scalogram or response approach.

Another problem of the judgement method is to do with the validity. It is difficult to find standards to measure validity. The most common effort has been to compare opinions of respondents as discussed on Thurstone's comparative judgement.

Response Approach

The Response approach deals with intersubject and interstimuli differences, i.e., influence of respondents' attitude and also of stimuli. The preference expressed by the respondent is assumed to be affected by the stimulus as well as by his attitudes towards the attribute. Therefore, the respondents and stimuli are given values. Respondents may be asked whether they agree with the stimuli or prefer one stimulus to another. At the time of tabulation of the data derived from the stimuli by the respondents, response is deduced from them. Many of the following analysis are subgroups of the response approach. There have been a number of methods of evaluating the attributes, but the self-report attitude scales are the most common.

The response approach may be known as scalogram analysis. The qualitative stimuli are scaled. This approach differs from the judgement method in the sense that it does not necessarily assume homogeneity among the responses, and it does not assure the order of stimuli. Scalogram analysis is used to determine whether a meaningful rank order of the respondents' attitudes can be determined. On the basis of the responses, a score is determined to measure the individual attitudes. There may be different scales to measure such attitude, viz., equal appearing intervals, summated ratings, semantic differential, staple scale, rating scale and other techniques.

1. Equal Appearing Intervals

The respondents are biased by the design and form of the questionnaire. Positive questions may result in different responses than those of negative questions. Similarly favourable and unfavourable attitude questions will not give the same type of answers because the attitudes of respondents are influenced by the frame of questions or administration of the interview. Therefore, the questions are divided into equal parts to represent different types of attitudes. For example, if the attitudes are influenced by positive and negative questions, the questionnaire is equally divided into two parts. Dividing the questionnaire in such parts is known as using equal appearing intervals. It is the purpose of equal interval scaling to develop values for the statements so that we can assess a person's attitude.

Scale construction: Thurstone developed this method of equal appearing intervals on the assumption that even though people could not assign quantitative measurements to their own attitudes, they could tell the difference between the attitude represented by two different statements and could identify the items. The scale is constructed in the following way:

1. The researcher assembles a large number of statements concerning the psychological object of interest. These may be obtained by unstructured responses from a large number of persons who may extend to a thousand.
2. Several judges, i.e., 20 are asked to classify the statements independently into eleven "equal" groups ranging from most favourable to least favourable with regard to a specified attribute. The sixth point or pile will be the neutral point.
3. The frequency distribution of ratings for each statement is studied and statements giving widely scattered ratings are eliminated.
4. Scale values of each item are computed as the mean or median position weighted by the judges, frequencies.
5. One or two statements from each of the 11 piles are selected for the final scale. Those statements with the narrowest range of ratings are preferred. Thus, the statements having a relatively small dispersion are selected and 20 to 25 items are finally obtained.
6. The statements using 20 to 25 items are presented in random order in the final questionnaire. The respondents are asked to check only those with which they agree.
7. The respondents' mean or median of the scale values is finally taken as the score on the attribute being measured.

The 11 points scale may be presented in the following form:

Unfavourable Neutral Favourable

1 2 3 4 5 6 7 8 9 10 11

The most unfavourable pile is expressed as 1 and the most favourable pile is expressed 11. The neutral pile represents neither positive nor negative as expressed by 6th pile. The distance between two piles is always equal. Therefore, the scale is known as equal appearing intervals.

Several criticisms have been levelled at the Thurstone scales. Thurstone scales are not widely used in marketing research because of the time consuming task of preparing them. The preparation of long tests of statements and the rating of these statements by a number of judges are influenced by their own attitudes. To avoid the problems, the scale should not be used as interval scales as originally intended, but as ordinal scales. Some researchers may prefer median to mean to analyse the scale. Some of the respondents may select similar piles but their attitudes may not be uniform. Similarly some respondents may have large dispersions but their attitudes may be uniform. The respondents are not allowed to express their feelings. The degree of intensity of agreement is not identified in this scale.

2. Summated Ratings (Likert Scale)

The Likert method of summated ratings removes the criticism of equal appearing intervals. The intensity of degree of feelings is also recorded by this method.

Scale construction: The format of the scale for the summated ratings method is the same as that for construction and use. Instead of giving only those statements with which they agree, respondents are asked to indicate the degree of agreement or disagreement with each of the statements. Each degree of agreement/disagreement is given a numerical score and the respondent's total score is computed by summing up these scores from all the statements. In brief the Likert summated scale is discussed below:

1. The test items used are classed *a priori* as favourable or unfavourable. No attempt is made to find an equal distribution of test items and scale items.
2. A pretest is conducted. In the pretest, the respondents indicate agreement or disagreement with every item. For example, strongly disagree; disagree; neither agree nor disagree; agree and strongly agree. There qualifications may be given numerical weight and as -2, -1, 0, +1 and +2 respectively.
3. The score of a respondent represents the algebraic summation of weights associated with each item checked. In the scoring process, weights are assigned such that the direction of attitude is consistent throughout the survey. For example, if +2 is assigned to strongly approve for favourable items, +2 should also be given to strongly disapprove for unfavourable items.
4. The researcher is allowed to select those items which appear to discriminate "best" between high and low scores. Test scores for each item, i.e., using scores for only the highest and lowest quartile of subjects, and comparing mean differences over each item may be done for the said purpose.
5. The items finally selected are those which have demonstrated "best" among high versus low total scores.

The procedure has illustrated 5 degrees of each point; but it can be more than that.

Example of Likert Summated Rating Form

Powder Orange Juice

	Strongly Disagree	*Disagree*	*Neither agree nor disagree*	*Agree*	*Strongly Agree*
1. Powdered Orange Juice, I like.					
2. It is a mess to make.					
3. It sticks to the ribs.					
4. It is expensive.					
5. It is rich in vitamins.					

The score to each item is assigned as given in rule number 2 and 3. The sum of scores from all the statements provide the total scores for the respondent. Thus, respondents having a strong favourable attitude towards powdered orange juice could receive a score of 10, as +2 is for strong favourable degree of each of the five items mentioned above. The unfavourable attitude to any point may properly take place in the summated ratings because the unfavourable attitude will be assigned negative value. Mean value and coefficient of correlation may be used in this scale.

The difference in mean score if positive will indicate that the statement is a discriminating one. The mean score for each statement for the favourable attitude group will exceed the mean differences near zero are poor statements and should be eliminated. The product moment correlation of each item with the total score will be a useful method of analysis of the scale. Those items that have the highest correlation with the total are the best, and those that have correlation with near zero should be eliminated.

Use: The direction of its use is the same as the directions employed to generate a score to screen statements. The statements after modifying the original list are randomly ordered on the scale form to mix positive and negative scores. The respondents are asked to indicate their degree of agreement/disagreement. They find it easy to respond because the response categories do allow the expression of the intensity of the feelings. The respondents' total score is simply the sum of the scores on each statement. This scale is very useful over the equal appearing interval scale because it measures the intensity or degree of agreement or disagreement. The scale though states the comparative figure is not in a position to measure accurately the intensity or degree of the statement. Comparisons are made to determine whether the person has a positive or negative attitude toward the object. Norms are not developed for comparing subjects to determine who has the more favourable attitude. One can simply compare the raw scores of the subjects.

Since Likert scales are of the ordinal type, it gives rank to attitude rather than measuring the difference between attitudes. However, it is more discriminating and reliable than the Thurstone scales because of its larger range of responses. The Likert scales suffer from the disadvantages of no sound evidence on the comparative validity. Nonetheless Likert summated ratings are simpler to use than the Thurstone scale.

3. Semantic Differential

The semantic differential has been used for measuring the brand and image. It facilitates development of descriptive profiles for comparison with competitive items. The semantic differential scale grew out of researches at the University of Illinois and was developed by Osgood and his associates. It enabled the researcher to probe into the intensity and content of respondents' attitudes toward image and attitudes of marketing practices and policies.

The original semantic differential scale consisted of many bipolar adjectives to secure people's reactions to the objects of interest. It was observed that the reactions to the bipolar scales were correlated, and later on three basic uncorrelated dimensions were developed for the variations in ratings, viz., evaluation dimension, potency dimension and activity dimension. Evaluation dimension demonstrates good-bad, helpful-unhelpful, sweet-sour, warm-cold and so on. Potency dimension includes bipolar items such as powerful-powerless, strong-weak, deep-shallow and so on. Activity dimension consists of adjective pairs such as fast-slow, alive-dead, noisy-quiet and so on. The semantic differential technique suggests that an appropriate sample of adjective pairs should be selected for the object for each of the evaluation, potency and activity dimensions. The object can be compared to other objects using this technique. The semantic differential technique can be illustrated as below.

Semantic Differential Scaling Form

Reliable	..	..	..	..	Unreliable
Friendly	..	..	..	..	Unfriendly
Warm	..	..	..	..	Cold
Deliberate	..	..	..	..	Careless
Powerful	..	..	..	..	Weak
Well known	..	..	..	..	Little known

The respondent may be given a set of pairs of antonyms, the extremes of each pair being separated by seven equal intervals such as seven point scale such as extremely powerful, very powerful, slightly powerful, both powerful and weak, slightly weak, very weak and extremely weak. More bipolar adjectives are used to measure the intensity and content of the attitude. The approach in marketing has been different. Instead of applying the basic adjective pairs to the objects of interest, marketers have developed their own areas of interest. Marketers have used phrases to anchor the ends of the scale. Some of these phrases have been attributes possessed by the product. Instead of attempting to generate evaluation, potency and activity scores, marketers are interested in developing a profile for the brands, stores, companies and others. Marketing studies have tended to follow the Likert approach to scale construction rather than the Semantic differential. A researcher generates large list of bipolar adjectives or phrases. This attitude can be expressed in positive and negative statements. The negative phrase generally appears at the right side of the scale and the positive phrase at the left side of the scale as given in the previous figure. To avoid a biased attitude, the sides can be changed in subsequent items.

The scale is administered to the sample of subjects. Each respondent will be asked to read each set of bipolar phrases and check the segment which represents the degree of the characteristic involved which most closely coincides with their opinion of the product or other items being rated. The end positions are usually defined for the respondent in the instructions as being very closely descriptive of the object, the central position as being neutral and the intermediate positions as slightly descriptive and quite closely descriptive. There is no reason why the space between the opposing adjectives must be divided into seven segments. Any number will work if it does not get so large as to represent distinctions too small to be meaningful to respondents. Many researchers now use an even number of segments to force respondents to take a position. The neutral midpoint in a semantic differential seems to attract many respondents to avoid discriminating scores. Many researchers develop their own scales for specific projects.

The basis for the selection of opposing adjectives to use is the purpose of the project at hand. Opposing adjectives must be such as to be readily understood as being opposites by respondents. Pairs of adjectives must be selected that are relevant to the attitude to be measured. There is need for inclusion of all factors affecting a particular attitude. The use of a total score obtained as an indication of the overall attitude towards a brand assumes that all the important factors that determine consumer attitudes towards a brand have been included and that they are all of relatively equal weight.

Semantic differential is used to develop an image profile. It provides a good basis for comparing images of two or more items. When it is used, it is presumably serving as a scale on which some underlying attitude is measured. Semantic differential technique is used for comparing corporate images of product classes, comparing brands and services of competing suppliers, determining the attitudinal characteristics of purchasers of particular product classes or brands, and also for analysing the effectiveness of advertising and other promotional stimuli on attitude change. The semantic differential procedure provides a convenient, reliable and popular method of scaling procedures.

Semantic differential is not free from defects. The rudimentary item analysis is critical when comparing the scores. The total scores may be meaningless if the items employed in generating the scores are inappropriate. It cannot analyse internal consistency. Its validity is so doubtful that it is not recommended for overall attitude measurement. It may be very useful for image descriptive purposes. The total scores may be meaningless if the items employed in generating the scores are inappropriate. It is the ease with which semantic differential scales can be developed or the ease with which the findings can be communicated.

4. Stapel Scale

Stapel scale is a modification over semantic differential scale. It differs from the semantic differential scale in the sense that adjectives or descriptive phrases are tested separately instead of simultaneously as bipolar pairs; points on the scale are identified by number. Sometimes, there are ten scale positions rather than seven. The scale is divided into five positive points and five negative points. The respondent may select a plus number for the positive adjectives and minus number for the negative adjectives. The advantages of this scale are that it frees the researcher from the need of developing bipolar adjectives. The respondent may either agree or disagree to the statement. He may not remain undecided as there is no mid-point of neutral attitude. Only even scales are recorded and neutral points are excluded. The total of all the scores of all adjectives gives the summation of the scores of the respondent. The score represents his position on the continuum of agree-disagree toward a statement.

The stapel scale, like the semantic differential scale, is the study of consumers' attitudes on the pattern devised by Likert. This technique has not been as popular as the semantic differential scale. The total score will reveal very nominal meaning unless accompanied with certain statements. Marketers have assumed the positive of many psychological scaling specialists who believe interval scaling allows more powerful methods of analysis. The marketers have found such scalings more fruitful and productive.

5. Q-Sort

Q-sort technique is based on the Thurstone scale but differs from that in several aspects at the later stage. The objective of Q-sort is to compare individuals. This technique is parallel to the judgement of Thurstone's equal appearing interval except that the subjects respond to each stimulus in terms of their attitudes toward it, and not in terms of its degree of favourableness, and the subjects are instructed to place a specific number of statements in each category.

The respondents are given a large number of items and are asked to place them in eleven piles (scales) from most favourable to least favourable as indicated in the following table.

Distribution of Q-Sort Items

Number of statements	4	8	16	24	28	40	28	24	16	8	4	
Most favourable	0	1	2	3	4	5	6	7	8	9	10	Least favourable

Unlike the Thurstone technique whose objective was to develop scale values assuming judges could place the statements in various piles (scale) according to items' favourableness and unfavourableness, the Q-sort technique requires the respondent to express his degree of agreement or disagreement with the item. If he agrees most favourably the item is placed in one extreme. The respondent should place a preassigned number in each pile usually preset so as to result in an approximately normal distribution over the whole range. Each pile is given a "score value." Interest centers not on total subject scores but the degree of similarity among various subjects. The similarity may be determined by correlation analysis.

The Q-sort procedure is used to classify subjects in terms of "similarity" with regard to the attitude being measured.

6. Rating Scales

There are different rating scales having their distinctive features. But, one common feature is found in all the rating scales: "The rater places the person or object being rated at some point along a continuum or in one of an ordered series of categories; a numerical value is attached to the point or the category".[1] There are three main rating scales — graphic rating scales, itemized rating scales, comparative rating scales.

1. Graphic Rating Scales

This is the most widely used technique. The researcher or the respondents themselves make mark (✓) at the appropriate point on a line that runs from one extreme of the attribute

1. Claire Selltiz, Lawrence S. Wrightman, and Stuart W. Cook: *Research Methods in Social Relations*, 1976, pp. 403-404.

or characteristic in the question to the other extreme. Scale points with brief descriptions may be indicated along the line-example of graphic rating scale are given below:

Detergent	Use Regularly	Use occasionally	Might use	Probably never use	Would never use
Soap A					
Soap B					
Soap C					
Soap D					

Listed above are several brands of detergent products. The respondents check in one of the spaces beside each brand how they think about using the brand. Many different scaling devices can be used with this type of rating scale. The respondent places a mark ✓ or X in one box which indicates how much he likes or dislikes. The more he likes it, the bigger the number he should give it and the more he dislikes it, the smaller the number he should give it. There is no right or wrong answer. Only the opinion of the respondents count. The scores of each brand will indicate their popularity. If the scores of each brand are wide, their marketability can be known.

A graphing rating scale is easy to use and provides opportunity for fine discrimination of degree. It is easy to construct. It provides an opportunity to make fine distinctions and discrimination. Some argue that to measure small changes in attitude a fine scale is needed and it requires more points on the scale. If there are more points, the consumer cannot distinguish between several points. In practice a scale of 5 to 6 per positive adjective is more suitable. For more effective use, the researcher is advised to avoid end statements which are so extreme that they are unlikely to be used, and place descriptive statement as close as possible to the numerical points on the scale.

2. Itemised Rating Scale

The itemised rating scale is similar to the graphic rating scale without the benefit of direct comparison. The itemized rating scale is distinguished by the fact that the rater must select from a more limited number of categories, usually five to seven and even ten in rare cases. The categories are ordered in terms of their scale positions and each category usually has an attached verbal description. Likert's statement serves as a five-point itemized rating scale. A semantic differential adjective pair is a seven point scale, and an itemized rating scale used to ascertain importance values. It is given in the following example:

Itemized Rating Scale

Attribute of Detergent 'A'	*Not Important*	*Somewhat Important*	*Fairly Important*	*Very Important*
Economical				
Fair and Cleanliness				
Convenient				
Durable				

The detergent soap has been judged at various points on the scale. There may be 7 points judgement rather than 4 points judgement as given above. The more clearly defined the categories, the more reliable the ratings. How much specification is needed depends on the fineness of distinctions required. The itemized rating scale is easy to construct and use, although it does not permit the fine distinctions possible with the graphic rating scale.

3. Comparative Rating Scales

Comparative scales involve relative judgements in that raters form their judgements of each attribute with direct reference to the other attributes being evaluated. The Q-sort method of scale construction is an example in that each attribute was compared to all other attributes. The rater may be asked to estimate the ability of an individual to do a certain kind of work as compared to the total group of persons engaged in a particular kind of work. In a comparative rating scale, the respondents are instructed to divide some given sum among two or more attributes on the basis of their importance. For example, in the itemized rating each attribute may be assigned 50 marks. If any attribute is to be given more importance, the attribute is assigned more marks. The comparative scales require more judgements from the individual than either the graphic of itemized scale, as they tend to eliminate the empty effect. The comparative scaling method allows more insight into the relative ranking.

❖ ❖ ❖

CHAPTER 9

SAMPLING PROCEDURES

1. **OBJECTIVES OF SAMPLING**
2. **SAMPLING PROCESS**
3. **PROBLEMS ASSOCIATED WITH SAMPLING**
4. **SAMPLING METHODS**

   (i) NON-PROBABILITY METHOD

   (ii) PROBABILITY METHOD

   NON-PROPABABILITY METHODS

   (A) CONVENIENCE SAMPLING

   (B) JUDGMENT SAMPLING

   (C) QUOTA CONTROL SAMPLING

   PROBABILITY METHODS

   (A) SIMPLE RANDOM SAMPLING

   (B) STRATIFIED SAMPLING

   (C) CLUSTER SAMPLING

   (D) SYSTEMATIC SAMPLING

   (E) AREA SAMPLING

SAMPLING PROCEDURES

Sampling has become a very common idea. Everyone is accustomed to draw conclusions about a large group on the basis of a small group known as a sample. For example, we test the warmth of our coffee by taking a sip. In marketing research too, we try to draw conclusions on the basis of a sample for the whole group known as universe. After defining clearly the problems to be researched and developed an appropriate research design and data collection instruments, the next step in marketing research is to select those elements from which the information will be collected. One way to proceed would be to collect information from each member of the population of interest by completely canvassing the population. A complete canvass of the population is known as a census. An alternative may well be to collect information from a portion of the population by taking a small element from the larger group. Information collection from the sub-set, i.e., sample is relevant to the larger group. The relevance of the inference made from the sub-set to the population depends upon how a sample of the elements was chosen.

Population in marketing research is not related only to people. It can refer to a manufacturing firm, retailer, wholesaler or any subject of interest. Population is defined as a totality of cases that conform to some designated specifications. The specifications define the elements that belong to the larger group and those that are to be excluded. The marketing researcher should define explicitly the target group of interest, and more carefully, that he has actually sampled the target population. The sample has certain advantages and disadvantages over a census study.

Advantages of Sample

1. Lower cost is the major advantage of a sample. The cost of gathering information is a compelling factor in favour of sampling. A full enumeration of any large population will be prohibitively costly. Sampling is economical and efficient. Fewer people need to be interviewed. A smaller staff is required to collect, process and tabulate the information. The training and supervision of a larger staff is also not required in the sampling.
2. Sampling saves time. Decisions have a time constraint. Management can wait no longer for arriving at a particular conclusion on the basis of census study which warrants almost correct information, whereas the complete count will be obsolete by the time the census is completed and information processed. In a census study, it would be necessary to recruit, train and supervise a large number of enumerators if the field work to be completed within a reasonable period of time. The time saving advantage is especially important for the marketing management.
3. When small samples are used, it becomes possible to devote more attention to each member to check the member's accuracy and depth. Thus it is said that the researcher should choose a sample over a census for purposes of accuracy. A census involves a larger field staff which may attract more non-sampling errors. This is the reason why samples are used to check the accuracy of the census.
4. The sampling technique is also used in situations in which the measuring of a particular element from a group will destroy the elements or render them useless

after examination. For example testing the quality of cloth, which requires rigorous testing and makes the cloth suitable for sale.

5. Sampling is used in those cases where a census is impossible. For example, examining all the electric bulbs and pens etc. In biological study of all fish and plants is impossible.

Disadvantages of Sampling

1. Sampling demands an exercise of great care for correct and representative results. When the characteristics of population units vary widely, a very large sample is required to give relief information about the population.
2. Sampling requires proper training and supervision of the field force. It may involve additional cost and time.
3. Probability and non-probability samples are used in marketing. Unless the researchers are well aware of their applicabilities and utilities they may select wrong samples. The purpose behind the sampling is that it should be representative of the universe or population of interest.

1. OBJECTIVES OF SAMPLING

The sampling needs appropriate data as efficiently as possible. The objectives of the decision-maker should be served by the sampling process.

1. The sampling is chosen for having representative data of the population with which management is related. The purpose is to have a cross section containing the key characteristics in the same proportion as they exist in the population. The management may need different objectives to be fulfilled. The sampling may be varied to serve those objectives.
2. The sampling is required to satisfy the decision-maker's reliability requirements. Sufficient accuracy in the sample is possible for stable results.
3. Sampling is unavoidable. Sampling can reduce the time and effort for getting information for most decisions, and for a given cost may be more accurate than a complete enumeration of the universe. To save time, effort and cost the researcher may use sampling. It is too much to lavish on time.
4. Sampling is required for higher standards of study. The researcher knows that sampling would obtain precision beyond that warranted by the universe. Appropriate sampling is needed for fresh and recent data. Large samples or complex sampling may be avoided because they require too much time and data.

2. SAMPLING PROCESS

A sample is merely a selected subset of the population. The means of obtaining the sample from the population is termed as sampling method. The term population means the set of items which form a total group, i.e., a complete list of all subjects. Alternative terms include the universe, population and the sampling frame. A population is the complete set of all relevant items from which a sample is drawn. It is also known as an aggregation of the elements or items. The census is the gathering of information about all elements in a population. There are five steps of the sampling process. Items or elements are those units about which information is collected and which provide the basis of analysis.

1. Defining the population or universe is the first step of the sampling process. The defined population is known as target population. After defining and identifying the population, study design has been spelled out to gather data. The population's attributes must be described in terms readily determinable in the field. Well defined population will indicate the members or units to be included in the sampling-process. These units are known as sampling units.
2. The second step in the sampling process is to establish a frame of that population. The frame serves as the boundaries that circumscribe the population. The researcher has to see that every element or unit must have a chance of being selected in the sampling units. The sample must have geographical coverage to make it representative. With the objectives of the study, the sampling process will vary from study to study. A listing of every element or unit of the population would constitute a perfect sampling frame. The sampling frames define the survey population.
3. The sampling process should be designed in such a way that the results are representative and stable. The selection of units to be included in the sample must be representative. This is done on the basis of both probability and non-probability methods. Probability methods are those in which the population elements or units have known chances of being selected for inclusion in the sample. The probability sampling adheres to a precisely specified system that permits no bias selection. Randomness is one of these selection processes. On the other hand, non-probability methods are those where sampling units are either purposefully or accidentally selected in a non-random manner. Accidentally selected means the sampling units are selected conveniently. No attempt is made to select a representative sample. In brief, probability methods are more scientific and more-efficient in obtaining accurate sample-units.
4. The sampling process requires selection of an appropriate sample-size which is discussed in detail in the next chapter. The appropriate size of sample will give correct information with the least cost and effort.
5. Planning of the sampling should be prepared before execution. All the instructions pertaining to collection of primary data should be completed before the sampling procedure. There is need of a pretest of sampling units to arrive at correct information.

3. PROBLEMS ASSOCIATED WITH SAMPLING

The sample is part of the universe. A census is a complete count of the universe. The universe under study is described by a small set of measurements called parameters. The notion of "universe" is a conceptual entity. The universe is defined to suit our needs. The same physical entities — a group of consumers may be described in a variety of ways; it is usually some characteristics and not the individual person, which we are interested in measuring.

Even if measuring instruments were sufficiently precise, no two things would be exactly alike. Samples thus provide only estimates of the parameters describing the universe. The estimation of samples is known as statistics. Thus, there is bound to be a difference between statistics and parameters. There are also some errors which may be present in parameters. They may arise on account of defining, observing, collecting and tabulating of data.

The problems related to sampling are the sample results that provide useful estimates about the characteristics of the population from which the sample was drawn. The accuracy and reliability of the sample data are affected by two different types of errors — sampling errors and non-sampling errors. This can be represented in the following formula:

$$\bar{x} = \mu \pm E_s + E_{ns}$$

where x represents the resultant value obtained from the sample and μ represents the true, but unknown, characteristics of the population. The E_s are discrepancies due to a sampling error, and Ens are discrepancies caused by a non-sampling error. The variation between the actual population characteristics and the resulting sample value is due to the size of E_{ns} and E_s.

1. Non-sampling Error

The non-sampling errors may arise due to defining, observing, collecting and tabulating of data. They may be false or inaccurate reporting of the desired data, non-response, poor selection of field-workers and so on. Even if a complete enumeration of the population is undertaken, non-sampling errors might exist. This is the reason why the non-sampling errors may become larger when the size of the sample increases because of the possibility of a non-response rate, interview errors and data processing errors. These errors cannot be totally eliminated. However, Benjamin Lipstein has given some guidelines for minimising non-sampling errors. The sample should be limited to execute easily. It means the size of the sample should be such as may be handled easily. Consistent with the objectives of research, the sample should be the smallest possible. The questionnaire should be restricted to the main issue. It should be pretested before use. The interviewer himself should practice the interviewing questionnaire to evaluate the fatigue involved in answering the questionnaire. Therefore, he should try to minimise the respondents' fatigue. He should rotate key questions to discover when respondent fatigue begins. Only those questions should be asked, which can be answered by the respondents. Cumbersome and touchy questions should not be asked.

The sampling problems also involve the problems of defining the universe, variables and sample design. The universe is to be identified by the researcher. The definition of the universe depends on the research objectives. The variables to be studied must be defined clearly. Problems may also arise on account of sample design, i.e., determining sampling units, sample size and estimating universe characteristics from sample data.

2. Sampling Error

Sampling errors are related to the selection of samples. It is the difference between the sample value and the true value of the population. It is difficult for a smaller group or sample of a population to be exactly representative of the population, some degree of sampling error is bound to be present there. This is due to sampling variations. Sampling errors are also known as experimental errors which are based on the differences in the estimates which would occur if the repeated samples from the same universe and using the same procedure are taken. The size of the sampling error is related to the size of the sample, and the variability in the universe. The reliability refers to a measure of the sampling error which is the result of chance, i.e., the laws of probability. The sampling error can be reduced by increasing the size of the sample as it is the difference between the universe parameter and sample statistics. The range of the sampling error can be defined at a given confidence level.

4. SAMPLING METHODS

Sampling techniques can be divided into the two broad categories of probability and non-probability samples. Probability sampling methods are those in which every item in the universe has a known chance or probability of being chosen for the sample. A sampling distribution is the probability distribution of a specified sample statistic for all random samples of a given size from a specified universe. Probability samples are distinguished non-zero chance of being included in the sample. Non-probability sampling methods are those which do not provide every item in the universe with a known chance of being included in the sample. Probability sampling as a method provides a way to measure the sampling error which the non-probability sample does not measure. The probability sample lays much emphasis on procedure, and the non-probability sample places reliance on the person handling the sample-units.

(i) Non-probability Method

Non-probability samples involve personal judgement somewhere in the selection of sample-units. Sometimes, even field-workers can influence the selection of sample elements. Non-probability selection can be either opportunistic or purposive. Opportunistic choice is done at sheer convenience. There is no specific method of choosing the sampling elements. Non-probability samples are also known as purposive samples as the population units are deliberately designated. These samples may be convenience samples, judgement samples and quota samples.

(a) Convenience Sampling: In convenience sampling selection, the researcher chooses the sampling units on the basis of convenience or accessibility. It is also called accidental samples because the sample-units enter by accident. This is also known as a sample of the man in the street, i.e., selection of units where they are. Sample units are selected because they are accessible. For example, in testing a potential new product, the sample work is done by adding the new product to the appropriate shops in the locality. Purchasing and selling of the new product is observed there.

The convenience samples may not be representative of the target population, but they are selected on being conveniently approachable. This sample is used for special situations in marketing research. There is no exact way of determining the representativeness of the chosen sample. The convenient units' characteristics differ significantly from the less "convenient units" characteristics. A convenience sample is not used for descriptive or causal research studies. This is used for exploratory designs where quick and inexpensive methods are required. It may also be useful where pretest of the questionnaire may be required to help ensure question comprehension, and to detect errors that may arise in the research design.

(b) Judgement Sampling: Judgement sample is deliberately undertaken for the purposes of research. This is also known as purposive sampling. The sample elements are selected because it is felt that they are representative of the population of interest. Thus, the key feature of judgement sampling is that population elements are purposively selected. The term "judgement" has been used to label two quite different sorts of deliberate choices. One is known as sampling by opinion. The researcher should know which members of the universe would constitute a proper cross section representing the parameters of pertinence.

The judgement sampling is used for the study of sales personnel for a corporation in which certain analysis of top grade, medium-grade and low-grade is conducted. The judgement sample would be representative of each of the three strata. This is not a scientific method. Other forms of judgement selection may use statistical judgement in which the criteria for selection are specified, and data on these factors are scrutinised to find out the population units specific to the purpose of the study. The choice of sample units is deliberate or purposive and not random or per chance conforming to the specifications.

The judgement sampling is not fixed. It may be changed as per need. If a member of a panel drops out, the researcher may take another person of similar attitudes. Here the characteristics of the members of the sample are specifically mentioned.

(c) Quota Control Sampling: In the commonly used method of quota control sampling, known parameters are used to describe the population. The field workers select a sample that conforms to these parameters. Each field worker is assigned quotas of the number of units. It is representative by selecting sample elements in such a way, that the proportion of the sample elements possessing certain characteristics are approximately the same as the population characteristics.

For example, the investigation of the popularity of a certain brand or commodity amongst the consumers may require quota sampling. In this example, the quota as per income, age, and locality may be selected. Considering the total number of units in each group, the sample units may be proportionately selected for representative study. Thus, the sample units in each group may be totalled to find out the total sample-units. This method of sampling has the advantage that the sample will conform to the chosen parameters of the population. The quota is correctly filled. It is therefore said that the quota control sampling is safer than that of probability selection. The field worker must be honest and select the quotas with the exact numbers of persons with the characteristics prescribed. If the relevant characteristics are not listed properly, no full proof method could be revealed. Stratified data of different quotas may not be easily available. Many of the units if missed cannot be revealed by the researcher.

Quota control sampling is widely used in the marketing system. This sample is widely used for economic studies also. A panel or quota is selected to study the opinion or attitudes of people. This form of sampling is a well-balanced sample and obtains high response rates by mail. The units of sampling are selected through direct mailing, using directories and lists through current panel members who are asked about their friends and also with personal interviews. A deliberate procedure is followed to find or to screen individuals who may cooperate with the interview. The chief advantages of panels are sampling efficiency costs and the saving of time. It is also possible with the panels to find out shifts of behaviour over a period of time. The panels have certain disadvantages. The panel may not accurately represent the whole market. The panel-members may not cooperate for a longer period. Substitute panel members may not be available in the original form and with similar characteristics.

The quota control sampling as claimed by some researchers to be representative may not be truly representative because the sample may be very far off with respect to some important characteristics of the population, vastly different from the population concerning some characteristics not explicitly compared, and may over represent a particular area or group. When the data collected from the quota control sampling is biased, it is difficult to correct them. However, it has been used in marketing research for some specific purposes where sample units are almost uniform.

(ii) Probability Method

Probability sampling calculates the likelihood of any given population element to be included in a sample. The sample elements are selected by chance or randomising devices. The primary reason for considering probability samples is that the sample error associated with the sample procedures can be determined easily. It allows objective assessment of the reliability of the sample result which is not possible with non-probability samples. The probability sampling may be simple random sampling, stratified sampling and cluster sampling.

(a) Simple Random Sampling

Probability sampling is the only sampling technique available which will provide an objective measure of the reliability of the sample estimate. The simple possible probability sampling method is called simple random sampling. In simple random sampling, every possible sample unit has a known and equal chance of being selected. This approach may be used in marketing studies when the entire population is listed and the sample units might be chosen readily by some randomised sampling. Simple random sampling is the easiest probability sampling method to understand more complicated ideas involved. The process of selecting a simple random sample guarantees that every universe item has an equal chance of being selected. Random sampling uses a random table for selection of sampling units. There is another method of selecting a random sample drawing the units randomly. Suppose there are 1,00,000 units in the target group and 1,000 units are to be selected for sampling purposes. All the 1,00,000 units of the target population are numbered and put in one bowl. One chip containing one number is drawn and its number is noted for sampling purposes, and the chip is again replaced in the bowl and mixed altogether. The second draw is made next time and the process is repeated until all 1,000 units are drawn.

Simple random sampling is very greatly related with the parent population, the derived population and confidence interval.

Parent Population: The parent population proves useful for exploring the notion of sampling distribution. This population can be described by certain parameters. A parameter is a characteristic or measure of a parent or target population. A parameter is a fixed quantity that distinguishes one population from another. We can calculate the parameter of the parent population. The quantities of values are fixed. Relying on a census, one can select a sample and use the values calculated from the sample for estimating the values of the parent population or original target group of study. One should estimate the sample values and variances to find out the population value. For example, if μ denotes the mean population income, σx^2 the variance of incomes and x_i is the mean value of sample one and N is the number of population elements, then

$$\mu = \frac{\sum_{i=1}^{N} X_i}{N}$$

$$\sigma^2{}_x = \frac{\sum_{i=1}^{N} (X_i - \mu)^2}{N}$$

Thus, μ is the parameter of the parent population.

Derived Population: The derived population is different from the original population or parent population in the sense that the derived population is based on the sample values. A statistic is a characteristic or measure of a sample. We use a calculated statistic to estimate the parameter. The value of the statistic depends on the particular sample selected from the parent population. Different samplings yield different statistics. The derived population i.e., total of all possible sample values can be a useful value of the parent population. Thus,

$$\bar{x}_k = \sum_{i=1}^{n} \frac{X_i}{n}$$

where $\bar{X}_k$ is the derived population, k refers to the sample number, $\bar{x}$ to the sample average and n to the sample size. The researcher will make use of the concept derived population, in making references from the sampling distribution. The derived population is defined as the population of all possible distinguishable samples. If any part of the sampling plan is changed, the derived population will also change. Similarly, if the method of selecting sample-elements is changed, the derived population will also change.

The statistic is unbiased when its average value equals the population parameter. For example all added sample means are divided by the number of samples, i.e., average mean values of all samples to get the mean of the population. For example,

$$\frac{\sum_{k=1}^{L} x_k}{L} = E(\bar{x}) = \mu$$

where L equals the number of possible samples. If the value is unbiased, a particular estimate may be very far from the true population value. Variance of mean income can be calculated by taking the deviation of each mean around its overall mean, squaring and summing the deviations and then dividing by the number of samples. Thus,

$$\sigma^2_x = \frac{\sum_{k=1}^{L} (\bar{x}_k - \mu)^2}{L}$$

whereas σ^2_x is the variance of mean incomes and L denotes the number of possible samples.

The distribution of the estimates of the sample is in contrast to the variable in the parent population. Sampling distribution of the statistic is the single most important statistic for drawing inferences. If the researcher knows the sampling distribution for the statistics, he is in a position to make an inference about the corresponding population parameter. If he knows only a particular sample estimate that will vary with repeated sampling and has no information how to vary the samples, it will be difficult to devise a measure of sampling error associated with the estimate. The sampling distribution of an estimate describes how the estimate will vary with the repeated sampling, and it provides a basis for determining the reliability of the sample estimate. Thus, with known probabilities of inclusion of any population element in the sample, the researchers are about to derive the sampling distribution of different statistics.

The mean of all possible sample means is equal to the population mean in case of simple random sampling. The variance of sample means is related to the population variance by the formula:

$$\sigma_{\bar{x}}^2 = \frac{\sigma^2 N - n}{n N - 1}$$

It is true when sampling units are selected from a finite population without replacement. In the case of sampling from an infinite population or from a finite population with replacement, the expression will be $\sigma_{\bar{x}}^2 = \frac{\sigma^2}{n}$. The distribution of the sample means is mound shaped and symmetrical as known by the Central Limit Theorem. It shows that if simple random samples of size n are drawn from a parent population with mean μ and variance σ^2, then the sample mean ($\bar{x}$) will be approximately normally distributed with mean equal to μ and variance equal to σ^2/n. The approximation will become more and more accurate if the sample size (n) becomes larger. Thus the distribution of sample means will be normal if the sample is large enough regardless of the shape of the parent population. In the case of normal distribution of variable of parent population the means of sample will be normally distributed. If the distribution of the variable of the parent population is symmetrical, the samples of small size will produce means normally distributed. On the other hand, in the case of highly skewed distributed variables of the parent population, samples of large size are needed. In sufficiently large size samples, the sample mean is usually normally distributed. In the Central Limit Theorem, we assume the normal curve of population variables.

Confidence Interval Estimates: In practice, only one sample is drawn, and inference to the parent population is made thereupon as it is not possible to make any sample study. Researchers like to determine a range of values within which they can be fairly sure that the true value lies, i.e., the determination of the interval within which the values may lie. The theory of simple random sampling provides methods for establishing such a range or interval estimate. Thus, the sample estimates may permit evaluation of the reliability of values. It is possible to measure the sampling error associated with estimates such as mean, percentage etc. This estimate will give limits within which the universe value may fall.

There may be several samples and their values will also give limits within which the population value may lie. Such values of random samples will give the frequencies of occurrence which is also known as random sampling distribution of the estimate or value. This is generally called sampling distribution. The knowledge of the sampling distribution makes it possible to predict the behaviour of the sampling estimate and provides a basis for determining the reliability of the sample estimates. The sampling distribution of the mean will be approximately a normal distribution. The sample means tend to cluster around the universe x mean. Given positive and negative deviations of equal magnitude samples, the more closely will the sample means cluster around the universe mean. If a universe is normally distributed, the proportion of the universe items located between any two limits is determined by the distance of those limits from the universe mean measured in terms of standard deviation (σ). Since sample means will be approximately normally distributed about the universe mean, it is stated that the deviation of sample means from the universe mean differs with certain laws, i.e., the Central Limit Theorem. When applied to the sampling distribution of the mean, the standard deviation is known as standard error of the mean. If the mean of the sampling distribution is the population mean and is expressed by μ and it's the standard deviation by $\sigma\bar{x} = \frac{\sigma}{\sqrt{n}}$, the Central Limit Theorem says that 68.26 per cent of the sample mean will be within $\pm\ \sigma\ \bar{x}$ of the population mean, 95.45 per cent of the sample mean will be within $\pm\ 2\ \sigma\bar{x}$ of the population mean and 99.73 per cent of the sample mean will be within $\pm 3\sigma\bar{x}$ of the population mean. The σ or standard error or standard deviation of the population is expressed as

$$\sigma = \sqrt{\frac{\varepsilon x^2}{N-}}$$

where

σ = Standard deviation

x = Deviation of an item from the universe mean.

N = Number of items in the universe.

The standard error of the mean of a simple random sample is obtained by the formula:

$$\sigma\bar{x} = \frac{\sigma}{\sqrt{n}}$$

whereas

$\sigma\bar{x}$ = Standard error of the mean.

σ = Standard deviation of the universe.

n = Number of observations in the sample.

The interpretation of the interval limits is that if a large number of random samples is selected and the interval limit is computed each time; about 95 per cent of the interval-limits, at which the standard deviation at a positive and negative side, will cover the universe mean. The confidence limits or interval limits of other estimates are also interpreted in the same way as discussed above. The interval constructed from a particular sample includes the population mean. Confidence in the estimate arises because of the procedure and not because of a particular estimate. The accuracy of a specific sample is evaluated by reference to the procedure by which the sample is drawn. Statistical inference procedures rest on the representativeness of the sampling plan. The probability samples allow an estimate of the precision of the results. The estimates will tend to cluster about the true value. The greater the standard error of the statistics, the less precise the procedure. The confidence level applies to the procedure and not to a particular sample result.

(b) Stratified Sampling

A stratified sampling is the probability sampling wherein the parent population is divided, into mutually exclusive and exhaustive subsets, and a simple random sampling is then chosen independently from each subset or groups or stratum. The division of strata is mutually exclusive and exhaustive. Every population element is assigned to one and only one stratum. The parent population can be divided into any number of strata. The procedure to select two elements for the stratified sample is like the selection of a sample random sample.

Reasons for Stratification: Stratification in marketing research is used for greater reliability. A very small proportion of the universe contributes heavily to the estimate. Unless a very large and simple random sample was used, there will be an expectation that the extreme members of the universe will be represented. Thus, a relatively small sample taken from each stratum would provide a good estimate of the mean of the stratum. If the proportion of the universe included within each stratum was unknown, the estimated means of these strata could be weighted together to provide an estimate of the mean of the total population.

The second reason for stratification is that information may be required about the components of the universe. For illustration, the study of coffee consumption may require stratification of the population into geographical regions, city, family size, income group and so on. Similarly, there may be other examples where the stratification of the universe may be desirable. Other example may be various sub-universes or strata of a universe which may have their distinctive features that may be very useful for marketing research. Similar to the simple random sampling, the stratified sampling may have derived population, sampling distribution, confidence interval estimate, and precision of stratified samples.

Derived Population: The derived population of all possible samples of stratified sampling can be selected along with the mean of each sample. Every possible combination of sample units is no longer a possibility, since every continuation of two units from the same sub-universe is precluded. If the stratified random sampling has 100 possible sample combinations, there will be 190 possible combinations of simple random sampling. Thus, the stratified sampling is more restrictive than the simple random sampling. Equal probability of selection is a necessary but not a sufficient condition for simple random sampling.

Sampling Distribution: Stratified sampling can produce a more concentrated distribution of estimates. It can produce sample statistics which are more precise and have smaller error. The characteristics of sub-groups can be known particularly from the population with rare segments. A small subset will account for a large proportion of the behaviour of interest in marketing. It becomes essential that the sub-group be adequately represented in the sample. The distribution of variables in each stratified sample is made in the same way as was done in the case of the simple random sample.

Confidence Interval Estimate: Establishing a confidence interval with a simple random sample. The degree of confidence desired (z) as a point estimate of the population mean (a) by the sample mean x, and also an estimate of the amount of sampling error associated with the sample mean. The spread in the distribution of sample means can be equal to $\sigma\bar{x} = \frac{\sigma}{\sqrt{n}}$ when the population variance can be known.

Since a stratified random sample is just a group of simple random samples, the mean estimate of the sample is unbiased. The means of the individual stratum can be combined and weighted into an unbiased estimate of the total population mean. Thus, the estimate of the universe mean is simply a weighted average of the strata means. The weight assigned to each stratum is the proportion of universe items included in that stratum. So the population mean would be estimated by multiplying each stratum mean by its assigned weight, adding the results, and dividing by the sum of the weights. Thus $x_k = w_1x_1 + w_2x_2 + \dots w_kx_k$.

The confidence limits for a universe mean can be estimated with standard deviation or standard error. Therefore standard deviation of the stratified sampling is first calculated, and then similar to simple random sampling, it is multiplied by two and three respectively to arrive at confidence limits at both 95.45 per cent and 99.73 per cent levels of confidence. The total of population standard deviation is calculated to find out the standard error of the population based on the stratified sampling. The estimate of the standard of each stratified random sampling mean is first made to calculate an overall standard error of the population. The quantity σ^2 is the variance, i.e., the standard deviation squared of the sample in strata 1 and n_1 in the number of observations in that stratum. Similarly the sample variance of stratum 2, i.e., σ^2_2 with sample size n_2 is also known. The weighted standard deviations are used to multiply their respective values and all the summation of each stratum added. The figure thus arrived at is divided by the total of elements of a stratum.

The estimate of the standard error of the total population required or variance is thus calculated as below:

$$\sigma^2 = \frac{\sigma_1^2 w_1^2}{n_1} + \frac{\sigma_2^2 w_2^2}{n_2} + \ldots \frac{\sigma_k^2 w_k^2}{n_k}$$

Thus, the standard error of population mean in

$$\sigma = \sqrt{\sigma^2}$$

So the confidence interval at

(i) 68.26 per cent of the sample means will be within $\pm\sigma$ of the population mean.

(ii) 95.45 per cent of the sample means will be within $\pm 2\sigma$ of the population mean.

(iii) 99.73 per cent of the sample means will be within $\pm 3\sigma$ of the population mean.

Precision of Stratified Samples: The stratified sampling offers an opportunity for reducing sampling error or for increasing precision. The sampling error is calculated by standard error or standard deviation (σ_x). The smaller the $\sigma_{\bar{x}}$, the lesser the sampling error, and more precise will be the estimate by expressing a narrower confidence interval. The total size of the population and the size of each stratum is fixed. The smaller the variance of the estimate, the lesser will be the sampling error. The variance of the estimate by strata depends on the variability of the characteristic within the strata, i.e.,

$$\sigma \bar{x}_k{}^2 = \frac{\sigma_k^2}{n_k}$$

where σ^2_k is the sample variance within the kth stratum and n_k is the size of the sample selected from the k_{th} stratum. The estimate of the mean can be made more precise to the extent the elements of the strata are homogeneous. The characteristics of interest display a certain amount of variation in the population but the investigator cannot influence the fixed characteristics of the population. The only alternative left to the researcher is to divide the elements of the population into strata so as to increase the precision with which the average value of the characteristic can be estimated. The researcher should divide the population into as disparate strata as possible. If the researcher is successful in partitioning the population in several strata containing exactly equal elements of each stratum, there will be less error with the estimate of the population mean. The variability that exists between strata does not enter into the calculation of the standard errors of the stratified sampling.

Issues in the Selection of Stratified Random Samples

In the stratified random sampling, three important issues are considered, i.e., bases of stratification, number of strata and sample size. The sample size is discussed in the next chapter.

Bases of Stratification

The strata are based on the criteria which divide the population into sub-groups or sub-universes. The criteria may be the characteristics of interest. The best basis is the frequency distribution of the principal variables. The stratification may be on the basis of a single, simple variable or a compound variable depending on such matters as availability of detailed information. It is desirable to make up strata in such a way that the sampling units within the strata are similar to the possible extent. One way of doing this is to employ a great many very small strata. The creation of additional strata is often expensive in terms of sample design, data collection and analysis.

It is desirable to use a stratification system which will maximise differences in stratum means for the key survey variables of interest. In marketing research, stratification of variables takes place on the bases of geographical location, population, income, age and so on. The cadre of employees, production-techniques and other internal factors may also be taken as bases of stratification.

Number of Strata

Since the calculation of the standard error of estimate provides some bias to the number of strata, the various strata should be made as homogeneous as possible. There should also be as many strata as possible. Each stratum mean can be estimated with high reliability and precision. Practical problems limit the number of strata used. The inclusion of additional strata may involve greater cost which may outrun the benefits.

Types of Stratified Sampling

The stratified sampling may be of three types: proportionate stratified sampling, disproportionate stratified sampling and quota sampling. The stratified sampling costs more than the simple random sampling but the former is more precise than the latter.

Proportionate Stratified Sampling

Proportionate stratified sampling is one where the number chosen in each stratum is proportionate to its share of the total population. This method provides an equal chance of inclusion as fully as with simple random sampling. The number of observations in the total sample is allocated among the strata in proportion to the relative number of units in each stratum in the population. For example, there are five strata containing 10 per cent, 20 per cent, 30 per cent, 25 per cent and 15 per cent elements of the total population. Therefore, each stratum must have sample units proportionate to their involvement in the total population, i.e., 10 per cent, 20 per cent, 30 per cent, 25 per cent and 15 per cent.

Stratified selection tends to be more efficient than simple random sampling. The problem of under or over sampling the data is avoided. This reduces the sampling error.

The important point under this ample is that the information on the composition of the whole population should be currently accurate. The stratified samples should be done in correlation between criteria and data. The researcher should know the relative sizes of each stratum in order to determine the number of sample observations.

Disproportionate Stratified Sampling

Disproportionate stratified sampling involves balancing the criteria of strata size and strata variability. Strata having more variability are sampled more than proportionally to their relative size. On the other hand, strata having homogeneous elements are sampled less than proportionately. The sample size for each stratum should be determined. A stratum that is characterised by great variability will require a large number of observations to produce a precise estimate of the stratum mean. There is possibility of greater precision when the various strata are sampled proportionate to the relative variability of the characteristic as compared in proportion to their relative size in the population. A disproportionate stratified sample requires more knowledge about the population of interest than does a proportionate stratified sample. In this case, the researcher should have more efficient estimates than proportionate sampling. If the sample-units are heterogeneous, the disproportionate stratified sampling will be more useful.

Quota Sampling

The quota sample refers to the selection of sampling units as per quota or judgement. It is based purely on the judgement or personal discretion of the researcher to fix a quota of sample units from each group. Therefore, it has no objective assessment of the degree of sampling error, confidence interval estimates and statistical tests of significance. On the contrary, the stratified sampling units are selected on probability and statistical verification. So, it has minimum sampling error and high precision and confidence. On the whole, the stratified sampling and quota sampling involve division of the population into segments or subgroups and selection of elements from each segment or subgroup.

(c) Cluster Sampling

We have seen in the previous sections that simple random sampling and stratified random sampling involve enormous cost when dealing with a large number of sample units. Therefore, the researcher may use cluster sampling rather than simple and stratified sampling. The cluster sampling, i.e., the smaller first samples from the population is being used for detail and cheaper study. The clusters may be a city, households, or geographical location. The sampling of clusters from the population is done by simple or stratified random sampling. From these clustered samples, the constituent units are sampled by random procedures. For example, the parent population is divided into mutually exclusive and exhaustive subsets known as clusters. A random sample of the cluster is selected. If the researcher uses population elements in the cluster for the sample, it is known as one-stage cluster sampling. But if a sample of elements is selected in a probabilitical manner from the selected clusters, the procedure in known as two-stage cluster sampling.

The cluster sampling and stratified sampling are similar in some forms. Both involve the division of the population into mutually exclusive and stratum exhaustive subgroups known as a cluster although the criteria used are different. In the former case it is mainly locality, city, household and some other geographical units, while in the latter case, it is mainly income, education and other socio-economic characteristics. In the cluster sampling, the researcher chooses the sample of subgroups and in stratified sampling, a sample of elements is selected from each subgroup.

In a sample of subgroups with cluster sampling, each subgroup is treated as a model of the population. If the characteristics of each subgroup are exactly according to the population, then one subgroup can serve the purpose of sampling. In cluster sampling, the subgroups are usually heterogeneous. But this is not always necessary. In practice, the defined clusters are homogeneous rather than heterogeneous in characteristics of interest. The homogeneous subgroups produce less ideal cluster samples from the point of view of statistical efficiency.

Relative statistical efficiency of the two sampling systems depends on the degree of similarity among items in each cluster. The greater the similarity of the observations in the cluster, the less efficient will be the cluster sampling. The greater the dissimilarity among the observations in a cluster, the more efficient will be the cluster sampling. The relative statistical efficiency is a relative notion by which a sampling plan can be compared with other samples. A sampling plan is more efficient than the other, for the same size sample, if the former produces a smaller standard error. If the characteristic of interest is the mean, the sampling plan that produces the smallest value of σ_x for a given size of sample will be statistically efficient than comparable stratified samples or simple random samples, because the standard error of the cluster sample is more than those of stratified and simple random samples. With the minimum similarity clusters the standard error of the means of the cluster samples is zero, i.e., each cluster has the same mean. In this case, the cluster sampling will be more efficient than the simple random sampling. But in almost all cases the cluster sampling has more standard errors and is therefore statistically less efficient. The relative cost per observation in the cluster sampling is comparatively less than that of other samples. This is known as economic efficiency.

Simple cluster sampling may be either more or less efficient statistically than simple random sampling, depending on the degree of intra-cluster heterogeneity. Clusters are often constructed in such a way that the observations within a cluster are relatively homogeneous. Simple cluster sampling will be less efficient statistically than simple random sampling. The lower relative cost of obtaining observations in cluster sampling often offsets the loss in statistical efficiency. Thus, the net efficiency is often greater in the cluster sampling. The cluster sampling may be systematic and area samples.

(d) Systematic Sampling

Systematic sampling is a very important form of cluster sampling. It offers one of the easiest ways of sampling. For example, every item of the population is selected to form sampling units. In this case, the items of population are chronologically arranged. This nth item is randomly selected for the first, and the next item will be selected after n number. Systematic sampling is one-stage cluster sampling as the subgroups are not sampled but all the elements in the selected clusters are used.

Advantages: A systematic sample may be more representative than a simple random sample. It is easier to choose a random start and select every nth item thereafter than to make a simple random selection. This technique is well-known for its simplicity. It is less subject to error than the simple random selection. It may be used for selecting items within strata in a stratified design. The mean of a systematic sample is an unbased estimate of the universe mean since each of the five possible samples shown has the same chance of being chosen and their average is equal to the universe mean. Systematic sampling operates much like a stratified random sampling. The degree to which the systematic sample may be more representative than a simple random sample depends on the clustering of objects within the sample.

Disadvantages: The systematic sampling may select only one cluster of the population although there may be several clusters in the universe. The sampling error, therefore, may be very high and cannot be evaluated properly. It may be possible to obtain an unbiased estimate of the sampling error by drawing a number of systematic samples instead of one. There may be a possibility of selecting impracticable units of the population. In a practical situation, it may be easy to determine whether a periodicity is present or to evaluate its significance.

(e) Area Sampling

The researchers may develop a design which may involve the initial sampling of groups of elements or clusters followed by the election of elements within each selected cluster. The clusters are made up of individual units which constitute mutually exclusive and exhaustive categories or subsets which are randomly selected by the researcher. If the phenomena sampled have fixed and known locations, they may be grouped by identifiable geographic areas and the sample drawn is known as area-sampling. The number of units to be taken from each area can be specified and made proportional to the share of the total population located in each area. If all the areas are included in the sampling, this will be a true probable sample. This is a form of stratified sample based on locations. It assumes that the geographical distribution is a proper cross section of the population. The population and relevant data of each area must be known to the researcher. Area sampling is very complex, and some of the methods of area sampling are discussed here.

One stage area sampling: In the case of one stage area sampling, the areas selected for the sample are completely enumerated. It is assumed that elements in each area are uniform. One approach to the problem is to choose a simple random sample of n city blocks from the population of N blocks and determine the characteristics of the sample units. After the study, the findings are generalised in relation to the larger population. The probability of any household being included in the sample may be given as n/N since it equals the probability. Since units within each cluster-block tend to be rather homogeneous, the members of the households within each block tend to be quite similar with regard to such characteristics as income, ethnic background, occupation and so forth. The researchers form clusters so that the units within each cluster vary as much as possible and select a large number of clusters in order to obtain a more representative picture of the population for the geographical area. Since each household on the selected blocks is included in the sample, the procedure is known as one-stage area sampling. Each subsector cluster is mutually exclusive and exhaustive. The cost of data collection will be low because of the concentration of households within an area.

Two stage Area sampling: In two stage area sampling, one selected area may not be useful; the elements associated with a sample area may be sub-sampled. This method of sampling in which the sample units are themselves sampled is called two stage sampling as there are two clusters, i.e., cluster and sub-cluster within the cluster. For example, there are 8 blocks in a district and all the blocks have some households. Suppose 10 households are to be selected, there will be 80 households in the sample study. It is not essential that a similar number of households may be selected from each block. There may be a different number of households in each block. The product of the block sampling fraction (first stage sampling fraction) and the household sub-sampling fraction (second stage sampling fraction) will be equal to total probability. If the researcher wishes to sample second stage units at a rate of 1 in x then y cluster and sub-clusters will be 1/xy. This is observed by selecting first stage units at a rate of 1 in y, and second stage units from the selected first stage units at a rate of 1 in x. Thus, the overall section probability will be :

$$1/xy = 1/x \cdot 1/y$$

The costs of data collection dictates that a second stage sampling fraction will be high. Many households may be selected from each block with a high sampling fraction ratio. This reduces field work and travel costs. Since it is expected that the blocks will be relatively homogeneous in character, it is desirable to have very few households from a particular block.

Whenever clusters are of differing sizes, it is essential to use a modified design called probability proportionate to size (PPS). If a proportional representation is desired, a weighting procedure must be followed so that the sample members proportionately represent the number of households in each cluster. Thus the probability of households in a block is equal to the number of blocks to be chosen multiplied by the product of block probability and within block household probability. The probability proportionate to size (PPS) is utilised to ensure that large clusters are represented in the sample. It can also produce estimates that are more precise when there is great variation in the number of second stage units in relation to the first stage unit.

Multiple Area Sampling: When the sample-units are wide and varied, the population target may be divided into areas from which selection would be made. The blocks of small rural sections would be selected thereafter and finally the sample units may be selected. Specifically it can be stated that the sample of cities may be divided into geographical location, the sub-sample of blocks may be selected from the sample cities and then from each sub-sample or blocks, households may be selected. The actual sampling plan will depend on the characteristics of the specific problem, resources and ingenuity of the researcher. For example, all countries and metropolitan sections might be stratified by educational levels, by percentage employed in manufacturing or by other significant characteristics. There may be a large number of classes, sub-classes and cross sectional classes. This technique tends to improve greatly the probability of getting proper representation of all the factors associated with these samples and sub-samples.

❖ ❖ ❖

CHAPTER 10

SAMPLE SIZE

1. **DETERMINING SAMPLE SIZE (MEANS)**
2. **DETERMINING SAMPLE SIZE (PROPORTIONS)**
3. **STRATIFIED SAMPLE SIZE**
4. **SAMPLE SIZE IN NON-PROBABILITY**
5. **OTHER DETERMINANTS OF SAMPLE SIZE**

SAMPLE SIZE

After selecting the specific type of sampling the next important consideration is determination of the sample size. The researcher may need some means of determining the necessary size of the sample before starting collection of data. The present chapter will discuss determining the sample size of probability and non-probability samples. The objectives of research have been the guiding lines for determining the size of the sample while considering the amount of time, money and personnel involved in the administration of the specific sample size. There are various other factors to determine the sample size such as sampling error, inefficiency, cost and so on. The researcher while deciding the appropriate size of the sample compromises all the factors affecting the sample size. The decision to decide the sample size must be scientifically made and should not be done arbitrarily because of the risks involved. The sample size should be neither too large nor too small. The sample size should be decided on some specific theories. The determining of standard error of the estimate becomes essential for deciding the sample size. Besides, consideration of precision of the estimate is also required for the sample size. The desired degree of confidence is also considered for the sample size. We shall discuss the sample size for estimating means, sample size for estimating proportions, stratified sample size, non-probability sample size and other factors determining the sample size.

1. DETERMINING SAMPLE SIZE FOR ESTIMATING MEANS

The sample size for estimating means is decided on the basis of acceptable errors, confidence level, standard deviations, sequential sampling, cost and multiple objectives.

1. Acceptable Errors: There may be several errors in the sample size. The researcher will have to decide those errors which may be acceptable to the executive. For example, if the marketing executive desires to spend Rs. 10,000 per month on advertisement, he may willingly spend ± 10% of the said expenditure. The deviation is decided on the basis of the acceptable mean of the expenditure. A large size error would be unacceptable. Therefore, the management will have to determine various errors related to the sampling procedures. How many errors will be acceptable to the management are decided before planning the sampling. The sampling techniques and errors related to samples and to non-sample techniques are discussed in detail in the next chapter.

2. Confidence Level: The next factor influencing the sample size is deciding the confidence level. The larger the size of the sample, the larger will be the confidence level of the estimate. In case of a 100 per cent sample of the population, the confidence of the estimate will be a 100 per cent accurate. But the study of all elements of the population will be too costly and impractical. Therefore, a smaller size sample is selected for calculating the estimate. In practice, the management may decide on a 90 per cent, 95 per cent or 99 per cent confidence level. A confidence level of 95 per cent is desirable for all purposes. The remaining 5 per cent risk is acceptable. Depending on a 95 per cent confidence level, the size of the sample may be determined. In case of the mean estimate, the size of the sample is decided by the following formula:

$$\sigma\bar{x} = \frac{S}{\sqrt{n}}$$

where $\sigma\bar{x}$ is the estimate of the standard error of the mean and S is the sample standard deviation and n is the size of the sample. We have seen that $\pm 2\ \sigma x$ is the interval at 95.45 confidence level to decide a specific estimate. If we assume that we want $\pm 10\%$ of the estimate, the x would be

$$2\sigma\bar{x} = 10$$

$$\sigma\bar{x} = \frac{10}{2}$$

$$\sigma\bar{x} = 5$$

Thus if the standard deviation of the sample is 45

$$\sigma\bar{x} = \frac{S}{\sqrt{n}}$$

$$5 = \frac{45}{\sqrt{n}}$$

$$n = 81$$

But in practice, the standard deviation of the sample is unknown before selection of the sample. It is a typical case. The researcher tries to know from past studies.

3. Standard Deviation: The standard deviation of sample (s) can be estimated by the pilot study, past studies and the ranges of distribution. A pilot study may be conducted and the estimated standard deviation of the pilot sample may be used to determine the size of the sample. The previous studies already conducted may also prove to be a guideline to determine the sample size. The range of distribution with assumed standard deviation may provide a base for the calculation of standard deviation. With the interval in mind, the standard deviation may be estimated by dividing the range by 6, as practically all values at 99.7 per cent of confidence will include the mean $\pm$ 3 times the standard deviation of the population. We can illustrate this with the standard deviation of past studies. If the standard deviation (s) is assumed to be 60 and the acceptable error is estimated at $\pm$ Rs. 10, the sample size at 95 cent confidence level will be

$$\sigma x = \frac{S}{\sqrt{n}} \qquad 2\sigma\bar{x} = 10$$

$$5 = \frac{60}{\sqrt{n}} \qquad \sigma\bar{x} = \frac{10}{2} = 5$$

$$\sqrt{n} = \frac{60}{5}$$

$$n = 144$$

Thus, the sample size will include 144 units for 95 per cent confidence level with mean expenditure of $\pm$ Rs. 10.

Now, if the standard deviation of 144 units of selected sample comes to 80, the sample size will be

$$\sqrt{n} = \frac{S}{\sigma x}$$

$$\sqrt{n} = \frac{80}{5}$$

$$n = 256$$

Thus, the addition of 112 units will be a useful and appropriate sample size for the consequent researcher.

4. Sequential Sampling: The previous sampling has shown that the sampling units were drawn prior to the drawing of the actual sample and has a fixed size. But the sequential sampling known as sampling analysis differs from the previous samples in the sense that it does not make an advance determination of the sample size. In this case, the researcher obtains measurements on one unit or the population at a single time. A group of population units is also measured at a time. The measurements of each group are cumulated. With the probable error and the cumulated results, the size of the sample can be decided. If the error is too large, the study of additional groups continues until the standard error is reduced to a minimum level.

The sample size may vary according to the need of the management and standard error. It is not fixed. In testing the hypotheses, sequential sampling reduces the required sample size as compared to the fixed sampling. When the sequential sampling is applied, the survey costs may be reduced. The utility of sequential sampling in marketing is not very useful because there is need of a randomly selected sample or cross-section study. If sampling is from a heterogeneous and non-uniformity population, cross-section may be useful. No small group of sample will be sufficient. There may be need of additional groups of samples to reduce standard error which may involve more cost. By the time the next sample is taken into study, the report of the previous study may be outdated. Considering the utility of the continuing sampling, the sequential sample is utilised in the marketing study.

5. Cost: The cost factor is a very important factor in determining the size of the sample. The budget for research should be properly decided. The management may not like to exceed the sample size because of cost constraints and may remain satisfied with a lower level of confidence. For example, if the cost of sampling per unit is Rs. 20 including cost of field work, training and supervision, coding, editing, tabulation and writing the report, the management may select only 400 units if the budget or research is merely Rs. 8000. If the cost of research is more than Rs. 8000, the management may either cancel the research study or select another research approach or consider the original study approach. On the other hand if the management considers retaining the research study, it may reduce the confidence level from 99 per cent to 95 per cent and thus reduce the sample size. Thus,

$$\sigma\bar{x} = \frac{S}{\sqrt{n}}$$

where $\sigma\bar{x}$ is the standard error of the mean, s is the standard deviation of the population and n is the sample size. Here the standard error of the mean is expressed in terms of money, i.e., ± Rs. 10. If the standard deviation is 100, the factor for 95 per cent confidence is 1.96 of standard deviation. Thus, the actual size of the sample would be

$$\frac{10}{1.96} = \frac{100}{\sqrt{n}}$$

$$\sqrt{n} = \frac{196}{10}$$

$$n = 384 \text{ (Approx.)}$$

The total cost of the budget been reduced from Rs. 8000 to Rs. 7680 = (384 x 20).

Another alternative may be to increase the allowable error from a lower level to a higher level provided it does not affect the attitude of the respondents. For example, if the error is increased to 15, the sample size will be

$$\sigma\bar{x} = \frac{S}{\sqrt{n}}$$

$$\frac{15}{1.96} = \frac{100}{\sqrt{n}}$$

$$\sqrt{n} = \frac{196}{15}$$

$$n = 169 \text{ (Approx.)}$$

Thus, the total budget will be reduced from Rs. 8000 to Rs. 3380 = (169 x 20).

6. Multiple Objectives: The sample size may vary according to the objectives of the research. There may be several objectives of marketing research. So, the sample size may vary as per distinctive objectives. Apart from these objectives, statistical variables are also taken into consideration, viz., confidence level, desired precision, estimated standard deviation and so on. These may also affect the sample size.

2. DETERMINING SAMPLE SIZE FOR ESTIMATING PROPORTIONS

It is also necessary to determine the sample size for a problem involving proportions. This deals with the percentage of frequency of occurrence. The standard deviation is computed considering the proportions of the happening of a particular event. If the frequency of occurrence is known as p and the frequency of non-occurrence is known as 1, the standard deviation of the proportion may be

$$\sigma p = \sqrt{\frac{pq}{n}}$$

The sample size is determined as discussed earlier. The precision and population size have been the deciding factors for determining the sample size. The precision can again be expressed absolutely or relatively. Absolute precision involves that the estimate will be within plus or minus of the true value, i.e. ±5 percentage points of the true value. If the sample elements are selected independently and if the sample size is small, the correct distribution of the sample proportion will be binomial. It is convenient to employ the normal approximation for estimating the sample size. After the sample is drawn and the sample proportion determined, the researcher determines the confidence interval. One observes that the distribution of sample proportions is centered about the population proportion. The level of precision is equal to the number of standard deviations of the population proportion. The standard deviation is the standard error of the proportion.

1. Absolute Precision: The sample size is decided with the formula as noted above. For example, if frequency of occurrence, i.e., p is 60 and the confidence level is 95 per cent. If the allowable error is 2% in estimating the population proportion; the sample size will be calculated as

$$\frac{0.02}{1.96} = \sqrt{\frac{.60 \times .40}{n}}$$

$$\sqrt{n} = \sqrt{\frac{.60 \times .40 \times 1.96}{0.02}}$$

$$n = 2308 \text{ (Approx.)}$$

2. Relative Precision: The sample size may increase with a higher precision. This has been the case of absolute precision. Similarly, the sample size may be decided on the basis of relative precision. A population proportion can be estimated on a specification of the relative precision estimated. Relative precision means that the size of the interval will be a function of the value, i.e., within a certain per cent of the value regardless of the confidence level. If the relative precision is to be specified within ± 10 per cent, it means that if the proportion is 20, the interval will be .20 ± 10%, i.e., 0.18 to 0.22. The formula of relative precision is

$$rp = s\sigma p$$

where r is the specified relative precision, p is the probability of the occurrence, s is standard deviation of the mean and p is the standard error of the population. Thus

$$rp = s\sqrt{\frac{p\,(1-p)}{n}}$$

Substituting the value of σp

$$n = \frac{s^2}{r^2}\left(\frac{1-p}{p}\right)$$

For example, if the population proportion is 0.2, the level of confidence at 95 per cent is 1.96, the desired level of relative precision r = 0.10; the sample size will be

$$n = \frac{(1.96)^2\,(.8)}{(.10)^2\,(0.2)} = 1600 \text{ (Approx.)}$$

3. Population Size: In discussing the sample size we have ignored the population size. Ignoring the size of the population will be a significant factor if the population is very large. The nearer the sample size to the population size, the lesser the sampling error. The sample size based on population size is not very significant if the population units are exactly of the same value of their characteristics. For example, if the value of a unit is the same or almost the same, then it would be immaterial to select 1,000 or 10,000 out of 1 lakh population units. It is very important to note that the size of the sample is affected by the variability of the characteristics of the population. The more variable the characteristics, the larger the sample needed to estimate it with some specified level of precision. Thus the population size may affect the sample size indirectly on account of variability. The larger the population, the greater the scope of variation in the characteristic. Although a rule of thumb of 5 per cent of the population elements are considered for the sample size, there is not much reliability about this. The following formulae have been used to estimate the sample size on the basis of population size.

$$n = \frac{NZ^2(pq)}{NT^2 + Z^2(pq)}$$

Where

n = adjusted sample size

Z = Level of confidence

T = Allowable tolerance of variation

N = Population size

P = Probability of occurring the event

q = Probability of non-occurring the event

Suppose: Population units = 1000

Level of confidence at 95 per cent = 1.96

Allowable tolerance of variation = 0.05

Probability of occurring the event = 0.60

Probability of non-occurring the event = 0.40

Substituting the values, the sample size will be

$$n = \frac{1000\,(1.96)^2\,(0.60 \times 0.40)}{1000\,(0.05)^2 + (1.96)^2\,(0.60 \times 0.40)}$$

$$= \frac{921.984}{5 + .921984}$$

$$= \frac{921.984}{1.421984}$$

$$= 648 \text{ (Approx.)}$$

3. STRATIFIED SAMPLE SIZE

The sampling study has depended much on the stratified sample to reduce the sampling error. Sample size may have a number of strata or clusters. The researcher will have to deal within strata variability, and within and between cluster variability in calculating the sample size. Since allocation of the population members into strata confines each subsample's variance within the range of values in each stratum, the sampling error is reduced to a very nominal level. The standard error has a determining affect on the sample size. The stratified sample size may be proportional or disproportional. While one stratum may contain 0.05% of the population size, the other may contain 0.08%, 0.10% and so on. The percentage may vary as per requirements and situations. In case of stratified sampling, only the size of the stratum is used as a guide for allocating the total sample. The size of stratified sampling may be calculated as below:

$$n_i = \frac{N_i}{N} - n$$

Where

ni = Number of sample units from Stratum i

Ni = Total number of units in the stratum i

N = Total number of units in the Population

n = Sample size desired

The advantage of proportional allocation is that it leads to an estimate which is computationally simple. For calculating the weighted estimates, the weighted calculation of each stratum is totalled. Thus, standard deviation of all the

$$\sigma\bar{x}st = \sqrt{\sum_{i=1}^{k} W_i^2 \frac{\sigma i^2}{ni}}$$

Where

$$Wi = \text{Weight of Stratum } i = \frac{Ni}{N}$$

σi = Standard Deviation of the i stratum

k = Total number of strata

The disproportional stratified sample may be a more desirable method if the standard deviation of the observation in each stratum is known. Thus, the standard deviation of the mean of a disproportionate stratified sample

$$\sigma = \sigma\sqrt{\frac{(W\sigma)^2}{n}}$$

The cost per observation did not enter into the formula for calculating the sample size although cost exerts a direct impact. If the cost per observation or variability is not the same for each stratum, there is need of determining sample size by considering the precision. Cost per observation by subgroup is considered for calculation of sample size.

4. SAMPLE SIZE IN NON-PROBABILITY

Beside the probability selection, non-probability selection is also taken into account. The probability selection does not apply to purposive selection. The size of the non-probability sample is selected in a subjective manner. The researcher selects a size because he feels that the size will be appropriate and the response pattern will be formed. In many studies, the financial factor is the single factor to decide the sample size based on non-probability judgement. In the quota sample, some criteria are taken into account for deciding the sample size. In many theories of non-probability sampling, the researcher considers the statistical significance, sampling error, method of sample selection, representation of sampling and other factors. The researchers should base their sampling size in relation to the statistical significance of the findings.

5. OTHER DETERMINANTS OF SAMPLE SIZE

The probability and non-probability sample size may be decided by some other method. The variability of elements within the population has become a very important factor to decide the sample size. The more variable the strata or cluster, the larger the sample taken from the population. The research budget and cost per unit of researcher are very important factors in all sorts of probability and non-probability samples to decide the sample size. Cost exerts a direct impact on the stratified or cluster samples. Unequal costs per observation by strata or by cluster are also taken into consideration for deciding the sample size. The researcher, therefore, makes an initial estimate of the cost. The precision is also taken account of besides the cost and variability to determine the sample size. The tolerable error, variance of stratum, confidence level etc. are also considered to decide the sample size. The respondents' attitude may also influence the sample size. In case of mail surveys some respondents may not reply. Although there are several ways and means to increase the response rate, some questionnaires may remain unattended by the respondents. Thus, the sample size may be restricted with the willingness of the respondents to respond to the questionnaire. In this case, it is clear that the sample size may increase if the researcher takes greater initiative to increase the response rate. He may adopt modern techniques of handling questionnaires, sending postal surveys and approach the respondents with monetary incentives, non-sensitive issues, and so on. The response may increase if the prequestionnaire letter, questionnaire with cover letter and follow up letter are sent from time to time. Even if the questionnaire is unattended, a second questionnaire and a third follow up letter may be sent to the respondents. These attempts will increase the sample size.

❖ ❖ ❖

CHAPTER 11

DATA COLLECTION AND FIELD FORCE

1. TASK AND FUNCTIONS IN DATA COLLECTION
2. ERROR SOURCES
   1. NON-SAMPLING ERRORS
      - (A) NON-OBSERVATION ERRORS
        - (i) NON-COVERAGE
        - (ii) NON-RESPONSE
      - (B) OBSERVATION ERRORS
        - (i) FIELD DATA COLLECTION ERRORS
        - (ii) OFFICE PROCESSING ERRORS
3. SAMPLING ERRORS
4. MANAGING THE FIELD WORK
   1. SELECTION
   2. TRAINING
   3. SUPERVISION
   4. CONTROLLING
   5. EVALUATING

DATA COLLECTION AND FIELD FORCE

The research design, methods of data collection, preparation of questionnaire and administering the questionnaire, sample design and sample size have been discussed in previous chapters. The data collection after application of these methods may not give accurate results unless the field force works properly. The research directors may develop their own organisations or can contract with a field work agency to do the job. The field work may involve the selection, training, supervision, control and evaluation of their job. A successful gathering of field data depends both on the thoroughness of the plans and faithful execution of the plans. Data collection and other activities involved in preparation of the questionnaire may cause errors. Therefore, at the data collection stage, there should be at least two primary objectives, viz., maximising the relevant information, and minimizing errors within the given constraints of time, money and environment.

1. TASKS AND FUNCTIONS IN DATA COLLECTION

There may be several means of data collection, viz., observation, personal interviewing, telephone interviewing and mail survey. These techniques may be properly utilised for collection of data.

1. Observation

The observation method deals with obtaining information that is already recorded or dealt with objects. Field force can obtain data for the said objective. The effort, time and cost of collecting these data may be high, but the data may be more accurate and relevant to the objective. The accuracy of data also depends on the observers' capacity which may perceive and record people's behaviour properly. The observer has to record the behaviour of the respondents and record the data for research purposes. Instruction, training and supervision have a great effect on the observation. Therefore the selection, training and supervision of the field force are very important functions of marketing research.

2. Personal Interview

The personal interview obtains a greater range of data although it is more expensive and time consuming. The errors arising on account of personal interviewing may be minimised by sampling the designated areas or locations, administering the questionnaire strictly according to instructions, recording the responses precisely, properly processing and editing of data and completing the field work within the budgeted time and money. The interview should be conducted after establishing sufficient rapport or level of understanding with the respondents. Interviewing involves stimuli and deeper understanding of the problems. The interviewer has to interpret and collect the information as per the objectives. The information differs from interviewer to interviewer. The interviewer, therefore, has to be very apt and experienced to collect adequate and proper information from the respondents. Where proving the information is needed, great reliance is placed on the interviewer's intelligence. The experienced and intelligent interviewer may reduce the non-sampling errors to a greater extent. The interviewing technique, therefore, has much impact on the validity and reliability of data.

3. Telephone Interviewing

Telephone interviewing may not have many field errors. The respondents can be easily met and the interview speeded up. It is also less costly. The rapport with the respondents is developed unseen. The interviewer should keep the interview moving slowly and steadily. The interviewer can avoid errors if he is experienced and talented.

4. Mail Surveys

Mail surveys though easy to handle suffer from various impersonal defects. The chances of field errors are extremely high because the questionnaire is filled without proper guidance and personal assistance. The mail surveys are handled with precaution and wide coverage.

2. ERROR SOURCES

We have noted that the research should be conducted to achieve the objects of research with a minimum of errors. Potential errors should be avoided to the possible extent. The sources of error may be broadly divided into two categories, i.e., Non-sampling Errors and Sampling Errors.

1. Non-sampling Errors

We have discussed sampling errors in detail in the previous chapter. The sampling distribution arises because of sampling errors. The sampling error can be reduced by increasing the sample size. Non-sampling errors consist of many kinds of errors that may arise in research. The survey may be a sample or universe. Non-sampling errors do no mean that these are related with universe study only, but they may arise in case of sampling study also because the non-sampling errors are incurred on account of the research process. The errors may be random or non-random. Random errors produce estimates which may vary from the time value. Non-random and non-sampling errors may produce more mistakes. They tend to bias the sample value beyond the population parameter. Non-sampling errors occur because of errors in the research process, viz., defining the problems, collection of data, tabulation and interpretation of data. They may also arise because of the inexperience of the field force conducting the research.

The behaviour of non-sampling errors is unpredictable. One can know about the sampling error but cannot rely upon the trend of the non-sampling error. Sampling errors may decline with the increase of the sample size but non-sampling errors may not decrease with the increase of the sample size. It has been observed that the non-sampling errors may increase with the increase of the sample size. The direction of the sampling error can be estimated if the probability sampling is applied, but the direction of non-sampling errors cannot be estimated. The non-sampling errors may distort the reliability of sample estimates because of improper use of statistical tools. The confidence interval therefore, will be faulty. Non-sampling errors are not simply a matter of theory but they exist in almost all sorts of researches. It is not possible to eliminate them altogether even though more sophisticated samples are used. Since non-sampling errors are unaffected by the sample size, the increase in the sample size may not reduce the non-sampling errors. It is observed that increasing the sample size reduces the sampling errors but increases the non-sampling errors and ultimately the confidence intervals may be redundant. Therefore, a proper balance should be maintained between the sample size and non-sampling errors; the non-sampling errors can be reduced by application of appropriate tools and techniques of research. The researchers with knowledge and experience can also reduce the non-sampling errors.

Types of Non-sampling Errors

There are two basic types of non-sampling errors, viz., non-observation and observation errors.

(a) Non-observation Errors

Non-observation errors result from a failure to obtain data from parts of population units. They may be incurred because part of the population of interest is not included, or some of the respondents have not responded. The non-observation errors may be of two types: *(i)* non-coverage errors and *(ii)* non-response errors.

(i) Non-coverage Errors: Non-coverage indicates failure to include some units or entire sections of the defined population. They are excluded because of zero probability and not on account of a deliberate attempt. Deliberate and explicit exclusion of sections of the larger population from the survey population is not discussed in the present category of non-observation. Actually they are among the field of observation errors. Survey objectives and practical difficulties determine the deliberate exclusions. Some units may be excluded because of practical survey difficulties. In this case, while calculating the non-coverage rates, members deliberately and explicitly excluded from the sample should not be counted in the survey populations.

Non-coverage is a problem which occurs on account of some difficulties. For example, in a telephone survey, only persons having telephones are contacted to reply to the questions. Non-coverage is also a problem in mail surveys if the mailing list is inadequate. There is also a chance of non-coverage in the case of personal interview because the map may be old and may not reveal all the areas, block and villages. The interviewer may select the most accessible sampling units contrary to random selection. This means a portion of the intended population is unrepresented while the easily accessible population is over represented.

The interviewer's attitude to selecting a particular population can cause non-coverage errors. The interviewer may select persons having high income and low income with certain unknown bias. In case of a quota sample, this problem becomes more complex and elaborate. The interviewer may find it difficult to locate respondents who have the prescribed characteristics.

Errors may also arise on account of duplication in the list of sampling units. This is called an overcoverage error. Units having multiple entries in the sampling frame have a higher chance of being included in the sample. There may be some errors for distinguishing active purchasing and inactive purchasers. Non-coverage errors may also occur on account of non-existence of clear, convenient and complete sampling.

Non-coverage error poses two problems, viz., to find out its magnitude and the methods of reducing it. The magnitude of non-coverage can be estimated with certain criteria. The criterion can be established through an auxiliary quality check of the results, or some reliable and current studies. The population census may also be used to check the magnitude. The second problem of reducing the non-coverage error can be solved by improving the quality of the sampling frame. Consulting the latest map and checking the quality and representativeness of a mailing list are the important methods of reducing the magnitude of the non-coverage error. The most important method is through the selection of sampling units and adjustment of the results. The sampling and adjustment method are quite technical and fall largely in the domain of the sampling specialist. Since non-coverage bias or error is a non-sampling error, it cannot be dealt with life a formula-like standard error, an increasing sample size and so on. It cannot be totally eliminated but can be reduced by improving the sampling frame and employing a sampling specialist to help reduce the non-coverage errors through the sampling procedure and adjust through analysis and interpretation.

(ii) Non-response Errors: Non-response error represents a failure to obtain information from elements of population selected for study. The respondents have not replied to the questions for several reasons. It is different from the non-coverage error because the covered respondents have not replied. Non-covered respondents are not within the purview of the non-response errors. The distribution of opinions on the subject may be different for the respondents than for the non-respondents. The distribution of returns by socio-economic groups differs from the population. It is very difficult to know before administering the questions who will respond and who will not respond. Non-response error can arise with studies employing personal interviews, and with varying degrees or mail surveys. The non-response errors may occur on account of not being at home, refusals and incompetence of the researcher.

(a) Not-at-Home: The interviewer may not meet the respondents at the place of interview because the respondents do not remain at the place. Generally the interviewer visits the home of the respondents to record the answers, but if they are not available there, the interviewer cannot get the response. The percentage of those not at home depends upon the nature of the designated respondent and the time of the interview. Married women with young children are generally found to be at home. Single persons are generally "not-at-home" during daytime. It is easier to find a responsible adult at home. Efforts are made to reduce the incidence of those "not-at-home." The interviewer should make an appointment in advance. This should be adhered to with the executives because they are busy persons. The non-response problem owing to those "not-at-home" is acute. Small samples with four to six callback are more efficient than large samples without callback. If the first callback is not met with respondents, the interviewer may leave a self-administered questionnaire with a self-addressed stamped envelope. The interviewer can note the time when the respondents will be available at home. He can visit the respondents when they are present at home. The interviewer should record the time and data when the designated sample member will be available at home. The sample-members can be grouped according to the estimated amount of time they are at home. The estimates may be unbiased and the variance of the estimate can be obtained.

The "not-at-home" problem can be avoided by approaching the neighbour's house in case the designated member is absent. In the telephone survey the next name in the telephone directory may be called upon for questioning. The proportion of reported "not-at-home" is likely to depend on the interviewer and the judgement he uses in scheduling the callbacks. The interviewing training and techniques may reduce the errors of "not-at-home." The effectiveness of the interviewer to contact "at home" respondents can be measured by the proportion of the number of sample units contacted to the total number of sample units approached. This measures the interviewer's persistence. This requires additional training on the part of the interviewers to reduce errors.

(b) Refusals: The refusals refer to those respondents who do not respond to the interviewer's calls. The rate of refusals will depend on the nature of the respondents, the acceptability of the research, and the situations and time of contact. The refusal problem is acute in the case of mail surveys because of the non-response bias and non-receipt problem. Those respondents who do not respond to the mail survey are approached personally. It has been observed that the respondents differ from non-respondents in respect of socio-economic characteristic such as education, income, culture, mental status, age, occupation etc. Educated people generally reply to the questionnaire. Similarly adults and professionals reply to the questionnaire. The impact of refusals is demonstrated in the form of systematic bias which can be predicted by experienced interviewer.

The auspices of research may also influence the refusal rate. The respondents may react differently to different research agencies. If the respondents are contacted when they are busy, tired or sick, the refusal rates may be very high. The subject of the research has some impact on the refusal rate. Persons interested in the subject may respond at a higher speed than the persons not interested in the subject. In case of an opinion survey, persons at a distance may cooperate easily. The non-response errors are sensitively related to the information. The socio-economic characteristics of the interviewer also affect the refusal rate. It has been observed that the refusal rate can be minimised through follow up steps.

(c) Increasing Initial Response Rate: The nature and attitude of the respondents may be beyond the control of the interviewer. The target population or sample may contain different education levels, cultural and occupational backgrounds and income levels. The interviewer and respondents' behavioural relationship may influence an error. The respondents' cooperation can be sought with the interviewer by stating the value of the research and the importance of their participation. The interviewer can be trained to approach the respondents with dedication to obtain information from them. If the respondents do not cooperate on account of secrecy, they should be told that their names would be kept confidential. If the interviewers are motivated, they can devote much time and energy for collecting the data. If the non-response is biased owing to the sponsor's names, the respondents should not be told the name of the sponsor.

(d) Follow-up: The non-response errors are mainly due to flexible and temporary reasons which can be reduced by follow up actions. If the non-response bias is on account of business and the sickness of all the respondents, the interviewer may approach them at a different time when the respondents are free from problems. In a mail survey, the follow up letters may be sent to them. The training and motivation of the field staff can reduce the non-response errors, particular in the case of sensitive research. They will diagnose the non-response error and reduce the source of refusals. If the respondents do not return the first questionnaire, the second and third follow up letters may be sent to them.

(e) Adjusting the Results: Even if after follow up and other techniques the non-response errors are not minimised, the results may be adjusted. The problem of non-responses may be adjusted by segregating the results of respondents from non-respondents. For example, if the mean of the respondents is x_r and that of non-respondents is $\overline{x}_{nr}$ and their respective numbers are p_r and p_{nr}; the mean of the universe (p) can be calculated as below:

$$x = \frac{p_r \overline{x}_r + p_{nr} \overline{x}_{nr}}{p}$$

The crude adjustment of the initial results may be arrived at by inflating the result of the responded units. The differences between estimates before follow up, estimates after first follow up and estimates after second follow up are calculated to find out the impact of the follow ups. If there is no significant difference between these estimates, the estimate of the original study may be accepted for research purposes. If there is a significant difference, the original estimate is adjusted accordingly. The original result may be extrapolated to include the non-respondents.

The past studies may be used as a guidance to adjust the non-response results. This procedure may be suited to similar studies. Sometimes, non-response may be due to unawareness of the answers. The interviewer may set a limit of how to respond to the questions. In case of sensitive questions which may embarrass the respondents, the randomised response model may be selected. This model includes one of several paired from questions which one pair is selected at random to be asked from the respondents. When a few questions are unanswered the reply becomes usable with reference to other answers of the questions.

(b) Observation Errors

Observation errors occur because of inaccurate information, errors in collection of data, errors in processing of data, and errors in the analysis and interpretation of data. These errors are more difficult to reveal and remove than the non-observation errors. The researcher may not be aware of the observation errors. The observation error may simply be the difference between the reported value and the true value. The detection of an observation error places the researcher in an awkward position because the error occurs owing to this inefficiency. The observation errors are of two types: Field errors and Office errors.

(i) Field Errors: The field errors occur on account of the behaviour of field workers. These errors may be due to difficulties and weaknesses in the survey procedures, collection of data and behaviour of the researcher. The interviewer's and respondents' behaviour actions and reactions may influence the field errors. Their characteristics, psychological factors and behavioural factors are important instruments in influencing field errors. The background characteristics of the interviewer and respondents are age, education, socio-economic status, race, religion, culture, tradition etc. Similarly the psychological factors influencing the field errors may be perceptions, attitudes, expectations and motives of the interviewer and respondents. Behavioural factors may cause errors in asking questions, in proving, in motivating and in recording responses by the interviewer and respondents. The perception and attitude are a predisposition to behaviour. The behaviour of the interviewer and respondents decides the success or failure of the interview. During the interview process, the interviewer gets some cues from the respondents on which he can base his interview. The interaction pattern of the interview deserves special mention. The inter-connections of various background characteristics and psychological factors influence the behavioural factors. Their linkage creates complex behaviours of the interviewer and respondents. Their perception, attitude and motivation may be utilised to achieve success in the interview-technique.

The psychological factors of perceptions, attitudes, expectations and motivations of the respondents cannot be perceived directly but can be referred to as having been perceived in behaviour. The perceived behaviour is also influenced by the background characteristics such as age, income, the socio-economic level and so on. But they may cause erroneous inferences. Respondents and interviewer make such inferences as assist them to understand each other. The "interviewer-interviewee interaction" may offer valuable insight on how response errors can be potentially reduced. This model may also be applicable to mail surveys and telephone interview. The background factors, psychological factors and behavioural factors are the main causes of field errors which are discussed in detail.

(a) Background Factors: The background factors such as age, sex, colour, caste, education, socio-economic status, race, religion etc. affect the responses significantly. The previous researches have shown that diverse-caste interviewers obtain more information. The working class and middle class can secure more information than their counterparts. Young interviewers and female interviewers are apt to get more information. Similarly respondents of different background characteristics may have better chances of collection of data. Apart from the background characteristics, the interview-technique may also influence the interview-results. Since the interviewer's background influences the result, he should try to minimise the bias. This requires proper selection, training and motivation of the field force.

(b) Psychological Factors: The psychological factors such as the perception, attitudes, expectations and motives of the interviewer and respondents affect the response rate. If the interviewer is asking such questions and such moods are welcomed by respondents, he can secure more answers from the respondents. The interviewer's psychological factors can influence the response bias to a large extent. The psychological behaviour of the interviewer is conditioned by the background factors. The background factors may be sorted out by proper selection and recruitment methods of appointing the interviewer. The psychological factors can be avoided by proper training. A well trained interviewer will contain these psychological factors, and avoid their influence on the respondents' behaviour and also on the final result. The interviewer should be trained to ask the questions in such a way that the answers are given in unbiased manner. The instructions to the interviewer should be given in a clear and unambiguous form. The interviewer should finally check up the questionnaire and answers given by the respondents.

(c) Behavioural Factors: The behavioural factors such as errors in motivation, in recording responses etc. may cause both adequate and inadequate responses, as well as accurate and inaccurate responses. When the questionnaires are simple and structured, the interviewer may follow the rules. The interviewer has plenty of opportunity to compromise sampling instructions, to reword questions, and to record the responses, in his own manner. Errors in asking questions, errors in recording questions, and errors due to cheating are important errors on the part of the interviewer. The errors in asking questions may be acute in case of open ended questions. The probing may also cause errors. The content and timing of the probes may differ. The difference in answers may be due to different probing method. The initial questions and rewording of the questions may influence the response. When there are alternative responses to a question, the interviewer's bias may influence the result.

The interviewer has to see that the respondents are motivated and kept interested to answer. The incompatible and irresponsible interviewer may cause some errors. The interviewer may derive the answer through cheating. The errors checked with the respondents may reveal the cheating. The chances of cheating are high in case of key questions and filling the answer at a later stage, in a group interview, inaccessible respondents and a contaminated atmosphere. If the interviewers are dishonest and are interested in higher wages, they may inflate the figure of the respondents without contacting them. The fictional names may be completed with wrong information. The training and motivation of interviewers may reduce the field errors.

Minimising Fieldwork Errors

There are some important measures which can minimise the fieldwork errors, namely, proper selection and training of fieldworkers, cost control and evaluation of the interviewers. The selection, training and supervision of fieldworkers are discussed in the next sections. In the present section we shall discuss administrative control, quality and cost control and evaluation of interviewers.

(i) Administrative Control: The administrative control is related to the date and quotas of starting and completions of field work. The list of materials is prepared before despatch by the fieldworkers to the respondents. The daily work of field-survey is reported to the supervisor or the central command office. The time taken and work performed by each and every field worker will provide a platform for comparison. Thus, the slow field worker can be identified and motivated to speed up his work. Mistakes can be corrected because the interviewer can know the problem and difficulties before they become serious.

(ii) Quality and Cost Control: The quality and cost may be controlled by the supervisor. In many research organisations, supervisors play an important role in conducting the appropriate research. The central office or the representatives of the central office may have adequate control on the field work. The local supervisor may contact the field workers. He has close contact with the interviewers. The supervisor can keep daily records of calls not at home, the number of refusals and completed interviews by the interviewers. The cost per call can also be estimated in this way. The supervisor can also control quality and detect cheating.

(iii) Evaluation of interviewers: The interviewers' activities are evaluated to find out the efficient interviewers, and to build, gradually, a better field force. If any interviewer is found falsifying questionnaires, he may be dropped immediately. The causes of drawbacks in the interview should be revealed immediately so that they can be improved for further interviews. The questions may be embarrassing or awkward, the instructions may be unclear and ambiguous, and the situations may demoralise the interviewers. Export interviewers with sample interviews can improve the results. The interviewers can be rated on several grounds such as cost, refusals and for following instructions.

Total cost per completed interview is the basis for comparison of the interviewers. Interviewers working in similar conditions can be compared. The cost may vary as per coverage by different interviewers in cities, suburban and rural areas. The percentage of refusals can be compared among interviewers. The interviewers may be graded on the basis of mistakes made by each of them. The unsatisfactory answer, ambiguous answer may be better than non-response. The interviewer's individual record may be used for comparison and evaluation of his activities.

(iv) Office Errors: These errors are related not only with the collection of data, but they may occur in relation to the editing, coding, tabulation, analysis and interpretation of data. These errors can be reduced to a considerable extent with proper analysis and interpretation. The office errors have been discussed in the chapter concerned with the analysis and interpretation of data. The background factors and psychological factors have a significant influence on the office errors.

3. SAMPLING ERRORS

Sampling errors have the difference between the observed values of a variable and the long run average of the observed values in repetitions of the measurement. The sampling error reflects the fact that the different possible samples will produce different estimates of the parameter. The sampling error can be reduced by increasing the sample size. It has been discussed in detail in previous chapters.

4. MANAGING THE FIELD WORK

Management of the field force can play a significant role in marketing research. It can reduce not only the errors but can help the successful achievement of the objectives. The importance of effective management of the field force becomes great when a large number of consumers with varied tastes, attitudes and interests are to be interviewed. Managing the field work involves selection, training, supervision, controlling and evaluating.

1. Selection of Staff

Job specifications of the research project are prepared before selection of the staff. The specifications will decide what type of field worker will be able to meet the job requirements. Since data are to be collected at different places, interviewers from the respective localities should be appointed to match the specific needs of the interview. Qualified interviewers should be selected for the purpose.

Job Specification: The interviewers' job require proper handling of job conduct, job skills and initiative. Since the interviewers have to interact with people having varied backgrounds and psychological behaviours, they have to be well versed in conduct. They should be fully skilled for conducting the interview. They must know how to file the entries and analyse the information. The interviewer should have the ability and willingness to follow instructions and policy. The initiative of the workers will inspire the field force to work without frustration. They will acquire personal motives to derive adequate information, and analyse this for the benefit of the marketing management.

Qualifications and Experience: Qualification and experience are considered for recruitment of the staff for field work. These qualifications may be age, education experience, acquired knowledge, aptitudes, intelligence and so on. Age is used as an index of health and vigour. Experience and educational qualifications provide the base for successful completion of the job. Acquired knowledge reveals the candidates' capacity to take up the challenge. The aptitude and interest of the candidate must be evaluated before appointment because these factors are essential for dealing with human-behaviour. Positive attitudes and interest may be required to conduct the job successfully. Adventure, reflective thinking, clean environment and clear understanding are the various factors necessary to evaluate the interest and aptitude of the field workers. The field force should possess some basic qualifications and interest such as physical fitness, attentiveness, persistence, endurance, self-reliance, gregariousness, benevolence and so on. The temperamental characteristics of the interviewers must be known to the appointing authorities so that they may seek these tenets in a candidate and select the most suitable candidates for the field work. The temperamental features may be dominance, self-confidence, calmness, composure and poise, cheerfulness, emotion, agreeable outlook, cooperative behaviour and tolerance. They must also possess decision-making ability, executive ability, fine personal characteristics, divergent new views, flexibility, reliability, responsibility, adjustability and organisational and technical knowledge pertaining to research and interviewing.

Suitable Personnel: The selection of suitable staff is essential for the purpose of marketing research. The staff may consist of science and commerce and engineering graduates. The computer operators and programmers may be more suitable persons for research purposes because they have knowledge of mathematics, the ability of visualisation and quantitative reasoning, and the capacity to deduce, have an imaginative approach and mechanical capabilities. The sociologists and psychologists may be suitable for conducting interviews. Commerce graduates may be necessary for office work such as typing, secretarial work, telephone operators and other clerical jobs. Similarly supervisors selected must be competent enough to supervise the job of interviewing. They should also possess technical competence, leadership qualities, power of expression and understanding, persuasiveness and judgement.

Selection Procedure: Selection procedure consists of defining management philosophy and company objectives, also selection standards and tools. There are different selection methods for obtaining the information necessary to make a relevant judgement for appointments. The biographical questionnaire must be obtained to know the education, experience, age and other background factors. The written test, interview and psychological test are applied to evaluate candidates for suitable jobs. The tests may be conducted to examine whether the candidates are aware of sample design, sample techniques, interviewing techniques and so on. Suitable tests may reveal the appropriate persons for undertaking marketing research.

2. Training

After the selection and appointment of interviewers, training to meet the research challenges is very essential. They have to deal with the socio-psychological factors and may face rebuff and frustration at several points. Training will motivate and inspire them for taking up the job as a more challenging and interesting responsibility. Although the selection is made on a scientific basis, training becomes essential for practical learning of the job. The basic aptitude and qualities may be properly utilised with training. The interviewers are given practical insights into field work concepts, and can attain the objectives of the interviewing with necessary attitudes and motivations. The training includes a discussion of the various kinds of questionnaire and their layout and instructions. It may be a package programme consisting of written instructions on how to locate and approach respondents to establish rapport, to ask questions and to obtain and record accurate answers. It reveals the length of time required to execute the field plan, to conduct the field work and meet the unexpected problems.

Training Programme

The training programme of the interviewer may consist of developing the questionnaire, training place, demonstration, case method and practicing the interview. The training programme starts with the development of the questionnaire wherein cumbersome and complex questions are eliminated. The training place is decided so that the interviewer can very well understand the training procedure. The instructor demonstrates the interviewing technique. He performs the interview-activities and then asks the trainees to perform the job. The cases of interviewing are discussed mutually and the techniques of interviewing are explained to the trainees. After theoretical discussions and practical demonstration, the trainees are asked to undertake the interview. If any mistakes occur there, the instructor tries to remove them. The training programme discusses the entire job of the interviewer. Location of the respondent, introducing and establishing rapport, asking questions, obtaining adequate information and processing and analysing the collected data, are the various functions of interviewers which are explained to the trainees for the efficient performance of the interviewing. The interviewers are told how to introduce themselves and how to establish rapport. The leading questions are framed and formulated for the interviewers. The interviewers are trained how to ask questions and obtain adequate information.

The pretesting of the questionnaire, simplifying the interview procedures and instructing field workers should be included in the training programme. An adequate pretest is essential for conducting the full study. The pretest will reveal whether the interviewers would understand and respond to the questionnaire and whether the interviewers can administer it. The nature of the information to be collected including categories of answers, problems to be encountered, sample segments, the time required and problems involved in organising the field force are the various factors which are pretested before pertaining to the final interview. The pretest will reveal the planning errors, interviewers' mistakes, procedural defects, non-proper sequence, awkward expressions, leading questions and weak stimulation. During the course of the training interviewers can understand these factors and try to avoid them.

The trainees should be told how to simplify field work. They should be told about multiple choice questions and desired categories of response. They are told various ways of improving the design and legibility of questionnaires. The instructional materials should in good times be handed over to the trainee-interviewer. Instructions should be given in clear and distinct terms. The instructions involve time, schedule of survey, persons to be employed, respondents to be interviewed, the technique of introducing and developing rapport, methods of asking questions, and probing and encouraging responses. How the questionnaire is to be studied and completed, and determination of the quality of the interview should be explained to the trainees. The trainees are also told how to reduce errors and biases. Mailed train, i.e., sending instructions by post is not a very effective method of training. Personal training has become an important tool of the training process. Primary training, both in job training and advanced training should be adopted to make the interviewers more competent in conducting market research.

3. Supervision

The interviewers generally face various problems and disappointments. They require constant supervision and motivation. They have to maintain a certain uniform standard of work and avoid differences. The supervisor should be appointed to work at the spot. He should work with the interviewers. He should assist the interviewers for mapping, prelisting addresses and conducting the interview. He may appoint a local interviewer for getting information. The supervisor should maintain regular contact with interviewers and try to help them from time to time.

4. Controlling

There are numerous functions in interviewing and survey work to be performed by the interviewers. They require proper control and supervision. They should be carefully scanned to determine their success and failure. The controlling techniques may be of two types: scheduling and validating. The scheduling must be initiated in advance wherein appointing the dates for interviewing, coordinating activities and finalisation of work are mentioned. The time and cost are decided while preparing the schedule. Validation refers to verifying whether the interviewers are submitting authentic interviews. The supervisor or the office staff should determine whether instructions are studied and understood, and the reported interviews are genuine. He has to appraise the quality of the interviewing and report. The cheating can be reduced through checks by the supervisor or by preparation of the response cards or by close scrutiny of interviews. The interviewers should be told that their work will be evaluated and graded. This will create a sense of responsibility and proper working by the interviewers.

5. Evaluating

The evaluation work is done by the supervisor in the field and by the executives in the office. Since the majority of the interviews are conducted without the supervisor, the completed questionnaires are checked. Occasional checking by the interviewers will ensure proper working and detection of cheating. Another interviewer is sent to the respondent's home to check whether the interview was carried out or not. The completed questionnaire may be used for rating the interviewer. He may be evaluated on cost, non-response to errors and instructions followed. The call back method may be more useful for evaluation of work. This involves the supervisor's checks of each interviewer on a sample basis. The respondents should not be aware that the interviewers are being checked; because this will create doubts in the minds of the respondents and they may not cooperate with the research work.

❖ ❖ ❖

CHAPTER 12

PROCESSING OF DATA

1. PREPARING RAW DATA
2. EDITING
3. CODING
4. TABULATION
5. SUMMARY OF DATA

PROCESSING OF DATA

The processing of data is a significant function of marketing research. After collection of data, the researcher turns his focus of attention on their analysis and interpretation. The analysis of data involves processing of data, examination of differences, investigation of associations and measuring associations. The purpose of analysis is to see the data in the light of hypothesis and prevailing theories to draw conclusions. The task of analysis is to get appropriate combinations of data and reading them in the light of verification and falsification of hypothesis. The analysis and interpretation of data are performed together. It is very difficult to draw a line between them. Analysis of data involves organising data in a particular manner, and interpretation governs the ideas of analysis. Interpretation is the method for deriving conclusions from the data analysed. Analysis of data is not complete unless interpreted. Interpretation is inextricably interwoven with analysis. It is a special aspect of analysis rather than a distinct operation. This is a particular research operation which brings to light the broader findings or conclusions of the research process.

The processing of data involves preparing raw data, editing, coding, tabulation and preparing a summary of the data.

1. PREPARING RAW DATA

The collection of data may be a significant part of marketing research, but more significant is weeding out the relevant data from the mass of the data. Unless the data collected are processed, they will be of no use to the researcher. The data collected are in raw form unless they have been processed and analysed. A set of procedures is established to maintain accurate and reliable information. Editing and coding individual questionnaires, establishing categories into different responses, tabulation and such other factors may be planned in the processing of data. The data of all questionnaires are recorded on a single questionnaire to reveal the total form of information and data. If the form is a panel diary, the panelist records the responses. In the case of observation study, the processor may record the data on the set form. Thorough preparatory work is done before starting of actual processing of data. The task of preparatory work is decided at the design stage. Uniform categories for statistics and qualitative responses are decided at this stage to decide significant categories. The classification technique is decided before editing, coding and tabulation. Full understanding is required of the purposes of the project and the problems encountered in gathering and analysis of data.

2. EDITING

The main purpose of editing is to eliminate errors and confusion. The editing is done mechanically to avoid personal biases. Editing involves the inspection and correction of each questionnaire or observation form. The analysis, therefore, may be hampered because of poor editing. Editing plays an important role in helping the evaluation of the field force, the utility of the questionnaire and the survey operation. It provides a platform to improve the operation of research activity. The editing may be done in two stages — the field editing and office editing.

1. Field Editing

The field editing is a preliminary editing done to detect the glaring omissions and inaccuracies in the data. It is useful for controlling the field force and removing misunderstanding.

The field editing is done immediately after collection of data because the interviewers then have a fresh memory about the lapses and wrong statements of answers. The preliminary editing should be done by a field supervisor. The editing is done to find out completeness, legibility, comprehensibility, consistency and uniformity. The completeness-check involves scrutinizing the data form to ensure that no questions or sections or pages are omitted. When some questions are left unanswered the supervisor should try to know the reason for this. The questions may be left out on account of oversight or not knowing the answers. Such questions are corrected by observing another questionnaire. Therefore, such unintelligible abbreviations should be clarified by the supervisors. The incomprehensible questions should be clarified at this stage. The inconsistencies of the answers indicate errors in collection and recording of the data, ambiguity in instrument or carelessness. The responses should be recorded in uniform units. If required, the interviewers should recontact the respondent and verify the puzzled and inconsistent records. The editor should be familiar with field interviewing procedures and instructions. Adequate checks should be built into the editing and coding procedures. These checks will be more effective during the early stages of field work. Different coloured pens may be used for editing purposes. The editor should not destroy the original data by erasure. The wrong entries should be underlined with a red pen to mark them as answers that are not required or answers that are to be modified. A preliminary check must be made before final editing and coding.

2. Office Editing

The office editing is done after the field editing. This implies a complete and thorough scrutiny of the questionnaire. There should be expert editors in the office to evaluate and examine the completed returns of the respondents. There may be a division of labour for editing purposes, and each editor may be assigned a particular portion of the questionnaire. The office editors decide what to do with the data rather than follow up the procedures of interviewed responses. They are more concerned with incorrect and incomplete answers.

The incorrect answers may be detected easily when two or more questions are inconsistent. The handling of such answers depends upon the nature of the inconsistencies. The incorrect answers may also be verified by observation. When the answers are given in an ambiguous manner, serious efforts are made to rectify and complete them by consulting another questionnaire. The earlier answers may form a basis for the correction of the incorrect answers.

Many incomplete answers are known from the responses of "don't know." It is a very difficult answer because it reflects a variety of answers. It may represent a lack of knowledge or of memory. The respondents may leave the questions blank intentionally or unintentionally. Such "don't know" answers may be dealt with by distributing them proportionately among other categories, or estimating the answers from other data, or showing them as a separate category. There cannot be any clear cut rule for handling incorrect and incomplete answers. However, with the analysis and observation of other questionnaires, the incorrect and incomplete questions can be rectified and modified for the analysis and interpretation of data.

Classification: Sometimes, there may be several answers to a question. All the alternative questions should be categorised, edited and tabulated for analysis purposes. Unless these answers are classified, they are difficult to tabulate. Dichotomous and multiple choice questions have a specific category of answers. Open questions can fall in different categories. There may be several unspecified answers, and classification of these answers becomes a difficult task. The researcher should establish different categories for the respective answers. The answers should be carefully edited to review and place them in meaningful categories. The classification will serve as a basis for tabulation. Without referring to these categories, the purposeful analysis may not be done. Therefore, all alternative questions should be grouped into a systematic and orderly manner. The working hypotheses may be compared with these answers and their acceptability can be established. The researchers should establish specific categories to deal with satisfactory solutions of the problems. The product quality, brand, price, competition and different types of consumers can be studied by proper classification of the responses.

3. CODING

Coding consists in assigning symbols and numerals to each answer. Coding is the technical procedure by which data are categorised. Through coding, the raw data are transformed into symbols and numerals that may be tabulated and counted. The transformation is based on certain criteria and judgements.

The first step in coding is specifying the answers into categories or classes. The assigning of numbers or symbols to these categories is done thereafter. The number of symbols depend on the research problem to be investigated and researched. The order, the person assigning codes, may develop some rules for coding purposes. The categories or classes should be exhaustive. Every response should be placed into a particular category. Since the responses to a question may be several, the category may be divided into sub-categories and their respective codes may also have several sub-codes. The coding may be done at the time of convenience of the interviewer. Responses may be easily coded by the interviewer with a check-list, and technique and the coding of dichotomous answers may be easy because of the check-list, but coding of open ended questions can be very difficult. The coder will find alternative responses to the open ended questions. There may be a possibility of inconsistency and errors in coding answers to such questions. If one coder is assigned the coding of the full questionnaire, he may find solutions to such inconsistency. When several coders do the job of coding, comparison of their work can remove the inconsistency. In coding, the use of numerals is a commonly accepted principle rather than assigning letters to them. The number should be taken as such and no numeral should be assigned to them.

More problems of coding may arise when the official coders are entrusted to assign codes to the responses because they have inadequate knowledge of the field. Coding of complex data may be effectively performed by the office coders as they have adequate knowledge of research methods. Uniformity, comparability and personal attention can be observed in case of office coders. The coding done by interviewers or supervisors may serve several purposes because they have more information on which to base their judgement. Time and cost may be saved. The problems of coding may arise on account of inadequate data, nature of the data, inefficient coder etc. The inadequacy of data can be overcome by careful editing of data, and careful and close examination of the data. The interviewers might have misunderstood the instructions and may not have recorded adequate information. The proper selection, training and motivation of interviewers may reduce the problems at the level of codification of data. At the time of editing the editor should edit the data in the light of completeness, legibility, comprehensibility, consistency, relevance and uniformity of data. Trained and experienced people may avoid some of the problems of coding. It is necessary to check the reliability of coding. The more structured the data to be coded, the higher will be the reliability of coding.

Machine tabulation requires a different type of coding. The data should be expressed in numerical symbols. It has used punch cards. In order to tabulate by machine, the data must be key-punched onto computer cards. The key-punching operation occurs after each of the questionnaires has been edited and coded, and usually it is performed by a person other than the person who undertook editing and coding. The editor should know what position on the card is to be punched for each answer. The key-punch operator has to convert the specified codes into a number of holes punched in a computer card. Thus, the mechanical tabulation requires a special type of coding of data.

4. TABULATION

Tabulation is a part of the technical process of statistical analysis that consists of counting the number of cases that fall into the various categories. The results are summarised in the form of statistical tables. The raw data was divided into groups and sub-groups. The counting and placing of the number and data in a particular group and sub-group are done thereafter. Tabulation depends on establishing categories for raw data, and editing and coding of responses. Experienced researchers plan tabulation while collecting the data. They become sufficiently familiar with the research problem. They prepare the tabulation plan by using the experiences of other researchers. In exploration researchers, a better and safer procedure is utilised for data collection.

Tabulation involves the activities of sorting, counting and summarising of data. Tabulation may take the form of a simple tabulation or cross tabulation. In simple tabulation, a single variable is counted. A separate table for each variables may be prepared, but the related dependent and independent variables are put together in the simple tabulation. Cross tabulation includes two or more variable which are treated simultaneously. The tabulation may be done entirely by hand or entirely by machine or by both hand and machine. The deciding of tabulation methods depends upon the number of tabulations required and the number of cases in each tabulation.

The tabulation form is decided taking into consideration the purposes of study and use of statistical tools, viz., mean, median, mode, standard deviation and so on. Improper tabulation may create difficulties in the use of these tools. Each tool has some difficulties and limitations. Therefore, the tabulation may vary as per the requirements, of statistical tools. Percentages are the ratios that are highly useful for purposes of analysis. The tabulation is changed as per percentage or ratio analysis. The absolute amount along with percentage to total amount reveal the actual position of a particular phenomenon. The percentage should be used with precaution because the average of percentage, too large a percentage or too small a percentage etc. may cause difficulties in analysis and interpretation of data.

Sorting and Counting of Data

The sorting and counting of data are done in several ways. The hand tabulation may require the following methods of sorting and counting.

Table 12.1
Sorting of Data

Income (Rs.)	*Tally Marks*	*Frequency*
1000	~~IIII~~	5
1500	~~IIII~~ III	8
2000	~~IIII~~ ~~IIII~~ II	12
2500	~~IIII~~ ~~IIII~~ ~~IIII~~ I	16
3000	~~IIII~~ ~~IIII~~	10
3500	~~IIII~~ II	7
4000	III	3

The above method has been commonly utilised for sorting of data for all sorts of variables. A variable is known as the characteristics which is capable of taking different values. It varies from observation. A variable may be of two kinds: Discrete and continuous. A discrete variable assumes only integral value or complete numbers only. A continuous variable assumes any values between two integers. The frequency is distributed as per the related variable as shown in the above table.

The tabulation may include the table number, title, head note, stub, caption, stub entries, body of the table, footnote and source. The following example explains the components of the table.

Table 12.2

Title . . . .
Head note . . . . (unit of measurement)

Stub	Caption	Total
Sub-entries	Body of the table	. . . .
Total	. . . .	. . . .

Footnote: . . . .

Source: . . . .

The table must have a clear and brief title. The head note, usually the measurement unit, is placed at the top of the table in the right hand corner in a bracket. The stub indicates the row titles or the row headings and is placed at the left hand column. The caption indicates what each column is meant for. The stub entries are sub-groupings of the stub. The body of the table gives full information of the numeral and frequency. The footnote gives special information about a particular item. A star (*) may be put on a particular number or word to explain their meaning. Sometimes the star (*) is put to explain that the figure is provisional. The source may indicate from which organisation the data is borrowed if the is secondary data.

Kinds of Tabulation

The tabulation may be of several kinds, viz. *(i)* Simple or one-way tabulation *(ii)* Cross or two way tabulation and *(iii)* High order tabulation.

1. Sample or One-Way Tabulation

Some questions contain information which may be useful to tabulate individually. The dichotomous scale or multiple choice questions which allow only one answer may use the one-way tabulation or univariate tabulation. The question is predetermined and consists of counting the number of responses falling into and consists of counting the number of answers may be put in the form of percentage. There may be two types of univariate tabulation: *(i)* open question with only one response and *(ii)* multiple responses to open and multiple choice questions.

(i) Open question with only one response: Categories are established for responses to open questions, and individual responses are read and coded according to the pre-established categories. If an open question gives only one answer, tabulation may be of the following type:

Table 12.3

Number of Children per Family

Number of Children	*Family Number*	*In percent*
0	10	5
1	30	15
2	70	35
3	60	30
4	34	7
More than 4	16	8
		100

Problems may arise when there is no response or fall in the "don't know" category. The researcher should be ready to deal with such responses while following the tabulation process. If a large number of "don't knows" are observed, they should be properly placed in the table. The don't know answers may be due to a poor questionnaire and interview technique. There may be some legitimate "don't know" answers. The "don't know" answers may be due to confusion, giving less importance to the questions. The inclusion of "do not know" answers may specifically mention its place in the tabulation. The exclusion of the "don't know" answer from the tabulation may not represent other categories.

(ii) Multiple Response to Open and Multiple Choice Questions

There may be some questions which may allow respondents to give more than one answer. Such questions present a different tabulation problem because the responses need not be total to 100 percent. There may be duplication of answers. The overlap or duplication may be ascertained. The researcher will have to determine the number of additional or unduplicated responses. It can be explained from Table 12.4.

Table 12.4
Preference of Television

Reasons	*Frequencies*
News	60
Advertisement	45
Film	80
Small Stories	75
Music and Song	50

The answers are duplicative because an audience which prefers news may also prefer small stones, music and song and other items. The answers are not exclusive and distinctive. The relative importance of each of the factors may be deduced to a common base.

The univariate tabulate can be used to locate blunders, outlines and to determine the empirical distribution of the variables. The tabulation introduces a spurious sense of accuracy and may impair the analysis. The reasonable and proper method of tabulation may avoid all these problems. The outliers are observations that exclude specific factors from the unique observation. The analysts should know how to study the univariate tabulation. The distribution of frequencies will reveal the characteristics. The histogram may be used from the frequencies distributed. Thus the typical characteristics of the data may be observed. The empirical distribution may be compared with the theoretical distribution or statement. A prior model, posterior model, polygon can be observed by the univariate tabulation. The mean, median and mode can be calculated from such tabulations. Graphs and interpretation of the tabulation may be possible by such tables.

2. Cross Tabulation or Two-Way Tabulation

Cross tabulation or Two-way tabulation or Bivariate or multivariate tabulation is that form of presentative of data which includes two or more variables. All the columns and rows as mentioned in univariate tabulation are also present in the multivariate tabulation except that two or more variables based on two or more questions are also included. The multiresponse questions are properly treated. All the variables are separately understood and observed before their tabulation in combined form. It is an important mechanism for studying the relationship among and between variables. In this tabulation, the data of several variables are divided into groups and sub-groups so that the behaviour of the dependent variable can be understood. Since this tabulation is commonly used in marketing research, it is known as the "bread and butter" of applied research. The cross tabulation or multivariate tabulation may be used as a common and comprehensive method of various analyses. Researchers using sophisticated tools of analysis may also adapt multivariate tabulation to get a glance of the findings in more observation. Some researchers may use only this tabulation to arrive at specific conclusions. The tabulator, analyst and researchers must have a comprehensive knowledge of the preparation of the tabulation. The number of variables decides the number of groups and sub-groups. The larger the number of variables, the larger will be the groups and sub-groups in the multivariate tabulation.

Illustration: In marketing management, the use of cross tabulation has been very common. Several important conclusions can be drawn from the observation of the table. For example, the popularity of "Brand A" milk powder may be studied amongst an income group. Suppose 1000 families have been observed as per Table 12.5.

Table 12.5

Use of Milk Powder "Brand A"

Number of Families

Income Range per month (Rs.)	*Number of children per family*							*Total*
	0	*1*	*2*	*3*	*4*	*5*	*More than 5*	
Below 1000	10	00	15	18	23	30	50	146
1000-2000	20	10	17	20	25	35	55	182
2000-3000	40	20	25	28	40	45	65	263
3000-4000	25	5	12	15	27	40	60	184
4000-5000	13	4	13	10	20	30	40	130
More than 5000	12	1	8	9	15	20	30	95
Total	120	40	90	100	150	200	300	1000

Table 12.5 reveals that the milk powder "Brand A" depends not only on the income but also on the number of children per family. The milk powder is also more popular amongst the family with no children for their self-consumption. It is clear from the table that 120 families out of 1000 families use milk powder although they have no children whereas a family having upto 3 children do not depend on milk powder. It shows that they want to feed their children on pure milk. In Indian conditions, it is correctly realised that children are mostly breast-fed or depend on cow milk or buffalow milk. Persons with Rs. 2000-Rs. 3000 per capita income are more accustomed to use milk powder. Persons below this income range either do not like milk powder, or cannot afford milk powder, or have been fed on cow or buffalows to get pure milk. Persons above this income range can afford pure milk and do not depend much on milk powder. There may be several other conclusions based on the multivariate tabulation.

If the multivariate tabulation is converted into percentage, the analysis becomes easier and quicker. The percentage is calculated in terms of factors affecting the phenomena. In the above example, income and number of children have been causes of affecting the use of milk powder. There may be some other factors affecting the statement which can be analysed by preparing such multivariate tabulation. Although this provides a basis of analysis and insight into the relationship, it should not be considered as a final analysis. It is a very good start for the analysis. There may be various factors influencing the subject of the study. Therefore, the subgroups may be decided on the basis of these factors. There may be three or more variate tabulations. In the above group the age of the children may be the third factor to decide its influence on the fact or statement. In every group the figure may be changed to the base of 100 to indicate the percentage of the each sub-group to its group, and also the percentage of groups to the total.

The multivariate tabulation can be presented in a more refined and clear way to indicate the effects of each factor. The tabulation is modified as per the objectives of the research. The relationship between various variables is also established and is exposed to observation and clear analysis. The cross tabulation reveals the relationship between the related variables and also between non-related variables to reveal how far they are unrelated. Thus, the existence and non-existence of several relationships can be revealed with the cross tabulation.

Proof of Relationship

The relationship between two variables can be proved by initiating a third variable. Similarly the three variate relationships can be substantiated by introduction of the fourth variable. Thus, the original multivariate tabulation is tested and examined by the introduction of a new variable. There may be some unexpected happenings apart from the theoretical statement. These unexpected relevations can be tested by initiating an additional variable which may prove or disprove the new findings. Thus, the original hypotheses may be expected by the empirical study of the factor, or they may be rejected by this study and new hypotheses may be developed as per the analysis of the cross tabulation. Moreover this tabulation may reveal some limiting conditions. This may reveal that the particular phenomena are limited on account of certain factors. This tabulation may also reveal some other needs of the population. Two or more factors affecting the needs can be known by deep observation of the cross tabulation or by restructuring of the tabulation. The correlation between two variables or between the third and the first two variables can be known by this table. More elaborate analysis is possible if the data are available.

The utility of the third variable can be revealed only if data are collected pertaining to that variable. If data are available the restructuring of the cross-tabulation by the introduction of the third variable will uncover some relationships and conclusions. There may be the introduction of more variables to examine the relationships of existing variables.

There is a possibility of concluding unrelated variables as related variables. The analysis may conclude that there is no relationship, or that there is some relationship between two or more variables when in a practical situation there is no or some relationships. The cross tabulation or multivariate tabulation may reveal the real relationship. The real relationship may be disclosed by adding one or more variable to the existing variables. The cross tabulation can be appropriately prepared if the related data are collected. If tabulations are to be done by machine, the analyst should plan carefully which bivariate and multivariate tabulations may be useful. The preferred information should be tabulated initially and other information at a later stage.

3. Higher Order Tabulation

Higher order tabulation incorporates several kinds of information whether related or unrelated. It is a composite tabulation ready for other operational tabulation. The first column may indicate the time and the rest of the columns may refer to other information allowing to the time. For example, demographic characteristics may reveal several characteristics year-wise, viz., population, density of population, education, sex, occupation, religion and so on. The tabulation may provide unlimited information. This tabulation does not serve a specific purpose, but it is used for all purposes. It is therefore, a general type of table not in the least concerned to a specific purpose of research. This tabulation provides comprehensive subject matters and data of all sorts of information of a subject. This is useful for the researcher to select the related data and ignore the unrelated data.

Mechanical Tabulation

Mechanical tabulation involves the use of a machine. It helps us to organise the work more speedily and accurately. The machine or equipment to be used for tabulation purposes is costly; so, it is used only when a large number of questionnaires are to be tabulated. Mechanical tabulation transforms all the entries in the questionnaire in numerical terms or codes, records all the entries on the punch card by punching holes, sorts out the cards and tabulates the data by use of a machine. Each card is given a number in which the respective person's age, sex, education, income etc. are noted.

The relevant information and data are punched on the card and the card is sorted by the sorting machines. Each card is verified by reading its punched holes. The special machine called a verifier is used for verification of the punched data. The punched cards are placed in the sorting machine after verification. The sorting machines sorts and tabulates the information. The data are totalled up and printed on the blank sheets. The automatic machine does the sorting, aggregating, tabulating and printing.

Advantages

(1) Mechanical tabulation facilitates speed up of the work. It may be more expedient.

(2) It facilitates cross-classifications and tabulation. The correlation may be easily computed with the machine.

(3) Mechanical tabulation may be used for periodic studies or surveys of repeated data.

(4) The sorting and counting may produce errors if done by the human hand; but the mechanical tabulation can avoid the errors.

(5) Mechanical tabulation provides enough scope for prompt and adequate analysis.

Disadvantages

(1) The cost of mechanical tabulation is very high. Machine tabulation involves greater cost since the charges for punching, sorting and tabulating are very high if hired mechanical tabulation is undertaken. Purchasing of a machine for tabulation is very high.

(2) Mechanical tabulation demands despatching of raw data to some offices far away from the project office. This may cause inconvenience to the researcher and supervisor.

(3) The hand tabulation provides sufficient scope for personal analysis and observation, but the mechanical tabulation may not provide such benefits.

The mechanical tabulation may be useful for prompt decision but may not serve the purpose of psychological study. In psychological research, various complex and cumbersome data may be required; tabulation of which with a machine may not give the correct result.

Computer Tabulation

Tabulation done by a computer is known as computer tabulation. A computer includes the entire variety of machines that electronically record, store and perform any calculations from the simple to the most complicated data. It prints or displays its results from the tabulated and analysed data. Computers may be of several sizes. Computer models can be developed to suit the research data. The computing personnel write the programmes and executes them. The computers may be both hardware and software.

The marketing researchers should have knowledge of hardware which is usually of a digital type. It processes information represented by means of a coded character. There may be binary digits which may be represented in two states from 0 to 1. Input, the first step is the central processing unit which performs the task. There may be reading of punched card processing of the cards. Information can be read into the computer on magnet tapes which can contain million kinds of information on a standard real. Drum and disc types of memory may provide inputs. It may also come directly from an on live-typewriter-like keyboard or direct sensors. After feeding the data into the computer, it goes to the central processing unit which is the heart of the computer. It contains the main trunk lines upon which all information flows. It is a control device and operation unit. The operation unit provides all the fundamental operations of arithmetic and the logical capability to compare. The storage or memory unit of the computer is an array of tiny rings based on a magnetic or non-magnetic system. It stores linary information that may be related to the decimal or alphabetic code. Through a series of pulses, the molecules in the cores are oriented and reoriented. The memory disc can store as many as billions of characters and information. The fourth function of a computer is related to the output. The output may come out on cards, and takes on a drum-disc memory unit from the central processing unit. Since the researcher may like the result printed, this is done by the line printer. It can print various types of reports or tabulation. It can prepare multiple copies. The punched cards are now replaced by pencil marks which is done by special and heavy pencils that will pass an electric current. The computer senses the information written on the card and computes the data through its central processing unit.

The software computer refers to the systematised and managed computer which electronically operates within its systems and sub-systems. It contains programme interpretation and an operating system. The application is known as packaged programmes which provides instructions on how to carry out a series of operations. Biomedic (BMD) has been a more common package programme of marketing research. Recently a statistical package for the social sciences (SPSS) has been more popular in marketing research. It can be used on line as well as on batch operation. It provides a completely interactive mode of usage as contrasted with running each programme. Marketing research has become very easy and accurate with the application of a computer.

5. SUMMARY OF DATA

The tabulation provides a comprehensive picture of the analysis. The analysis requires a summary of the tabulated data. The summarised form of data facilitates the required statistical calculations. Such summary presentation make the data intelligible and easy for analysis. Statistical methods used for summarising the data are known as descriptive statistics. The central tendencies are typical tool to summarise the tabulated data. The arithmetic mean, median and mode are important measures of summarising the data. Therefore, they are well-known as the measurement of the central tendency. Although the central tendency is not free from drawbacks, it is being commonly used to summarise the data. The calculation of dispersion describes the summarised data. The dispersion may be measured by calculating range, quartile deviation, mean deviation and standard deviation.

❖ ❖ ❖

CHAPTER 13

DATA ANALYSIS: PRELIMINARY CONSIDERATIONS

1. **CHOICE OF ANALYSIS TECHNIQUE**
2. **FACTORS DECIDING APPROPRIATE TECHNIQUE OF ANALYSIS**
3. **NATURE OF ANALYSIS AND INTERPRETATION**
4. **SUMMARISING THE DATA**
5. **OVERVIEW OF STATISTICAL PROCEDURE**

DATA ANALYSIS: PRELIMINARY CONSIDERATIONS

The application of appropriate statistical tools to collected and tabulated data is an important function of data analysis. Before application of the tools, some basic considerations should be understood by the researcher. The collected data and information cannot be properly interpreted unless they are converted into significant statistical information. The fundamentals of data analysis should be known to the researchers. The data analysis may involve a charting of the sequential relationships between the stages and principal methods, a description of each method and its formula and a sorting of the result produced to bring into light the quantitative meaning of data.

The data analysis requires understanding of mathematical and statistical procedure. Mathematical expression is simply an alternative to verbal ones that are much more efficient in being expressed quickly in numbers. It is clear and specific avoiding the ambiguities and nuances. The qualities are expressed in numbers. The statistical procedure or tool tries to interpret the qualitative significance of the data. The quantitative analytical methods have been very useful for interpretation and inference for research purposes.

1. CHOICE OF ANALYSIS TECHNIQUE

The choice of analysis technique involves two basic questions: (1) what meanings should be obtained from the data with reference to the specific problems, and (2) which statistical tools are most useful in revealing those meanings that are feasible with the particular data. The researcher should have acquired skills of analysis of data. Intelligent researchers can derive benefits in several ways. The researcher should find out various alternative techniques or analysis, and select the most appropriate technique of analysis for the purpose of the research. In many research-fields, the averages and percentages may be useful techniques, and in other research areas, correlation and regression analysis will be most suitable. The scaling techniques may also be different for different purposes. For some researches, use of a particular technique may be totally inappropriate.

2. FACTORS DECIDING APPROPRIATE TECHNIQUE OF ANALYSIS

The appropriate technique of analysis depends upon the type of data, the research design and assumptions underlying the test statistics.

1. Type of Data: There may be several types of data, viz., nominal, ordinal, interval and rated which are dealt with separately in analysis. The nominal scale is used for categorising the objects. Nominal scale assigns words such as favourable or unfavourable to categorise the respondent. A numeral is assigned to each category to represent a distinct category. The nominal scale remains undistorted under a one to one substitution of the numerals. The normal arithmetical operations are not meaningful for nominally scaled variables. The mode is an appropriate measure of the central tendency for this purpose. The ordinal data requires a higher level of measurement than the nominal data. There may be categories A,B,C and so on for the ordinal data. For example, category A for good, category B for average and category C for poor and so on. The ordinal scale assigns an average in order of preference using ordinal values, e.g., first, second, third and so on. The structure of an ordinal scale is undistorted by any one to one substitution. Such as good

= 30, average = 15 and poor = 10 and so on. Thus, there is a significant difference between these categories. The median and the mode are used for ordinal data. The assignment of numerals to objects using an interval scale reflects the magnitude of the differences and one can determine how much more one category is higher than the other category. The comparison can be made using differences between the two objects. The interval scale contains the arbitrary zero. The normal arithmetical operations are meaningful with this scale. Similarly mean, median and mode are appropriate measures of the interval data. The ratio scale has a natural zero and characteristics of equal intervals. It provides a common base for comparison. The ratio scale is undistorted under proportionate or scalar transformations. The effect of transformations by a particular factor can be easily measured. The statistical measures used for internal data may be appropriate for ratio analysis.

The analyst must be careful to select appropriate measures of statistical tools for the given data. They should produce a scale which should be equally placed. The calculation of the mean is not appropriate with ordinal data. An appropriate scale with appropriate procedures of measurement will give appropriate results. The understanding of the level of measurement is crucial for proper analysis and interpretation and when the data are parametric they are distributed around their mean or central value in a symmetrical fashion. Non-parametric data do not conform with the normal curve of provability.

2. Research Design: The important questions for deciding a statistical tool is an understanding of the research design. This involves the dependency of observations, the number of observations per object, the number of groups being analysed and the control exercised over the variables. The research design requires understanding of sample independence, number of groups, number of variables and variable control.

(i) Sample independence: The researcher should know the nature of the sample. The dependent and independent variables should be understood before analysis of the data. The experimental design may necessarily have two such variables. The measurement of effectiveness can be assessed by correlation analysis. The before and after measurement data can be the basis of comparison to find out the impact of measurement. A paired difference test for statistical significance may be useful for analysis. In analysing associative relationships, two types of variables are considered: criterion and predictor variables known as dependent and independent variables. The researcher may investigate the interrelationships and interdependence among all variables.

(ii) Number of Groups: When there are a number of groups of study, the control group should be separated from the experimental groups. Different statistical tools should be used for different groups. The mean difference between two groups will not serve the purpose. The variance analysis may be useful tools of interpretation of data. Thus, the number of groups and their nature as per research design determine the need of a particular tool analysis.

3. Number of Variables: The number of variables also determines the analysis procedure. The attitude of the respondents can be determined by appropriate tools of analysis. The exposed and unexposed variables may require different statistical procedures. The attitude measurement may be a legitimate measure of effectiveness of a particular variable. The differences in attitudes and in variables of two groups will reveal the measurement of a particular factor. If the univariate test does not reveal the significant difference, there may be multivariate tests to measure the differences. Small and non-significant differences may indicate real differences. The favourable and unfavourable results may be taken for understanding the controlled group and the experimental group. The differences between unfavourable and favourable results may be difficult to be revealed, although multivariable statistical procedures may help disclose the differences. A larger number of measurements may reveal more errors and differences. The number of variables to be analysed is the relationship between variables.

4. Variable control: The control of variables that affect the result requires a proper tool of analysis. It lays emphasis on the differences in attitude between two groups. The experimental group keeps the controllable variable within limits to find out the result of the experiment and minimise its impact. The effective method is to make the experimental and control groups equal with respect to randomisation and combination. The statistical procedure is used for controlling the effect of control variables. The errors can be known by finding the differences between two groups, i.e., experimental groups and control groups. The regression analysis may be used to test the impact of variables on other variables. Thus the suitable statistical procedure is decided by considering the type of data and research design.

Assumptions Underlying Test Statistic

The assumptions underlying the test statistics will decide the method of analysis. The test of difference in the control group and experimental group will decide the tool of analysis. The test may be used in this case. The assumptions are that each variable or factors of each variable are drawn independently. It is assumed that the individuals composing the experimental group are drawn from a population with an unknown mean and unknown variance, and the control group comes from a population with an unknown mean and unknown variance. The attitudes toward the product are normally distributed in each of these populations. The variances of the two populations are considered equal. The test comparing two means assumes that the data have an equal interval. It is therefore assumed that the samples are independent, and that there is normal distribution of the characteristics of interest in each population; these are equal variances in the two populations and the interval or ratio is scaled data.

The test is more sensitive to certain violations of the assumptions. It works well with respect to violations of normal distribution, but is quite sensitive to violations of equal variance. It is surprising that little attention is paid to the variances, and to violation of normal distribution. The level of measurement can be ascertained through an analysis of the measurement procedures. The assumptions should be satisfied for analysis purposes. If assumptions are not satisfied, the analysis can use different tests which satisfy the assumptions. Researchers may examine whether the facts arrived at are due to chance or according to the analysis. Therefore, they resort to some kind of test of statistical significance. The researcher should know the association between two or more variables. He should investigate the strength of the association and the functional form of association. Whether or not samples of such data are statistically significant must be judged by tests. A large number of marketing data cannot be inherently parametric. So the ranking process is utilised for analysis and interpretation.

3. NATURE OF ANALYSIS AND INTERPRETATION

The application of analytical methods to data is known as analysis. Statistical methods are applied for getting logical inferences. The success of the application of methods depends on the honesty of the researcher in selecting the appropriate formula and data inputs, and also on the understanding of the formula and its application. There are various functions of analysis, viz., assembling the data, bringing the data along with the application of statistical tools and selecting appropriate analytical methods including examination of differences, analysis of experimental data and investigation of association.

Interpretation means bringing out the meaning of data, or converting data into information. The research process is approached as one draws conclusions from the data analysed. The whole investigation culminates in drawing inferences that lead to conclusions of the problems. This requires a high degree of interpretation skill. There are two methods of drawing conclusions, induction and deduction. In induction, the statement is drawn from observed data to specific conclusions. It means that conclusions are drawn from a general to a particular phenomenon. The deductive reasonings start from some general laws and conclude to a particular conclusion. It means deduction comes from a general to a particular law. For example, man is mortal. Since Mr. Ram is a man, he is mortal. It is deduction. Similarly, for induction reasoning, the researcher observes a large number of persons that they are dead. So we conclude that Mr. Ram will also die. From separate instances of observations, there may be generalised conclusions. Thus, the nature of scientific norm is to provide a bridge between theory and research. It provides that deductive reasoning is towards observation and inductive reasoning is from observation. Both logic and observation are essential for interpretation. From the inductive and deductive methods, numerous inferences can be drawn. It may be an indirectly derived conclusion. It may influence evidence from which to draw conclusion from the evidence. The major concern is that the conclusions drawn should be valid. Accurate evidence will give accurate conclusions.

The Interrelationship between Analysis and Interpretation

The success of interpretation depends upon the proper analysis and vice versa. In the absence of proper analysis, the interpretation will not be appropriate. Similarly, improper interpretation will cause improper analysis. The proper collection of data, relevant and suitable analysis, and appropriate interpretation will lead to correct conclusions. If there is a mistake at any stage the subsequent function will be faulty. Improper methods of data collection will not provide relevant and proper analysis. Similarly, suitably collected data but wrongly analysed data will not arrive at correct interpretation and conclusions.

It should be noted here that proper analysis will not necessarily result in proper interpretation. The interpretation depends on the experience of the researchers and the methods utilised for interpretation. There are various factors interacting and acting to influence the decision. A different analytical technique may be used for interpretation. Proper analysis and proper interpretation may infer right conclusions and suggestions. Analysis and interpretation are interdependent. The properly analysed data or sophisticated data may not infer right suggestions unless data are properly interpreted. The interpretation and the analysis are closely related. The result drawn on their basis should be statistically significant.

Proper Interpretation: Proper interpretation avoids errors and mistakes. The figure and analysis will not reveal the truth automatically. They require proper interpretation for which sound logic will be more concrete and helpful. The researcher should produce honest and sober interpretation, help the objectives and principles in the guidelines, be aware of the limitations of the research, recognise insignificant answers and tools of analysis, distinguish between opinions and facts, and find out the causes and effects. Good planning and anticipation pay off well in interpretation. The interpreter should have intimate knowledge of the problems under investigation in conjunction with the evidence. He should review the whole data collection process and reliability of the data before interpretation. The analyst must be unbiased and wise enough to select the relevant data. He should not hurry to draw swift conclusions from the raw data confusious data. The exaggeration and distortion of the interpretation should be avoided by the researcher.

4. SUMMARISING THE DATA

Before summarising the data, it is essential to bring the data into order i.e. into comparable form. The raw data collected from the field or secondary data are not in the shape of interpretation. The raw data may contain several data whether useful or useless, relevant or irrelevant. So the useful and relevant data must be weeded out from the jungle of useless data. The assumptions underlying the collection of data should be known to the interpreter and analyst. We have discussed these factors under processing of data. The important processes of summarising the data are (1) classification of data, and (2) frequency distribution and application of the appropriate statistical tool.

1. Classification

The first method of classification of raw data is bringing them into the array that lists all of them in numerical sequence. Setting up an array may not be difficult but in a larger number of data, legitimate and relevant data cannot be easily observed. Therefore, the second important method of classification is grouping the data into sub-classes. The important data may be revealed by classification by groups, and important inferences can be drawn from the classification of data. The classification can be known while collecting the data. The factors on which breakdowns or classification can be made may be anticipated. The objective of the research and nature of data may be considered as factors to decide classification. The following principles are also considered for classification:

(1) Number of groups: The number of groups and sub-groups should be substantial enough to record the possible differences in the data. The classification should not be too narrow to shadow important data nor too wide to diffuse the destructive nature of the data. The class-interval should be adequately devised to reveal the significant tendencies of the data.

(2) Inter-group similarity: The class-interval should be homogeneous. Responses classified in a particular category may be similarly placed to reveal the characteristics of each class.

(3) Recording of differences: The differences in responses between categories should be known. The dis-similarities should be substantially revealed by the grouping of the responses.

(4) Exclusive categories: The groups or categories should be mutually exclusive. They should be overlapping. The classification should be made in such a manner that a response can be placed in only one category.

(5) Exhaustive categories: The classification should be made to include all responses, viz., "Don't know", others and so on. If any response is not properly recorded, the analysis will be partially incorrect.

(6) Avoid extremes: Extreme answers should be avoided. Lack of specified interval limits may reveal the extremes of distribution. Open ended class intervals should be avoided because they will stretch the analysis unduly. The average value of the frequencies at extremes may misrepresent the data. Therefore, the class intervals at the extreme should be expanded comparatively to include larger frequencies.

(7) Width of class-intervals: The class-interval should be of equal size and width. It will give a consistent distribution of data. The equal breadth of the class-intervals will reveal statistically the correct information and will make the analysis easy. But, when the class-interval of equal size has very small frequencies, a larger class-interval should be made to include more frequency. Unequal width of class-interval may be possible when fewer categories may not include adequate information.

2. Frequency Distribution

The collected and classified data should be placed in a summarised form to reveal the result of the data. Summarised data will provide adequate information and inferences. Having decided the classification of data, the next step under summary of data is placing frequencies to each class-interval. The observation of data may be done as per class-interval. This means that the observations will be counted and will be placed in the respective class-interval is re-examined and reallocation is rechecked to examine their placement so that there does not arise any gap. If there are some gaps in frequencies, they are filled by the interpolation. The class interval and frequency distribution will give a definite shape of tabulation which may be of a discrete series or continuous series.

The frequency, may be put in definite data, i.e., the absolute frequency, relative frequency and cumulative frequency. There may be two open ends of class-intervals below... and above... to avoid the extremes at both ends. The mid-values in these are decided on the basis of other mid-values. The frequency distribution in these categories may be smaller depending upon the nature of the data. The odd numbers in cross-comparison may create difficulties in analysis. The simplification is required to compare the various categories within the frequency distribution. The distribution of data is compared with the previous data. The relative frequencies will provide comparative data. Therefore the absolute data is converted into relative data. When two or more variables are involved, there may be multivariate tabulation and they are inter compared. The frequency distribution requires proper understanding of the data and their relative importance so that the relevant data may be placed in suitable class-intervals before application of the statistical tool.

3. Application of Statistical Tools

The tabulated data can be further summarised by application of suitable tools, viz., central values, dispersion and cross-classification.

(i) Central Values: A single figure representing the total distributed frequency is known as central values. One cannot understand the values distributed throughout the class-intervals, so one value is calculated considering the total frequencies. Magnitudes of different sets of data can be compared with the central values or average. The average can be of five types, viz., mean, median, mode, geometric mean and harmonic mean.

(a) Mean: The mean, also known as the arithmetical mean, is calculated by dividing the sum of the values of the observations by the number of items observed. If data are of a continuous series, the mid values of the class-interval are multiplied by the respective frequencies, and then the products of each class-interval is aggregated and divided by the number of frequencies to arrive at the arithmetical mean. It can be expressed as below:

$$\bar{x} = \frac{fx}{f}$$

where,

x = Arithmetical mean

x = Midpoint of each class

f = Frequencies in each class

= Sum of the values.

The arithmetical mean can be computed even from unordered data. It can project the value of population also based on the sample study. It is effected by every value of observation. A change in value of observation will affect the vale of the mean. So, it is representative of all data. The mean value may be distorted too much by a relatively few extreme values. Thus, it may affect the average and the representativeness of data. The mathematical properties of the average have been important features of analysis and inferences. It is suitable for analysis and comparison as it can be used for further algebraic treatment; however, the abnormalities may influence the results.

(b) Median: Median is the value of the middle item of a series of observations when it is arranged in ascending or descending order of magnitude. The median is conveniently found for ungrouped data with the formula $\frac{N+1}{2}$. The median would be the value half way between the two central values. In class-interval the calculation of median is difficult as the actual values of the observations are lost in the class-interval. The formula for calculating the median may be as below:

$$M = l_1 + \frac{l_2 - l_1}{f_1} (m - c)$$

where,

M = Median

l_1 = The lower limit of the class in which median lies

l_2 = The upper limit of the class in which median lies

f_1 = The frequency of the data in which median lies

m = Middle item

c = Cumulative frequency of the group preceding the median group

The median is mid value, so one can say that it is representative. Unlike the mean, it can be computed from open-ended. It is not influenced by the extremes. If the distribution is highly skewed, the median value would be better value of central tendency. It is not affected by the value of observations but by the number of observations. So, extreme values whether high or low, will not distort the measure of the central tendency. When the class-intervals are of unequal size, the computation of the median may be more useful. Unless the data are arranged in ascending or descending order, the calculation of the median may be difficult. Therefore the simple frequency is counted into cumulative frequency. It is not suitable for further algebraic treatment. It is representative in the true sense as it does not evaluate the values of all observations. The mean is therefore considered superior to the median.

(c) Mode: The mode is the most common item of the series. It is the value which occurs most often. It is very easily determined when data are categorised in a frequency distribution as the mode is the category containing the greatest number of observations. The mode cannot be calculated from a series of individual observations unless it is converted into either a discrete or a continuous series. In the continuous series, the class interval having the maximum frequency would be the modal class. The modal class may be decided easily if there is only one class having maximum frequencies. If there are two classes having equal maximum frequencies, the modal class may be difficult to decide. It requires regrouping and reclassification. The mode is computed with the following formula:

$$Z = l_1 + \frac{f_0}{f_0 + f_2} \times (l_2 - l_1)$$

where,

Z = Mode

l_1 = Lower limit of the modal class

l_2 = Higher limit of the modal class

f_0 = Frequency of the class-interval just previous to modal class

f_2 = Frequency of the class-interval just after the modal class

The mode is easily calculated. It can be located even in an open ended question. The mode is used in day-to-day life. The mode is useful in marketing research. It is not affected by the values of extremes. Unlike the mean, the mode is the existing value although it may not be based on the total observations. It is not capable of further mathematical observations.

(d) Geometric Mean: Geometric mean is the nth root of the product of n items of a series. The formula for calculating the geometric mean is as below:

$$g = \sqrt[n]{m_1 \times m_2 \times m_3 \ldots m_n}$$

where,

g = Geometric mean

n = Number of items

m = Value of each item

It may be put in the following form also

$$g = \text{Anti log}\left(\frac{\log m_1 + \log m_2 + \log m_3 + \ldots \log m_n}{n}\right)$$

The geometric mean possesses mathematical properties. It possesses all the attributes of mean plus mathematical utility of the value. It is capable of further algebraic treatment. It is not affected by the fluctuations of sampling. It is not easy to calculate. It gives more importance of smaller values and less importance to higher values. It is not utilised in marketing research.

(e) Harmonic Mean: The harmonic mean is the reciprocal of the arithmetic average of the reciprocals of the values of its various items. Symbolically it would be,

$$h = \text{Reciprocal } \frac{\frac{1}{m_1} + \frac{1}{m_2} \ldots \frac{1}{m_n}}{n}$$

where, h = harmonic mean
m = values of each observation
n = number of observations

The harmonic mean satisfies the test of rigidity and preciseness. It is based on observation, and capable of further algebraic treatment. It measures relative changes and is useful in ratio and percentages. It is difficult to calculate. It does not serve many of the purposes. Therefore, it is not used in marketing research.

Use in Marketing Research

The use of central values in marketing research has been realised since the beginning. The researcher may be interested in knowing the average sales per shop, average consumption per month, average income of the consumer or of a society. The population parameter may be calculated with the help of the sample average. The average of the sample within a certain range may be taken as the population parameter. For example, if the average income of the population is to be computed, the researcher may select a sample, collect data on family income and calculate a relevant statistic which will be representative of the population. The sample estimate is considered as a point of the population although there may be some variances in the values of the sample and of the population. The total purchasing power of the community can be estimated on the sample average. If the sample is stratified the purchasing power of each income-class may also be estimated. The median purchasing power will reveal that half of population has more income than the median income, and half the population has less income than the median income. The mode will reveal the most common frequency. It will decide the place of the shopping centre and so on. There may be several methods of calculating the central values but each method may be suitable in a particular method to suit the situation, viz., consistency, efficiency, sufficiency and lack of bias. When the sample estimate is almost equal to the parameter, there is consistency in the values. The efficiency is observed when the sample size is almost equal to the parameter. The sufficiency of estimation is observed when all the information is properly utilised. The closeness of sample statistics of the population parameter is an indication of unbiased estimation. Therefore, an appropriate method of calculating the values should be decided to estimate the parameter based on the sample-statistics.

(ii) Dispersion: The central value is a point estimate whereby the nature of distribution of data is not revealed. The spread or scatter of the observations can be revealed by the measures of dispersion. Since the point value known as average value may not represent the whole observation, dispersion should be computed to know the nature of the data. The dispersion is measured by application of statistical tools such as range, mean deviation, standard deviation, variance and coefficient of variation.

(a) **Range:** Range is the simplest possible measure of dispersion. It is the difference between the values of the extreme items of a series, i.e., the difference between the highest and lowest values. The range can indicate the width of the observation values. The range is not based on all the observations of the series. It does not take into account the composition of a series or the distribution of items within the extremes. However, it is commonly used where the variation is not much. In quality control, range is used to measure variation in the quality of the units manufactured. In the marketing field, the price variation beyond the range may be rejected.

There may be a quartile range which measures the variation between the first quartile and the third quartile. The range between the third quartile and first quartile is known as the semi-inter quartile range. Their difference and aggregation may reveal the coefficient of quartile deviation. These ranges may be used in the marketing researches for knowing the differences between the highest and the lowest values.

(b) **Mean Deviation:** Mean deviation of a series is the arithmetical average of th[e] deviation of various items from a measure of central tendency. If the dispersion is calculat[ed] from the mean, the average of the dispersion is known as the mean deviation. It may throw light on the formation of the series and the dispersion of items round a central value while calculating the differences from the central value, when the algebraic signs are ignored. The mean deviation is known as the first moment of dispersion. Thus,

$$\delta = \frac{\varepsilon dm}{n}$$

where,

δ = Mean deviation from mean

d = Deviation from the mean

n = Number of items or observations

Similarly, the mean deviation may also be calculated from the median. Thus,

$$\delta m = \frac{\varepsilon dm}{n}$$

where,

δm = Mean deviation from median

dm = Deviation from the median

n = Number of items or observations

It is a more useful method of calculating mean deviation than that of mean deviation from mean. The mean coefficient of dispersion may be calculated by the formula $\frac{\delta}{a}$. The mean deviation is rigidly defined and is precise. It is based on all the observations. Since the algebraic signs are ignored, it cannot be used for further treatment. Therefore, standard deviation is calculated to measure the dispersion of data.

(c) Standard Deviation: The variance and standard deviations are calculated on deviations from the mean. The variance is defined as the average of the squared deviations of the difference from the mean. The square root of the variance is called the standard deviation. Thus,

$$\sigma^2 = \frac{\varepsilon d^2}{n}$$

where,

σ^2 = Variance

d^2 = Square of deviations from mean

n = Number of observation or items

The formula of standard deviation is as below:

$$\sigma = \sqrt{\frac{\varepsilon d^2}{n}}$$

The standard deviation is also known as standard error or mean error. It is often used to analyse its relationship to the mean of the observation. It is an important measure of symmetrical distribution. The standard deviation is commonly used for analysis purposes.

The standard deviation is used in marketing research to compute range. Thus $\pm\sigma$ covers about 67 per cent of the values, $\pm 2\sigma$ covers 95 per cent and $\pm 3\sigma$ about 99 per cent. Standard deviation possesses several important characteristics. It is based on all the observations of the data. It can be used for further algebraic treatment. It may be a representation of the observations. It gives more importance to extreme items and less importance to near the mean. However, the standard deviation cannot be computed from open ended classes.

(d) Coefficient of Variation: The standard deviation may not be comparable with other variables. So, the coefficient of variation is calculated for comparison purposes. The standard deviation is divided by the mean and multiplied by 100 to get the coefficient of variation. The formula may be stated as below:

$$V = \frac{\sigma}{a} \times 100$$

where,

V = coefficient of variation

σ = Standard deviation

a = Mean

The coefficient of variation may be used for analysis and interpretation of comparable as well as non-comparable data.

(iii) Cross Classification: The complicated statistical techniques may not be so useful for marketing research. Hence the cross-classification may reveal some important inferences. The observation or data may be tabulated in various groups and sub-groups as discussed in the previous chapter. The cross tabulation may be converted into a percentage.

In marketing research, factors such as sex, race, education, occupation etc. are stud they influence the purchasing power of customers. The difference may be expres absolute difference, relative difference and percentage of possible difference.

It is frequently used and highly flexible for studying the relationships be variables. There may be a large number of groupings as per the need of the object the research. The observation and reading of tabulation becomes difficult. Select appropriate sample size will make easy for cross-tabulation.

5. OVERVIEW OF STATISTICAL PROCEDURE

The researcher should review the statistical procedure to determine the appr technique. The important statistical methods decide whether the problem is of univ bivariate or multivariate nature. Univariate is that in which a single variable is analysed. Bivariate are those where some association is measured between two va simultaneously. Multivariate are those where relationships between three or more va are measured simultaneously. There may be two distinct emphases: the sear differences and of association.

1. Univariate Analysis

The univariate analysis is required where the problem is univariate. The univ analysis may involve several considerations, viz., level of measurement, single sam multiple sample, use of non-parametric statistics or parametric statistics, dependent or independent sample and application of suitable statistics-measurement.

(i) Level of Measurement: This is the most important consideration in uni analysis. If the data are nominal, ordinal, interval or ratio scaled, then different s measurements can be applied. If the data are nominal or ordinal, i.e., distribution free parametric statistical procedures will be suitable. Non-parametric statistical proc include the chi-square test, Mannwhitney median test, McNemar test etc. If the da either interval or ratio scaled, parametric statistical procedures may be applied. Z t test and variance are important measures of parametric statistic.

(ii) Single or Multiple Sample: The respondent should decide whether the sam should be single or multiple. There may be need of two samples to cross-check the variables Two or more samples may be taken to determine the validity and range of the mean. In the single sample, chi-square, Kolomogorov-Smirnov measurements will be suitable for the non-parametric test and for nominal and ordinal data Z test, then t test will be useful for parametric test interval or ratio scaled data.

(iii) Non-parametric or Parametric Statistics: The non-parametric statistic will be useful for distribution from data, viz., nominal and ordinal data. It includes chi-square test, Kolomogorov-Smirnov test, Fiedman two-way analysis of variance etc. Parametric statistics include Z test, t test and analysis of variance. The parametric statistics are applied to interval and ratio scaled data.

(iv) Dependent or Independent Sample: Whether the samples are dependent or independent depends on the specifics of the procedures employed to the sample. If the sample is selected without considering the samples already made, it would be an independent sample. If the affects of some factors are to be on some variables, a dependent sample may be selected. The measurements of affect of income on the demand of the ble require a dependent sample. The dependent sample may need McNemar, Codra st, Wilcoxon and Fiedman two-way analysis of variance and + test for non-parametric of nominal and ordinal data. The independent sample may use chi-square, Man-ney, median test, Kruskal-Wallies one-way analysis of variance for non-parametric test minal and ordinal data, and Z test, t test and analysis of variance for parametric test erval or ratio scaled data. The coefficient of concordance will be used for two or more al independent variables and one ordinal dependent variable. Spearman's rank lation and Kendall's rank correlation are used for one ordinal independent variable one ordinal dependent variable. In the rest of other associations, no statistical dures are applied.

nternal Data

In the case of two or more internal depend data, factor analysis and cluster analysis be used. Multiple regression analysis may be used for two or more interval independent ble and one internal dependent analysis. In case of one interval dependent and pendent variable, regression analysis may be suitable. In case of two or more interval pendent variables and one nominal dependent variables, discriminant analysis is used analysis and interpretation of data. In interval independent and ordinal dependent variables, no statistical procedure is applied.

Statistical Techniques of Association

The statistical techniques of association may be appropriate in their respective forms riables. For example, factors analysis with diverse variables and cluster analysis are ul for two or more nominal independent variables and a non-interval dependent ble. Multiple regression analysis (with dummy variables are used for two or more inal) independent variables and one interval variable. Contingency coefficient index dictive association may be useful for all nominal independent variables and nominal endent analysis. Kendall's coefficient of concordance is used for two or more external pendent variables and more ordinal dependent variables. Spearman's rank correlation d Kendall's rank correlation are used for one ordinal independent and one ordinal pendent variable. Factor analysis and cluster analysis are used for two or more interval dependent variables and non-interval dependent variables. Similarly multiple regressions analysis will be used for two or more internal independent variables and one internal dependent variables. Regression analysis is used for one interval independent, and one interval dependent analysis is used for two or more interval independents and one nominal dependent variable.

2. Multivariable Analysis

Bivariable analysis and multivariate analysis use an almost similar type of statistical procedure. The Bivariate has two variables or values whereas the multivariate has more than two variables. It requires additional considerations in choosing from among available procedures. This was the investigation of association and the determination of group differences. There are two factors to decide the type of techniques *(i)* the type of scale used and *(ii)* the role of the individual variables. There are independent variables and dependent variables. In dependent variables one or more of the variables is selected by the conditions of the problem, and there is need to investigate the way in which it depends on the other variates. In independent variables, the researcher is concerned with the relationship of a set of variates among themselves and no one is being selected in the form of a depende variable. These two factors interact to decide the use of a particular technique of analys These two variables may involve one or more variables in every type of nominal, ordi and interval data.

1. Nominal Data: There may be no need of a statistical tool in the case of nomi data of an independent variable and ordinal data of a dependent variable. One variab of nominal data of an independent variable and one variable of a nominal data o dependent variable may use a contingency coefficient index of predictive association. the rest of one variable of nominal data of an independent variable no statistical tool applied. In the case of two or more variables of nominal independent data, and interv dependent data, factor analysis with dummy variables cluster analysis are used for pri analysis, and multiple regression analysis with dummy variables may be used for on dependent variable. Similarly for nominal independent two or more variables and nomin one dependent variable, a contingency coefficient index of predictive association may b used.

2. Ordinal Data: There are only two variables of dependent and independe variables where statistical procedures are applied and in the rest of the variables no statistica tool is used.

❖ ❖ ❖

CHAPTER 14

TEST OF SIGNIFICANCE

1. SAMPLING STATISTICS
   (i) TESTING DIFFERENCES BETWEEN TWO PERCENTAGES
   (ii) TESTING DIFFERENCES BETWEEN CONTINUOUS VARIABLES
2. DIFFERENCES BETWEEN SETS OF DATA
   (i) CATEGORIAL VARIABLES
   (ii) CHI-SQUARE ANALYSIS
   (iii) ANALYSIS OF VARIANCE
3. GENERAL HYPOTHESES TESTING PROCEDURE
4. NON-PARAMETRIC STATISTICS
   (i) NOMINAL DATA
   (ii) ORDINAL DATA
5. PARAMETRIC STATISTICS
   (iii) INTERNAL DATA
   (iv) RATIO SCALED DATA

TEST OF SIGNIFICANCE

When the data have been tabulated and summary measures calculated, it is desirable to find out whether observed differences between categories indicate any actual difference or whether they occurred as a result of chance. There may be a number of statistical techniques for analysis of observed differences. One of the methods may be tests of significance, i.e., whether differences represent true differences or have occurred by chance. A variety of statistical methods have been developed to help researchers to test the significance of differences. The researcher should be aware of observed differences, use of standard error, confidence limits and sampling statistics. Except sampling statistics, we have discussed all the methods. Sampling statistics may be used for testing differences between continuous variables and also statistics to be used for small samples.

1. SAMPLING STATISTICS

The sampling statistics may differ for different purposes. They may be applied for testing differences between two percentages and for testing differences between continuous variables.

1. Testing Differences between Two Percentages

A research finding may be commonly expressed in percentages. Such finding may be useful for comparison and understanding the differences between two groups. For example, expenses of large families and of small families can be easily compared with the percentage. The researchers can conclude on the basis of sample statistics that this difference will exist in the population also. The sampling statistics are commonly applied to two situations, viz., *(i)* hypothesized percentage and *(ii)* different subpopulations.

(i) Comparing observed percentage with hypothesized percentage: The researchers may be interested to know the differences between the observed percentages and the hypothesized percentages. It may revaluate the differences. One may assume that 40 per cent of the consumers like bottled tomato sauce, 30 per cent of the consumers like fresh tomato sauce and 20 per cent like mixed sauce, while the remaining 10 per cent do not like sauce at all. This assumption of the hypothesis may be tested by actual observation of the sample. The sample may reveal the preference which may vary from the assumed percentage. One can find other samples to test the significance of the difference or may use standard deviation to find out whether the difference between the assumed percentage and observed percentage is significant. The observed percentage in the above example may be that 30 per cent of the consumers like bottled tomato sauce. Since the researcher is interested to know about the use of bottled tomato percentage and hypothesized percentage. The standard error of the hypothesized percentage can be calculated as below:

$$\sigma = \sqrt{\frac{pq}{n}}$$

where,

σ = Standard error of a percentage.

p = Hypothesized percentage or proportion of the universe with the characteristics being studied.

q = The probability of non-happening of the event.

n = Size of sample.

Substituting the values, we get,

$$\sigma = \sqrt{\frac{.40 \times .60}{600}}$$

$$= \sqrt{.0004}$$

$$= .02 \text{ or } 2\%$$

The standard error of the difference between hypothesized percentage and observed percentage can be calculated by the following formula:

$$Z = \frac{\text{hypothesized percentage} - \text{observed percentages}}{\sigma}$$

$$= \frac{40\% - 30\%}{2\%} = \frac{1}{2} = 0.5$$

The standard error of the observed difference (Z) has been 0.5 in this example. Thus the observed difference of 10 per cent is significantly high, as we have examined already that $\pm 3\sigma$ covers 99 per cent of the population. In this case $\pm 3 \times .5$ is merely 1.5 which is below the 10 per cent difference. The significant difference shows that the variances are due to subjective approaches, i.e., the liking of the people for the bottle tomato sauce.

(ii) Comparing two observed percentages: The significance of the difference between two samples may reveal the value of the observed percentages. The effectiveness of the publicity can be judged by the two samples: prior to the administration of the publicity and after the administration of the publicity. The difference between two samples with application of statistical procedure will reveal whether the difference was on account of publicity or on account of the sample size. For example, it was revealed with the 500 sample that 20 per cent of the population use pure milk. With the administration of publicity of Prag Milk Distribution, 70 per cent of the population started to purchase pure milk, as became clear from the observation of 600 samples. Thus it is to be observed whether a higher per cent of the population used milk on account of increased publicity, an increase in percentage is merely due on account of variation in sample units and size. The standard error may be used to find out the significance.

$$\sigma d = \sigma_1^2 + \sigma_2^2$$

where,

σd = Estimated standard error of the difference.

σ_1^2 = Estimated standard error of the percentage of first sample.

σ_2^2 = Estimated standard error of the percentage of second sample.

The standard error of percentages of the occurrence of the event is calculated.

$$\sigma = \sqrt{\frac{pq}{n}}$$

where,

σ = Standard error of the percentage.

p = Percentage of occurrence of the event.

q = Percentage of non-occurrence of the event.

n = Sample size.

Substituting the values of percentages and size in both the samples, the estimated standard error of the difference may be calculated as below:

$$\sigma d = \sqrt{\left(\frac{pq}{n}\right)^2 + \left(\frac{pq}{n}\right)^2}$$

$$= \sqrt{\frac{.5 \times .5}{500} + \frac{.7 \times .3}{600}}$$

$$= \sqrt{\frac{25}{500} + \frac{.21}{600}}$$

$$= \sqrt{\frac{1.50 + 1.05}{3000}} = \sqrt{\frac{2.55}{3000}} = \sqrt{.00085}$$

$$= .029 \text{ (Approx.)}$$

$$= 2.9 \text{ per cent}$$

Thus, the estimated standard error of the difference comes to 2.9 per cent. The observed difference expressed in the numbers of standard errors (z) may be

$$Z = \frac{\text{Hypothesized percentage} - \text{Observed percentage}}{\text{Estimated Standard error of the difference}}$$

$$= \frac{70\% - 50\%}{2.9\%} = \frac{20\%}{2.9\%} = .69$$

There is a chance of falling the standard error within the limit of $\pm 3z$, i.e., $3 \times .69 = 2.07$. The difference as shown above is more than this. Thus, the effect of publicity has been vividly observed. The publicity has undoubtedly increased the sale of pure milk. The sampling table of estimate and standard error has been prepared to find out the significance of the difference.

2. Testing Differences between Continuous Variables

When the research series are expressed continuous variables such as income, age, preferences etc. the analysis procedure will be slightly modified. The formula for continuous variables will be:

$$\sigma a = \frac{\sigma}{\sqrt{n}}$$

where,

σa = Estimated standard error of the mean.

σ = Standard deviation of the sample.

n = Number of observations in the sample.

First the standard deviation of the continuous series is calculated with the following formula:

$$\sigma = \sqrt{\frac{fd^2}{f}}$$

where,

σ = Standard deviation of the continuous series.

f = Frequencies of each class interval.

d = Deviations from the mean.

Suppose the standard deviation of 100 samples is 9, the estimated standard error of the mean (σ_a) will be

$$\sigma a = \frac{\sigma}{\sqrt{n}} = \frac{9}{\sqrt{100}} = \frac{9}{10} = 0.9$$

Thus the standard error of the differences of two continuous series may be calculated

$$\sigma d = \sqrt{\sigma a_1^2 + \sigma a_2^2}$$

where,

σd = Estimated standard error of the difference.

σa_1^2 = Estimated standard error of the mean of first sample.

σa_2^2 = Estimated standard error of the mean of second sample.

After calculating the estimated standard error of the difference the hypothesized or estimated difference is converted into the observed difference expressed in numbers of standard error i.e., Z will be calculated by the following formula:

$$Z = \frac{\text{Hypothesized or Estimated mean} - \text{Observed mean}}{\text{Estimated Standard error of the difference}}$$

After calculating the observed standard error of the difference the significance of the difference is interpreted as illustrated earlier. The table of standard errors and their distribution is not applicable to small samples. The theory of normal distribution is applicable in the scale of a large sample. In the case of a small sample, distribution will be useful.

2. DIFFERENCES BETWEEN SETS OF DATA

The sampling statistics dealt with two variables. But there may be more than two variables which may be placed in a tabulated column. The researchers have to study the data and make comparisons of the figures in two columns of data, in two rows and in two different tables. The statistical tests of significance designed for sets of data can determine whether the two sets of data are really different, or whether the differences could easily be attributed to sampling variation. Categorical variables, chi-square analysis and analysis of variance can be the tools of tests of significance.

1. Categorical Variables

Marketing data are generally presented in table or column form; the different rows and columns frequently display categorical variables. There are some variables which can be presented in terms of classes or categories. There may be various variables such as income, consumption expending, sex etc. which can be put in a continuous category. Although there may be no basis of distinction between continuous variables and categorical variables, the researchers try to identify them.

2. Chi-Square Analysis

Chi-square is used to study the divergence of actual and expected frequencies. The coefficient of contingency is calculated to find out whether there is any association between the variable and experimental factor known as attributes. This is the measure of the actual difference between observed and expected frequencies. The importance of such measures is very great in sampling studies where the influence of sampling size or unit may influence the result. In sampling, the perfect measures may not be expected. It will reveal the extent to which the difference between actual and observed frequencies can be ignored. If there is no difference between actual and observed frequencies, the value of chi-square will be zero. If there is a difference between the observed and the expected frequencies, the value of the chi-square will be more than zero. The values of chi-square under different conditions are usually given in the table. If the actual value of chi-square is more than that given in the table, it indicates that the differences between actual and observed values is not due to fluctuations but on account of other reasons.

The chi-square analysis indicates that the observed difference may be either on account of per chance or due to sampling variation. If the calculated value of chi-square is very small as compared to its tabular value, it indicates that the divergence between actual and expected frequencies is very low. On the other hand, if the calculated value of chi-square is very big as compared to its tabular value, the difference between actual value and expected value is very big.

The chi-square analysis can be used if the following four conditions are fulfilled:

1. There may be two observed sets of data or one observed set of data and one hypothetical set of data. These data may be expressed in table form or in frequency distribution form.
2. The two sets of data are based on sample size.
3. Each cell in the data contains an observed or hypothetical count.
4. The different cells in a row or column can represent either continuous variables or categorical variables. The continuous variable data should be placed into classes or categories.

Process: The chi-square is applied in the following processes:

1. The Chi-square statistic is first calculated, which summarises the differences between the two sets of data.

2. The degrees of freedom associated with the data are determined.
3. Using the table value and calculated value of Chi-square it is determined whether the calculated value of Chi-square statistic falls within the value of the table.
4. If the table value and calculated value are the same, the value of Chi-square will be zero and is not significant. In the same manner, if the calculated value does not fall within the range of the table value, the difference between the two sets of data are judged to be significant.

(i) Comparing two frequency distributions: The Chi-square may be used to find out the significant change between two variables. The two frequency distributions can be compared with the help of Chi-square analysis. For example, the pattern of consumption of coffee may be studied. It may have been revealed that 20 per cent were heavy consumers, 30 per cent moderate consumers, 5 per cent light consumers and 35 per cent non-consumer in 1980. If it is to be examined whether the consumption pattern has changed, 1000 samples were selected, and it was found that 220 households were heavy consumers, 370 were moderate consumers, 200 were light consumers and 210 were non-consumers. The figure for comparison purposes may be put in the following figures.

Table 14.1
Coffee Consumption Pattern

Consumption category	*Number of household in each category Study of*		
	1990	*1985*	
Heavy consumers	220	200	(20% of 1000)
Moderate consumers	370	300	(30% of 1000)
Light consumers	200	150	(15% of 1000)
Non-consumers	210	350	(35% of 1000)
	1000	1000	

The 1990 study may be known as actual or observed study, and that of 1985 as expected study. Since it is expected that there is no change in consumption pattern, the study of 1985 is known as expected value.

The Chi-square analysis is used to test whether there is an actual difference between the studies of observed and expected values. Before applying the Chi-square analysis, it is necessary to calculate the value of statistics which summarises the data. Thus, the summary of data also known as Chi-square statistics is calculated with the following formula:

$$X^2 = \Sigma\left[\frac{(f - f_1)^2}{f_1}\right]$$

where,

x^2 = The value of Chi-square statistics.

f = The observed frequency.

f_1 = The corresponding expected frequency.

The summation sign indicates that the equations are added up. There can be four items as mentioned above. The Chi-square statistics may be calculated as below from the above table.

$$X^2 = \left[\frac{(220-200)^2}{200} + \frac{(370-300)^2}{300} + \frac{(200-150)^2}{150} \frac{(210-350)^2}{350}\right]$$

$$= \left[\frac{20^2}{200} + \frac{20^2}{300} + \frac{50^2}{150} + \frac{-140^2}{350}\right]$$

$$= \left[\frac{400}{200} + \frac{4900}{300} + \frac{2500}{150} + \frac{19600}{350}\right]$$

$$= 2 + 16.33 + 16.67 + 56$$

$$= 91$$

The second process as explained above is deciding the degree of freedom associated with the observed set of data. The degree of freedom is decided by the number of examples, hence 4 sets of data or cells. Therefore the degree of freedom would be 4 – 1 = 3. The third process of data is observation of table value. The table value based on the Chi-square table at 3 degrees of freedom is 12.84 at 99% of significance. Thus the difference between the observed value and the expected value is significant, and it had not been an account of sample-fluctuations as the calculated value of X^2 = Chi-square (91) is more than that of the table value (12.84) at 99% per significance and 3 degrees of freedom. So, it can be concluded that the consumption pattern of coffee has improved significantly during the period of five years (1985-1990).

(ii) Comparing an observed frequency distribution: with a hypothetical one: Observed frequency and hypothetical frequency can be tested by Chi-square analysis to reveal the significance of the observed data. The Chi-square can be used to verify the hypotheses or some statements. For example, the producer knows that his share of the market in different regions had been 20 per cent in the South, 25 per cent in the West, 30 per cent in West-Northern, 40 per cent in the Central, 35 per cent in the East and 15 per cent in the north-eastern regions in 1985. In 1990, he wants to know whether his share of the market has declined or increased or has not changed at all. For the purpose, he has selected 100 samples from each cluster or region and it was revealed that his share of the market at present has been 15 per cent in the South, 30 per cent in the West, 40 per cent in West-Northern, 50 per cent in Central, 30 per cent in the East and 10 per cent in the North-East.

The management should analyse whether the data are significantly different from the expected frequency or on account of sampling-variations.[1] With the formula given above, the Chi-square is calculated as below:

$$X^2 = \Sigma\left(\frac{(f - f_1)^2}{f_1}\right)$$

Table 14.2
Analysis of Share of Market

Regions	*Share of Market*	
	Observed frequency 1990	*Expected frequency 1985*
South	15	20
West	30	25
West-North	40	40
Central	50	40
East	30	35
North-East	10	15

Substituting the values, we get

$$X_2 = \Sigma\left[\frac{(15-20)^2}{20}+\frac{(30-25)^2}{25}+\frac{(40-30)^2}{30}+\frac{(50-40)^2}{40}+\frac{(30-35)^2}{35}+\frac{(10-15)^2}{15}\right]$$

$$= \frac{-5^2}{20}+\frac{5^2}{25}+\frac{10^2}{30}+\frac{10^2}{30}+\frac{10^2}{40}+\frac{-5^2}{35}+\frac{-5^2}{15}$$

$$= \frac{25}{20}+\frac{25}{25}+\frac{100}{30}+\frac{100}{40}+\frac{25}{35}+\frac{25}{15}$$

$$= 1.25 + 1 + 3.33 + 2.5 + .71 + 1.67$$

$$= 10.46.$$

The degrees of freedom = n–1 = 6–1 = 5.

The table value of Chi-square at five degrees of freedom and 90 per cent of level of significance is 11.07. Thus the calculated value of Chi-square is less than the tabular value even at 90 per cent level of significance. This shows that the market share of the producer has not significantly increased. The increased value is attributed to sampling fluctuations.

(iii) Comparing two large tables of data: The Chi-square can be used to compare the similarities and differences. There may be different consumption patterns and income ranges which may go on changing every time. To study the influence of a particular factor on other factors requires data of different times. A large number of data are compared to reveal the significant difference of two factors. The degree of freedom is calculated by R rows and C columns, i.e., (R–1) (C–1) = degree of freedom. The analysis is made in the same manner as discussed already, viz., the calculated value is compared with the table value. If the calculated value is less than the table value, the difference between the observed values and expected values is insignificant, and the difference is attributed to the sampling variations. On the other hand, if the calculated value is more than the table value, the difference is significant and the hypothesis is accepted. The difference is not on account of the sampling fluctuations but on account of the attributes, i.e., factors affecting the difference.

The Chi-square test is also applied to the frequency distribution table (one row and C column or R rows and one column) and table form (R rows and C columns). The Chi-square analysis can be applied to many of the different types of categorical data. There may be several examples where Chi-square may be useful, e.g., market segments, advertising, sales territories etc. The number of customers in each category may be used for analysis purposes. It has been considered a very useful technique for marketing researches and the establishment of significance of the differences between observed and expected data.

3. Analysis of Variance

The variance analysis is made for analysing a large set of experimental data. The Chi-square analysis may be applied to survey data placed into categories and classifications after the collection of data. On the other hand, analysis of variance is applied to a set of data collected in an experimental setting. The data drawn from an experiment are tested under similar conditions to evaluate the effectiveness. There may be different rows and columns of data. Each row may contain different treatment of the variables. Similarly, different columns may represent different treatments of the variables. Each cell represents data from a sample which has been subjected to the specific treatment represented by the cell's column and row variables.

The next difference between analysis of variance and Chi-square analysis is that the former applies to one set of experimental data whereas the latter applies to two sets of data to test their significance of difference. Researchers can use analysis of variance to determine if the variation observed down the rows or across the columns have occurred by chance owing to the sampling process. If the differences are real and attributed to some treatments, they can be calculated with the help of variance. As has been mentioned the square of standard deviation is variance. It means the arithmetical average of the squares of deviation taken from the mean is variance. The application of variance can be illustrated from the following examples.

The effect of advertisements on the sale of a particular product can be given in table form:

Table 14.3
Advertising Media

(in thousand units)

Regions	*Newspaper*	*Radio*	*Television*	*Fair*	*Salesmen*
North	30	35	40	30	38
West	35	40	45	32	40
South	40	45	50	35	48
East	45	48	55	40	50
Central	25	20	35	15	22

The Chi-square can reveal the differences between them; but the variance analysis will reveal how far the different advertisement media have affected the sale in different regions. It will reveal whether the sales differences observed across the columns, i.e., media-wise sales are due to the different advertising media or only due to sampling variation. Similarly it will reveal whether the sales differences observed down the rows or region-wise are due to the difference in the features of regions or only due to sampling variation. Thus, the researchers can reveal whether the differences between rows or columns have occurred by chance or due to the sampling process. If it can be revealed that the differences are really on account of factors other than the sampling variation, it can be concluded that the differences are real and attributed to some other factors. The variance analysis is concerned with significant differences within one set of data rather than significant differences between two sets of observations. The above sets of data under different media can be a guideline to present data or experimental variables.

There may be several samples and sub-samples which can be presented in the cross-table as illustrated above and analysed in a systematic manner. The experimental variables may be before experiments and after experiments. The respondents are interviewed before the experiment and also after the experiment. The derived data will reveal how far the experiment has influenced the respondents. In the above example, each media may be divided into two variables, i.e., before the advertisement and after the advertisement. It will be revealed how far these media would influence the sales in different regions. The variation can be calculated from the deviation with the mean.

Table 14.4.A

Total Sale without Administration of Advertising Media

(In thousand units)

	Salesman						
Regions	*A*	*B*	*C*	*D*	*E*	*Total*	*Row Mean*
North	20	25	30	25	30	130	26
West	25	30	20	35	30	140	28
South	10	35	30	45	20	140	28
East	15	30	25	40	30	140	28
Central variation	5	5	10	15	5	40	8
Total	75	125	115	160	115	590	
Column Mean	15	25	23	32	23		24

Table 14.4.B

Effect of Advertisement

(In thousand units)

	Salesman						
Regions	*A*	*B*	*C*	*D*	*E*	*Total*	*Row Mean*
North	40	45	35	30	40	190	38
West	45	50	30	40	55	220	44
South	30	55	40	50	45	220	44
East	25	35	30	45	35	170	28
Central	15	10	20	25	10	80	16
Total	155	195	155	190	185	880	35
Column Mean	31	39	31	39	37		

The formula for calculating the variance,

$$V = \frac{(x - x)^2}{n}$$

where,

V = Variance

x = Vale of individual item

a = Arithmetic mean

n = Number of items

The variance of row can be calculated by applying the above formula. The variance is calculated firstly by getting variation and secondly by degrees of freedom. Thus,

$$V = \frac{\text{Variation}}{\text{Degree of Freedom}}$$

where,

V = Variance

Variation = Square of difference between the items and respective average

Degrees of Freedom = n-1 where n is the size of sample

Row Variation = C [Σ (row-mean – total mean)]

where,

C = Column – number.

Substituting the values, we get

$$\text{Row Variation} = 5[(26-24)^2 + (28-24)^2 + (28-24)^2 + (28-24)^2 + (8-24)^2]$$

$$= 5[2^2 + 4^2 + 4^2 + 4^2 + 16^2]$$

$$= 5(4 + 16 + 16 + 16 + 256)$$

$$= 5 \times 308 = 1540$$

Column Variation = R [Σ (Column mean – total mean)]

where,

R = Row number

Substituting the values, we get

$$\text{Column Variation} = 5[(15-24)^2 + (25-24)^2 + (23-24)^2 + (32-24)^2 + (23-24)^2]$$

$$= 5(92 + 1^2 + 1^2 + 8^2 + 1^2)$$

$$= 5(81 + 1 + 1 + 64 + 1)$$

$$= 5 \times 148 = 740.$$

The interaction variation is calculated by subtracting row variation and column variation from the total variation. The total variation is calculated as below,

Variation = Σ (x – a)

x = The value of each item

a = The mean of all items

Since the total mean or mean of all the items are calculated as 24, the total variation will be the summation of all variation (x – 24). Thus,

$$\text{Total Variation} = (20-24)^2 + (25-24)^2 + (30-24)^2 + (25-24)^2 + (30-24)^2 + (25-24)^2 + (30-24)^2 + (20-24)^2 + (35-24)^2 + (30-24)^2 + (10-24)^2 + (35-24)^2 + (30-24)^2 + (45-24)^2 + (20-24)^2 + (15-24)^2 + (30-24)^2 + (25-24)^2 + (40-24)^2 + (30-24)^2 + (5-24)^2 + (5-24)^2 + (10-24)^2 + (15-24)^2 + (15-24)^2$$

$$= 4^2 + 1^2 + 6^2 + 1^2 + 6^2 + 1^2 + 6^2 + 4^2 + 11^2 + 6^2 + 14^2 + 11^2 + 6^2 + 21^2 + 4^2 + 9^2 + 6^2 + 1^2 + 16^2 + 6^2 + 19^2 + 19^2 + 14^2 + 9^2 + 19^2$$

$$= 16 + 1 + 36 + 1 + 36 + 1 + 36 + 16 + 121 + 36 + 196 + 121 + 36 + 441 + 16 + 81 + 36 + 1 + 256 + 36 + 361 + 361 + 196 + 81 + 361$$

$$= 2880.$$

The variation in samples may be due to salesman (row) variation and also due to region (column) variation. There may be other factors to influence the variation which is calculated by the interaction variation.

$$\text{Interaction Variation} = \text{Total Variation} - \text{Row Variation} - \text{Column Variation.}$$

$$= 2880 - 1540 - 740$$

$$= 600.$$

Thus,

$$\text{Total Variation} = \text{Row Variation} + \text{Column Variation} + \text{Interaction Variation.}$$

$$= 1540 + 740 + 600$$

$$= 2880.$$

This shows that the row variation, i.e., variation due to salesmen effectiveness is very high, e.g., 1540 followed by the column variation, i.e., variation due to regional potentialities, e.g., 740. There are also some variations on account of other fluctuations to the extent of 600. The interaction variation is unaccounted for by either the variation due to the rows or the columns. Since it is unaccounted variation, it is also called residual variation. It is called interaction variation because it may have been caused by interaction of row variation and column variation. Their mutual treatments would also have been affected by the interaction variation. Similarly, from the variation, the variance can be calculated as given in the previous page. Thus,

$$\text{Row Variance or } V_r = \frac{\text{Variation}}{\text{Degrees of Freedom}}$$

$$= \frac{1540}{5-1} = \frac{1540}{4} = 385$$

$$\text{Column Variance or } V_c = \frac{740}{5-1} = \frac{740}{4} = 185$$

$$\text{Interaction Variance } V_{it} = \frac{\text{Variation}}{(R-1)(c-1)} = \frac{600}{(5-1)(5-1)} = \frac{600}{16} = 37.50$$

$$\text{Total Variance or } V_t = \frac{\text{Variation}}{R \times c - 1} = \frac{2880}{5 \times 5 - 1} = \frac{2880}{24} = 120$$

Thus,

Analysis of Variance Summary

Variation Source	*Variation*	*Degrees of Freedom*	*Estimated Variance*
Row Variation	1540	4	385.00
Column Variation	740	4	185.00
Interaction Variation	600	16	37.50
Total	2880	24	120.00

It reveals that there is wide variance in the case of the row item, i.e., salesman. It provides that the effectiveness of the salesmen can influence the total sale to a large extent. The column variance, i.e., the variance on account of region has also some influence on the total sale as it is more than the total variance, i.e., 120. The regionwise variance has been 185. The influence of other factors has been very nominal, i.e., 37.50. However, the fact cannot be ignored that there is no influence of any other factors. Other factors may also influence the total sale but they are negligible.

The effects of advertisements on the sale variations can also be analysed in the same manner. The figures are taken from table 14.4.B.

$$\begin{aligned}
\text{Row Variation} &= 5[(38-35)^2 + (44-35)^2 + (44-35)^2 + (28-35)^2 + (16-35)^2] \\
&= 5(3^2 + 9^2 + 9^2 + 7^2 + 19^2) \\
&= 5(9 + 81 + 81 + 49 + 361) \\
&= 5 \times 581 = 2905.
\end{aligned}$$

$$\begin{aligned}
\text{Column Variation} &= 5[(31-35)^2 + (39-35)^2 + (31-35)^2 + (38-35)^2 + (37-35)^2] \\
&= 5(4^2 + 4^2 + 4^2 + 3^2 + 2^2) \\
&= 5(16 + 16 + 16 + 9 + 4) \\
&= 5 \times 61 = 305
\end{aligned}$$

$$\begin{aligned}
\text{Total Variation} &= (40-35)^2 + (45-35)^2 + (35-35)^2 + (30-35)^2 + (40-35)^2 + (45-35)^2 \\
&\quad + (50-35)^2 + (30-35)^2 + (40-35)^2 + (55-35)^2 + (30-35)^2 + (55-35)^2 \\
&\quad (40-35)^2 + (50-35)^2 + (45-35)^2 + (25-35)^2 + (35-35)^2 + (30-35)^2 \\
&\quad + (45-35)^2 + (35-35)^2 + (15-35)^2 + (10-35)^2 + (20-35)^2 + (25-35)^2 \\
&\quad + (10-35)^2 \\
&= 5^2 + 10^2 + 0^2 + 5^2 + 5^2 + 10^2 + 15^2 + 5^2 + 5^2 + 20^2 + 5^2 + 20^2 \\
&\quad + 5^2 + 15^2 + 10^2 + 10^2 + 0^2 + 5^2 + 10^2 + 0^2 + 20^2 + 25^2 + 15^2 \\
&\quad + 10^2 + 25^2
\end{aligned}$$

$$= 25 + 100 + 0 + 25 + 25 + 100 + 225 + 25 + 25 + 400 + 25 + 400 + 25 + 225 + 100 + 100 + 0 + 25 + 100 + 0 + 400 + 625 + 225 + 100 + 625$$

$$= 3925$$

Thus,

$$\text{Interaction Variation} = \text{Total Variation} - \text{Row Variation} - \text{Column Variation}$$
$$= 3925 - 2905 - 305$$
$$= 715$$

So,

$$\text{Row Variance or } V_r = \frac{\text{Variation}}{\text{Degrees of Freedom}} = \frac{2905}{5-1} = \frac{2905}{4}$$

$$\text{Column Variance or } V_c = \frac{305}{5-1} = \frac{305}{4} = 76.25$$

$$\text{Interaction Variance or } V_{it} = \frac{715}{(5-1)(5-1)} = \frac{715}{16} = 44.69$$

$$\text{Total Variance or } V_t = \frac{3925}{5 \times 5 - 1} = \frac{3925}{24} = 163.54$$

Analysis of Variance Summary

Variation Source	*Variation*	*Degrees of Freedom*	*Estimated Variance*
Row Variation	2905	4	726.25
Column Variation	305	4	76.25
Interaction Variation	715	16	44.69
Total:	3925	24	163.54

This statement reveals that the variation of row, i.e., variation on account of effectiveness of the salesman has been very high. The regional potential has also revealed the variation but it is less than the total variance. The influence of other or miscellaneous factors has been very nominal, i.e., 44.69.

The statistical test of significance can be employed to analyse the variance. This test is known as F test.

$$F = \frac{\text{Estimated variance whose significance is being tests}}{\text{Interaction estimated variance}}$$

Thus, the F test of Row variation can be calculated as

$$F = \frac{726.25}{44.69} = 16.25 \quad \frac{4 \text{ degrees of freedom}}{16 \text{ degrees of freedom}}$$

The table value of F distribution at 95 per cent confidence at 4 degrees of freedom of numeration (Row items) and 16 degrees of freedom of denominator (Interaction) has been 3.01. Thus, the calculated value of F is higher than the tabular value of F. It shows the effectiveness of salesman is significantly higher and has also influenced the total sale alongwith the advertisement.

Similarly the column variance can be tested with F test.

$$F = \frac{\text{Estimated variance of column items}}{\text{Interaction estimated variance}}$$

$$= \frac{76.25}{44.69} = 1.71$$

It shows that the calculated value of F is less than the tabular value. It means that the variation in regional data has been significant. It has been on account of sampling variations.

Analysis of variance can be used to evaluate the results of the experiment. The researchers can use the methods described above. The F test has been used to test the significance of variation in several fields with the help of the above calculation. If the calculated value falls within the range of tabular value of F, it is on account of the sampling variation. The differences in the samples are not on account of experiments. On the contrary, if the calculated value is more than the tabular value, the difference is undoubtedly on account of the experiment factor. The categorical variables such as difference, colour, advertisement, cities and packaging can be examined with the use of variance analysis.

3. GENERAL HYPOTHESES TESTING PROCEDURE

The researchers are interested in knowing whether the researcher results are statistically significant. They want to know whether the difference occurred by chance or by the factors to be examined. Therefore tests of significance are applied to examine the differences. It becomes essential to know whether sample results supported a hypothesis about the population or they suggest that the hypothesis should be rejected. The testing of hypothesis may involve the following steps:

1. Select null hypothesis.
2. Select the appropriate statistical test.
3. Select the desired level of significance.
4. Determine the probability of occurrence.
5. Calculate the value of the test statistic.
6. Draw a statistical conclusion.

These procedures are summarised in the present section.

1. Null Hypothesis

The null hypotheses or alternative hypotheses are the statements that are made between relationships or differences existing between the variables. The relationships or differences found may be due to sampling. The sample study is done to support the null hypothesis or reject the null hypothesis. When the null hypothesis is rejected, another alternative hypothesis is developed and tested again to examine the alternative hypothesis. A hypothesis is an explanation held after careful canvassing of known facts, in full knowledge of other explanations that have been offered and with a mind open to a change of view. The null hypothesis in its simplest form asserts that there is no difference between two samples. The alternative hypotheses and the null hypotheses together constitute the framework for the statistical testing of hypotheses.

2. Appropriate Statistical Test

The statistics are used to come to a decision about a hypothesis. Statistical test is a model and a measurement requirement. The researchers must have knowledge of several statistical tests and their underlying assumptions and utilities. The probability distribution will decide the statistical tools to be applied to test the null hypothesis.

3. Desired Level of Significance

After selecting the appropriate statistical test, the next step is to decide the level of significance. Since a sample is not a total coverage of population, there is need for deciding the level of significance, because then it would be difficult to be certain that the decision to accept or reject a hypothesis is appropriate. The probability of accepting or rejecting a null hypothesis is called the level of significance. The level of significance, also known as alpha (α), depends on how much risk the researcher wants to take in accepting or rejecting the null hypothesis. The level of confidence may be 90 per cent, 95 per cent and 99 per cent which may also represent level of significance 0.10, 0.05 and 0.01 respectively. Higher level of confidence means lower level of significance. The researcher should decide the level of confidence before using a particular statistical tool or test of significance.

4. Probability of Occurrence

After deciding the level of significance, the next step is to determine the probability of occurrence of the test statistics under the Null hypothesis using the sampling distribution specified. The sampling distribution includes all possible values that a test statistic can work under the null hypothesis. The area of rejection will be composed of a set of possible values which are so extreme that when the null hypothesis is true, the probability is very small. There may be tabular values of different probability distribution, e.g., cumulative normal distribution, t distribution, F distribution and so on. The calculated value is compared with the tabular value to find out the significance.

5. Value of the Test Statistic Appropriate for the Sampling Distribution

The actual data analysis starts after deciding the probability of occurrence. The appropriate formula is used for the appropriate statistical test and the critical value is calculated. There are different statistical tools suitable in some specific situations. Thus the data are analysed and statistical values are calculated.

6. Statistical Conclusions

The null hypothesis may be accepted or rejected based on the calculated value and table values. The sampling distribution is considered as part of null hypothesis. If the calculated value falls beyond the table-values, the hypothesis is accepted, and vice versa is used for rejecting the hypothesis.

The statistical tools which are used for testing null hypothesis may be non-parametric statistics and parametric statistics. Parametric measures have been commonly used. These tests are based on models with some assumptions. If the assumptions hold good, these tests may offer a more powerful tool for analysis. This is a well-known fact that tools are based on the interval scale. The application of the interval scale has been commonly used in different areas of knowledge. But with the development of behavioural sciences, we need different techniques as the interval scale does not measure many psychological and sociological variables. The marketing research deals with these psychological and sociological variables for which the traditional interval scale has not been of much help, although the use of the interval scale is still very common in marketing research.

Many of the marketing researches are based on ordinal and nominal scales. The ordinal scale may indicate descriptors which may appear to the scale developer to reflect equal increments of the characteristics when some parametric statistical tests, e.g., t-test and F-test are distorted rather dramatically when the assumption of linearity is violated, the nominal and ordinal scales may be useful. The interval scale is more useful to develop descriptors which reflect equal increments of the characteristics, and the linearity assumptions are slightly distorted. Where only ordinal measurement exists, the interval scale can attempt the true relations among variables and cannot lead to overestimation of results. Where the parametric tools may prove more powerful, more sensitive and more cleanly interpretable statistics, as compared to the ordinal scales, the interval or other parametric scale may be used for proper analysis and interpretation.

The researchers may provide measurements on the interval scale, but the respondents may not understand the measurements. They may answer on the ordinal scale or nominal scale. Thus, the responses will have to be dealt with on the non-parametric scales i.e., the ordinal scale or nominal scale, although the analysis could have been done on parametric tools on the interval scale or ratio scale. Sometimes assumptions pertaining to the interval scale may prove inappropriate, then the use of the interval or ratio scale becomes essential. The subsequent sections will discuss the types of tests and the problems to which they are applicable. The non-parametric statistics are discussed first followed by the parametric statistics.

4. NON-PARAMETRIC STATISTICS

The non-parametric statistics may be of two types: Nominal Statistics and Ordinal Statistics. These statistics are dealt with in detail in the subsequent paragraphs.

1. Nominal Statistics

The nominal statistics involve the test of the goodness of fit, contingency table, McNemar Test and Cohran Q-test.

(i) Goodness of fit test: The goodness of fit test can be done by application of Chi-square test. In marketing research, some expected patterns are given, the observed frequencies should be in accordance with the expected frequencies. It is essential to know the difference between them and also to know the significance of the difference. In other words, it is desirable to know whether the observed frequencies are good or not. The goodness of fit technique is used to test whether a significant difference exists between the observed data and expected tendency. The expected pattern of the data are known from some theories or previous researchers.

For example, a manufacturer sells brand A detergent powder to different families. It was observed that the purchasers of detergent A were 20 per cent small income range family, 40 per cent medium income range family, 35 per cent large income range family and 5 per cent highly income range family. The manufacturer introduces another brand of detergent soap cake. He expects that the selling pattern of detergent powder will also continue in the case of detergent cake. He selects 1000 families of the said four strata. He observed that the buyers of detergent cake have been 250 small income range families, 450 medium range families, 280 large income range families and 20 highly range families. The manufacturer is interested to know whether the observed families of soap cake have followed the pattern of detergent powder. Here, the null hypothesis is developed that the buying pattern of detergent powder will continue to remain in the case of detergent soap cake. Thus the expected buyers will be 20/100 of 1000 = 200 in small income range families, 40/100 of 1000 = 400 medium income range families, 35/100 of 1000 = 350 large income range families and 5/100 of 1000 = 50 highly income range families. The comparison of expected buyers and observed buyers will reveal whether the null hypothesis, i.e., expected pattern will be followed in the observed frequency is accepted or rejected. It can be put in a table.

Table 14.5
Comparison of Observed and Expected Frequencies

No. of families

Income Range of families	*Observed frequencies (f)*	*Expected frequencies (f_1)*	*$(f-f_1)^2$*
1. Small	250	200	2500
2. Medium	450	400	2500
3. Large	280	350	4900
4. Highly	40	50	900
Total:	1000	1000	10800

$$\text{Chi-square or } X^2 = \Sigma\left[\frac{(f-f_1)^2}{f_1}\right]$$

where,

f = Observed frequencies.

f_1 = Expected frequencies.

Substituting the values, we get

$$X^2 = \left[\frac{(250-200)^2}{200} + \frac{(450-400)^2}{400} + \frac{(280-350)^2}{350} + \frac{(20-50)^2}{50}\right]$$

$$= \frac{50^2}{200} + \frac{40^2}{400} + \frac{70^2}{350} + \frac{30^2}{50}$$

$$= \frac{2500}{200} + \frac{2500}{400} + \frac{4900}{350} + \frac{900}{50}$$

$= 12.50 + 6.25 + 14 + 18$

$= 50.75.$

The Chi-square analysis will be complete when compared with the degrees of freedom which are calculated as (n–1) where n stands for the number of observation. In the above table, it is 4–1 = 3. The statistical distribution is determined by its degrees of freedom V. The level of significance or α is also decided to determine the limit base for acceptance or rejection of null hypothesis. Since the sample does not study all the population significance, the level should be decided to know the confidence level. Suppose in this case the confidence level is 99 per cent of level of significance or $\alpha = 0.01$, the table value of Chi-square at 3 degrees of freedom would be 11.34. The calculated value of 50.75 is higher than the table value 11.34. Thus the null hypothesis is rejected, and it is concluded that the observed frequencies are not following the expected frequencies distributions. The difference is on account of some significant factors. The population distribution can be estimated by the Chi-square goodness of fit.

(ii) Contingency Table: The Chi-square test is also applicable to two variables to test the relationship between them. The previous section was related with one variable. Cross tabulation may also use the Chi-square test to analyse the two variables. The Chi-square contingency table technique can be used to determine an association between the data or sets of data or some standards. The Chi-square test assumes that there is no relationship between the two variables. Technically, a null hypothesis is developed whereby it is ± stated that there is no relationship between the variables, i.e., the two variables are not contingent upon one another. The calculated value of Chi-square is compared with the critical value of Chi-square mentioned in the standard value. If the calculated value exceeds the critical value also known as table value, the null hypothesis, i.e., there is no relationship between the two variables which is rejected. On the other hand, if the calculated value falls within the critical value, the null hypothesis is accepted, i.e., there is some relationship between the two variables. When null hypothesis is rejected the difference between sample and chance expectation is too large to be attributed to random error. The Chi-square will reveal whether there is a relationship between the two variables, but it does not determine the strength of the relationship.

The dependence of variables on some factors may be determined by the chi-square test. For example, the researcher may be interested to know the relationship between income range and the use of different television sets. It starts with the null hypothesis, i.e., there is no relationship between income range and sets of television.

The null hypothesis, i.e., the income range and television sets are independent. The expected probability of occurrence of the event income range (A) and television sets (B) is the product of separate probability for A and B. For example

$$P = (AB) = P(A)\ P(B)$$

The probability of A is calculated by the formula, i.e., $\frac{nA_1}{n}$ where nA_1 is the total of first row and n is the total number. For example

$$\frac{nA_1}{n} = \frac{1000}{4000} = \frac{1}{4}$$

Similarly the probability of B is also calculated by the formula, i.e., $\frac{nB_1}{n}$ where nB_1 is total first column and n is the total number. For example

Table 14.6

Income Range and Television Sets

(No. of families)

Income Range per month	*36Cm(B&W)* Observed frequencies	*36Cm(B&W)* Expected frequencies	*36CM-C* Observed frequencies	*36CM-C* Expected frequencies	*11.4CM(B&W)* Observed frequencies	*11.4CM(B&W)* Expected frequencies	*11.4CM-C* Observed frequencies	*11.4CM-C* Expected frequencies	*Total*
Below 2000	50	295	150	112.50	500	230	300	112.50	1000
2000-4000	300	295	350	112.50	120	230	30	112.50	1000
4000-6000	400	295	450	112.50	120	230	30	112.50	1000
Above 6000	430	295	500	112.50	50	230	20	112.50	1000
Total:	1180	1180	450	450.00	920	920	450	450.00	4000

$$\frac{nB_1}{n} = \frac{1180}{4000} = \frac{59}{200}$$

The joint probability $P(A_1B_1)$ i.e., probability of the first row and first column

$$P(A_1B_1) = \frac{nA_1}{n} \times \frac{nB_1}{n} = \frac{1}{4} \times \frac{59}{200} = \frac{59}{800}$$

Thus the frequency of probability of occurrence of first row and first column is

$$E(n_{11}) = np(A_1B_1) = 4000\left(\frac{59}{800}\right) = 295$$

The expected frequency of each cell can be calculated directly by the following proportion

$$E(n_{11}) = nP(A_1B_1) = n\ P(A_1)\ P(B_1)$$

$$= \frac{1000 \times 1180}{4000} = 295$$

Similarly, the expected frequency of each can be calculated such as in case of 2000-4000 income range and 36CM (B&W) frequency will be

$$= \frac{1000 \times 1180}{4000} = 295$$

In case of 2000–4000 income range and 36 CM-C, the frequency will be = $\frac{1000 \times 450}{4000}$ = 112.50. The frequencies of other cells may also be calculated in the same manner. Since the total of each column is 1000, it is 1000 in every case.

The value of Chi-square is calculated with the following formula

$$X^2 = \Sigma\left(\frac{(f - f1)^2}{f_1}\right)$$

where,

X^2 = Chi-square

f = Observed frequency

f_1 = Expected frequency

Substituting the values, we get

$$X^2 = \frac{(50-295)^2}{295} + \frac{(150-112.50)^2}{112.50} + \frac{(500-230)^2}{230} + \frac{(300-112.50)^2}{112.50}$$

$$+ \frac{(300-295)^2}{295} + \frac{350-112.50)^2}{112.50} + \frac{(250-230)^2}{230} + \frac{(100-112.50)^2}{112.50}$$

$$+ \frac{(400-295)^2}{295} + \frac{450-112.50)^2}{112.50} + \frac{(120-230)^2}{230} + \frac{(30-112.50)^2}{112.50}$$

$$+ \frac{(430-295)^2}{295} + \frac{(500-112.50)^2}{112.50} + \frac{(50-230)^2}{230} + \frac{(20-112.50)^2}{112.50}$$

$$+ \frac{245^2}{295} + \frac{37.50^2}{112.50} + \frac{270^2}{230} + \frac{187.5^2}{112.50} + \frac{5^2}{295} + \frac{237.5^2}{112.50} + \frac{20^2}{230}$$

$$+ \frac{12.50^2}{112.50} + \frac{105^2}{112.50} + \frac{110^2}{230} + \frac{82.5^2}{112.50} + \frac{135^2}{112.50} + \frac{387.5^2}{112.50}$$

$$+ \frac{180^2}{230} + \frac{92.5^2}{112.50}$$

$$= \frac{60025}{295} + \frac{1406.25}{112.50} + \frac{18900}{230} + \frac{35156.25}{112.50} + \frac{25}{295} + \frac{56406.25}{112.50}$$

$$+ \frac{400}{230} + \frac{204.25}{112.50} + \frac{11025}{295} + \frac{113906.25}{112.50} + \frac{12100}{230} + \frac{6806.25}{112.50}$$

$$+ \frac{18225}{295} + \frac{150156.25}{112.50} + \frac{32400}{230} + \frac{8156.25}{112.50}$$

$$= 302.83 + 2861.11 + 233.91 + 449.98$$

$$= 3897.83$$

The degrees of freedom or V = (R–1) (C–1)

= (4–1) (4–1) = 9

where R represents the number of rows and C represents the number of columns. Assuming .01 level of significance, the table value X^2 at 9 degrees of freedom is 21.67. Thus, the calculated value of X^2 is more than the critical value of the standard table. Thus the null hypothesis of independence of two variables is rejected. It means both variables are dependent on each other. The Chi-square test hereby reveals that the purchase of a particular television set is influenced by the income range of the purchasers. However, it does not tell us the strength of the relationship or the difference. The Chi-square test is most widely used in marketing research.

Precautions: The Chi-square tests should be used with precautions. Since it deals with frequencies, the percentage figure is converted into an absolute figure. The X^2 distribution is used for discrete variables. Therefore, the continuous series are first converted into discrete variables for application of the Chi-square test. If too many expected frequencies are small, the value may be highly inflated as discussed in the previous section. Small samples may generate a large Chi-square value. Therefore, the sample should be reasonably large. If the size is small, the expected and observed frequencies may not have normally been distributed. It is a presumption that there is nominal distribution. Therefore, a rule of thumb of at least 50 sample units has become essential. Each cell must have some values which should not be less than one. The Chi-square test would be appropriate for analysing observation related to the pretest post-test experience.

(iii) McNemar Test: The McNemar Test is applicable for pretest-post-test research design when the data are measured nominally, and 2 × 2 contingency table is involved. This technique is used to test the effectiveness of a particular treatment. The null hypothesis is developed to test the change in the variable after treatment. Suppose the treatment of the advertisement is to be examined on brand x and y of a particular product, e.g., processed fruit:

Table 14.7

Effect of Advertisement

No. of families

		After Advertisement		*Total*
		Brand x	*Brand y*	
Before Advertisement	Brand x	200 (A)	50 (B)	250
	Brand y	100 (C)	650 (D)	750
	Total:	300	700	1000

The data in each cell is put after observation. The change between first and second observation appear in cells B and C. The family purchasing brand y before the advertisement relating to brand x and after the advertisement of brand y is placed under the cell 'B.' Similarly, families purchasing after advertisement of brand x and before advertisement of brand y in cell 'C.' After advertisement of brand x and before advertisement of brand x, the number of families are the same, i.e., 'A.' They are not influenced by advertisement because they purchase the same brand after the advertisement as well as before the advertisement. Similarly after the advertisement of brand y and before the advertisement of brand y, the number of families are the same, i.e., 'D.' This means they are not affected by the advertisement. The advertisement does not influence cell A and D. The number of families within these cells are the same before and after treatment of the advertisement. B and C have shown changes in the purchasing behaviour.

The test will begin with the null hypothesis that there is no change in behaviour after the advertisement. In other words, the change in behaviour after the advertisement has been proportionate to the behaviour before the advertisement. The proportion change in one brand will be the proportion change in the other brand. Therefore, the null hypothesis will examine the cases of B and C. The McNemar test modifies the X^2 test as below:

$$X^2 = \frac{[(C-B)-1]^2}{C+B}$$

where X^2 = Chi-square of McNemar test.

(C–B) = The absolute value of the difference between C and B frequencies.

1 = Correction for continuity is subtracted from the difference to compensate for the use of the continuous Chi-square distribution.

C + B = The summation of frequencies put in cell C and B.

Since the continuous series cannot be suitable for the Chi-square test, they are converted into discrete series; one is essentially used for correction. The subtraction of one from the absolute value of the difference between C and B before squaring is necessary, because Chi-square is a continuous distribution which is used to approximate a discrete distribution. Substituting the values in the formula, we get

$$X^2 = \frac{[(C-B)-1]^2}{C+B}$$

$$= \frac{[(100-50)-1]^2}{100+50} = \frac{(50-1)^2}{150} = \frac{49^2}{150} = \frac{2401}{150}$$

$$= 16.00$$

The degree of freedom or V = (R–1) (C–1)

= (2–1) (2–1)

= 1

Assuming the level of significance or $\alpha = 0.05$, the critical value of standard X^2 table will be 3.84. Even at the level of significance or $\alpha = 0.01$, the critical value is less than the calculated value, i.e., 6.63. Thus, the calculated value of the McNemar test comes to 16.00 which is much higher than the table value at 1 degree of freedom at 0.01 level of significance. If the calculated value falls within the table value, the null hypothesis is accepted, and if the calculated value falls beyond the table value, the null hypothesis is rejected. Thus, the calculated value 16.00 is more than the table value 6.63. So, the null hypothesis, i.e., the advertisement has no impact on the sale of brand x and y and has been rejected. This shows that the advertisement has been successful in turning the purchaser of y brand to brand x.

The McNemar test has been useful for analysing the pre-test and post-test experiment. It is also useful for analysing samples of matched pairs. The basic assumption under the use of McNemar test is that both the variables are dependent. It can be used only for two variables.

(iv) Cochran Q-test: It has been mentioned earlier that the McNemar test is not useful for series involving more than two variables. The Cochran Q-test may be useful in such circumstances. The samples can be related because each variable may serve as its own control in several sets of observation. The variables can be matched and can be assigned different treatments. For example, the manufacturer of ceiling fan is interested to know the impact on the buyers over the discount in prices during several seasons. A particular year may be divided into four seasons, viz., May to July, August to October, November to January, February to April. Suppose the discount varies from zero percent, 10 percent, 20 percent, 15 percent respectively during the said four seasons also known for analysis purposes as A, B, C and D. The success of price-discount is that it has increased sale. The success may be denoted by 1 and failure of price discount, i.e., it has not increased more than the average sale of the season may be denoted by 0. If ten cities are inquired the impact of discount may be noted in the following table.

Table 14.8

Price Impact on the Seasonal Sale

	Seasons				
City	*A*	*B*	*C*	*D*	*Total*
1	1	0	1	0	2
2	1	0	1	1	3
3	0	1	1	1	3
4	0	1	1	0	2
5	1	1	0	0	2
6	1	0	1	0	2
7	0	1	0	0	1
8	0	1	1	0	2
9	1	1	0	0	1
10	0	0	1	0	1
Total:	5	6	7	2	20

The test will start with the null hypothesis that there is no difference on account of price-discount. The alternative hypothesis is that the price-discount affects the sale. As mentioned above the affect is denoted by 1 and non-affect is denoted by 0. The hypothesis can be related.

$$H0 : P_1 = P_2 = P_3$$

This means the null hypothesis states that the probability of each item is equal.

$$Ha : P_1 \neq P_2 \neq P_3$$

This indicates the alternative hypothesis whereby the probability of each items is not equal. Thus the cochran Q-test will be

$$Q = \frac{k(k-1)\,[\Sigma(C-a)^2]}{\Sigma R(K-R)}$$

where,

Q = Cochran Q-test.

k = Number of experimental conditions.

C = Total number of success in the column.

a = Average of C.

R = Total number of success in the Row.

Substituting the values, we get

$$Q = \frac{4(4-1)\,[(5-5)^2 + (6-5)^2 + (7-5)^2 + (2-5)^2]}{(4-2) + 3(4-3) + 3(4-3) + 2(4-1) + 2(4-2)}$$

$$= \frac{4 \times 3\,(0^2 + 1^2 + 2^2 + 3^2)}{4+3+3+4+4+4+3+4+4+3}$$

$$= \frac{12(14)}{36} = \frac{168}{36} = 4.67$$

A short cut formula is also used to calculate Q

$$Q = \frac{(k-1)\,[k\Sigma C^2 - (\Sigma C)^2]}{k\Sigma R - \Sigma R^2}$$

$$= \frac{(4-1)\,[4(5^2 + 6^2 + 7^2 + 2^2) - (5+6+7+2)^2]}{4(2+3+3+2+2+2+1+2+2+1) - (2^2 + 3^2 + 3^2 + 2^2 + 2^2 + 2^2 + 1^2 + 2^2 + 1^2)}$$

$$= \frac{3(4 \times 114 - 400)}{4 \times 20 - 44} = \frac{3(456 - 400)}{80 - 44} = \frac{3 \times 56}{36} = \frac{168}{36}$$

$= 4.67$

The degrees of freedom or V = k–1 = 4–1 = 3. The level of significance is assumed at 10. The table value of X^2 at 3 degrees of freedom is 6.25 whereas the calculated value is 4.67. It means the null hypothesis is accepted as the calculated value and falls within the critical value of the table. The null hypothesis is not rejected. It means that the price-discount has no impact on the season sale. The reduction in price during some seasons does not increase the sale significantly.

2. Ordinal Statistics

The previous section has discussed nominal statistics which was applied to nominal data. The nominal data is a categorised object. A letter of numeral is assigned to each category so that each number represents a distinct category. It remains undistorted under the one to one substitution. For example, 1 number may be assigned for a Male and 2 number may be assigned to a female. Here 1 and 2 have no distinctive feature. They are only indicative. It does not mean that two is twice better or worse to one. It may also be indicated by A and B. The ordinal data represents a higher level of measurement than the nominal data because the numerals reflect the order as well as the identification of the objects. For example, students may be classified into good, average and poor denoting the numbers 1, 2 and 3 respectively. The order may be reversed. To indicate a higher order, a higher number is also denoted. Only an order is implied by the assignment of numerals. No significant magnitude of the differences in scale can be assigned. The ordinal statistics are used for analysing ordinal data. There may be several ordinal statistics but the important statistics such as the Kolmogorov-Smirnov Test, Median Test, Man-Whitney U Test, Kruskal-Wallies Test, Wilcoxon Test and Friedman analysis are discussed in this section.

1. Kolmogorov-Smirnov D Test

This test is also known as Kolmogorov-Smirnov one sample test and is similar to the Chi-square test of goodness of fit. It is concerned with the degree of agreement between the distribution of observed values and some specified theoretical distribution, i.e., expected frequencies. It is chosen because it compares the distribution on an ordinal scale. The test is applied to test the preference hypothesis and under cumulative frequency distribution. It will test whether the distribution is due to chance or as a result of preference.

This test will reveal whether there is any kind of preference. It represents a natural ordering and tests them under preference hypothesis and cumulative distribution function. The maximum deviation is determined and involves a test statistic. For example, the manufacturer may be interested to know the effect of a coloured package. The researcher may inquire from 200 buyers and was shown different coloured packages, i.e., red, green, blue and white. It was observed that 80 preferred a colour package, 60 preferred a green colour package, 40 preferred a blue colour package and 20 preferred a white package. This can be put in the table for comparison purposes.

Table 14.8
Observed and Expected Distribution

Colour	*Observed Number*	*Observed Proportion*	*Observed cumulative Proportion*	*Theoretical Proportion*	*Theoretical Cumulative Proportion*
Red	80	0.40	0.40	0.25	0.25
Green	60	0.30	0.70	0.25	0.50
Blue	40	0.20	0.90	0.25	0.75
White	20	0.10	1.00	0.25	1.00

The researcher may be interested to know whether such a divergence between the observed frequencies is due to chance or really occurred on account of preference. The Kolmogorov-Smirnov Test known as D test focuses on the largest absolute value of the deviations among observed and theoretical proportions:

$$D = \text{Maximum } [F_o(X) - S_n(X)]$$

where,

D = Kolmogorov-Smirnov Test

$F_o(X)$ = Cumulative frequency distribution under null hypothesis (H_o) for any value x and is the proportion of cases expected to have scores equal to or less than x.

$S_n(X)$ = Observed cumulative frequency distribution of a random sample of N observations where X is any possible score.

Thus, this test involves specifying the cumulative distribution function that would occur under the null hypothesis and comparing that with the observed cumulative distribution function. The null hypothesis is that there is no preference for the various colours. Thus, it is expected that 0.25 of the sample size would prefer any colour because there are only four colours. Thus difference in the observed frequency and expected frequency will be

	$F_o(X)$	–	$S_n(X)$	=	(Difference in going sign)
Red	0.25	–	0.40	=	0.15
Green	0.50	–	0.70	=	0.20
Blue	0.75	–	0.90	=	0.15
White	1.00	–	1.00	=	1.00

If the level of significance is 0.05, the critical value of D for a larger sample is given by 1.36/n where n is the sample size. Thus, in the above example the critical value will be 1.36/200

$$\frac{1.36}{14.14} = 0.096$$

The calculated value of D is 0.20 at the maximum which is higher than the critical value 0.096. Thus the null hypothesis, i.e., the colour that does not impact the sale preference is rejected. It reveals that the colour of the packaging influences the preferences of the buyers. The purchasers prefer a particular coloured package. The D test will examine the preference of the people. It is useful technique of testing preference although Chi-square goodness of the fit test may also be used to test the preference. D-test is preferred procedure and more powerful than Chi-square test. It is easier to compute and does not require a minimum expected frequency in each cell as in the case of Chi-square. It may also be used to determine whether two independent samples have been drawn from the same universe. It is a very useful technique to test the preferences of the consumers. It may also be used for experimental variables, i.e., two observed variables. The maximum deviation may be used to test the difference between the pre-test and post-test variables.

2. Median Test

The median test is the simplest method to test the differences of ordinal data. This is used for testing whether two independent groups differ on the basis of deviations from the median. The null hypothesis that two random samples have been drawn from the population with the same median is also determined by the median test. The test can be used when the samples are independent and the measurement scale is ordinal. The null hypothesis, i.e., medians of two samples are the same can be tested by this method. The procedure is that the two different samples or more samples are combined into a single distribution and the grand median for the sample is obtained. Each median in each sample is compared with the grand median. If a particular median is more than the grand median, it is assigned a plus category, and if the value of the median is less than the grand median, it is assigned a minus category. The null hypothesis says that observations falling in each category will have the same median in all the samples and population.

The median test may be applied to review the deviations in the different samples. The manufacturers may be interested to know whether the customers are satisfied with after sale service or dealers' behaviour. The researcher may develop a number of Likert-type statements which encompass a full range of service and dealers' behaviour. The data are collected on the ordinal scale and no interval measurement is possible. The researcher may mail the questionnaire to both types of customers who have availed of after the sale services of the manufacturers and dealers' service. The questionnaire can furnish information pertaining to both types of services, viz., after sale service and dealers' service. The information can be arranged in table form.

Table 14.9

Scores of After Sale Service and Dealers' Service

Raw Scores		*Combined Rank arranged in Descending order*	
After Sale Service	*Dealers' Service*	*After Sale Service*	*Dealers' Service*
75	82	85	85
63	53	80	82
67	76	75	79
54	79	67	76
35	84	63	70
85	65	54	68
52	68	52	65
80	70	38	60
28	36	35	53
38	60	28	36

Grand Median = 66

Above grand Median = 4 6
Below grand Median = 6 4

The combined median is calculated after rearranging the data of after sale service and dealers' service.

1.	85	11-65
2.	84	12-63
3.	82	13-60
4.	80	14-54
5.	79	15-53
6.	76	16-52
7.	75	17-38
8.	70	18-36
9.	68	19-35
10.	67	20-28

The tenth item is 67 and 11th item is 65. Thus the grand median is 66 as

$$\frac{67+65}{2} = \frac{132}{2} = 66.$$

Table 14.10

Scores of After Sales Service and Dealers' Service Above and Below Median

	After sale Service	*Dealers' Service*	*Total*
Above grand median	4 (a)	6 (b)	10 (a+b)
Below grand median	6 (c)	4 (d)	10 (c+d)
	10 (a+c)	10 (b+d)	20 (a+b+c+d=n)

The calculation X^2 on median test can be done with the following formula.

$$X^2 = \frac{n[ad - bc) - \frac{n}{2}]^2}{(a+b)(c+d)(a+c)(b+d)}$$

where,

X^2 = X^2 based on median test.

n = The total number of observations.

a = Above grand median of first variable.

b = Above grand median of second variable.

c = Below grand median of first variable.

d = Below grand median of second variable. The difference between (ad-bc) ignores the plus and minimum sign.

Substituting the values, we get

$$X^2 = \frac{20[4 \times 4 - 6 \times 6) - \frac{20}{2}]^2}{(4+6)(6+4)(4+6)(6+4)}$$

$$= \frac{20[(16-36)-10]^2}{(10)(10)(10)(10)}$$

$$= \frac{20[(20-10)^2}{10000} = \frac{20 \times 100}{1000} = \frac{2000}{10000} = 0.5$$

The degree of freedom or V = (R–1) (c–1)

= (2–1) (2–1) = 1

The table value of critical value at one degree of freedom and at 0.05 level of significance is 3.84. The calculated value 0.5 falls within the table value 3.84. Thus, the null hypothesis is accepted, i.e., there is no difference between after sale service and dealers' service. There does not appear any difference in satisfaction in both the types of services.

Thus, the median test is very useful for testing the preference or changes in the services or attitudes.

3. Mann-Whitney U-Test

The Mann-Whitney U-test is a powerful test for treating the ordinal data which can be ranked. It is also used with interval data when the t=test may not be used and the variable is normally distributed in the two parent populations. This test is an alternative of the test. If the data are really ordinal and can be ranked, the U-test is a more appropriate method, but if it is meaningful to separate the observations either above or below the grand median, the median test may be a more useful technique of analysis.

This test assumes that the two population distributions are identical. It employs the actual rank of the observations as means for testing the hypothesis, i.e., the two samples are identifically distributed. The ranking is done to each item and they are counted for the purpose of analysis. We illustrated the use of U-test in the previous example. First assign rank to each of the combined observations in terms of magnitude. Secondly add up the ranks associated with the observations in each sample. Thirdly use the U-test formula.

Table 14.11

Scores of After Sale Service and Dealers' Service

Raw Scores		*Combined Rank assigned in Magnitude to each item concerned*	
After Sale Service (n_1)	*Dealers' Service* (n_2)	*After Sale Service* (R_1)	*Dealers' Service* (R_2)
75	82	7	3
63	53	12	15
67	76	10	6
54	79	14	5
35	84	19	2
85	65	1	11
52	68	16	9
80	70	4	8
28	36	20	18
38	60	17	13
$n_1 = 10$	$n_2 = 10$	$R_1 = 120$	$R_2 = 90$

The Mann-Whitney U statistics is defined as smaller of

$$U_1 = [n_1 n_2 + \frac{n_1(n_1+1)}{2} - R_1]$$

$$\text{or } U_2 = n_1\, n_2 - U_1$$

$$\text{or } U_3 = n_1\, n_2 + \frac{n_2(n_2+1)}{2} - R_2$$

where,

U = The Mann-Whitney U value.

n_1 = Number of items in first variable.

n_2 = Number of items in second-variable.

R_1 = Total of rank magnitude of first variable.

R_2 = Total of rank-magnitude of second variable.

Substituting the values, we get

$$U_1 = n_1 n_2 + \frac{n_1(n_1+1)}{2} - R_1$$

$$U_1 = 10 \times 10 + \frac{10(10+1)}{2} - 120$$

$$= 100 \times \frac{110}{2} - 120$$

$$= 100 + 55 - 120 = 35$$

$$U_2 = n_1\, n_2 - U_1$$

$$= 10 \times 10 - 35 = 100 - 35 = 65$$

$$U_3 = n_1\, n_2 + \frac{n_2(n_2+1)}{2} - R_2.$$

$$= 10 \times 10 + \frac{10(10+1)}{2} - 90$$

$$= 100 + \frac{110}{2} - 90$$

$$= 100 + 55 - 90 = 65.$$

Thus, the smaller of these three values is 35. Thus the Mann-Whitney U value is 35. It is revealed that the smaller the value of R, the larger will be the value of U. Thus the larger the difference between the two variables, the smaller will be the U. If the two items are totally non-identical, the value of U will be the lowest one. On the other hand if the two items are identical the value of U will be very high. We have assumed that the null hypothesis is that the two variables are identical. The alternative hypothesis is that the two variables are not identical.

The calculated value of U is compared with the critical value of U given in a standard table. If the calculated value falls within the range of critical value, the null hypothesis, i.e., that the two variables are identical is rejected. On the other hand if the calculated value is more than the table value, i.e., critical value, the null hypothesis is accepted. At the 0.05 level of significance (α), the critical value of U is 64 for a two tabled test. Since the calculated value (35) is below the table value (64), the null hypothesis, i.e., that there is no difference in the two variables is rejected. But it was revealed by the median test that there was no difference in the two types of services. However, if the U test is compared at 0.01 level of significance, the null hypothesis will be accepted as the calculated value of U will be higher to the table value. The Mann-Whitney U test is more powerful than the median test because the former uses more of the information contained in the sample rather than using a point value as in the median test. Therefore, the Mann-Whitney U test is more scientific than the median test. This test assumes that both samples consist of continuous random variables. The correction factor may be used if there are too many tied scores. The U test is differently used than those of other tests. Null hypothesis will be accepted if the calculated value falls beyond the critical value and vice versa.

4. Kruskal-Wallis Test

The Mann-Whitney U test is applicable only in two variables; but there may be more than two variables. So the Kruskal-Wallis H test may be used for more than two independent samples. There may be k sample from each of the k populations. It assumes also the same null hypothesis, i.e., that the samples are identical or the samples are drawn from the identical populations. It requires that the random variable has underlying continuous distributions.

This test involves the same procedure as discussed in the Mann-Whitney U test with the only difference that ranking is done combining all the variables instead of two variables. It consists of combining the scores from the k samples into one large distribution, ranking them, and then obtaining the sums of the ranks for each of the k samples.

For example, the publicity agent may be interested to know whether there is some significant difference between television, radio and newspaper publications. He may collect information from ten customers from each on a rating scale of effective criteria. The raw score of each media is obtained and is given in the following table.

Table 14.12

Evaluation of Media of Advertisement

Raw Scores			*Combined Ranks in Descending order*			*Rank-Magnitude in each Media*		
Tele-vision	*Radio*	*News-paper*	*Tele-vision*	*Radio*	*News-paper*	*Tele-vision* R_1	*Radio* R_2	*News-paper* R_3
35	30	25	58	60	59	21	25	27
40	51	27	55	56	57	15	10	26
20	53	31	52	54	49	30	8	24
58	54	33	50	53	33	3	7	22
38	56	32	45	51	32	18	5	23
39	60	49	40	44	30	17	1	12
50	37	57	39	41	27	11	19	4
45	36	59	38	37	25	13	20	2
55	41	22	35	36	24	6	16	29
52	44	24	20	30	22	9	14	28
$n_1=10$	$n_2=10$	$n_3=10$	Total observation or n		$n=30$	$R_1=143$	$R_2=125$	$R_3=197$

We start with the null hypothesis, i.e., there is no difference among the advertisement media. If the null hypothesis is true, there will be an equal number of evaluation of each media, i.e., the sum of ranks would be equal. But they are not equal, so an adjustment would be needed to make the sum of ranks to allow for this truth. Thus, the Kruskal-Wallis H test is given as

$$H = \frac{12}{n(n+1)}\left(\Sigma\frac{R^2}{n}\right) - 3(n+1)$$

Substituting the values, we get

$$H = \left[\frac{12}{30(30+1)}\Sigma\frac{143^2}{10}+\frac{125^2}{10}+\frac{197^2}{10}\right] - 3(30+1)$$

$$H = \frac{12}{930}\left(\Sigma\frac{20449}{10}+\frac{15625}{10}+\frac{38809}{10}\right) - 3 \times 31$$

$$= \frac{12}{930} \times 7488.3 - 93$$

$$= 9662 - 93 = 3.62$$

The computed value of X^2 at 0.05 level of significance and 2 degrees of freedom (V = k–1 = 3–1 = 2) is 5.99. This reveals that the null hypothesis is accepted as computed value 3.62 and falls within the range of table value (5.99). Thus, there is no significant difference between the effectiveness of advertisement media.

5 Signed Rank or Wilcoxon T Test

The signed rank or Wilcoxon T test is applicable to pretest post-test experiment when the assumptions underlying the parametric tests are not justified. This test is complementary to the Mann-Whitney U test when the two ordinal samples are related. This test is basically suitable to ordinal data; but it can be applied for t or Z test of interval or ratio data if the parametric assumptions are not applicable to them.

This test is useful for pre-test and post test experiments. For example, the manufacturer may be interested to know the impact of advertisements on the services rendered by the dealers to the consumers. A questionnaire is framed to ask for satisfaction on the ordinal scale, i.e., whether the customers are satisfied with the dealers' services. The answers are ranked. The ranks for all dealers are counted and placed as raw scores for each dealer. After an advertisement, the same questionnaire is administered to the customers and the customers are required to rank their satisfaction. The scores of rank obtained by each dealer are recorded in their respective names. The difference of the pre-test and post test scores, without regarding the algebraic sign, are noted and ranked. Then, the differences are ranked in order and the magnitude of rank assigned. The differences of plus sign and of minus sign are noted. The smaller of the two differences are taken as the value of T which is compared with the critical value to compare its significance.

The two scores of pre-test and post test advertisements are recorded in Table 14.13.

Table 14.13
Satisfaction with the Dealers' Services

Dealer	*Before Adver-tisement*	*After Adver-tisement*	*Difference in scores*	*Overall Rank of the difference*	*Ranks of difference*	*Ranks of difference*
1	40	45	5	5	5	
2	45	48	3	4	4	
3	30	40	10	7	7	
4	32	50	18	10	10	
5	46	42	–4	2		2
6	47	44	–3	3		3
7	35	51	16	9	9	
8	38	53	15	8	8	
9	48	55	7	6	6	
10	50	43	–7	1		1
	Total:				49	6

The ranking is done from the smallest value, i.e., 7 in the above example. The plus deviations and minus deviations are separated. Their sums are taken to decide the smallest value. In the above example 6 is the smallest value which is associated with the negative differences. This test starts with the null hypothesis, i.e., there is no difference in dealers' service after advertising and before advertising. The alternative hypothesis will be that there is significant difference between the two variables, i.e., after the advertisement and before the advertisement. The test is one tailed, the argument is similar to the Mann-Whitney U test. The critical value of T at 0.025 level of significance and for a sample of 10 is 8. The calculated value (6) is smaller than the table value (8). Thus, the null hypothesis is rejected. In other words, there is a significant difference between before the advertisement and after the advertisement variables. In tests such as Mann-Whitney U test and signed Rank or Wilcoxon Test, the null hypothesis is rejected if the computed value is less than the critical value, as the U value or T value are the smaller values and their respective differences would be larger. We have noted that the smaller the R value, the larger would be the U value. So, the U and T tests are different from other tests. In these two cases the null hypothesis is accepted when the calculated value is more than the critical value, but in other cases the null hypothesis is accepted when the calculated value is less than the critical value.

6. Friedman Analysis of Variance

The Friedman analysis of variance by ranks is used to test the situations involving more than two sets of related samples. It is an extension of signed rank or Wilcoxon test whereby only two variables are to be examined. This test is useful if the samples are related through some causes or matching or because of repeated observations of the same objects. This test may be used to test the variables often used. For example if the changes in dealers' services are to be examined every year, this test may be a very useful technique. There may be other matched services, e.g., customers' after sale services which may be examined by this test. This test may be used in k samples from the same population or one sample from k populations.

The first step in this test is to rank the values by rows than by columns as discussed earlier. The raw scores are converted into ranks. The highest score for each dealer is scored one in each row, and the lowest score in the k row will be kth as there are k samples. Respective scores of each column are totalled to apply X^2 test. For example, if the manufacturer is interested to know the satisfaction of the customers dealer-wise for the last 4 years. He may prepare a questionnaire and may administer every year to get the score. If there are 10 dealers to be examined, their respective scores for each year of the four years are given in the table and they are marked row-wise.

Table 14.14

Customers' Satisfaction as per Dealer in Four Years

Dealer	Row Scores				Ranks for the year			
	1984	*1986*	*1988*	*1990*	*1984*	*1986*	*1988*	*1990*
1	42	50	55	53	4	3	1	2
2	45	46	50	52	4	3	2	1
3	35	36	40	42	4	3	2	1
4	37	38	42	43	4	3	2	1
5	39	40	45	42	4	3	1	2
6	40	42	47	45	4	3	1	2
7	43	45	52	51	4	3	1	2
8	32	35	38	40	4	3	2	1
9	47	45	53	54	3	4	2	1
10	30	32	35	36	4	3	2	1
	Total:				39	31	16	14

The test proceeds with the null hypothesis that there is no difference in scores during the time. If the null hypothesis is true, the distribution ranks will be relatively equal throughout the period of analysis. If the null hypothesis is false, there has been change in satisfaction rank over the period of time. The alternative hypothesis is that there is variation from one year to the other year. The related statistics of X^2 will be calculated with the following formula:

$$X^2 = \frac{12}{n\,k(k+1)}\ \Sigma R^2 - 3n(k+1)$$

where,

X^2 = Value of Chi-square.

n = The number of matched subjects.

k = The number of matched observations or conditions.

R = The sum of the ranks of each column.

Substituting the values, we get

$$X^2 = \frac{12}{10(4)\,(4+1)}\ [\Sigma\ 39^2 + 31^2 + 16^2 + 14^2] - -3(10)(4+1)$$

$$= \frac{12}{200}\ [1521 + 961 + 256 + 196] - 150$$

$$= \frac{12}{200} \times 2934 - 150$$

$$= 176.04 - 150 = 26.04$$

The critical value of X2 at 0.05 level of significance and 3 degrees of freedom (k–1) is 7.81. Since the calculated value (26.04) is more than the critical value (7.81), the null hypothesis is rejected. The alternative analysis that there is significant difference is accepted. The difference over the period of time has been significant. The dealers' services have given satisfaction in recent years as compared to the previous years.

5. PARAMETRIC STATISTICS

Assigning of numerals to objects is related with the parametric statistics. It tells how much more a number is higher than the other one. The parametric statistics include interval scale and ratio scale. The interval scale has an arbitrary zero whereas the ratio scale has a natural zero. The statistics discussed upto this stage are applicable to the nominal or the ordinal data. If the continuous variables are converted into ranks or classifications, these statistics can be used with interval or ratio scaled data. The higher scaled data are transformed into classifications or rank ordered data. Converting the data into an ordinal or nominal data means losing valuable information. Therefore, the researcher should not discard information for the sake of ordinal or nominal data unless there is justification for doing so. In other words, if the assumptions underlying the appropriate parametric test do not apply, a lower powered test with less rigid statistical assumptions, i.e., nominal or ordinal statistics may be used. Therefore, a powerful statistical test which is appropriate to the circumstances should be used. The researcher should be aware of the conditions and situations which may justify use of the parametric statistics. The parametric statistics may be (1) interval statistics and (2) Ratio statistics.

1. Interval Statistics

The interval statistics may deal with the absolute data. There are equal differences between two and more points on an interval scale. Z and t tests are techniques for measuring such differences. In brief, these tests may be applied when measurement scales are interval, the data are parametric, the observations are independent, and two or less groups are involved. The researcher may decide whether to use Z test or t test. Z test is applied where the population standard deviation is known, or the sample size is greater than 30, and the population standard deviation is unknown. The t test is appropriate when the sample size is less than 30 and the population's standard deviation is unknown. The researcher must consider the alternative hypothesis is stated in one specific direction, or a two tailed test, i.e., a situation in which the alternative hypothesis is stated in both ends of the sampling distribution is used. Both one and two tailed tests may be employed in the testing hypothesis.

The hypothesis therefore may be related to one mean or two means.

1. Hypothesis about one Mean: With the help of a sample mean, some statements about the parent population are made. The mean calculation of a distribution is generally required in the marketing field. For the purpose of several marketing decisions, the estimation of population mean is required. Since the population mean cannot be calculated, the sample mean is taken as approximately equal to the population mean. The study of the sample mean may accept or reject the null hypothesis. These hypotheses may be listed with certain statistical significance because the range of the sample mean may reveal the scope within which the population mean may befall. There is a confidence level to accept the range of estimate. In marketing research we used, may be 90 per cent, 95 per cent and 99 per cent. These are known as level of significance as 0.10 per cent, 0.05 per cent and 0.01 per cent respectively. The sample mean (x) is expected to be equal to population mean (μ). Therefore, the sample variance σx^2 is also expected to the population variance σ2.

(i) Application of Z test: The Z test is applied with the following formula:

$$Z = \frac{\overline{X} - u}{x}$$

where,

Z = Number of standard deviations for the desired level of significance.

$\overline{X}$ = Mean of the sample.

μ = Mean of the population or hypothetical mean.

σx = Estimate for the standard error of the mean.

The standard error of the mean or $\sigma\overline{x}$

$$\sigma\overline{x} = \frac{S}{\sqrt{n-1}}$$

where,

S = Standard deviation of the sample.

n = Number in the sample.

The Z statistics is used to test the significance of the sample mean but it is appropriate if the sample is drawn from a normal population. If the variable is not normally distributed, the sample is large enough for the Central Limit Theorem. One problem arises here that the standard error of the mean (σ) is unknown as the parent population variance is unknown which is equal to $\frac{\sigma}{\sqrt{n}}$. So, the standard error of the mean is estimated from the sample data. Thus, the estimate will be $\sigma\overline{x} = \frac{s}{\sqrt{n}}$ where s is the unbiased sample standard deviation, i.e.,

$$\sigma\overline{x} = \frac{s}{\sqrt{n}}$$

and

$$s = \sqrt{\frac{\Sigma(X - \overline{x})^2}{n-1}}$$

where,

s = Standard deviation of the sample.

X = Actual item.

$\bar{x}$ = Mean of the sample selected.

n = Number in the sample.

The Z test statistic is used to know the significance of the mean. For example, the mean of the soap cakes is 50 mm, and the expected mean of the soap cake is 55 mm. If the sample size has been 626, the sample standard deviation is 20. The Z test will examine the significance of the difference between the observed mean and the expected mean, i.e., they are technically known as the sample mean and population mean. The unbiased estimate of the error of the mean ($\sigma\bar{x}$) will be

$$\sigma\bar{x} = \frac{s}{\sqrt{n-1}}$$

where

$\sigma\bar{x}$ = Unbiased estimate of the standard error of the mean.

s = Standard deviation of the sample and

n = Number of samples.

Substituting the values, we get

$$\sigma\bar{x} = \frac{20}{\sqrt{626-1}} = \frac{20}{25} = 0.80$$

The number of standard deviations for the desired level of significance (Z) is calculated as below:

$$Z = \frac{\bar{X} - u}{\sigma\bar{x}}$$

where,

Z = Number of standard deviation for the desired level of significance.

X = Mean of the sample.

μ = Mean of the population or hypothetical mean.

$\sigma\bar{x}$ = Unbiased estimate of the standard error or the mean.

Substituting the values, we get

$$Z = \frac{50-55}{.80} = -\frac{5}{.8} = -6.25$$

This value is compared with the critical value of Z statistics, i.e., 1.96. Since the calculated value ignoring the sign is more than the critical value, the null hypothesis is rejected. Thus, the true measurement of 50 mm. is not approximately equal to the expected measurement. The difference cannot be assigned to the random fluctuations. The difference was significant.

(ii) Application of t-test: We have seen in the previous chapter that the standard error of the mean ($\sigma\bar{x}$) is

$$\sigma\bar{x} = \frac{s}{\sqrt{n-1}}$$

where,

s = Standard deviation of the sample.

n = Sample size.

or

$$s = \sqrt{\frac{\Sigma(X-x)^2}{n-1}}$$

where,

X = Item of the sample.

$\bar{x}$ = Sample mean.

n = Sample size.

The t distribution at (n–1) degrees of freedom in the small sample, i.e., less than 30 will be

$$t = \frac{(\bar{x}-\mu)}{s_x}$$

Before using the t test, the researcher must ascertain whether the distribution of the variable in the parent population is normal or asymmetrical. He must know whether the sample size is large or small. If the variable of interest is normally distributed, the test statistics will be $\frac{(\bar{x}-\mu)}{s_x}$ where $s\bar{x}$ is standard deviation of the sample. This test is true whether the sample size is large or small. For small samples, t test with n-1 degrees of freedom is used although it may be used for 30 or more observations. The t test is compared with the critical value of the table of normal deviation when analysing large samples. Since it is an unknown factor, t is the useful technique to analyse the normal curve. In case of a large sample the denominator n instead of n-1 may be used to calculate s_x such as

$$s_x = \sqrt{\frac{(X-\bar{X})^2}{n-1}} \text{ or } \sqrt{\frac{\Sigma(x-\bar{x})^2}{n}} \text{ or } \sqrt{\frac{\Sigma d^2}{n-1}}$$

$$t = \frac{\bar{x}-\mu}{s_{\bar{x}}} = \frac{\bar{x}-\mu}{\sqrt{\frac{\Sigma d^2}{n-1}}}$$

In case of a large sample, the value of t can directly tell us whether the difference between the actual and observed mean is significant or not. If the calculated value of t is more than 3, the difference is obviously very significant, and even if it is more than 1.96

the difference is significant at 5% level of significance. In case of small samples, the use of the table serves the purposes. In a small sample, t is denoted as the relationship between the standard error of the mean, and the difference between the observed and actual mean. Thus, t in small samples will be

$$t = \frac{\bar{x} - \mu}{s_x}$$

where,

t = The t value of small samples.

x = The calculated mean value.

μ = The observed mean value.

s_x = The standard error of the mean or $\frac{S}{n}$

$$s = \sqrt{\frac{\Sigma(X - x)^2}{n-1}} \text{ or } \sqrt{\frac{\Sigma d^2}{n-1}}$$

Thus,

$$t = \frac{\bar{x} - \mu}{s_x} \text{ or } \frac{\bar{x} - \mu}{\frac{S}{n}} \text{ or } \frac{\bar{x} - \mu}{\frac{\sqrt{\frac{\Sigma d^2}{n-1}}}{\sqrt{n}}}$$

$$= \frac{\bar{x} - \mu\sqrt{n}}{\sqrt{\frac{\Sigma d^2}{n-1}}} \text{ or } \frac{(\bar{x} - \mu)}{S}\sqrt{n}$$

The above calculation is theoretically correct when the population is normally distributed. When the population is not normally distributed, the t test will not be applicable. If the variable is highly skewed in the parent population and the sample is small, the t test becomes inappropriate. In this case, either the variable has to be arranged in normally distributed frequency or the distribution free statistics may be used.

In the large sample, the t test may be used if the sample size is large enough so that the samples mean X is normally distributed because of the operation of the Central Limit Theorem. The greater the degree of asymmetry, the larger should be the sample size. The sample standard deviation ($\hat{S}$) is a close estimate of the parent population standard deviation (σ). A larger sample size will reduce the difference between sample and population standard deviations.

The t test will be applicable to test the deviation from the theoretically accepted norms. For example, the marketing manager may be interested to know the effectiveness of 10 salesmen. It is expected that at lest 100 units must be sold by each salesman every day. Their actual sale per day will reveal whether they are effectively selling the products or not.

Table 14.15

Effectiveness of the Salesmen

Salesman	*Units sold per day*	*Salesman*	*Units sold per day*
1	95	6	135
2	105	7	123
3	120	8	117
4	125	9	107
5	130	10	93

The null hypothesis, i.e., where there is no difference between the actual sale and expected sale is the starting point for the purpose of analysis. The average (x) of the units sold per day becomes $\frac{1150}{10}$ = 115 and standard deviation of the sample (10 salesmen) or $\hat{S}$ is

$$\hat{S} = \sqrt{\frac{\Sigma(X-x)^2}{n-1}} = \sqrt{\frac{1624}{10-1}} = \sqrt{180.44} = 13.43$$

Therefore the standard error of the mean or $S_{\bar{x}} = \frac{\hat{S}}{\sqrt{n}} = \frac{13.43}{\sqrt{10}} = 4.25$

Thus the value of t will be

$$t = \frac{\bar{x}-\mu}{s_{\bar{x}}}$$

$$= \frac{115-100}{4.25} = \frac{15}{4.25} = 3.53$$

The t value may also be calculated by the short-method.

$$t = \frac{(X-\mu)\sqrt{n}}{\hat{S}} = \frac{(115-100)\times 3.16}{13.43} = 3.53$$

The critical value of t at (n–1 = 10–1 = 1) degrees of freedom is 1.833, since we have taken one tailed test whereas the critical value is of two tailed tests. The level of significance, i.e., 0.05 should therefore be increased to 0.10 level of significance. Thus, the value of t at 0.10 level of significance and 9 degrees of freedom is 1.833. The calculated value 3.53 is more than the critical value (1.833). It suggests that the null hypothesis, i.e., there is no difference between the observed frequency and expected frequency should be rejected. It means that the salesmen were more effective in selling a higher number of units per day, i.e., 115 on an average. The difference cannot be attributed to the sampling variations. If the sample units were large, the Z test may be used instead of the t test.

2. Hypotheses about Two Means

The Z and t tests may be used to test two variable means. There may be three cases to consider the hypotheses. The two parent population variances are known, whereas the parent population variances are unknown and cannot be assumed equal.

(i) Variances are known: Since the population variances change more showly than the population mean, the old variance can be used as the known population variance. The consumption pattern revealed in the previous years may be used as the basis of comparison of the present consumption pattern. The previously determined variances may be known as known variances which may be used for testing the differences. For example, the marketing manager may be interested to know the consumption of coffee among the lower strata and higher strata of the people. It was realised that average consumption per day for the lower strata may be 10 grams, and for the higher strata may be 15 grams. We start with the null hypothesis that there is no difference between the consumption of coffee of the lower strata and of the higher strata, i.e., $H_o : \mu_c = \mu_h$. There may be the alternative hypothesis $H_a : \mu_c = \mu_n$. The average consumption mean of coffee of the lower strata and the higher strata, i.e., $\bar{x}_e$ and $\bar{x}_h$ are normally distributed. The two samples are large enough so that the Central-Limit Theorem is operative. The test statistics will be

$$Z = \frac{(\bar{x}_1 - \bar{x}_2) - (\mu_1 - \mu_2)}{\sigma\, \bar{x}_1 - \bar{x}_2}$$

where,

Z = Calculated value of Z test.

x_1 = The sample mean for the first variable, i.e., lower strata.

x_2 = The sample mean for the second variable, i.e., higher strata.

μ_1 = The unknown population mean of the first variable.

μ_2 = The unknown population mean of the second variable.

$\sigma\bar{x}_1 - \bar{x}_2$ = The standard error of estimate for the difference in means and is equal to $\sqrt{\sigma x_1^2 + \sigma x_2^2}$

where,

$$\sigma x_1^2 = \frac{\sigma^2}{n_1} \text{ and } \sigma x_2^2 = \frac{\sigma 2^2}{n_2}$$

σ_1^2 and σ_2^2 are known population variances of the first variable, i.e., lower strata and second variable, i.e., higher strata in the above examples. If $\sigma_1 = 2$ and $\sigma_2 = 3$. The variances may be $\sigma_1^2 = 2\times2 = 4$ and $\sigma_2^2 = 3\times3 = 9$. Assuming $\bar{x}_1 = 10$ and $\bar{x}_2 = 15$ grams in the random sample of 100, we can evaluate whether the difference is a real one or on account of sample variations. Thus the Z test can be calculated as below:

$$Z = \frac{(\bar{x}_1 - \bar{x}_2) - (\mu_1 - \mu_2)}{\sigma\bar{x}_1 - \bar{x}_2}$$

The standard error of estimate will be

$$\sigma\bar{x}_1 - \bar{x}_2 = \sqrt{\sigma x_1^2 + \sigma x_2^2}$$

$$= \frac{\sigma_1^2}{n_1} + \frac{\sigma_2^2}{n_2}$$

Since $\sigma_1^2 = 2^2 = 4$ and $\sigma_2^2 = 3^2 = 9$; the standard error will be

$$\sigma\bar{x}_1 - \bar{x}_2 = \sqrt{\frac{2^2}{100} + \frac{3^2}{100}} = \sqrt{\frac{4}{100} + \frac{9}{100}} = \sqrt{.13} = 0.367$$

Thus,

$$Z = \frac{(10-15) - (\mu_1 - \mu_2)}{0.367} = \frac{-5.0}{0.367} = -13.5$$

Since we assume under null hypothesis that $u_1 = u_2$; the u1-u2 = 0, the critical value of Z is 1.96 at 0.05 level of significance. The calculated value (13.5) is more than the critical value (1.96 or 3 at 99% confidence). Here we ignore the algebraic signs. Thus, the null hypothesis, i.e., that there is no difference between the two strata about consumption of coffee is rejected. This reveals that the consumption of coffee is significantly higher in the case of the higher strata than that of the lower strata.

(ii) Variances are unknown: In the case of unknown variances of two populations, the standard error of the test statistics i.e., $\sigma\bar{x}_1 - \bar{x}_2$ is also unknown, as $\sigma\bar{x}_1$ and $\sigma\bar{x}_2$ are unknown. They have to be estimated. The population standard deviation is estimated as per the formula of sample standard deviation $(\hat{S}_1^2)$

$$\hat{S}_1^2 = \frac{\Sigma(x_1 - x_1)^2}{(n_1 - 1)}$$ will be to estimate σ_1^2 and

$$\hat{S}_2^2 = \frac{(x_2 - \bar{x}_2)^2}{(n_2 - 1)}$$ will be to estimate σ_2^2

The estimates of standard error of the means will be

$S_{x_1} = \frac{\hat{S}_1}{\sqrt{n}}$ and $S_{x_2} = \frac{\hat{S}_2^2}{\sqrt{n}}$. So the general estimate of the standard error of test statistics or $\sigma\bar{x}_1 - \bar{x}_2$

$$S_{\bar{x}_1 - \bar{x}_2} = \sqrt{S_{x_1} + S_{x_2}} = \sqrt{\frac{\hat{S}_1^2}{n_1} + \frac{\hat{S}_2^2}{n_2}}$$

$$= \sqrt{\hat{S}^2\left(\frac{1}{n_1} + \frac{1}{n_2}\right)}$$

The two parent population variances can be assumed equal to

$$\hat{S}^2 = \frac{\Sigma(x_1-\bar{x}_1)^2}{n_1-1} + \frac{\Sigma(x_2-\bar{x}_2)^2}{n_2-1}$$

$$= \frac{\Sigma(x_1-\bar{x}_1)^2 + \Sigma(x_2-\bar{x}_2)^2}{n_1+n_2-2}$$

Where $\hat{S}_2$ is the pooled sample variance used to estimate common population variance. Thus the appropriate test statistics will be t test.

$$t = \frac{(\bar{x}_1-\bar{x}_2)-(\mu_1-\mu_2)}{S_{\bar{x}_1-\bar{x}_2}}$$

This is the t distribution at $n_1 n_2^{-2}$ degrees of freedom. Since, the null hypothesis assumes $\mu_1 = \mu_2$

$$t = \frac{\bar{x}_1-\bar{x}_2}{S_{\bar{x}_1-\bar{x}_2}}$$

The marketing management may be interested to know whether the plastic container or the glass container of a particular brand of medicine would be better for storing in a particular shop. For this purpose he may select 10 samples containing plastic containers, and other independent 10 samples containing glass containers. Their respective units in the shops are given in table 14.16, and t test is used to examine whether there is any significant difference between the two containers.

Table 14.16

Shops having containers of Medicines

(In thousand units)

Store	*Plastic container*	$(x_1-x_1)^2$	*Glass container*	$(x_2-x_2)^2$	*Store*	*Plastic container*	$(x_1-x_1)^2$	*Glass container*	$(x_2-x_2)^2$
1	12	$2^2=4$	10	$7^2=49$	6	20	$6^2=36$	52	$5^2=25$
2	10	$4^2=16$	12	$5^2=25$	7	21	$7^2=49$	23	$6^2=36$
3	8	$6^2=36$	13	$4^2=16$	8	22	$8^2=64$	25	$8^2=64$
4	13	$1^2=1$	15	$2^2=4$	9	23	$9^2=81$	21	$4^2=16$
5	7	$7^2=14$	20	$3^2=9$	10	14	$6^2=36$	19	$2^2=4$

The test starts with the null hypothesis that there is no difference between a plastic container and a metal container. The formula of t test is given as below:

$$t = \frac{(\bar{x}_1-\bar{x}_2)-(\mu_1-\mu_2)}{S_{\bar{x}_1-\bar{x}_2}}$$

$$\bar{x}_1 = \frac{\Sigma x_1}{n_1} = \frac{140}{10} = 14.0$$

$$\overline{X}_2 = \frac{\Sigma x_2}{n_1} = \frac{170}{10} = 14.0$$

$$S_{\overline{x}_1 - \overline{x}_2} = \sqrt{S_{\overline{x}_1^2} + S_{\overline{x}_2^2}} = \sqrt{\frac{\hat{S}_1^2}{n_1} + \frac{\hat{S}_2^2}{n_2}}$$

$$\hat{S}_1^2 = \frac{\Sigma(X_1 - \overline{X}_1)^2}{(n_1 - 1)} = \frac{301}{10-1} = \frac{301}{9} = 33.44$$

$$\hat{S}_2^2 = \frac{(X_2 - \overline{X}_2)^2}{(n_2 - 1)} = \frac{248}{10-1} = \frac{248}{9} = 27.56$$

Thus,

$$S_{\overline{x}_1 - \overline{x}_2} = \sqrt{\frac{33.44}{10} + \frac{27.56}{10}} = \sqrt{\frac{61.00}{10}} = \sqrt{6.1} = 2.46$$

Substituting the values in the formula of t test

$$t = \frac{(\overline{X}_1 - \overline{X}_2) - (\mu_1 - \mu_2)}{S_{\overline{x}_1 - \overline{x}_2}}$$

$$= \frac{(14 - 17) - (0)}{2.46}$$

$$= \frac{3}{2.46} = 1.27$$

The calculated value of t (1.27) is less than the critical value of t at ($n_1 + n_2{}^2$ = 20-2 = 18) degrees of freedom and 0.05 level of significance (2.101). Thus the null hypothesis, i.e., there is no difference between a plastic container and a glass container is accepted. The marketing manager may therefore decide that there is no difference between a plastic and a glass container. He may select any container for packaging the medicine.

(iii) Samples are related: The related samples can be analysed to find out the significant difference between them. For example, the manufacturer may be interested to know the impact of colour on the sale of school bags to children. There may be earth colour and other colours. The manufacturer may not produce bags or different colours. He may select only one colour for manufacturing purposes. Before starting to manufacture a particular colour bag, he may require to find out the impact of colour on sales. He may select 10 shopkeepers and record their sales of different colours as given in the table.

Table 14.17

Sale of Bags per Shop in Thousands

Shop	*Earth colour* (x_1)	*Other colour* (x_2)	$(x_1-\bar{x}_1)^2$ $(x_1 = 48)$	$(x_2-\bar{x}_2)^2$ $\bar{x}_2=31$	*Shop*	*Earth colour*	*Other colour*	$(x_1-\bar{x}_1)^2$ $\bar{x}_1=48$	$(x_2-x_2)^2$ $\bar{x}_2=31$
1	50	30	$2^2=4$	$1^2=1$	6	46	29	$2^2=4$	$2^2=4$
2	56	32	$8^2=64$	$1^2=1$	7	43	26	$5^2=25$	$5^2=25$
3	52	36	$4^2=16$	$5^2=25$	8	47	27	$1^2=1$	$4^2=16$
4	53	38	$5^2=25$	$7^2=49$	9	48	31	0=0	0=00
5	45	28	$3^2=9$	$3^2=9$	10	40	33	$8^2=64$	$2^2=4$
								= 212	= 134

The pooled estimate of the common variance is

$$\hat{S}^2 = \frac{\Sigma(X_1 - \bar{X}_1)^2 + (X_2 - \bar{X}_2)^2}{n_1 + n_2 - 2}$$

Substituting the values, we get

$$\hat{S}2 = \frac{212+134}{10+10-2} = \frac{346}{18} = 19.22$$

and

$$S_{\bar{x}_1-\bar{x}_2} = \sqrt{\hat{S}^2\left(\frac{1}{n_1}+\frac{1}{n_2}\right)}$$

Substituting the values

$$S_{\bar{x}_1-\bar{x}_2} = \sqrt{19.22}\left(\frac{1}{10}+\frac{1}{10}\right)$$

$$= \sqrt{19.22}\left(\frac{2}{10}\right) = \sqrt{19.22+0.20}$$

$$= \sqrt{19.42} = 4.406$$

The value of t will be

$$t = \frac{(\bar{X}_1 - \bar{X}_2) - (\mu_1 - \mu_2)}{S_{\bar{x}_1-\bar{x}_2}}$$

$$= \frac{48-31-0}{4.406} = \frac{17}{4.406}$$

$$= 3.85$$

The table value at 18 degrees of freedom and 0.05 level of significance will be 2.101. Thus, the null hypothesis, i.e., there is no difference between earth colour and other colours is rejected, because the calculated value is more than the table value. The earth colour is more acceptable among the school children. The bags of different colours are related because they are found in the shops and children have opportunities to select from amongst them.

The standard deviation is calculated to test the significance between the two related samples. The deviations between the two samples are calculated as below:

Deviation between Two Samples

Shop	*$(x_1-x_2)^2$ = d*	*$(d-\bar{d})^2$ $\bar{d}$ = 17*	*Shop*	*(x_1-x_2) = d*	*$(d-\bar{d})^2$ $\bar{d}$=17*
1	50–30 = 20	3^2 = 9	6	46–29 = 17	0^2 = 0
2	56–32 = 24	7^2 = 49	7	43–26 = 17	0^2 = 0
3	52–36 = 16	1^2 = 1	8	47–27 = 20	3^2 = 9
4	53–38 = 15	2^2 = 4	9	48–31 = 17	0^2 = 0
5	45–28 = 17	0^2 = 0	10	40–33 = 7	10^2 = 100
	= 92	= 63		= 78	= 109

The calculated mean difference

$$\bar{d} = \frac{\Sigma d}{n} = \frac{170}{10} = 17$$

The standard error of the difference

$$Sd = \sqrt{\frac{172}{10-1}} = \sqrt{\frac{172}{9}} = \sqrt{19.11} = 4.32$$

The test statistic is

$$t = \frac{\bar{d} - D}{Sd / \sqrt{n}} = \frac{17-0}{4.29/\sqrt{10}} = \frac{17}{4.29} \times \sqrt{10}$$

$$= \frac{17 \times 3.16}{4.29} = 12.5$$

The calculated value 12.5 is more than the t table value 2.101. The null hypothesis, i.e., there is no difference between each colour and other colours is rejected. The manufacturer should produce earth colour school bags as these are more popular among the school children.

2. Ratio Scaled Data

The procedure for testing the difference between two population proportions is the same as has been discussed to test the differences between means. The test for the difference between two population proportions is basically a large sample problem. The samples from each population must be large enough to bring the binomial distribution of sample proportions. So, the np and nq must be more than 10 for each sample where p is the proportion of successes and q is the proportion of failures and n is the sample size. The manufacturer of different items of breakfast cereals and non-cereals may be useful for the school children. He classifies them mainly into two breakfast items: cereal food stuff and non-cereal food stuff. For this purpose, he has selected 300 school children from Northern India and 200 school children from Southern India. In the Northern part of India about 0.55 of the 300 school children used cereal food stuff. So in this case the p_1 is = 0.55, and in the southern part of India, the users of cereal food stuff was $p_2 = 0.4$. The manufacturer may be interested to know whether there are regional differences in the consumers' preferences to the cereal food stuff.

The marketing manager may test the null hypothesis, i.e., there is no difference in the cereal consumption. It may be placed as $H_o : \pi_1 = \pi_2$ where H_o refers to the null hypothesis, π_1 is the proportion of school children who indicated a preference for the cereal in the Northern part of India and π_2 is the proportion of school children who indicated a preference for the cereal in the Southern part of India. The alternate hypothesis, i.e., there is significant difference between the two proportions is also expressed as $H_a : \pi_1 \neq \pi_2$. The Z test formula is used to examine the differences.

$$Z = \frac{(p_1 - p_2) - (\pi_1 - \pi_2)}{\sigma p_1 - p_2}$$

where

$\sigma p_1 - p_2$ is the standard error of the difference in the two sample proportions. It is calculated with the following formula:

$$\sigma p_1 - p_2 = \sqrt{(p_o q_o)\left(\frac{n_1 + n_2}{n_1 n_2}\right)}$$

where,

$$p_o = \frac{n_1 p_1 \; n_2 p_2}{n_1 + n_2} \quad \text{and } q_o = 1 - p_o$$

and

$n_1 p_1$ = The total number of school children who preferred the cereal in the first sample (region).

$n_1 p_2$ = The total number of school children who preferred the cereal in the second sample.

p_0 = The pooled estimate of p of both samples.

Substituting the values

$$p_0 = \frac{300 \times .55 + 200 \times .40}{300 + 200} = \frac{165 + 80}{500} = 0.49$$

and $q_0 = 1 - .49 = 0.51$

The standard error of the difference ($\sigma p_1 - p_2$) will be

$$\sigma p_1 - p_2 = \sqrt{(p_o q_o)\frac{n_1 + n_2}{n_1 n_2}}$$

$$= \sqrt{\frac{.2499 \times 500}{60000}} = \sqrt{0.0020825} = 0.0456$$

Now

$$Z = \frac{(0.55 - 0.40)}{0.0456} - 0$$

We have assumed the null hypothesis, i.e., there is no difference between the two proportions, e.g., $\pi_1 = \pi_2$

So, $\pi_1 - \pi_2 = 0$

$$= \frac{.15}{.056} = 3.29$$

The critical value at 0.05 level of significance is 1.96 which is smaller to the calculated value (3.29). Since the calculated value is greater than the critical value, the null hypothesis is rejected. Now it is well established that there is a significant difference between the two proportions. The school children in the Northern part of India use more cereal than those in the Southern part of India.

Analysis of Variance

The previous sections have analysed only two sets of samples to test their significant differences between the two samples. There may be more than two samples and researchers may face several problems. Therefore, they use variance. In such situations, the most commonly used procedures for testing the significance of the difference among several means are known as Analysis of Variance (ANOVA). This analysis is described in detail in the succeeding chapters. The null hypothesis may discuss several samples as equal. The sum of squared deviations are calculated rather than the sample variances. An individual score in any sample can differ from other scores. The differences can be attributed to two sources. Some individuals may be in different treatment groups and other samples may be under other treatment or experiments. So the measure term of the sum of squares between groups reflects the contribution of different treatments to intergroup differences. The treatment may also differ because of chance variation or individual differences. The sum of squares within groups reflects the intergroup difference.

❖ ❖ ❖

CHAPTER 15

ANALYSIS OF ASSOCIATIONS

1. ASSUMPTIONS:
   - (i) DEPENDENT AND INDEPENDENT VARIABLES
   - (ii) CATEGORICAL AND CONTINUOUS VARIABLES
2. MEASURING ASSOCIATIONS (DEPENDENCE METHOD):
   - (i) CROSS TABULATION
   - (ii) SIMPLE CORRELATION AND REGRESSION ANALYSIS
   - (iii) MULTIPLE CORRELATION AND REGRESSION ANALYSIS
   - (iv) RANK CORRELATION COEFFICIENT
   - (v) CONTINGENCY COEFFICIENT
   - (vi) DISCRIMINANT ANALYSIS
   - (vii) CANONICAL CORRELATION
3. MEASURING ASSOCIATIONS (INTERDEPENDENCE METHOD):
   - (i) DISCRIMINANT ANALYSIS (DETAIL)
   - (ii) FACTOR ANALYSIS
   - (iii) CLUSTER ANALYSIS
   - (iv) MULTIDIMENSIONAL SCALING
   - (v) PLANNING REQUIREMENTS FOR EFFICIENT ANALYSIS

ANALYSIS OF ASSOCIATIONS

There are several situations in which the researcher may be interested to know whether a relationship or association between two or more variables exist. The strength and functional structure of the relationship is also investigated. This chapter will discuss various techniques of measuring the associations. Before discussing the techniques, we will discuss the assumptions underlying the variables and data.

1. ASSUMPTIONS

The prime assumption for analysis of associations is that the data are obtained from surveys and not from experiments. The data are from very large samples, i.e., in excess of 100. The data are obtained from a number of variables and are not limited to one variable. There may be multivariate techniques to obtain these data. The variables are due to several factors. There may be dependent and independent variables and categorical and continuous variables.

1. Dependent and Independent Variables

Dependent variables are those variables which are affected by other factors such as the sale may increase on account of advertisement product quality, low price and so on. Here the sale is a dependent factor and the data related to the sale are dependent variables. The independent variables are uninfluenced by the factors. These variables influence the dependent variables. In brief, the independent variables may be treated as causes of dependent variables. In the above example, the advertisement, product quality and low price etc. are the independent variables which are controlled by management. The dependent variables depend upon the independent variables. The income, family size, education etc. are independent variables which influence the consumption pattern of the people. The consumption pattern will be the dependent variable.

2. Categorical and Continuous Variables

The data tabulated may be either categorical or continuous. The categorical variables are those which can only be measured in terms of classes or categories. They can more conveniently be measured in categories rather than on a continuum. The frequencies cannot be broken in parts. Sex, education, purchases can be measured in categories or discrete. The discrete series are formed from items which are capable of exact measurement. The units are not capable of division. Each unit of data is separated and complete. These data are discussed and analysed in different manners.

Continuous variables are those variables which can be measured on a continuum rather than in classes or categories or discrete series. The continuous variables are put in continuous series whereby the statistical units are capable of division and may be measured in fractions of any size. They can be divided into a limitless number of sub-divisions. In discrete series statistical units are either not divisible or are not divided. If the units are divided, they lose their identity. The age and measurement in kilograms can be divisible, and therefore, put in a continuous series. Where exact measurement is not possible, the information is tabulated in a continuous series.

2. MEASURING ASSOCIATIONS (DEPENDENCE METHOD)

The association between two variables can be measured by applying various techniques. These techniques may be used in dependent as well as independent variables. Some of the techniques may be useful for only a dependent variable or others may be used for independent variables. The important techniques of measuring associations may be cross tabulation, simple correlation and regression analysis, multiple correlation and regression analysis, rank correlation coefficient, discriminant analysis and canonical correlation.

1. Cross Tabulation

Cross tabulation consists of multiple variables and are used for summary analysis of all factors. The cross tabulation is used to indicate data in which both the dependent variable and the independent variables are categorical. The correlation and regression analysis are commonly used in situations where both the dependent variable and the independent variables are continuous. The marketing researcher may be interested to know the impact of various variables on a particular factor. He may like to know the product consumption, brand preference and brand switching and ultimate impact on the sale-volume. The larger income, family size and other factors may be independent variables and the consumption pattern may be the dependent variable. There may be null hypothesis that these factors influence the dependent variable.

The multivariate data can be analysed by a number of statistical methods. The multivariate data consist of one dependent variable and more than one independent variables. Multivariate can be analysed with the cross tabulation.

The simple tabulation may revel only the fact, but the cross tabulation reveals the causes of the fact. For example, the simple tabulation may reveal that 30 per cent of the Indian population view television. The cross tabulation based on income, education, occupation, location and electricity may reveal the percentages of viewers of television. It may reveal why only 30 per cent of the Indian population view television. If one cross tabulation does not reveal all the factors, another cross tabulation with significant data may be used for revealing the important factors of the phenomenon. The cross tabulation may serve the purpose of fact finding and causal relation analysis; but there is a practical limit to the use of cross tabulation. There may be a limitation on account of the small number of independent variables. There may not be enough information to prepare adequate independent variables. It requires a large number of data for preparation of cross tabulation. This is the reason the cross tabulation generally has only three or four variables. It may be illogical to relate nonassociative data to find out the cause and effect relationship. If the data are not related, the cross tabulation may reveal a spurious result. However, the cross tabulation may reveal significant relationships between two variables which are logically related. The multivariate data can be combined in a cross tabulation to reveal the relationships between the variables.

2. Simple Correlation and Regression Analysis

Correlation is the measurement of the degree to which changes in one variable are associated with changes in another variable. When the dependent variable is related to a single independent variable, this is a case of simple regression, and when the dependent variable is related to multiple independent variables, multiple correlation is established. When the two variables are related, some summary value is needed to express the degree of association. This central value is called the correlation coefficient. The correlation coefficient can be measured with direct method and also with the regression method. It is based on the difference between the observed values of each variable and its arithmetical mean. It is measured with the help of a diagram where the two straight lines of the two variables coincide, the correlation coefficient is taken to be at the point. A perfect positive correlation will be +1.0 and a perfect negative correlation will be –0.1, whereas other values of correlation will be within the range of +1.0 and –1.0.

The coefficient correlation is calculated with the algebraic formula, as given below, of x and y variables

$$r = \frac{\Sigma XY}{\sqrt{(\Sigma X^2)\,(\Sigma Y^2)}}$$

where,

r = Coefficient of correlation.

x = Deviation of each case from the mean X.

y = Deviation of each case from the mean y.

ΣXY = Value of covariation.

x^2 = Square of each X deviation.

Y^2 = Square of each y deviation.

The calculated value will reveal the magnitude of the relationship. If r calculated falls between 4 and 8, the relationship is moderate. If the value is more than 0.8, it indicates a strong relationship. If the r is less than 0.4, the relationship is a weak one. The researcher may like to analyse the correlation by calculating the coefficient of determination which is the square of the coefficient of correlation or r^2. This is the proportion of variance in the dependent variable that is associated with or determined by the independent variable.

The significance of correlation can be tested by calculating t value and standard error. The t value is calculated by the following formula:

$$t = \frac{r\sqrt{n-2}}{1-r^2}$$

where,

t = Calculated value of student's t

n = Number of sample size.

r = Coefficient of correlation.

If the calculated value of t is more than the table value the null hypothesis is rejected. The null hypothesis is that the variables are not related. If the calculated value exceeds the table value, the null hypothesis is rejected and it is established that the variables are related.

The correlation may be used with precaution because one may be tempted to conclude the relationship between unrelated variables. This tool should be used to establish the relationship between one and other variables where the cause and effect relationship exists. There must be a logical relationship between two variables.

Simple Regression

Regression and correlation analyses are important techniques for studying the relationship between two or more variables. The two terms are used interchangeably, but there is a difference in purpose. Correlation analysis involves measuring the closeness of the relationship between two or more variables. Regression analysis refers to the techniques used to derive an equation that relates the criterion variable to one or more predictor variables. It considers the frequency distribution of the variable when one or more predictor variables are fixed. Correlation analysis is concerned with the strength of a relationship, whereas regression analysis identifies the relationship between variables in the form of an equation in which one can predict one variable on the behaviour of the other variable. It should be noted here that there is nothing in correlation analysis or any other mathematical procedure. It is only the measure of the nature and degree of association or covariation between variables. The regression analysis may be done by plotting the data on graph-paper. It is the line of regression that will reveal the value of x at the behaviour of y and vice versa.

The line of regression has been used to measure the functional relationship between two variables. It is the slope of the linear relationship that measures the behaviour. It is known as slope parameter. It is computed with the following formula:

$$Y = a + bx$$

This formula is based on the average (a) and growth rate (b) as calculated in the time series. The x value of y can also be calculated in terms of the coefficient of correlation, standard deviations and the mean of the two series.

$$y - \bar{y} = r \frac{\sigma y}{\sigma x} (x - \bar{x})$$

where,

r = Coefficient of correlation.

σy = Standard Deviation of y variable.

σx = Standard Deviation of x variable.

For example if the coefficient correlation between price and sale is –0.8 and the standard deviation of the price (σx) is 4 and the standard deviation of the sale (σy) is 8, the regression coefficient of price on sale will be

$$b_{xy} = r \frac{\sigma x}{\sigma y}$$

Substituting the values,

$$b_{xy} = -0.8 \frac{4}{8}$$

$$= -0.4$$

Similarly, the regression coefficient of sale on price will be

$$b_{yx} = r \frac{\sigma y}{\sigma x}$$

Substituting the values,

$$b_{yx} = -0.8 \frac{8}{4}$$
$$= -0.8 \times 2$$
$$= -1.60$$

Thus, if the price changes by 1, the sale will change by 1.6. Since there is negative correlation, the reduction in price will increase the sale. This will reveal by what rate the sale will increase if the price is reduced. The standard error of the estimate can be calculated to find its unbiased estimate. The standard error of the estimate will be

$$\frac{Sy}{x^2} = \frac{(y-\bar{y})^2}{n-2}$$

The above formula and regression coefficient are applicable only in the linear system. In multilinear and curvilinear data, these formulae are not applied. For these data, different methods of a more sophisticated nature are used.

3. Multiple Correlation and Regression Analysis

The simple correlation and regression analysis decides the internally scaled variables. Analysis of variables reveals several important factors. They should be analysed in relation to other factors. It will predict the behaviour of some phenomena. The factors influencing the dependent variable can be analysed systematically with the help of multiple correlation. It includes the influence of more that one independent variable affecting the dependent variable. The influencing factors may be regregated in important parts. The use of a computer helps to handle several variables at a time influencing one dependent. In the multiple correlation, the primary subscript identifies the criterion variable and predictor variables. The coefficient of multiple correlation is denoted by R whereas the simple correlation is denoted by r. The coefficient of multiple determination is represented by R^2. It represents the proportion of variation in the criterion variable as per variation in the predictor variables. It is always expressed in a positive number. For example, $R^2 = 0.755$ between the sales and other factors has been calculated to reveal that the sale will increase if other factors vary by 75.5 per cent. This relationship can be tested by using the F test. The F can be calculated by the following formula:

$$F = \frac{R^2\ (k-1)}{1-(R^2\ /n-k)}$$

Where n is the number of observations and k is the total number of variables. If the calculated value of F is more than the critical value, the null hypothesis is rejected. The null hypothesis is developed so that there is no relationship between the variables. If the null hypothesis is accepted, it will reveal that there is no significant relationship between the variables. On the other hand, if the null hypothesis is rejected, there is a significant relationship between the variables.

Multiple Regression

The multiple regression constructs an equation that will enable one to estimate values of the criterion variable from the given values of the predictor variables. In simple regression there is only one criterion variable and predictor variable whereas in the multiple regression, there are more than one predictor variable. For example, if there are three predictor variables, the regression equation may be

$$y = a + bx_1 + cx_2 + dx_3$$

Where y is the criterion variable or dependent variable of which value is to be estimated; x_1, x_2 and x_3 are the predictor variables or independent variables; a is the intercept parameter in the multiple regression equation and b, c and d are coefficients of x_1, x_2 and x_3 respectively. The coefficients are calculated with their respective mean and sum of deviations from the mean as discussed in the simple regression.

Multicollinearity

The predictor variables or independent variable are more than one and they are not correlated among themselves. The analyst does not give more importance to any variable. The predictor variables and criterion variable are mutually exclusive. The researcher will evaluate a number of different regression equations as per his need. The level of the predictor variables can be set by the researcher. When the observation's result differs from a survey, the experiment's assumptions are violated. Higher incomes, for example, are associated with a higher education level. Multicollinearity is present in multiple regression when the predictor variables are correlated. Multicollinearity is a situation in which the predictor variables are correlated with each other as well as with the criterion variable. The greater the influence of multicolinearity, the smaller will be the separate effect of adding another variable. It reduces the efficiency of the estimates for the parameters. The effect of each predictor variable on the criterion variable declines as the correlation among the predictor variables increases. One must try to avoid the violation of the multicollinearity assumption to have good independent variables as predictors. The multicollinearity can be reduced by changing the independent variables.

Partial Regression and Correlation

The Coefficient of partial correlation indicates the proportion of variation in one variable as per change in another variable holding all other variables constant. The coefficient of partial determination, R^2 is also used for analysis purposes. It investigates the two variable relationship. The parameters of the model could be estimated from sample data employing the least square method. The regression equation may be expressed as below:

$$y = a + bx + bx_2$$

Whereas other variables are expected to remain constant. The value of y can be estimated by the least squares method. Assuming the multicollinearity assumption is satisfied, the coefficients of partial regression are interpreted as the average change in the criterion variable associated with a unit change in the appropriate predictor variable while holding the other predictor variable constant. In simple regression, the significance of the regression equation is determined by employing the t test. Similarly in multiple regression, the significance of the regression is examined by using the F test. The formula of F has already been described. Very little meaning can be attached to the coefficients of partial regression when multicollinearity is present. If the historical relationship between two predictor variables can continue, it may be easy to predict one variable. But when significant multicollinearity is present, the partial regression should not be used.

The multiple regression analysis requires some additional considerations which are not present in simple regression: *(i)* the coefficient of partial correlation and *(ii)* the coefficient of partial determination. The coefficient of simple determination can be expressed as

$$r^2 = 1 - \frac{\text{Unexplained variation}}{\text{Total variation}}$$

The unexplained variation is known by the square of standard error of estimate Sy_1. The standard error of estimate measures the variation in the criterion variable that was unaccounted for by the predictor variable X. Total variation was given by the variance in the criterion variable Sy_2. Thus,

$$r^2 = 1 - \frac{Sy_1^2}{Sy^2}$$

It measures the relative degree to which the association between the two variables can be used to provide information about the criterion variable. The standard error of estimate measures the variation still remains in the criterion variable y after the two predictor variables x_1 and x_2 have been taken into account. Since Sy_1^2 measures the variation in the criterion variable that remains after the first predictor variable has been taken into account, the ratio Sy^2/Sy_1^2 is a measure of the relative degree to which the association among the three variables y, x_1 and x_2 provides information about y. It is said that this ratio measures the relative degree to which x_2 adds to the knowledge about y after X_1. It is the basis for the coefficient of partial determination which is

$$r^2 = 1 - \frac{S_y^2}{Sy_1^2}$$

The square root of the coefficient of partial determination is the coefficient of partial correlation. When there are more than two predictors, many more coefficients of partial determination can be calculated. Each variable will have two primary subscripts indicating the criterion variable and predictor variable. If there are three predictor variables, there would be fixed subscripts.

4. Rank Correlation Coefficient

We have discussed correlation between interval data and ratio data; but when data are ordinal, different methods are applied to measure the correlation. One of them is Spearman's Rank correlation coefficient, r_s. The coefficient is appropriate when there are two variables both of them are measured on ordinal scale. For example, if the researcher is interested to know the correlation between purchasing habits and social order he may use the rank correlation coefficient. The social order can be measured in ranks as per the Likert Scale. The social class may be indicated in terms of education, income, marital status and so on. They are ranked first considering all these factors. The purchase behaviour is measured as per the amount of purchase. The result may be stated in the following table:

Table 15.1

Rank of Purchase Behaviour and Social Order

Households Behaviour	*Purchase Class*	*Social Squared*	*Difference*	*Difference*
1	6	5	+1	1
2	5	6	−1	1
3	3	3	0	0
4	8	9	−1	1
5	9	10	−1	1
6	10	8	+2	4
7	2	4	−2	4
8	1	2	−1	1
9	4	1	+3	9
10	7	7	0	0
				$\Sigma d^2 = 22$

The formula for calculating rank correlation is as below

$$r_s = 1 - \frac{\Sigma d^2}{n(n^2 - 1)}$$

where,

r_s = Rank correlation coefficient.

Σd^2 = Sum of the squared difference between the rank of the two variables.

n = The number of pairs of rank.

Substituting the values

$$r_s = 1 - \frac{22}{10(10^2 - 1)}$$

$$= 1 - \frac{22}{10 \times 99} = 1 - 0.022$$

$$= 0.978$$

It shows a high degree of correlation between purchase behaviour and social class. We start to test its significance with the null hypothesis, i.e., there is no association between purchase behaviour and social class, i.e., H_0, $r_s = 0$. The value of t is calculated to test the significance with the following formula:

$$t = r_s\sqrt{\frac{n-2}{1-r_s^2}}$$

$$= 0.978\sqrt{\frac{10-2}{1-.978^2}} = 0.978\sqrt{\frac{8}{1-956}}$$

$$= 0.978 \times \sqrt{181.82} = .978 \times 13.45$$

$$= 13.15$$

The table value or critical value at 8 degrees of freedom at 95 level of significance is 2.306. The calculated value of t, i.e., 13.15 is more than the critical value, i.e., 2.306. So, the null hypothesis is rejected and it is concluded that the purchase behaviour and social class are closely related.

Kendall's Tau

Kendall's Tau is an alternate measure of association between two ordinal variables. It has an advantage over the rank correlation because it can be generalised. Kendall's Tau or τ^2 is employed with the same type of data as the rank correlation coefficient uses. The data are rearranged for analysis purposes in an ascending or descending order.

Table 15.2

Purchase Behaviour and Social Class

Households	*Purchase Behaviour*	*Social Class*	*Sum of Natural Order*
8	1	2	+7
7	2	4	+4
3	3	3	+5
9	4	1	+6
2	5	6	+3
1	6	5	+4
10	7	7	+3
4	8	9	0
5	9	10	−1
6	10	8	0
			S = 31

It involves deciding the summation of natural order from the first household. The pair between 8 and 7 households reveals the social class 2 and 4. It reveals that there is natural order, i.e., +1. Similarly the pair 8 and 3 reveals social class 2 and 3, it is again +1. Thus the sum of natural order will be

Households	*Calculation*	*Sum of Natural order*
8	= +1 +1 −1 +1 +1 +1 +1 +1 +1	= +7
7	= −1 −1 +1 +1 +1 +1 +1 +1	= +4
3	= −1 +1 +1 +1 +1 +1 +1	= +5
9	= +1 +1 +1 +1 +1 +1	= +6
2	= −1 +1 +1 +1 +1	= +3
1	= +1 +1 +1 +1	= +4
10	= +1 +1 +1	= +3
4	= +1 −1	= 0
5	= −1	= −1
		0
		S = 31

The maximum possible score within n objects taken as pairs is given by the formula for the combination of n things taken at a time, i.e.,

$$C = \frac{n^1}{(n-2)\,2}$$

which is simplified by the expression $\frac{1}{2}$ n(n–1). Thus with the maximum possible score of 10 pairs would be = $\frac{1}{2}$ 10(10–1) = 45.

The Kendall rank correlation coëfficient τ will be

$$\tau = \frac{\text{Actual Total}}{\text{Maximum Possible Total}} = \frac{S}{\frac{1}{2}n(n-1)}$$

Substituting the values

$$\tau = \frac{31}{45} = 0.722$$

The statistical significance of τ can be examined by employing special table and calculating the value of z

$$z = \frac{\tau - \mu_\tau}{\sigma_\tau}$$

where,

$$\mu_\tau = \text{Mean} = 0$$

and

$$\sigma_\tau = \text{Standard Deviation} = \sqrt{\frac{2(2n+5)}{a\,n(n-1)}}$$

In the above example,

$$\sigma_\tau = \sqrt{\frac{2(2\times 10+5)}{9\times 10(10-1)}} = \sqrt{\frac{50}{810}} = \sqrt{0.0617} = .258$$

Substituting the values,

$$z = \frac{.722-0}{.258}$$

$$z = 2.8$$

The critical value of z at 0.05 level of significance and 8 degree of freedom is not more than 0.5. Thus, the null hypothesis is rejected and it is established that there is significant correlation between purchase behaviour and social class.

5. Contingency Coefficient

The contingency coefficient or C is a measure of the extent of association between two nominally scaled attributes. It has been observed that X^2 test is used to test the independence of nominally scaled variables in a rows and columns contingency table. The contingency coefficient is directly related to the X^2 test; it can be generated in the following formula.

$$C = \sqrt{\frac{X^2}{n+X^2}}$$

where,

C = Contingency coefficient

X^2 = Value of calculated Chi-square

n = The sample size

If the X^2 is calculated as 40.30, in the case of 200 households for purchasing specific articles, we can calculate the contingency coefficient as below:

$$C = \sqrt{\frac{40.30}{200+40.30}}$$

$$= \sqrt{\frac{40.30}{240.30}} = \sqrt{.16} = .4$$

The interpretation will only reveal whether this value is an indication of weak association or strong association. We can say it by comparing with its limit. When there is lack of any association between the variables, the coefficient of contingency will be zero, but it cannot be equal to one in case of perfect association. When the number of rows (r) is equal to columns, the upper limit, on the contingency coefficient for two perfectly correlated variables will be

$$= \sqrt{r-1/r}$$

If the r = c = 3; the value will be

$$= \sqrt{3-2/3} = \sqrt{\frac{2}{3}} = 0.816$$

Thus, the value of contingency coefficient will be between 0 to 0.816 from no association to perfect association. Similarly for the row and column having 5 will be

$$= \sqrt{5-1/5} = \sqrt{\frac{4}{5}} = \sqrt{.8} = .283$$

Two contingency coefficients are not comparable because they have no equal columns and rows. In the above example 0.4 is the contingency coefficients and the maximum value is 0.816. Thus the two variables are significantly associated.

6. Discriminant Analysis

The researcher may classify the data into several groups and sub-groups. There may be multiple categories. He has to establish a relationship between these factors so that forecasting may be possible for each category. By such a formula, he can discriminate between the members of groups. So it is known as discriminant analysis. It is the formula that can examine the relationship between the nominally scaled dependent variable and independent variables. The discriminant analysis can be used to predict a class or category. This analysis indicates a transformation of scores on individuals from a set of independent variables. For example,

$$Y = C_1X_1 + C_2X_2$$

where,

Y = Discriminant value of the element of the population.

X = Exploratory variable.

C = The weighted parameter specifying the relationship between X and Y.

A classification boundary between the two groups Y and Y_1 can be established by discriminant analysis. The analysis may reveal characteristics of variables. Multiple discriminant analysis may be made by computing a linear discriminant function. The ratio of the difference between the means of the two groups to the standard deviation within the group is estimated. This analysis will give an indication as to which factors are important. The multiple discriminant analysis can be employed to examine the difference between variables.

Index of Predictive Association

The contingency coefficient is not appropriate to be interpreted as Karl Pearson's coefficient of correlation. The coefficient of determination or r^2 indicates the proportion of the variance in one variable that is accounted for by covariation in the other. The contingency coefficient is not of that level. So, the index of predictive association is used to interpret. It is appropriate for nominally scaled variables. It can be illustrated by the following table.

Table 15.3

Predictive Association

	Actual Association					*Predictive Association*			
Factor	*A*	*B*	*C*	*Total*	*Factor*	*A*	*B*	*C*	*Total*
D	20	10	0	30	D	6	15	9	30
E	10	70	20	100	E	20	50	30	100
F	10	20	40	70	F	14	35	21	70
Total	40	100	60	200	Total	40	100	60	200

The predictive associations are calculated on relative ratio.

7. Canonical Correlation

There may arise occasions when the researcher may require determination of the relationships of several or a set of dependent variables to a set of independent variables.

It can be established by a canonical analysis. It is a composite association which may measure metric or non-metric data. It utilises a composite of the dependent variables and another composite of the independent variables. The independent and dependent variables can be equally cross established. Simple correlation between the dependent and independent composite variables can be calculated for developing canonical correlation. Weighted coefficients can be estimated if linear combinations of each set are formed and correlated in a simple linear correlation. It can relate that a particular set of composite variables may be highly correlated than other composites.

3. MEASURING ASSOCIATIONS OF INTERDEPENDENT VARIABLES

The previous sections have discussed techniques of measuring associations, and they predict one unknown variable to explain it on the basis of other variables. The interrelationships among all the relevant variables are estimated. The interdependence of variables have been ignored upto this stage. We consider the interdependence variables in this section under discriminant analysis, factor analysis, cluster analysis, multidimensional scalings and planning requirements for analysis.

1. Discriminant Analysis (Detail)

In the previous section we have described the discriminant factors in brief and that too in case of dependence series. In this section, we shall study the discriminant factors as applicable in interdependent variables. This is applicable mainly for analysing the group differences whether two or more groups differ from one another. It requires understanding of the nature of these differences. These may be different characteristics which are analysed. In case of a product, the customers may like to know the price, quantity, quality, design or brand. The socio-economic characteristics of the consumers also affect the purchase behaviour. The scaled data such as income, age, education etc. are decided for comparison purposes. Group differences tend to increase the correlation among the variables. Since the correlation is not direct, it is difficult to determine their impacts.

There may be several factors that influence the purchase behaviours, viz., characteristics related to product and characteristics related to the purchaser. These characteristics are also interdependent. For example, a good quality product may be known by a specific brand, and prices may be reasonable so that the product is purchased by the consumers. The consumers having a higher income may be well educated and may be willing to purchase that particular article. More income influences education and the purchase habit, but it does not mean that more purchasing implies more education and income. There will be more problems if there are several variables to isolate their impact on these factors. It becomes difficult to interpret the differences between two or more groups on each variable taken singly. It requires alternative methods of discussion. One alternative is to construct a linear combination, i.e., a weighted sum of the set of variables. The groups are ranked in terms of linear combination, i.e., a weighted sum of the set of variables. The groups are ranked in terms of linear combination and are examined in relative weights assigned to them. The pattern of weights gives a much more accurate account of the nature of group differences.

Discriminant analysis determines such linear combination as $3x + .7y + .2z$ and so on. The discriminant analysis was first described by R.A. Fisher in two group variables. Later on it was extended to three or more groups.

1. Two Group Variable: Under this method two groups are compared to disclose any discriminating factors because one group has been assigned the typical characteristics of a test. The impact of the characteristics is examined by comparing the two groups. Closer observation of the variable can reveal various important findings. The behaviour of the important factors can be estimated and sometimes linear combination may be established such as:

$$Y = V_1X_1 + V_2X_2$$

Where V_1 and V_2 can be arbitrary or can be derived in such a way as the variation in Y scores between the two groups is as large as possible while the variation in Y scores within the groups are as small as possible. The weights are derived with the following ratio.

$$\text{Ratio} = \frac{\text{Between group variation}}{\text{Within group variation}}$$

is the maximum. This may make V_1 and V_2 a linear progression. This function will reveal the weights to be applied to X_1 and X_2 as the distribution of Y scores and the largest separation between one group and other groups. The two sets of scores may be very different. Since groups are different, the generated scores are also different.

Researchers have decided to analyse the discriminant variable with two way functions *(i)* interpreting the discriminant function and *(ii)* classifying individuals using the discriminant function.

2. Interpreting the Discriminant Function: The researcher should carefully analyse the statistical significance which reveals that there is meaningful differentiation of the groups on the discriminant functions. The investigation will be worthwhile. For example discriminant function

$$Y = 0.89\, x_1 + 0.56\, x_2$$

may relate some functions between y and x_1 as well as x_2. The discriminant function can be analysed as the view of the contribution of each of the variables. The relative importance of each of the variables can be understood. The spurious effect of the measurement units can be eliminated by applying the weight that would predict the standardised form of comparison. Thus, the standardised weights can be compared to determine the relative contribution of the variables. The weights are not assigned where variables are approximately equal. But in many cases, the variables are not of equal importance, so weights are assigned to them.

I. Classifying Individuals using the Discriminant Function

Mean discriminant score for each group will assist interpretation of the discriminant function. There will be a separate regression equation for each variable.

The discriminant function may provide meaningful practical differentiation between the two groups. It is possible to apply the discriminant function to each individual. The variable should predict the behaviour of the score. If an individual's discriminant score is closer to the mean score, it can reveal the specific behaviour of the variable, and it is also easy to predict it. It can predict several other factors influencing the discriminant function. This procedure may have an upward bias in the procedure because the proportion may be overstated. There may be equal classification of the variables. There are also possibilities of multinormal and covariance of the matrics.

Three Group Variables

The discriminant functions may be analysed under three group variables. Some problems may arise when more than two groups are involved. The discriminant functions depend on k group and p variable. While deciding the number of discriminant functions, some rules are observed. If there are more variables p, than groups k, there will be at most k–1 discriminant functions. On the other hand, if the number of variables p is less than the number of groups k, there will be no more than p discriminant functions. The number of statistically significant discriminant functions can be less than the maximum number possible. For example if there are four variables and three groups, the maximum number of discriminant functions may be k–1 = 3–1 = 2. As illustrations:

$$Y_1 = 0.85X_1 + 0.32X_2 + 0.56X_3 + 0.47X_4$$

$$Y_2 = -0.68X_1 + 0.025X_2 + 0.53X_3 + 0.85X_4$$

The linear combinations of the four variables can be developed. They may provide maximum separation among all linear combinations. They may require the respondents' classification and key variables.

The statistical significance of these functions should be checked before they are employed to classify them. The mean discriminant scores must be known for each variable. The matrix maybe used to classify them. It may develop predictive validity. The management may be interested in determining the key variables for differentiating the classes of risk. The raw score coefficients cannot be useful. The discriminant functions were generally not applied to marketing researches; but recently, they have been used for measuring the effectiveness of communication-media. It may be useful to predict adopters and non-adopters of a new product, to predict purchase behaviour and advertising exposure. It may determine the relationship between personality variables and the consumer decision.

2. Factor Analysis

Factor analysis is one of the important analyses of interdependence. It seeks to resolve a large set of measured variables in terms of relatively few new classes known as factors. The factor analysis will reveal the underlying or latent factors that determine the relationship between the observed data, will also make evident relationships between data that had been obscure before such analysis, and will provide a classification scheme when data scored on various rating scales have to be grouped. In a factor analysis, the linear combination of the variables are determined that help in studying the interrelationship. The factors are linear combinations of data for which a line could be drawn to represent its dimension. It coordinates the distance of each observation or variable to obtain the factor loadings. The loadings are derived by the principle of regression analysis. In other words, they represent the degree of correlation between the particular variable and factor. The factor loadings may be placed in a matrix of correlations between the variable and the factors.

There may be various types of matrixes that may be used for rotation of the initial results and bring to light relationships not previously seen, and clarify the common factors underlying the data. Factor analysis is a complicated tool. The factor analysis reduces redundant attributes to bring the underlying construct which is known as the factor. The observed attributes and newly produced factors are revealed in the form of factor loadings which may be termed as coefficients within the matrix. If we square a factor loading, we may be able to evaluate the amount of shared variation between the attribute and the factor. The purposes of factor analysis are two: summarising the data and interpretation.

Summarising Data

The factor analysis summarises the data. It reveals the important questions or information by establishing correlation by establishing the correlation between variables and the measure of the covariation of the variables' objects. Many factor analyses are an implementation of standardised variables, avoiding unnecessary raw variables of differing units. By standardising the variables to mean zero and unit standard deviation, the effect of units of measurement on the final solution is removed. This may be expressed as under:

$$Z = \frac{X - \bar{x}}{s}$$

where,

Z = The standard score of the individual is the variable.
X = The Raw score of the individual on the variable.
x = The mean of the variable.
s = The standard deviation of the variable.

The factor loading matrix is one of the key outputs of a factor analysis. Consider the following variable factor correlations:

Table 15.4

Variable Factor Correlations

Variable	*Factor* 1	2	3
1	0.857	0.082	0.334
2	0.973	0.212	0.456
3	0.934	0.351	–0.222
Total:	2.764	0.645	0.568

The individual row-column entries are the correlations between the variables and the factors. For example, the correlation between factor 1 and variable 1 is 0.857. Similarly, factor 2 and variable 2 have 0.212 correlation. These correlations are called factor loadings. The table of loadings reveals that all three variables load heavily on factor F. The correlations between variable and factor, if squared, will indicate the proportion of variation in the variable that is accounted for by the factor.

Table 15.5

Covariance Factor

Variable	*Factor* 1	2	3
1	$(0.857)^2 = .734$	$(0.082)^2 = 0.007$	$(0.334)^2 = 0.112$
2	$(0.973)^2 = .947$	$(0.212)^2 = 0.049$	$(0.456)^2 = 0.210$
3	$(0.934)^2 = .872$	$(.351)^2 = 0.123$	$(0.222)^2 = 0.049$
Total:	2.553	0.179	0.371

The variance of the correlation has been given in Table 15.4. It indicates the proportion of variation. It focuses on how closely the correlations between the variables can be estimated. The proportion of the total variations in each variable accounts for the factors parallel to the regression analysis. In regression analysis, the problem is how to predict the value of the criterion variable at the given criterion variable. In case of factor analysis, the predictor variables are decided by estimating z score at a standardised criterion variable. There are three factor scores for each variable. In this example, we take the variable as the salesman. The management is interested to know the effectiveness of each salesman in the areas or factors of sales growth, sales profitability and new sales. The salesman one (variable 1) has linear combinations with factor one, i.e., sales growth (.734) with factor two, i.e., sales profitability (.007) and also with factor three, i.e., new sales (0.112).

In one factor model, the question is how well the original variables can be estimated using the first factor scores. The coefficient of determination employed lies in assessing the goodness of fit in a regression model. The coefficient of determination is given as

$$R^2 = \frac{\text{Explained Variation}}{\text{Total Variation}} = 1 - \frac{\text{Unexplained Variation}}{\text{Total Variation}}$$

Thus R^2, i.e., total variation is measured by the variance of the variable. If the criterion variable is to be estimated for each object, the difference between the estimated value and the actual value should be determined. If these residuals are squared and the squared results are summed up, the calculation will give the measure of unexplained variation. The factor analysis is based on similar calculation. The difference between the actual scores and the scores estimated using the first factor scores can be calculated. If these differences are squared and summed up, the result would be a measure of the unexplained variation. If this unexplained variation is divided by a measure of total variation and subtracted from 1, a measure of the goodness of fit can be known. The total variation is a standardised unit variance, i.e., 1. Thus, the sum of the residual squared when subtracted from 1 is the summary measure of factor analysis.

The above theory can be explained by the example of Table 15.4. The pairwise correlations between variables reveal covariability. For example,

$$(0.857)\ (0.973) + (0.082)\ (0.212) + (0.334)\ (0.456)$$
$$= .833 + 0.017 + 0.152 = 1.002$$

The factor estimate of two variables:

$(0.857)\ (0.973) = .833$

$(0.857)\ (0.934) = 0.800$

$(0.973)\ (0.934) = 0.908$

The factor estimate is quite close to the covariability. Thus, these estimates are quite good. The objective of a principal components analysis is to transform a set of interrelated variables into a set of unrelated linear combination of the variables. Similarly, other factors and variables are taken into consideration to decide several independent dimensions or components.

Interpretation: The above analysis has been the summary analysis of the data, but it does not provide the optimal solution. The interpretation of the factors is essential to underly the observed variables. Measures can be obtained for the variables across a set of objects. They reveal the common characteristics of the variables, underlying factors, and real observed variables as a result of underlying factors and isolating and identifying the factors. In the previous examples of the salesman, the relevant factors influencing the sale can be interpreted by calculating the factor score for each salesman. The best performing salesman may be known by ranking the factor score of each salesman, as the maximum score reveals the best salesman and the lowest score reveals the worst salesman.

The complete factor loading matrix which results from principal components can be a source of proper interpretation. The important factors can be revealed from this analysis. Table 15.4 has revealed that factor one is important in every variable, whereas other factors are not so important in these variables. Table 15.4 has also revealed that some of the factors are negatively correlated. A scatter diagram is used for presentation of the factor score at variable levels. It reveals how far a particular factor is important. It also signifies the differences between the factors. The axes can be rotated to reveal more important features of the factor variable analysis. Some analytic criteria may be used to transform the initial factor solution to understand the variables more specifically. Orthogonal rotations and oblique rotations may be used for rotation of the axes. The orthogonal, i.e., angle-preserving rotations may take the form of the quartimex and varimax. The quartimax is the simplification of the rows of the loading matrix, whereas the varimax is the simplification of the columns or factors.

Factor analysis has been used to develop consumer profiles that reflect their attitudes, activities, interests, opinions, perception etc. to predict their consumption behaviour. Factor analysis is used for psychographic research and demographic measures. Eating, drinking, living, reading and several other habits and preferences are analysed by the factor analysis. In marketing, factor analysis has been employed to determine the key attributes determining customer preference for a product, or assess the institutions' images, also job satisfaction of workers and so on.

3. Cluster Analysis

The marketing researcher becomes useful when the objects of study are classified into different segments known as a cluster. The cluster may be people, products, prices, distribution etc. The classification is made on the basis of similarities among the objects. For example, the researcher may be interested in grouping potential customers into homogeneous groups of marketing mix. The classification of groups may be based upon a variety of characteristics ranging from the socio-economic factors to sophisticated psychological factors. For example, the researchers may classify the data as per city assuming their socio-economic and psychological characteristics at par. If there is any difference in the findings, they can be attributed to the city as the influences of socio-economic and psychological characteristics are kept at the minimum. Reducing all the influencing factors to one, e.g., a city in the above case or two only may be a difficult problem for the researcher. It may also be impossible for the person to classify the influencing factors in some definite clusters or groups as they have composite effects on the object or result. Therefore, it becomes essential to combine the related and similar variables into the specific groups according to the objects. The above example may suggest that the "like" cities may be selected instead of cities having the same socio-economic and psychological characteristics as such features are not possible. Thus, "like" cities having approximately similar characteristics are selected for research purposes. The research may be test product marketing, price research, promotional campaigns, distribution system etc.

The characteristics may be of different measures. Therefore, it is essential to group them into standardised characteristics for grouping purposes. If the measurement scales are not standard ones, the grouping would change at the change of the variables. It will be difficult to analyse if the number of measures are changed. This is the reason that the cluster analysis requires measure of "similarity" or "likeness" of the objects for natural groupings.

The Euclidean distance measurements are used to minimise the differences between two variables. For example, the distance or the differences between City A and City B can be minimised by the following formula:

$$d_{A,B} = (X_{B_1} - X_{A_1})^2 + (X_{B_2} - X_{A_2})^2$$

where,

$d_{A,B}$ = Distance between A and B cities.

X_{B_1} = Coordinate of city B on the first dimension, e.g., average income.

X_{A_1} = Coordinate of city A on the first dimension.

X_{B_2} = Coordinate of city B on the second dimension, e.g., average population per Sq.Km.

X_{A_2} = Coordinate of city A on the said second dimension.

If there are three dimensions, it can be extended to the coordinates on the three dimensions. The average distance is developed by dividing the normal Euchidean distance by the number of variables. The distance is an inverse measure of similarity in that the larger the distance, the farther are the objects. A computer is used to measure the distances of several sample units. If there are 16 objects, there will be 16(15/2) 120 distances.

Clustering Methods

There may be three methods for developing natural groupings, viz., linkage procedures, nodal procedures and factor procedures.

1. Linkage Methods: The linkage methods may be several. Some of them, e.g., single linkage, complete linkage and average linkage are discussed here. In the case of single linkage method, the similarity values are arranged from the highest to the lowest figure. The objects having higher or lower coefficients are grouped together. The similarity value is recorded. The union of two objects, i.e., the admission of an object into cluster or the union of two clusters is by the criterion of single linkage. For example, the distance between A and B is 0.35, B and C is 0.25, C and D 0.40 and A and D 0.28. And so on. They can be arranged as per the highest to the lowest rank and can be a cluster in similar group having a group distance. For example, in cluster 1 cities A,C,F etc. may be put as per the class-interval of distance. Similarly, other clusters may be formed considering the distance intervals.

The complete linkage method assumes that an object joining a cluster at a certain similarity coefficient has link at the level. Complete linkage has a tendency to produce tight and compact clusters. The following table will reveal the complete linkage.

Table 15.6
Complete Linkage of Cities

A	B	C	D	E
A	00			
B	0.25	00		
C	0.32	0.22	00	
D	0.28	0.31	0.52	00
E	0.33	0.21	0.35	0.29	00

The above table reveals the distances amongst all the cities. This table does not reveal at a glance the highest and the lowest values. It requires the complete study of the table.

The average linkage is the middle value between complete linkage and single linkage. The average of all similarities between an object and a class of objects is calculated. This involves more calculation union when the average similarity between objects in distinct groups satisfies the criterion. As the composition changes, the average distances or similarities are calculated afresh.

2. Nodal Methods: The second method of clustering are nodal methods whereby grouping is done on the basis of local objects. The nodal methods may be several, some of them are discussed here. The focal objects are known as nodes for clusters. After selecting the focal objects, the remaining objects are then allocated to each cluster on the basis of similarity to the modes or focal objects. The basic principle behind the modal method is selection of modes on the basis of the least similarity or greatest distance. The lowest and greatest focal objects are the two polar modes. The rest of the objects are allocated as per similarity to the polar modes.

The second modal method is employing "Prime" mode which is the typical object. In other words, the prime mode is that object which includes the average characteristics of all the objects. The average based on the mean or median method is calculated to make it a typical object. For example, the characteristics of several cities may be known by their respective average income, average education and so on. The average of all the cities will be known as the prime mode. Other cities having average proximity to the prime mode will be grouped accordingly.

3. Factor Method: In the case of factor method, object by object factor method is known as Q analysis or inverse factor analysis. Variable by variable and object by object are the two types of factor analysis. Variable and object may create cross product of matrix and will be known as cross product factor analysis. The data may be summarised by rotating the simple structure.

Stages in Cluster Analysis: The cluster analysis involves five stages, viz., selecting and coding attributes, producing estimates of resemblance, clustering, testing the system and defining and naming the classes.

1. Selecting and Coding Attributes: The first step indicates the attributes to be employed to generate the natural groupings. We have seen in the previous sections that income, education etc. have been the attributes for grouping purposes. The Euclidean distances have been used for clustering purposes. Change in the characteristics used to define similarity will change the natural groupings characteristics. The marketing researchers generally used a large number of attributes which are unweighted or of equal importance. The attributes may be discrete or continuous. They may be dichotomous or multichotomous.

2. Producing Estimates of Resemblance: The types of statistics to be used to estimate the similarities are important in cluster analysis. We have seen that ratio and interval data use ratio and interval statistics, and non-parametric statistics are used for nominal and ordinal data. Income and population ratio scaled and have been grouped employing Euclidean distance. Similarly marital status, ethnic background, religion etc. may be based on the ordinal or nominal scales. They are measured by absent-present (0-1) attributes. The researcher may use a number of decisions to estimate the similarities for clustering purposes, but the selection of measurements to estimate the resemblance should be logical and practical. In dichotomous and multichotomous data, some methods except distance or product moment correlations are needed. Some sort of matching coefficient will be useful, because it represents the number of characteristics in relation to the number of comparisons. The negative positive or both kinds of matches may be used to measure the resemblance.

3. Clustering: We have already discussed the three methods of clustering, viz., linkage methods, nodal methods and factor methods. Any of these may be used for clustering the objects.

4. Testing and Defining: The researcher has the dual work of testing the system and naming the clusters. The system test measures whether the results offer a reasonable summary of the similarity, correlation and distance matrix. It estimates whether the individual clusters are sufficiently homogeneous, typically useful, and consistent with the input. The unions of any two objects may be affected by their links with the other objects. The acceptable clusters are defined and named. The researcher will analyse those variables which form memberships of the class. The defining and naming of clusters are done in such a way that other researchers and analysts do not confuse with the clustering. They may understand the purpose of cluster analysis.

The problem of determining homogeneous groups is a real problem in marketing research. When test marketing research or similar research is done, it becomes imperative to select those objects which are similar in nature. The use of cluster analysis is not very common in marketing research as compared with that of factor analysis and discriminant analysis.

4. Multidimensional Scalings

The Likert scale and the Stapel scale are unidimensional in nature. They measure perceptions or preferences in terms of a single dimension. Consumers' perceptions and preferences for a given product or brand may be multidimensional. For example, an automobile may be assessed by its luxuriousness dimension, sportiness dimensions and so on. Multidimensional scaling is an important statistical technique that represents such perceptions and preferences which are interdependent between responses and variables. There may be several approaches for analysing multidimensional data. The study of a product may involve analysis of the product-quality, brand, space, cost, colour and so on. This analysis may employ market clusters, segments and their sizes and so on. Such analysis may yield valuable results for determining marketing strategies. The attributes and non-attributes are examined for analysis purposes.

Multiple discriminant analysis is used to isolate a combination of attributes which discriminates groups and competitive products. There may be several discriminating factors according to multiple attributes and specific attributes which are segregated from the general attributes. There may be several categories or dimensions in which attributes may be grouped. The data may be placed on graphs depicting the multidimensional figures. The marketing managers may use the multidimensional figures for arriving at definite decisions for pricing, competition, quantity, distribution etc. The market structure analysis is possible with the multidimensional techniques.

Market Structure Analysis: The multidimensional analysis refers to the market structure analysis specifically. It may offer sufficient guidance for marketing decisions. We observe that the market segmentation work is more sophisticated because of greater dimensions for marketing decisions. For example, a consumer packed goods will involve several dimensions to meet the consumers' taste, interest and preferences. The general characteristics and technical factors are considered for analysis of market structure. It uses the consumer panel, purchasing behaviour, product class and demographic characteristics. The consumer research involves various independent consumer variables, purchasing behaviours and segmentation. It is a significant part of market structure analysis which may use analysis of consumer product, brand type of product and other dependent variables. The attitudinal factors are reduced to a smaller number of factors for analysis purposes. The independent variables such as attitudes, opinions, interest and other demographic factors are taken into consideration for analysis purposes. The correlation between product variables and independent variables is calculated to analyse the market structure. Canonical analysis is undertaken to develop a classification system of the consumers, e.g., the number, size, nature and consumption pattern of the consumers. The classification of consumers and their different attitudes may provide segment and matrix to analyse the several patterns of consumption.

Non-Attribute Analysis: Non-attribute data may be included under multidimensional scaling method. The non-attribute data are those data which are derived without perceiving or evaluation of the object. The object, e.g., product, brand, type etc. may not be described in terms of individual attributes. For example, the researcher may be interested to find out the popularity of different types of television, e.g., black and white television or colour television. The individual consumers are required to answer various questions pertaining to each type of product. On the basis of these answers black and white television may be ranked first and colour television may be ranked second. There may be several points of similarity between the two types of television and also other points of dissimilarity between the two kinds of television. These points can be plotted on the graphs to visualise the similar points and dissimilar points. Several dimensions may be created on the basis of these points. There may be other examples whereby several types of television of different companies may require to be ranked according to the judgement of the consumers from the most preferred to the least preferred. The summation of all the ranks as given by consumers, will reveal the rank from the maximum to the minimum ranks.

The multidimensional scaling technique is a very useful technique of marketing analysis whether the data is metric or non-metric. The attributes, variables and factor analysis may be usefully employed under the multidimensional scaling technique.

5. Planning for Analysis

The data should be properly analysed to interlink all steps of marketing research. In the natural way, all steps of marketing research are closely interrelated and therefore should be treated with proper statistical tools, specially for data collection, data processing and logical interpretation. The suitable planning of analysis involves the following steps:

1. The analyst should know the kinds of results on which the decision should be based. The purpose should be well-known specially in terms of market segments, attitudes and commodities.
2. The analysis should evaluate the methods of analysis which may be feasible for a particular situation and data. The statistical measurements should be determined thereafter for developing the decision model.
3. The parametric measurements should be used for analysing the parametric data. Similarly non-parametric measures are used for non-parametric data.
4. The sampling error is determined for analysis purposes. It will provide precision and clarification of the statement.
5. The measures should be selected after thorough examination and evaluation of the project planning.
6. The original plans for analysis should be remodified and adapted to suit the situation and data. It is possible that unexpected relationships may be revealed at the modified plans.
7. The analyst should be familiar with the outputs and limitations of each method of analysis to make quick and accurate decisions on the steps needed for the analysis.

❖ ❖ ❖

CHAPTER 16

ANALYSIS OF EXPERIMENTS

1. RANDOMISED OF EXPERIMENTS:
   (i) RANDOMISED BLOCK DESIGN
   (ii) COMPLETELY RANDOMISED LAYOUT
   (iii) RANDOMISED PAIRED COMPARISON
2. LATIN SQUARE DESIGN
3. FACTORIAL DESIGN
4. ANALYSIS OF COVARIANCE

ANALYSIS OF EXPERIMENTS

The previous chapters have highlighted the methods of analysis of significance, differences and associations of data. The experimental design of marketing research uses the cause and effect relationships. Therefore, there is need to measure cause and effect relationships between two or more variables. The statistical tools and methods are used in designing experiments and in analysing the data obtained from experiments. The experimental design of non-statistical character has been discussed already. Experimental design emphasizing random sampling and their treatment are discussed in this chapter. Randomisation assumes that the different groups of experimental units will be approximately equal. Any differences between the groups may be assigned to the experimental variable. The observed data for estimating cause and effect relationships can be analysed with the use of statistics and experimental variables. Experimental design generally uses the small samples. The researcher may assign test variables to experimental units using randomisation. He may apply test variables using an appropriate response variable. The results of each experimental variable are combined by using an average method. The confidence intervals are evolved for treatment of the variables. There may be other methods of treatments such as Latin Square Design, Factorial Design and Analysis of Covariance. All of these methods have their respective utilities and applications.

1. RANDOMISED EXPERIMENTS

The randomised experiments as discussed above have wide acceptability and utility in marketing research. Their detailed treatment can be classed under *(i)* randomised block design, *(ii)* completely randomised layout, and *(iii)* randomised paired comparison.

1. Randomised Block Design

Randomised block design assumes the treatment with the use of averages. There may be several extraneous factors distorting the experimental factor. Therefore, it becomes essential to segregate the distorting factors to the possible extent. This is possible with the use of randomised block design which involves the grouping of similar test units into blocks and assigning the treatment randomly to the units of each block. The assumptions behind this treatment are that the units within each block will be similar. The differences between blocks are taken into consideration with analysis of variance (ANOVA) to reveal the error mean which is the smaller square mean of the randomised design. For example, the researcher may be interested to find out the impact of advertising on sale. He has selected three rural areas and three urban areas. Thus, these six areas represent blocks. There may be some variations on account of economic and demographic factors of the areas. Therefore there are different treatments of advertising. The randomised block design is used to extract the external factors influencing the sale.

Table 16.1
Impacts of Advertisement on Sale

Increased no. units in thousand

	Treatment			Block	
Areas	*Newspaper*	*Television*	*Radio*	*Total*	*Mean*
1 Urban	5	3	6	14	4.67
2	6	4	7	17	5.67
3	4	2	5	11	3.67
4 Rural	3	1	4	8	2.67
5	2	3	3	8	2.67
6	4	2	5	11	3.67
Total	24	15	20		
Mean	4	2.50	3.33		
Total Mean	3.27				

The above table reveals that the sale has varied with ecological factors and advertisement media. The analysis of variance as discussed already assumes null hypothesis and aiternate hypothesis. For example, null hypothesis (H_0) assumes that there is no difference in treatment. It can be stated as

$$H_0 : \mu_1 = \mu_2 = \mu_3$$

The null hypothesis (H_0) for the blocks assumes that there is no difference in the sale increase area-wise. For example,

$$H_0 : \mu_1 = \mu_2 = \mu_3 = \mu_4 = \mu_5 = \mu_6$$

Equal for the blocked data is

$$SS = K \Sigma (\bar{X}_{BL} - \bar{X})^2$$

$$= 6[(4.67-3.27)^2 + (5.67-3.27)^2 + (3.67-3.27)^2 + (2.67-3.27)^2 + (2.67-3.27)^2 + (3.67\text{-}3.27)^2]$$

$$= 6[(1.40)^2 + (2.40)^2 + (0.40)^2 + (-.60)^2 + (-0.60)^2 + (0.40)^2]$$

$$= 6[1.96 + 5.76 + .16 + .36 + .36 + .16]$$

$$= 6 \times 8.76$$

$$= 52.56$$

The error is calculated

$$S\sigma = \Sigma(X_{ij} - \bar{X}_{BL} + \bar{X})^2$$

$$= (6 - 4.67 - 4 + 3.27)^2 + (3 - 4.67 - 2.50 + 3.2)^2 + (6 - 4.67 - 3.33 + 3.22)^2 + (6 - 5.67 - 4. + 3.27)^2 + (4 - 5.67 - 2.50 + 3.27)^2 + (7 - 5.67 - 3.33 + 3.27)^2 + (4 - 3.67 - 4 + 3.27)^2 - 1\ (2 - 3.67 - 2.50 + 3.27)^2 + (5 - 3.67 - 3.33 + 3.27)^2 + (3 - 2.67 - 4 + 3.27)^2 + (1-2.67 - 2.50 + 3.27)^2 + (4 - 2.67 - 3.330 + 3.27)^2\ (2 - 2.67 - 4 + 3.27)^2 + (3 - 2.67 - 2.50 + 3.27)^2 + (3 - 2.67 - 3.33 + 3.27)^2\ (4 - 3.67 - 4 + 3.27)^2 + (2 - 3.67 - 2.50 + 3.27)^2 + (5 - 3.67 - 3.33 + 3.27)^2$$

$= (-.40)^2 + (-0.90)^2 + (1.27)^2 + (-.40)^2 + (-0.90)^2 + (1.27)^2 + (-0.40)^2 + (-.40)^2 + (1.27)^2 + (0.40)^2 + (-.90)^2 + (1.27)^2 + (-1.40)^2 + (1.10)^2 + (.27)^2 + (-0.40)^2 + (-90)^2 + (1.27)^2$

$= .16 + .81 + 1.61 + 0.16 + 0.81 + 1.61 + .16 + .81 + 1.61 + .16 + .81 + 1.61 + 1.96 + 1.21 + 0.73 + .16 + .81 + 1.61$

$= 16.80.$

Table 16.2
Analysis of Variance

Variation	*Sum of squares*	*Degree of Freedom*	*Mean square*	*F-Ratio*
Block (Areas)	52.56	5	10.51	14.06
Treatment (Between group)	4.00	2	2.00	9.53
Error	16.80	10	1.68	
Total	73.36	17	14.19	

The calculated value of F (9.53) exceeds the critical value of F (4.10) at 0.05 level of significance. Since the calculated value exceeds the critical value, the null hypothesis is rejected. Thus there is a difference in the effectiveness of the advertisement. The advertisement has effected the sale.

An Alternative Method

The following method has been used to discuss the mean differences:

	X_j	$\overline{X}_j - \overline{X}_t$	$\overline{X}_j - \overline{X}_r$
X_N	4	1.50	0.67
X_R	3.33	0.83	
X_T	2.50		

Thus the treatment difference between $\mu_N - \mu_T$ and $\mu_R - \mu_T$ are significant and $\mu_N - \mu_R$ is not significant.

Efficiency of a Randomised Block Design

The effectiveness or efficiency of randomised block design has been realised by the researcher. It has increased precision for treatment. It has been compared with the completely randomised design. Use of mean squares from the analysis of variance for the randomised block design reveals its relative efficiency. The relative efficiency of the randomised block design is estimated by the following formula:

$$\text{Estimated Relative Efficiency} = \frac{(n-1)\,\text{BMS} + n(k-1)\,\text{WMS}}{(nk-1)\text{WMS}}$$

where,

n = number of blocks.

k = number of treatments.

BMS = Block Mean Square.

WMS = Weighted Mean Square or Error.

Substituting the value

$$ERE = \frac{(6-1)(10.51) + 6(3-1)(1.68)}{(6 \times 3 - 1)\,1.68}$$

$$= \frac{(5 \times 10.51 + 6 \times 2 \times 1.68)}{17 \times 1.68} = \frac{52.55 + 20.16}{28.56} = \frac{72.71}{28.56}$$

$$= 2.54$$

It shows that randomised block design is 256 per cent efficient as compared with completely randomised design. Therefore it is advantageous to use a randomised block design.

2. Completely Randomised Layout

When the principle of randomisation is assigned to the simplest experimental design, it is called the completely randomised layout (CRL). There may be two or more treatments. For example, the researcher may be interested to know the impact of the advertisement on the sale. He may select six stores for each type of advertisement, viz., television and radio. The sales may be recorded for six months after the advertisement for the 12 stores having administered one type of advertisement to six stores. Completely randomised layout is assigned to the experimental design. The first step in completely randomised layout (CRL) is assignment to the variable randomly experimental units. In the above example, the experimental variable is the advertisement, and experimental units are the stores.

The researcher first selects six stores randomly out of the twelve stores for experimental treatment. Secondly he will select randomly any of the two media of the advertisements. The stores are randomly assigned a number. Lastly the remaining six stores are assigned the remaining advertisement media. This step is called the completely randomised layout as no bias occurs in the assignment of treatment to a specific unit. There is an equal chance of assignment of treatment to any unit. It is observed that the twelve stores are alike in nature before treatment. After treatment of the experimental variable, the two groups of the stores will reveal varied degrees of sales. The impact of the experimental variable, i.e., the advertisement on the sale will reveal how far a particular advertisement can increase the sale. The average sale of each group before treatment and after treatment, will reveal the degree of the impact of a specific type of advertisement on the sale. The differences between the averages of the two groups will reveal the effect of a particular type of advertisement. The researcher may realise that the difference in sales between two graphs are random in nature. The genuine differences become known when several experiments at the same situations and conditions are effected and their impact on the sale are recorded.

Mathematical Calculation

As discussed above two experimental treatments, i.e., television advertisements and radio advertisements may be separately administered to the experimental units, i.e., stores. Measurements of the sale are done by recording the sale of each unit after six months of the advertisement. The following formula may be used for mathematical calculation of the Completely Randomised Layout (CRL)

$$Y = M + C$$

where,

Y = CRL or the observation for treatment.

M = The population mean of all observations subjected to treatment.

e = The experimental error or deviation from the population mean.

The population mean may differ because of the treatments. If there is only one type of advertisement, there will only be a population mean. If there are two treatments, the population mean will differ from the previous one. Similarly the random experimental error may also differ according to the difference in treatment. The experimental variables and experimental units may influence the population mean and experimental error.

Assumptions: The completely randomised layouts (CRL) have certain assumptions. It is assumed that the experimental errors are conceived normally, and distributed independently around the population mean. if they are measured with plus and minus from the mean, they will have an average value of zero, and the distribution of each set of experimental errors around the population mean will give the same standard deviation. The errors are approximately close to the normal distribution. The standard deviation of the sale on treatment of television is approximately equal to the standard deviation of the sale on treatment of radio advertisement.

Data Analysis

The completely randomised layout (CRL) can be analysed with the following data. The sale-increase because of the influence of the advertisement is recorded in the following Table.

Table 16.3
Impact of Advertisement on Sale

In thousand units

Stores	*Television (Sale)*	*Stores*	*Radio (sale)*
1	6	1	6
2	5	2	4
3	6	3	7
4	8	4	8
5	8	5	9
6	9	6	2
Average (M) $M_1 = 7$	42/6 = 7	$M_2 = 6$	36/6 = 6

The difference between averages M_1 and M_2 has been $(M_1 - M_2) = (7–6) = 1$. It reveals that the television has been more effective as the average of sale increase on account of television which has been one more than the average sale increase of radio.

Internal estimate of each mean is calculated to discuss the treatment's effect on a randomised basis. The above means and differences of the means are subject to sampling error as the stores are samples only. The universe analysis is not possible. There is need of calculating confidence intervals to provide an indication of the precision-result. The small sample may use t distribution for confidence interval analysis. The internal estimation is done with the following formula:

$$Y \pm t \frac{s}{\sqrt{n}}$$

where,

$\overline{Y}$ = Sample mean.

s = Estimated standard deviation of observations.

n = Number of observations.

t = Critical value at table 't.'

The critical value of 't' at 95 per cent confidence interval is 2.23 at 10 degrees of freedom 2(6–1) s is the calculated value of standard deviation of two observations. Thus

$$s = \sqrt{\frac{(S_1)^2 + (S_2)^2}{2}}$$

where,

S_1 = Standard deviation of television treatment.

S_2 = Standard deviation of radio treatment.

Substituting the values

$$s = \sqrt{\frac{2.4 + 5.2}{2}} = \sqrt{\frac{7.6}{2}} = \sqrt{3.8} = 1.95$$

The sample mean of the two observations has been 88/12 = 7.33.

$$Y \pm t \frac{s}{\sqrt{n}}$$

$$= 7.33 \pm 2.23 \frac{1.95}{\sqrt{6}}$$

$$= 7.33 \pm 2.23 \frac{1.95}{\sqrt{6}}$$

$$= 7.33 \pm \frac{4.3485}{2.45}$$

$$= 7.33 \pm 1.77$$

$$= 5.56 - 9.10$$

Thus, the confidence interval of the sale is between 5.56 to 9.10 thousand units of sale. The average sales increase on account of television has been 7, and of radio has been 6 which lie between the interval. Thus, the impact of both types of advertisement is real and television has been more effective for increasing sales.

3. Randomised Paired Comparison

The completely randomised layout (CRL) has been simple to understand and calculate but it is not very precise for statistical treatment. It has not been widely used in marketing research. There has been randomised block design (RBD) as discussed earlier for more precise analysis. The present randomised paired comparison (RPC) is often used in marketing research. It is observed that the sale may increase or decrease not only on account of advertising but also owing to other factors such as the socio-economic characters of the consumers, changes thereon, store size etc. may also influence the sale. These factors are well known as uncontrolled variables which contribute to the changes of the observations. They may, therefore, increase experimental bias and lack of precision. The researchers have to understand these factors. They should be competent enough to assess them in the light of experiment variables.

The randomised paired comparison (RPC) uses the principles for evaluating experimental treatments. Before assigning treatments, the experimental units are stratified on the basis of some factors contributing to the variability in experimental results. The units may be divided into two groups on the basis of similarity. For example, if there are different stores for study, they should be classified on the basis of the store size to avoid the influence of the size on the basis of the region. If such classification is done, their factors' influence may be minimised to arrive at the real result of the experimental treatment. Thus, this analysis will reveal a more accurate result as compared with a completely randomised layout.

After stratification of units into a similar class, the allocation of similar units to a specific group or pair will be randomly done. The numbering of the units in a specific pair is done randomly.

Table 16.4

Impact on Sales as Treatment of Price Discount

Sale Increase in thousand units

Store	*Price Discount 20%* *Treatment A*	*Store*	*Price Discount 15%* *Treatment B*	
1	10	1	8	+2
2	13	2	9	+4
3	12	3	10	+2
4	9	4	7	+2
5	8	5	6	+2
6	14	6	8	+6
Total	66		48	18
Mean $(\bar{Y}) = \bar{Y}_1 = 11$		$\bar{Y}_2 =$	8	$\bar{Y}_1 - \bar{Y}_2 = 3$

Standard Error: The next step is to estimate standard deviation for the purpose of knowing the experimental error. This is devoted by s_p to differentiate it from the corresponding error standard deviation s in CRL. The estimated error standard deviation, sp = is calculated by the following formula.

$$S_p = \frac{\Sigma(Z-\overline{Z})^2}{2(n-1)}$$

where,

S_p = The estimated error standard deviation.

Z = The difference in response between treatment A and treatment B in each pair.

$\overline{Z}$ = Sample mean of the Z values (paired differences).

Substituting the values,

$$S_p = \sqrt{\frac{\Sigma(Z-3)^2}{2(6-1)}}$$

$$= \sqrt{\frac{(2-3)^2+(4-3)^2+(2-3)^2+(2+3)^2+(2+3)^2+(6-3)^2}{2\times 5}}$$

$$= \sqrt{\frac{(-1)^2+(1)^2+(-1)^2+(-1)^2+(-1)^2+(3)^2}{10}}$$

$$= \frac{1+1+1+1+1+9}{10} = \sqrt{\frac{14}{10}} = \sqrt{1.4} = 1.18$$

The confidence interval in the randomised paired comparison (RPC) for the treatment A is calculated with the following formula:

$$\overline{Y} \pm t\frac{S_P}{\sqrt{n}}$$

$$= 11 \pm 2.23\ \frac{1.18}{\sqrt{6}}$$

$$= 11 \pm \frac{2.6314}{2.45} = 11 \pm 1.07 = 9.93 - 12.07$$

In the randomised paired comparison, the main focus is on the treatment difference.

$$= \overline{Y}_A - \overline{Y}_B \pm \sqrt{2}\,\frac{tS_P}{\sqrt{n}}$$

$$= 3.0 \pm \sqrt{2} \times 2.23 \times \frac{1.18}{\sqrt{6}}$$

$$= 3 \pm 1.41\text{x } 2.23\text{x } .48 = 3 \pm 1.51$$

$$= 1.49 - 4.51.$$

Since the average of the difference is 3 which lies between the above intervals, the impact of discount in price is effective to increase sale. The price-discount of 20 per cent is more effective in increasing the sale as compared to that of 15 per cent price-discount.

The randomised pair comparison is mainly used for evaluating two variables in marketing research experiments. This analysis may be used for more than two variables. This is also called group wise pairing matched or balanced pairs. The randomised pair comparison is used to control the experimental results by stratification. The pair comparison of two treatments is more precise than that of a completely randomised layout (CRL). Randomised pair comparison uses a pair of experimental units whereas a completely randomised layout does not use pairs for analysis. There is a different method of calculating experimental error, degrees of freedom and observations of units in RPC as compared to those of CRL. The randomised pair comparison can be extended to more than two variables, which is known as randomised block design (RBD) as discussed in the first subsection of the section randomised analysis of the experimental units.

2. LATIN SQUARE DESIGN

The marketing researchers are faced with multiple extraneous variables which distort the experimental analysis. The randomised paired comparison mainly involves two variables, and the randomised block design involves stratification of the experimental units into homogeneous groups to control the extraneous variables. These two methods are not very useful for analysis of experimental data. The Latin Square Design (LSD) is an improvement towards precision result on experimental analysis. The main features of Latin Square design are that the number of categories must be the same for two control variables, i.e., the number of rows and columns should be equal, e.g., 2×2, 4×4 etc., while the number of experimental groups should also be equal to the number of categories in the control variables. The experimental results are placed in the rows and columns. For example, the researcher may be interested to know the effect of advertisements on sale. He may select three stores and three 6 monthly periods for analysis as given in the following table.

Table 16.5
Latin Square Analysis

In thousands of sales units

Time Period	*Store*				
	1	*2*	*3*	*Total*	*Mean*
1	5(1)	3(2)	4(3)	12	4
2	8(3)	6(1)	5(2)	19	6.33
3	9(2)	7(3)	6(1)	22	7.33
Total	22	16	15	53	–
Mean	7.33	5.33	5	–	5.89

Note: Figures within brackets denote the number of treatments. Since there are three treatments, e.g., (1) Newspaper Advertisement, (2) Television Advertisement and (3) Radio Advertisement. These treatments are administered at random to each store and time.

The above table reveals the Latin Square. It has a balanced property as the treatment is free from differences between rows and columns. The Latin Square removes experimental errors arising on account of extraneous variation associated with rows and columns. It is proved with standard deviation which is the smallest in this design.

Analysis of Treatment

Time Period	Treatment 1	2	3
1	5	3	4
2	6	5	8
3	6	9	7
Total of Treatment	17	17	19
Treatment Mean	5.67	5.67	6.33

Substituting the values,

$$
\begin{aligned}
SS_{t_r} &= 3[(5.67-5.89)^2 + (5.67-5.89)^2+(6.33-5.89)^2] \\
&= 3[(-0.22)^2 + (-0.22)^2 + (0.44)^2] \\
&= 3[0.048 + 0.048 + .19] \\
&= 3 \times 0.28 \\
&= .84
\end{aligned}
$$

Error Sum of Squares (SS_E)

$$
\begin{aligned}
SS_E &= SS_T - SS_R - SS_C - SS_{t_r} \\
&= 28.87 - 17.49 - 9.51 - 0.84 \\
&= 28.87 - 27.84 \\
&= 1.03.
\end{aligned}
$$

The Latin Square method uses the analysis of variance to discuss the significance of particular factors, e.g., store, time or treatment (advertisement).

Table 16.7

Analysis of Variance

	Sum of squares	*Degree of freedom*	*Mean square*	*F-Ratio*
Rows (Stores)	17.49	t–1 = 2	8.74	17.14
Column (Time)	9.51	t–1 = 2	4.75	9.31
Treatment (Advertisement)	0.84	t–1 = 2	0.42	0.82
Error	1.03	(t–a)(t–2)=2	0.51	
Total	28.87	t^2–1 = 8		

The F ratio is calculated by the following formula:

$$F = \frac{\text{BMS (Between – Column Mean Square)}}{\text{WMS (Within – Column Mean Square)}}$$

where,

$$BMS = \frac{SS_B \text{ (Sums of Squares between Group)}}{n-1}$$

$$WMS = \frac{SS_W \text{ (Sums of Squares within Group)}}{N-n}$$

where,

N = Total number of observations.

n = Number of treatments.

Substituting the values

$$\text{Sum of Squares between groups or BMS} = \frac{SS_R}{n-1} = \frac{17.49}{3.1}$$

$$\text{Within group mean Square (Error) or WMS} = \frac{SS_E}{N-n} = \frac{1.03}{2}$$

$$= \frac{1.03}{2} = 0.51$$

$$F = \frac{BMS}{WMS} = \frac{8.74}{0.51} = 17.14$$

The calculated value of F ratio at 5 per cent level of significance and 2 degrees of freedom in case of store is 17.14, and also in case of time is 9.31 whereas the calculated value of F at 9.5 level of significance and 2 degrees of freedom is 0.82. The tabular value is 19.0 at the level and degree of freedom. This shows that there is no significant differences between the means.

Multiple Comparisons

The T method is also used for comparing the Latin Square method with the use of the following method

$$T = \frac{1}{\sqrt{n}} \quad t\sqrt{EMS}$$

where,

n = Number of treatment.

t = Critical value of F.

EMS = Error Mean Square.

Substituting the values

$$T = \frac{1}{\sqrt{3}} \times 19.0 \sqrt{.51}$$

$$= \frac{1}{1.73} \times 19.0 \times .71$$

$$= 0.58 \times 19 \times .71$$

$$= 7.82$$

Table may be constructed for the purpose of comparison of the treatment

$\bar{X}_j$	$\bar{X}_j$	$\bar{X}_j - \bar{X}_1$	$\bar{X}_j - \bar{X}_2$
$\bar{X}_3$	6.33	0.66	0
$\bar{X}_2$	5.67	0	
$\bar{X}_1$	5.67		

It shows the difference 0.66 below the T value of 7.82. Thus, there is no significant difference between the treatment.

Efficiency

The efficiency of the Latin Square can be obtained similar to the randomised design block with the following formula:

$$\text{Latin Square Relative Efficiency} = \frac{\text{RowMS} + \text{ColumnMS} + (t-1)\,\text{EMS}}{(t+1)\,\text{EMS}}$$

$$\text{Estimate (LS/CR)} = \frac{8.74 + 4.75 + (3-1)\,.51}{(3-1)\,.51}$$

$$= \frac{8.74 + 4.75 + 1.02}{2.04}$$

$$= \frac{14.51}{2.04}$$

$$= 7.11$$

The relative efficiency of the Latin Square design has been calculated as 7.11. This means, the same result would be obtained by 7.11 per cent of the present sample if they are not controlled. The result is consistent with the significant difference among the row means and the column means. This design may control the extraneous factors to arrive at the result due to the experimental factor. The experimenters can obtain a more precise estimate of treatment means with the use of the Latin Square Method because extraneous factors are properly analysed under this method. The confidence interval can be developed with the use of the error means. For example, the row interval, will be 8.74 ±.51. This means that the influence of period on the sale will be between 8.23 and 9.25 if other samples are taken into consideration. Similarly the value of the store will be 4.75 ± 0.51, i.e., between 4.24 and 5.26. The influence of treatment, i.e., advertisement is not very effective as its values are smaller than those of stores and time. The treatment confidence interval will lie 0.42 ± 0.51, i.e., –.09 to 0.93 which is very small. This analysis has revealed that the advertisement could not greatly influence the sales increase. It was the effects of the store and of time which influenced more sale.

The Latin Square Design has been usefully and precisely practiced in marketing research. It is in a position to control extraneous sources. The Latin Square Design is subject to limitations of creating an equal number of rows and columns. The analyst cannot create an unequal number of rows and columns because it assumes square blocks of data. This design has been widely used in marketing research as it controls the extraneous factors under reasonably realistic conditions. It requires that the resultant data must be sufficiently definite and reliable for statistical treatment.

3. FACTORIAL DESIGN

Factorial Design is a multivariate statistical technique that assumes the study of interrelationships among various factors. This design studies the effects of two or more independent treatment variables at a time. We have discussed in the previous two designs that there is only one treatment, e.g., advertisement, but factorial design tries to analyse more than one factor. It examines the impact that each independent treatment has directly on the dependent variable and vice versa as well as on their interactions.

It has been observed that the advertisement has not influenced the sale increase. The producers also have to reduce the price. Thus, there are two factors, i.e., an advertisement and price reduction required to influence sale, escalation. The researcher may be interested to know how much advertising and how much price reduction can increase the sales. What will be their influence on sales, separately as well as with the two factors.

There may be three null hypothesis, viz., *(i)* treatment of the advertisement (A) has no effect on sale, i.e., $H_0 : A = 0$; *(ii)* treatment of price (B) has no influence on sale, i.e., $H_0 : B = 0$ and *(iii)* treatments of advertisement and price have no effect on sale, i.e., $H_0 : AB = 0$. The alternative hypotheses are that their influences on sale are positive, i.e., $H_1 = A \neq 0$; $H_1 : B \neq 0$ and $H_1 : AB \neq 0$.

The impact of price reduction and advertisement can be observed in the following table.

Table 16.8

Impact of Price Reduction and Advertisement on Sales Increase

In thousand units

	Advertisement (A)			
Price Reduction (B)	*0.5 per cent increase in expenditure of Advertisement (A_1)*	*1.0 per cent increase in expenditure of Advertisement (A_2)*	*Price Total*	*Price Mean*
2 per cent reduction (B_1) in price	(7,8) 15	(9,10) 19	34	8.50
5 Per cent reduction in Price (B_2)	(12,13) 25	(14,15) 29	54	13.50
Advertisement Total	40	48	88	11.00
Advertisement Mean (A)	10	12		

Note: Figures within brackets are results or two periods, viz., first after 6 months and second after one year.

Treatment Cell
(Advertisement and Price Reduction)

	A_1B_1	A_1B_2	A_2B_1	A_2B_2	*Total*
Cell Total	15	25	19	29	88
Cell Mean	7.50	12.50	9.5	14.5	44

The impact of the advertisement and price reduction are discussed with the following formula.

Total Sum of Squares:

$$SS_T = \Sigma(X - \overline{X})^2$$

$$= (7–11.00)^2 + (8–11.00)^2 + (9–11.00)^2 + (10–11.00)^2$$

$$= + (12–11)^2 + (13–11)^2 + (14–11)^2 + (15–11)^2$$

$$= –4^2 + –3^2 + –2^2 + –1^2 + 1^2 + 2^2 + 3^2 + 4^2$$

$$= 16 + 9 + 4 + 1 + 1 + 4 + 9 + 16$$

$$= 60$$

Sum of Squares of treatment A

$$SS_A = b\, n\Sigma\, (X_A - \overline{X})^2$$

where,

b = Number of levels of treatment B.

n = Number of replications.

Substituting the values,

$$SS_A = 2 \times 2\, [(10–11)^2 + (12–11)^2]$$

$$= 4\, (–1^2+1^2)$$

$$= 4 \times 2$$

$$= 8$$

Sum of squares of treatment B

$$SS_B = a\, n\, \Sigma\, (\overline{X}_B - \overline{X})^2$$

where,

a = Number of levels of treatment A.

n = Number of replications.

substituting the values,

$$SS_B = 2 \times 2\, [(8.50–11)^2 + (13.50–11)^2]$$

$$= 2 \times 2\, (–2.50^2 + 2.50^2)$$

$$= 4 \times (6.25 + 6.25)$$

$$= 4 \times 12.50$$

$$= 50$$

Sum of Square of Interaction (AB)

$SS_{(AB)} = n\Sigma (\overline{X} + \overline{X}_t - \overline{X}_B)^2$

Substituting the value,

$= n [(11.0 + 7.50 - 8.50 - 10)^2 + (11.0+12.50 - 13.50 - 12)^2 (11 + 9.5 - 10 - 8.50)^2 + (11 + 14.5 - 12 - 13.5)^2$

$= 2 [(0)^2 + (-2)^2 + (+2)^2 + (0)^2]$

$= 2 (4+4)$

$= 2 \times 8$

$= 16$

Sum of squares of Error

$SS_E = SS_T - SS_A - SS_B - SS_{AB}$

$= 60 - 8 - 50 - 16$

$= 60 - 74$

$= -14$

Table 16.9

Analysis of Variance of Factorial Design

Sources of Variation	*Sum of Squares*	*Degrees of Freedom*	*Mean Square*	*F-ratio*
Advertisement (A)	8	(a–1) = 1	8	2.28
Price Reduction (B)	50	(a–1) = 1	50	14.29
Interaction	16	(a–1) (b–1)=1	16	4.57
Error	–14	ab(n–1) = 4	3.5	
Total	60	ab(n–1) = 7		

The critical value of F at 0.05 confidence level at degree of freedom of price and advertisement and 4 degrees of freedom of error was 7.71. It shows that the null hypothesis of no difference for price is rejected and the alternative hypothesis of significant difference is accepted. The effects of reduction have been positive although interaction has shown an insignificant. Though the price and advertisement together revealed insignificant difference, they have a wide difference as observed sale increase at 5 per cent reduction in price and one per cent increase in expenditure of the advertisement. The time factor also increased the sale as the price and advertisement have shown a more favourable effect after one year. The sale increase after six months but before one year has been comparatively lower than the sale after one year of treatment which is not revealed by the analysis. However, this analysis is more efficient than other methods of analysis.

4. ANALYSIS OF COVARIANCE

There may be some variables which are not controlled during the experiment. They may arise after administering the treatment. There maybe situations when the factors though very influential cannot be controlled by the researchers. Thus, there is need of *expost facto* analysis which is done by covariance in which the experimental results arising from extraneous variations can be properly adjusted. This is done by regression analysis which has been discussed under analysis of association in a previous chapter.

CHAPTER 17

PRESENTATION OF RESEARCH REPORT

1. ROLE OF REPORT
2. TYPES OF REPORT
3. CONTENTS OF THE REPORT
4. PRINCIPLES OF REPORT PREPARATION
5. VISUAL DEVICES IN REPORT-PREPARATION:
   (i) TABULAR DEVICE
   (ii) GRAPHIC DEVICE
   (iii) CHARTS AND MAPS
6. PRESENTATION AND COMMUNICATION
7. FOLLOW-THROUGH

PRESENTATION OF RESEARCH REPORT

The effectiveness of the research depends upon the methods of communication and presentation of the research report. Very useful research, if not presented in a suitable manner for the users of the research findings, may not serve its purpose. The users are not greatly interested in the research methodology, they will use only those findings which greatly interest them. They use those findings which are properly understood by them and solve their problems. Therefore, it is very essential to present the research findings in a very effective manner to meet the requirements of the marketing managers. It is accepted that properly conducted research may be presented effectively. The researcher may put the objectives of the research first, followed by suggestions on how to solve the problems or methods to attain the objectives. Properly conducted research can be presented effectively, but a haphazard manner of conducting the research process may not present the research report in an effective manner. The oral research report may not be properly understood. Therefore it is essential to present the report in black and white. The presentation of research findings can be studied under the role of the report, types of report, content of the report, principles of report presentation, visual devices in report presentation, presentation and communication methods and proper follow through.

1. ROLE OF REPORT

The research report gives an understanding of the data and conclusions. It suggests appropriate measures to solve the problems. The information and data obtained are placed in a logical manner to guide the action for corrective measures or to solve the problems. The goal of marketing research as given in the report will help one to understand the purpose and means of the research. It gives an insight to the marketing executive to use the research report in a systematic manner and logical sequence. The research report places the data and findings in an organised and suitable form. It reveals the systematic records and steps of the research. Future researchers can use the research report for their references and as guidelines for future action.

The research report should serve the purpose of the research. It should serve the needs and wishes of the executives. The executives if convinced of the usefulness of the research findings can implement them. The purpose of the report may be served if the findings are implemented by the clients. The executives should also know the limitations and weaknesses of the research report so that they can avoid them while using the findings. The report should be easier to understand and simple to implement because the executives are in many cases, in distant touch with the research. They may not ask for removing confusions and complexities of the research report from time to time. The qualitative research report may be very useful for the executives. The time, money and energy involved for conducting research report, therefore, will serve the purpose of research, and executives may wish to use it for their decision-making processes. The qualitative report has convincing effects on executives who may be prompted to take correct action. The communication system of the research report also influences the utility of the report. Appropriate communication methods may serve the executives' motive to implement the report. The research report may be oral or written. The oral report may not be useful for easy references and proper communication. Therefore, the researcher may prefer to prepare a written report.

2. TYPES OF REPORT

The research report may be oral or written. Oral report has face to face communication between the researcher and the clients. The researcher himself talks about the project and its findings. Oral reports are not greatly used owing to their limitations and their utility. The reports may also be progress reports and final reports. When the report is not finally prepared, its intermediate conclusion may be mentioned in the progress report which reveals how much work has been done and how much work remains to be done. The progress report is merely a memorandum in nature. According to the purpose of the report, it can be classified as a basic report, a report for publication, a technical report and a report intended for executives.

1. Basic Report

The basic report is the first report prepared on the research project. It is prepared by the researcher for his own use as a working paper for further study and findings. Only experienced researchers are accustomed to prepare such a report as a qualitative final report. Many of the researchers do not bother to prepare such reports. They prepare the final report which may be full of preliminary shortcomings. Unless basic reports are prepared and complete basic records are maintained, the final findings may not incorporate the necessary data and information. The final report may not be very useful. Therefore it is essential to prepare the basic report from time to time to record all available conclusions and findings.

2. Reports for Publication

During the course of research the researchers may prepare research papers suitable for publication in magazines, journals and news-letters. They may provide an insight into a problem. They get a feedback from the public and from experts. The research paper does not form part of the final report as it is generally written keeping in view the interests of the public and the outlook of journals. Research papers are published only in technical and concerned periodicals. The papers written for readers of general interest will have to be moulded in the language of common people. The research papers have proved very useful for the public, for new researchers and management. In India, many important journals in the areas of marketing, finance, industrial relations and management have been publishing research papers for the benefit of business, industry and professionals.

3. Technical Reports

Technical reports are prepared by specialised people, such as technically trained personnel and academicians. Such people prepare the reports in logical sequence, using relevant statistics and comprehensive data as appendices. The problems and hypotheses are properly researched and their findings are given in technical terms. There is a step by step interpretation of the findings. The sources of the data are properly acknowledged. Appendices and diagrams are given to substantiate the findings and conclusions.

4. Reports for Executives

These reports are the actual and final reports for the decision makers in the areas of marketing management. The researchers prepare the report keeping in view the objectives of the management. The reports for executives suggest the appropriate measures to be adopted by the management to solve problems or arrive at concrete decisions in management.

3. CONTENTS OF THE REPORT

The report should be presented in a readable and acceptable manner. The purpose of report writing is to suit the requirements of the clients for whom the report is being prepared. The report should contain the following elements:

1. Title page.
2. Table of contents.
3. Executive synopsis.
4. Introduction.
5. Methodology.
6. *(i)* Objectives.
   (ii) Research design.
   (iii) Data collection method.
   (iv) Sampling.
   (v) Field work.
   (vi) Analysis and interpretation.
7. Limitations.
8. Findings.
9. Conclusions and recommendations.
10. Appendix.
11. Bibliography.

The researcher follows the sequence of the content while preparing the research report.

1. Title Page: The title page refers to the subject of the report. It should be simple and brief. This page also indicates the name of the organisations for whom the report is being prepared. The data of preparation and the name of the persons writing the report are given on the title page.

2. Table of Contents: The table of contents is an outline of the order of the chapters, sections and sub-sections with their respective pages. If report includes a number of charts, figures, tables, maps, diagrams and graphs etc., a separate table for each category would immediately follow the table of contents.

3. Executive Synopsis: The synopsis or the summary is the most important part of the report because many executives will read only this part. It is a guide to those questions about which the executives would like more questions. It enables the executive to grasp the import the research. The synopsis precedes the details of the research report because it helps executives to read the summary first, and then read in detail if they require clarification on any point. The summary is a concise form of all the essential parts of the research report. It should include all the major facts, findings and conclusions. It is background information containing important results and recommendations. The recommendations may not be in very great detail but should contain all necessary information in broader headings and sub-headings. The purpose of writing an executive synopsis is to provide the reader with the minimal background of the results, conclusions and recommendations. The purpose of the research is also given in the synopsis. The synopsis must be in accordance with the main report. This is the reason why the synopsis is prepared after completion of the final report.

4. Introduction: The introduction provides background information. The reader needs to discuss points in the main report. A report with wide distribution requires a more extensive introduction. The introduction defines unfamiliar or technical terms. The vague terms are specifically delineated. It informs the reader about problems to be researched, purpose of the research, scope of the study, research methodology and the hypothesis to be tested. The sub-problems or hypotheses are explicitly stated. The relationship between the findings and the objectives of the research should be clearly established. The historical background of the research problems may be stated if relevant to understanding the problems. The research materials used to conduct the research are stated in the introduction.

5. Methodology: The purpose of stating the methodology is to describe the research procedure. This provides the objectives of the researcher and details the research design, data collection method, sampling, field work, analysis and interpretation.

(i) Objectives: The objectives of the research should be clearly specified before preparing the report. It will help understand the overall problem and solution thereof derived from the research. The methodology without stating the objectives of the research will not be properly understood. The objectives may be deduced into sub-objectives and hypotheses for the purpose of research.

(ii) Research Design: Research design denotes the description of the research technique. It defines exploratory, conclusive and experimental designs. They have their respective merits and demerits. The methodology will reveal why a particular design is being used for conducting the research.

(iii) Data Collection Method: The methodology reveals the methods of data collection. There may be primary sources and secondary sources of data collection. The researcher should explain why a particular method has been utilised to collect the data. A copy of the questionnaire may be included to demonstrate the method and form of data collection. The methods of interviewing are also given in the beginning of the report to reveal the technique of data collection.

(iv) Sampling: The universe study is not feasible for collecting adequate information and data. Therefore, sampling is done to collect data. The relationship between universe and sampling should be noted to clarify the nature of the data collected. The common terminology may be used for sampling as well as establishing a relationship between universe and sampling. The sampling units should be clearly defined and geographical limits should be specified. The confusion in defining sampling units should be avoided to the utmost possible extent. The sample size for each sub-sample and sample as a whole are important points for determining the authenticity of the result. The terms used for defining the size should be commonly understood and not be confusing.

The sampling is based on probability and non-probability methods. Each method has several techniques having their own advantages and disadvantages. The researcher should explain why a particular selection process has been used. The sampling units and size may be depicted on a map. For example, the number of villages selected in a particular district may be mentioned on the map. The map itself will reveal the coverage of the population by sampling.

(v) Field-work: The researcher should explain the quality and nature of the field force. The methods of their selection, training and motivation should be given before presentation of the final report because this will help in understanding the quality of the data collection and their interpretation in the light of their attitudes and merits.

(vi) Analysis and Interpretation: The methods of analysis and interpretation of the data and information are mentioned under the methodology. The usual statistical techniques are generally used for the purpose. If some special statistical techniques are used, they should be clarified by the researchers. The interpretation is based on logical sequence and use of statistical tools.

6. Limitations: The research methods and research reports may not be completely free from errors and drawbacks. There will be some limitations of the study, which should be known to the researcher and must be accepted while preparing the report. The hide out limitations may be dangerous to the research as well as to the executives because they may use the conclusions and recommendations without caring for the limitations which may prove to be a fatal organism while implementing the measures suggested by the research. Expressing the limitations of study actually delineate the research findings and suggests the areas within the research findings may more fruitfully be used. Explaining the limitations does not bias the results, rather it strengthens the findings and conclusions within the limits. The possible sampling errors and non-sampling errors are mentioned. They point out the areas and fields where the findings can be accurately applied and generalised. For example, research conducted in rural areas may not be perfectly applicable to urban areas. The limitations of the study should be explained in terms of the result so that research may create confidence amongst the users of the research report.

7. Findings: The findings of the study are presented in a logical sequence supported by adequate tables and findings. The findings may be presented in several chapters, sections and sub-sections. Each problem is discussed in a separate chapter. The irrelevant problems are ignored and relevant problems are thoroughly analysed with the help of collected information and data. The systematic presentation of the problems and their solutions based on the relevant statistics have been the common form of the findings. Region, State, social strata, economic levels and other sub-classifications have been the basis of presentation of the findings. Suitable tables, diagrams and charts are used to substantiate the findings. The findings and conclusions are also supported by the tables and figures put in the appendices. Only the summary and relevant tables are put in the main body of the findings. The details and basic statistics are given in the appendices. The findings are presented keeping in mind the objectives of the study.

8. Conclusions and Recommendations: The conclusions of the research-process are drawn by the researchers applying either the inductive or deductive method. The conclusions are scientifically tested statements and placed in a systematic manner. They verify the hypotheses or premises on which the research has been based. The conclusions are drawn according to the objectives and problems specified by the research. The step by step development of the conclusions is done under this section. The conclusions follow the natural findings. Conclusions denote that the researcher has complete knowledge of the research findings. Recommendations follow the conclusions. The knowledge of the situation and problem-finding solutions help appropriate recommendations. The researcher may recommend action only where it is necessary. Too much reliance on the recommendations is not permitted because the researchers would have recommended on some specific situations. Therefore, wherever recommendations are made, the situations and limits within which recommendations are made should be mentioned so that the executives may be aware of the situations and conditions for implementation of the recommendation.

9. Appendix: The appendix is placed at the end of the research report. These items are the main stream of the report. The detailed statement may relate to the comprehensive data, formula, detailed information such as the questionnaire, written interview instructions etc. It should be kept in mind that only those items of information and data should be placed under the appendix, which do not appear in the main report. If there is such information which is absolutely necessary for the main report and is put in the appendix, the clients cannot properly understand the recommendation and findings. Therefore, it is essential that such data should be placed in the relevant section and chapter. The main findings and conclusions can be presented graphically in the appendix. The graphs and charts put in the appendix highlight the main findings, but this does not mean that the relevant section and chapter should be devoid of the main findings and conclusions. Some researchers prefer to put the graphs and charts in the relevant sections to demonstrate the findings in reliable and suitable form.

10. Bibliography: The bibliography contains the detailed information on books, references, journals and other materials. The proceedings of the committees and references to the relevant portion of the findings may be given in this section. This is the last section of the report.

4. PRINCIPLES OF REPORT PREPARATION

The preparation of the research report is guided by objectives and methods of communication from the researcher to the clients. The report is tailor made for the readers or clients. As per the nature of the reader, the report may involve technical sophistication, general interest in the area and so many other relevant points. Reports are composed of words, numbers, graphs, charts and pictures. The researcher must be well versed in putting each of these components in such a way that readers may easily grasp and understand them. If the researcher can understand the modes and interests of the clients, he can prepare a very good report accepting or rejecting the findings; the researcher will start with the most interesting part of the research avoiding expressions and tactics. The research makes colourful and vivid presentation of the report for the instant decision makers. The report will be very comprehensive with complete data for the analytical types of the executives. The dynamic executives require a concise and correct report. Besides these varied requirements, a plain and straight-forward report must have some specific qualities. These qualities initiate some principles of report writing.

Principles of Report Writing

Report writing may involve the following principles:

1. Easy to Follow: The body of the report should be written in a self-evident and easy form. Every subject should be presented under different heads. There may be different sub-topics and sub-headings under one heading. The statement may be made in short and relevant paragraphs.

2. Clarity: Clarity in writing is as important as quality of communication. It is an art which is acquired after considerable experience. The vagueness should be corrected because vagueness may involve wrong decisions and faulty conclusions. The clarity may be observed by using a chart, pin-point sentences avoiding too much elaboration. Difficult words may be avoided. The precise word may serve the purpose. Incorrect grammar may discredit a worthwhile report. Uniform style and format may increase the clarity of the report. When the underlying logic is imprecise and fussy, the readers experience difficulty in understanding the report. There may occur a possibility of confusion and misunderstanding. The original drafts are rewritten and finally arranged under specific devices. Use of too much jargon, ambiguous work and critical expression may distort the clarity of the report.

3. Conciseness: The research report should be comprehensive as well as concise. The report should be long enough to cover all the components and objectives of the research project. But this does not mean that it should be too detailed and wide. It should not be too detailed unless it is really required to be extensive. The researcher should not try to impress the reader with all the information at his disposal. He should try to eliminate all unnecessary information and also such information which is commonly known to people. Conciseness can also be obtained by the style of writing. Duplication of words, use of unnecessary phrases, poor expression and long sentences should be avoided. The researcher should express his findings in as few words as possible.

4. Objectivity: The objectivity of the report should be kept in mind throughout the report. Irrelevant reports are damaging and clients cannot fulfil their targets. The research objective is decided keeping in view the management's judgement. It has sometimes been observed that the true research results have been avoided because they do not fit in with the management's judgement. The management will of course welcome those findings which suit it most. But this does not mean that the researcher should include only those interests which appeal to the management; he should present the correct picture of the findings with substantial evidence and support. He should defend his results. The researcher may be asked to participate in the formulation of problems. He may frame the objectives of the research accordingly and suggest to the management the solution of the problems. In many cases, the researchers are asked only to supply information rather than participating in the management. In such cases, they have to supply only information.

5. Stress on Practical Report: The report should be based on practical findings. It should not be theoretical statement. The evidence supporting the findings should be given in the report. The researcher should have a realistic viewpoint. Writing should be restricted to the practical findings and conclusions. Researchers should not write all those things which are supported by the practical findings.

6. Accuracy: The accuracy of the report requires accurate information and data. The accurate information and data if analysed properly and presented in a logical order will yield an accurate report. Accuracy needs careful handling of data, use of correct grammar, punctuation, spelling etc.

7. Completeness: A report will be considered complete when it includes all information which is required for the purpose of research. An incomplete report requires supplementary reports. If the report is formidable in size, it may not be useful. The interest and abilities of the researcher determine the completeness of the report.

8. Different Typography: A report may be prepared in different forms, colours and types to emphasise specific reports. The use of dots, exclamation marks, headlines and lead-lines may serve the purpose of specification. Contrasting colours are used to differentiate important reports. Numbers are expressed by numerals rather than in words. Visual devices may be used to give a dynamic approach to the report. These devices are supplements to the text report and are not used as a substitute for the report.

5. VISUAL DEVICES IN REPORT PREPARATION

The visual devices used in reports may be tabular devices, graphic devices and charts and maps.

1. Tabular Presentation

Statistical materials are presented in systematic tables. The statements of the findings are supported with tabular statistics. A table is the orderly arrangement of the data in rows and columns. The series of statistics are presented or analysed effectively to demonstrate important conclusions. Data may be ten important principles for tabular presentation.

1. Title: The title is a proper description of the presentation. It should be brief and colour. It should give a clear picture of the data and statement. Verbs and articles are omitted.

2. Number: All tables must have a number to show their position in the research report. The table number maintains the chapter number, head, subhead and important references.

3. Arrangement: The data and information should be arranged in a significant manner. They may be according to the chronological order, geographical divisions, significance and so on. Alphabetical arrangement is used for preparing the indexing. Similarly numerical designation may also be used.

4. Captions and Stubs: Captions indicate a column-title or column-heading. Each caption must state what each column indicates. Stubs indicate the row titles or row headings. They are placed at the extreme left hand column. Captions and stubs should be brief and descriptive. Stubs are described as a whole and their sub-classes are shown as sub-totals. If more than one line is required for a stub, the figures are placed opposite the first line. The miscellaneous caption is placed at the right hand side. The chronological columns should be placed from one side to another side in a definite order.

5. Units of Measurement: Units of measurement should be placed in the caption or at the side of the head title if the measurement is common for all data. Separate measurements may be used, if required, for each column.

6. Ruling, Spaces and Leaders: Ruling may be used according to captions and stubs to provide space for specific data to be inserted thereon. Skipping lines between different sections of the data may be used for clarity of the complicated data. Leaders are used with stubs to indicate the data with the statement.

7. Totals: Totals of columns and rows may be undertaken for specifications and analysis. Averages may be shown below the totals.

8. Sources: Below the table, sources of the data should be indicated to make it clear that the data are reliable. If they are primary data, they may be mentioned at the beginning of the report.

9. Footnote: A footnote gives special information about the table. Attention may be drawn to the footnote by placing a star or figures on the data. This is done to explain anything that cannot be incorporated in the table. It is shown immediately below the table before the source.

10. Emphasis: Emphasis may be placed on figures, stubs, captions etc. by using double lines, heavy lines or heavy types.

2. Graphic Device of Presentation

Graphic presentation being more technical in character represents the data more accurately and more usefully. It places greater and proper emphasis on the important parts of the research report. There may be different devices of graphic presentation. It is a visual aid to understanding tabular and expository materials. It should represent a complete picture of one central point or idea. The important graphic presentation may be line diagrams, bar charts, pictographs, pie charts, cartograms and map charts.

1. Line or curve diagrams: The line diagrams are used to show continuous functions or growth over a period of time. It is a very common type of chart to provide definite feeling of change. For construction of line or curve diagrams important rules should be followed. The scale may be placed either horizontally or vertically, with care. There may be two scales each for column and row presentation. For example, the sale may be shown in rupees on the horizontal scale, and the years of sale may be shown on the vertical scale. There should be as few lines as possible. The line dimensions should be portrayed without conflicting measures. The border should be heavier than the coordinates. Multilines should be specifically designed for each purpose. Too many curves plotted on a single chart become confusing and ineffective. Zero is considered the base lines, but if the figures fall below zero, there should be sufficient space to demonstrate the trend.

The line-graphs may be a histogram, range chart, and a band graph for a simple and discrete table. The continuous table may be presented on frequency distribution graphs which may be a histogram, frequency polygon, frequency curve and ogive curve.

Simple Line Graphs

The simple line graphs may be a simple histogram, range graph and band graph.

(i) Simple Histogram: A simple histogram is a technique used for plotting a time-series on the graph paper. The data are arranged according to the time of occurrence. Time is taken at the horizontal scale, i.e., the X-axis, and data are plotted at the vertical scale, i.e., the Y-axis. A simple line known as a histogram is plotted on the graph. First points are made according to time and related data. Secondly, the points are chronologically joined to form a straight line which indicates the movements of data according to time.

(ii) Range Graph: A range graph depicts data of two magnitudes according to the period of time. The difference between imports and exports can be known by the range graph according to the depiction of import and export figures. The gap may be shaded to emphasize the range. Similarly there may be two other related magnitudes to demonstrate the range graph, e.g., revenue and cost to demonstrate profit, minimum and maximum temperature to show the climate and so on.

(iii) Band Graph: The band graph is used to depict more than two magnitudes for a given period of time. Time is measured along the X-axis and other magnitudes are measured along the Y-axis. Progressive totals of the components are measured for depicting certain purposes. For example, the cost of production can be broken up to show the cost of row materials, cost of labour, cost of fuel, and the cost of machine's contribution. They may be progressively aggregated to demonstrate their effectiveness. The differences are shaded differently to demonstrate their magnitude. Starting from the lower level to the higher level of each magnitude collectively will show the band graph.

Frequency Distribution Graphs

Frequency distribution graphs may be histogram, frequency polygon, frequency curve and ogive curve.

(i) Histogram: The Histogram is drawn for the continuous variable which may be divided into suitable classes. It may take the form of a rectangle which represents the class interval with frequencies. The class interval may be represented on the Y-axis and their respective frequencies on the X-axis. Frequencies of each class are plotted as bar on the graph-scales to demonstrate the histogram.

(ii) Frequency Polygon: The frequency polygon is slightly different from the histogram. When the mid-points at the top of each of the rectangles of the histogram are joined, they represent the frequency polygon. The mid-points are joined with straight lines.

(iii) Frequency Curve: The frequency curve is different from the frequency polygon in the sense that the top points of the histogram in the former case are joined with the free-hand, whereas the top points of the frequency polygon are joined with a straight line. The frequency is plotted at the X-axis and the class interval at the Y-axis. The histogram is prepared accordingly. Mid-points of the rectangles are freely joined to make a curve. The frequency curve may be prepared without preparing the histogram by pointing the mid-value of the class-interval, i.e., frequencies at the mid class interval.

(iv) Cumulative Frequency Curve or Ogive Curve: The frequencies of each class are added up to plot the graph. The frequencies can be accumulated either upward or downward. They are respectively known as less than an ogive curve and more than an ogive curve. In many cases we adopt less than an ogive curve, i.e., the upward accumulation curve. It slopes upward to the right. It is known as a rising curve. It also shows the frequencies' direction and degree of the slopes.

3. Charts and Maps

Charts and maps are other visual devices to illustrate the report. The charts show how the data can move. The charts may be bar charts, pictographs and pie charts.

(i) Bar charts: Bar charts consist of bars running either vertically or horizontally with an individual bar for each observation. The individual bars have separate observations and magnitudes. Bar charts have become more popular than bar diagrams or line diagrams. The vertical charts are used for classified data and chronological quantity. In the case of qualitative and geographic data, horizontal bar charts are used to depict them more precisely. They may serve the purpose of showing the rate of change in continuous data. More than two series of data may be depicted by the use of component bar charts with distinctive shadings or colours. The positive and negative quantities may also be demonstrated with bar charts.

(ii) Pictograph: The pictograph uses tiny pictures or symbols to represent the idea or subject. This device is used to give a more vivid picture of the report. It is appropriate for bar-type charts. It is not intended for detailed study and precise measurement, but to give one short glimpses of the findings.

(iii) Pie Charts: The pie chart is presented in a circle dividing the charts in different components according to the needs of the distinctive data. The slices of the circle are also noted with the name and their percentage shares in the total circle. The slices are divided according to the proportion of their shares in the 360 degrees. The proportions are, therefore, calculated in accordance with the number of degrees of each angle of the slice.

(iv) Maps: Maps are used to show the figures in the geographical areas. Maps may be shaded in various ways. Income, population, production and other geographical presentations may be made with the help of maps. District maps may be used to show the magnitude of the data.

Consideration in the use of Visual Devices

Effective communication involves visual devices owing to several reasons because people are visually minded, retention is increased and visualisation encourages organisation. People grow up with visual influences from school life to career orientation. These influences encourage the organisation of several thoughts in systematic order. Misunderstandings recur less because of seeing and having the information simultaneously. While selecting the appropriate visual device, the following principles are taken into account. The visualised communication should be easy to comprehend. It should not be too complex. It is better to display one idea at a time. The size and location of the audience should be properly selected. Additional information may be written up on the surface of the medium of visual presentation. The pointer technique may be used to indicate a particular point or idea on the visual device. Similarly, the on and off technique, revelation technique and overlay technique. While using the presentation technique, the researcher should take into consideration the availability, the appropriateness and the effective technique.

6. PRESENTATION AND COMMUNICATION

The purpose of report writing is to present the report in a very effective manner. Since this involves communication of the findings and conclusions from the researcher to the clients, the principles of effective communication are followed in report writing. Report writing may not involve the use of words and phrases; the visual devices have proved very effective. Appropriate care should be exercised in preparing suitable reports keeping in view the interests of the executive and the perceptions of the readers. When there are a large number of diversified persons, the report writing becomes too complex. The report may be presented personally to the executives. The researcher may learn directly the reactions of the executives, the opposition and the skeptics.

The written report is very essential is serving the purpose of research. Several copies of the report may be prepared to present them to the executives concerned. It may also be used by other persons interested in the findings of the research. The research report before being finalised for presentation should be thoroughly discussed amongst the concerned authorities and researchers. The research report should have elaborate explanations and definitions. The important points and items should be stressed and anticipated by using effective communication.

Methods of Communication

There may be four methods of communication: *(i)* impromptu *(ii)* speaking from memory *(iii)* extremporaneous and (iv) reading from script. The impromptu and speaking from memory are not useful for communication of research findings. Impromptu becomes risky where accuracy is desired. Memory has memory lapses and fails to convey important information. The interception from any corner may distort the communication. Extemporaneous delivery is also not very useful. It should be prepared after thoughtful planning and organising the steps of presentation. The problem is that it is not written out in script form. The vital facts and figures are not written down before presentation. The advantages of extemporaneous communication are easiness, face to face communication, flexibility and better understanding.

Reading from the script is considered a useful method of communication. The researcher may read page by page, answer any questions that may come up and clarify all the doubts. He may express the findings with gestures, voice variations and with other indications. Effective communication involves the use of visual devices along with the written report.

7. FOLLOW-THROUGH

The efficiency of the research report should be evaluated after its preparation. Research decisions should be made with the benefits of the research report. The researcher should know the tasks and requirements of the company. The efficiency of the research may be maintained by follow-through activities. The principal researcher undertakes a careful review of the facts, findings and research report. He tries to find out the errors involved in finalising the research and preparing the research report. The inefficiencies and weaknesses afflicting the report should be avoided in order to present a clear report. There should be a systematic approach in establishing a checklist. There should be sufficient control to achieve the plans. The data should be valid and reliable. Logical and appropriate findings may be used for decisions. The decision-maker may accept the findings. In brief, follow-through involves control, validity, appropriateness and acceptability.

1. Control

The research work requires some control on various aspects such as time, costs, quality of work and other aspects of control. All aspects should be satisfied in accordance with the plans. The marketing research should audit its performance and should examine whether the goals have been fulfilled. The control includes the reporting of progress and corrective action. the planning is the basic standard of control; but the standard may lack reality and fact. So, the researcher should be competent enough to evaluate the performance in the light of plans, reality and fact. He should try to find out the causes of failure of non-achievement of objectives. If there are some faults at the planning stage, they should be avoided for future planning.

Time is the crucial factor to control the research and to complete it within the prescribed period. If the findings are presented too late, it will lose its value. The period of completion of the research work should be specified before the start of the work. It should be understood by the persons responsible for conducting the research. There should be a step by step time frame for each stage or research process. If any stage crosses the specified time, it should be checked initially so that the final stage may be completed within the specified time. If it is found that the research is being delayed on practical grounds the prescribed time may be extended. Cost-control is another important factor for controlling the research process. The costs of research should not exceed the benefits expected to be derived from it. The costs may involve several segments but only the labour cost, stationary cost and such types of other costs can be calculated. All the possible costs should be estimated before taking up the research work. The executive can get the research work conducted by an outside agency if the cost of hiring out a side agency is lower than that of conducting one's own research. The cost of hiring a particular agency should be compared with its benefits only for selecting a particular agency to conduct the research work. Determining the cost control is possible only after completing a few stages of the research work. Therefore, this is known as a posterior judgement. Identification and appraisal of the cost are essential to control the cost factor and to increase the efficiency of the marketing research. Quality is another factor involved in control. The field workers and outside agencies have to be controlled to retain a minimum level of quality. The data collection process and presentation of the findings after thorough analysis are to be constantly watched for quality preservation. Time and distance constraints are also considered for control quality. The quality of research can also be improved at the interpretation stages, by reviewing the data collection, process and the analysis technique. A final review is undertaken after the entire study has been completed.

2. Validity

Validity means correctness of various aspects of the research process. Errors should be prevented as far as possible, and their effects should be reduced to the extent possible whenever errors are incurred. A review will scrutinise such possibilities. Researchers are greatly interested in the validity of the findings. Whether the findings are valid can be interpreted in the light of their utility in the real world. The plausibility of the findings may be checked at every stage. The executive can test the findings on the grounds of their utility. The prediction or projection part of the research can be judged by the executives on estimation and on practical achievements in future. The researchers watch development over-time and watch whether their predictions come true or not. The findings may be considered hundred per cent valid if they are translated practically into action. The validity is the essential factor to evaluate the research findings.

3. Appropriateness

The appropriateness is also a factor for following through the findings. The findings should be derived in accordance with the objective. The problem-oriented research is considered appropriate. Inappropriateness will be observed if the findings are not related to the problems. Faulty communication between the researcher and the executive should be avoided to arrive at appropriate research findings. Wrong interpretations and conclusions should be avoided. The research should try to reduce the inappropriateness of the findings. Appropriateness mostly depends on the appropriate research process.

4. Acceptability

The executive may accept or reject the findings of the research. If the findings are accepted and executed by the decision makers, the test of acceptability is met. The researcher should prepare acceptable findings; but this does not mean that the research should be biased to appease the executives. The researcher should try to know the reasons why the findings would have been rejected by the executives. Therefore the researcher should always keep in touch with the executives to know their viewpoint on the direction and process of research. The acceptability factor should be kept into account by the researcher during the research process.

❖ ❖ ❖

CHAPTER 18

APPLICATIONS OF MARKETING RESEARCH IN INDIA

1. INTRODUCTION
2. MARKETING INFORMATION SYSTEM
3. SELECTED APPLICATIONS
4. MARKETING RESEARCH IN INDIA
5. FUTURE OF MARKETING RESEARCH

APPLICATIONS OF MARKETING RESEARCH IN INDIA

Marketing research has become an important tool for arriving at appropriate decisions in the field of marketing management. The underlying purpose of marketing research has been to serve people who may be executives, clients, consumers and other people interested in the findings of marketing research. The application of marketing research is an important aspect of execution techniques by people. The applications of marketing research have been analysed with reference to marketing information systems, selected areas of application, actual users of marketing researches and the future of marketing research in India.

1. INTRODUCTION

The marketing executives have several significant problems which require appropriate decisions. The critical problem areas have to be identified and given priority. The American Marketing Association has provided six areas of application of marketing research, viz., markets, products, sales force problems, distribution channel studies, advertising and other areas. Marketing research is a diverse function. There are mainly two parties connected with marketing research, i.e., client and researcher. The client may accept the appropriate report. The client generally has the decision-making authority or complete information on the goals and situation. He should inform the researcher about the problems. He should know the costs and the time taken for conducting the research. Since research results will be used by the clients, the researcher should be aware of the priorities related to decisions and problems. The researcher should know his target precisely and perform his work efficiently and sincerely. A valid and full report should be made by the researcher, who should avoid biases and prejudgments. He should know the clients' needs and should try to satisfy them accordingly. We have discussed in the previous chapters the sequence of steps in solving problems, viz., setting objectives, discovering problems, defining the problem, analysing the problem environment, searching and selecting alternatives, deciding on action and implementation of findings. The marketing information system is effectively used in marketing research.

2. MARKETING INFORMATION SYSTEM

The marketing information system influences the location and method of marketing research. The marketing information system is the same as the management information system (MIS) with the only distinction that the former applies to the marketing branch of management whereas the latter to the whole spectrum of management. The management information system has a network of computers. The present MIS is based totally on the computerised system. It has been used as mental processes for arriving at swift and unerring decisions. The MIS is considered as an extention of the scope of marketing research. It is used to solve all recurring problems. Marketing research can go beyond this and solve the non-recurring problems, too. The MIS may be used for a specialised department and may be used for monitoring and exploratory work; but the solution of complex problems would remain within the purview of the marketing research. The MIS and marketing research coordinate their functions and provide better service to the management.

The MIS is of significant aid to the marketing research for supplying data and analytical operations. It places the marketing research on immediate communication and relieves the researchers from the collection of routine data and reports. The marketing research cannot be replaced by the MIS as the latter has distinctive features over the former. The exploratory research, experiment research and descriptive research provide suitable information and reports to the management. The MIS provides data on regular basis rather than on a one time research. The research project is devised in a time of crisis and is carried out with urgency.

MIS Design Considerations

The main considerations of the marketing information system (MIS) are *(i)* information continuity, *(ii)* information aggregation, *(iii)* analytical sophistication, and *(iv)* computers. Information continuity refers to the time that elapses between the occurrence of an event and the inclusion of data. For example, if changes in inventory, sales etc. are recorded promptly, one can get accurate and upto date information of the subject. On the other hand, if the data are recorded periodically, the information can be obtained only after the elapse of the period. No information can be availed of before the expiry of the period.

Information aggregation relates to the details with which individual items are entered. for example, if the entry is aggregated with other items to produce a record of the amount, then there is considerable latitude in detail with the transactions entered. The data may vary by the type of entry. All small data are aggregated to produce wholesome data pertaining to the situation. Analytical sophistication refers to the types of models incorporated in the system. The lowest level of sophistication requires the computer to identify and retrieve the data. The computer may aggregate the data with other records. The analysis of the information and data may also be done at this stage. The computer can record and produce routine data. The exceptional problems and solutions are treated only with the marketing research.

3. SELECTED APPLICATIONS

We have discussed the individual steps involved in the marketing research project. Now we shall discuss how to use the tools of marketing research. This may include identifying market segments and the use of marketing steps for product research, advertising research, and market and sales analysis research.

1. Identifying Market Segments

Marketing research is not a panacea of all problems differing in nature and amount. There may be different types of problems for which specific marketing research may be designed. Therefore, it becomes essential to identify the market segment. Different consumption patterns may be observed according to differences in the locations, demographic characteristics, economic status, education pattern and so on. The marketers, therefore, do not find it profitable to try every individual and institution to make a customer. Some of them are either not consumers or consume very little for a profitable sale. The marketers have to find regular customers for similar uses.

Identification of groups of consumers implies finding consumers who are similar in their consumption patterns relating to a certain product or service. Identification also constitutes defining market segments or market segmentation. Groups of consumers having relatively homogeneous responses to marketing inputs are referred to as market segments. A segmentation scheme provides quantitative measurement of the size of different parts of the market. It may help product modification, price advertising, copy advertising media and so on. There may be two approaches of market identification: *(i)* consumer characteristics approach and *(ii)* product approach.

(i) Consumer Characteristics Market Segmentation

This is the oldest approach of market segmentation based on demographic characteristics, social class, consumption rates, personalities and so on. It has been observed that the socio-economic characteristics have closer association with the purchase rate of a specific product. Consumers in one group are compared with those in other groups to find out differences in them with respect to the purchase of particular products or brands or exposure to different advertising media. Besides demographic characteristics, sociological and psychological factors also influence the market segmentation. Consumers' life styles, interests and attitudes also influence market segmentation. In brief market segmentation based on consumer characteristics may be on the bases of (a) demographic measures and (b) psychographic measures.

(a) Demographic Measures: Demographic measures may be economic class, occupation, age, education and so on. Data relating to demographic measures may be collected by personal interview, telephone interviews and a questionnaire. It should be based on researches. One should not conclude that demographic measures discriminate perfectly between users and non-users. The size and nature of the family, education level of the family, and other demographic data have been used for marketing decisions.

(b) Psychographic Measures: Psychographic measures include attitudes, interests, beliefs, opinions and other activities. The psychographic data are collected using the criterion of agreement or disagreement. The statements written in random order are required to be arranged by the customers according to their interests and attitudes. The price consciousness, fashion consciousness, brand consciousness etc. are also considered while differentiating the customers. Group identification, its causes and degrees are considered under psychological measures. Researchers have shown that psychographic segments may fall under the category of traditionalist, discontended man, pleasure oriented man, ethical believer, achiever, he man and sophisticated man. Individuals may be classified as belonging to a particular group whose responses are similar. Data pertaining to psychographic market segmentation are collected on a large sample survey using a structured, disguised and self-completion on questionnaire. Psychographic segmentation has been useful for arriving at appropriate decisions specially for advertising designs.

(ii) Product Oriented Market Segmentation

Product oriented market segmentation includes identification of consumers of specific brands or products. It examines how consumers perceive different brands with regard to the different attributes they possess. It is a new approach to market segmentation. Several ideas have been coming in as a result of new researches, data collection, measurement techniques and so on. There may be two approaches of product oriented market segmentation, viz., *(a)* usage rate approach and *(b)* product attribute approach.

Usage Rate Segmentation: This approach identifies heavy, light and non-users of the said product in the light of demographic, psychographic and media usages. The purchase rate can be correlated with selected demographic variables to identify market segments. The use of a product may be based on marital status, number of children, education, age and also economic measures. Psychographic data are collected to establish the relationship between the uses of a product and different psychographic measures. It has been revealed by researches that a psychographic profile has supplemented a demographic profile. Psychographic data are collected using a structured and disguised questionnaire. Both the demographic and psychographic data can be used to differentiate between the users and non-users of the product. The product or brand attributes are also considered for deciding the market segments. Consumers, generally, determine the brand for usage by comparing the characteristics of different brands and products. Each brand or product has a distinctive position in the market. This form of market is called product or brand attribute segmentation. It focuses on how consumers perceive different brands or products. Such perceptions presumably form the basis for a purchase decision. The relative importance of the segments vary from person to person and may be used for a prediction of the market. Psychographic or demographic measures may be used separately for deciding the market mix. Scales may be developed to measure the characteristic and importance of the brand and product. The ranking of a particular brand is used for prediction of consumers' preference and buying behaviour.

Several techniques are available for collecting data. Multidimensional scaling may be used for collecting data. Multiple discriminant analysis and cluster analysis are commonly used for analysing such data. By rating the importance of different attributes, the differences between brands can be explained. The weighted combinations of attributes can distinguish the actual brands from the ideal brands. Product oriented market segmentation based upon consumers' perceptions has an added advantages over other segmentation approaches. Marketing managers can select target market segments and design effective media strategies for the segments.

2. Product Research

We have discussed the approaches of the identification of the market segments. There is need of a product line which can meet the needs of market segments when the product cycle moves towards a downfall. The marketer then has to rely on a new product to sustain the profit margin. It requires deeper research in the field of the product. The new product policy is very difficult. There is a need for finding those product opportunities which will generate a higher rate of return. This is possible by product research which may include developing product specifications, product testing and test marketing.

Developing Product Specifications

The product research aims to develop an overall product strategy based on market needs and the nature of industry. The optimum attributes of the product must be taken into account for developing product specifications. Researchers are required to determine product attributes. It is difficult to translate product attributes into a specific physical entity, because consumers cannot tell how a specific physical entity will serve the required attributes. The marketer, therefore, has to be very cautious while collecting the information pertaining to product attributes and product specification. He has to narrow down the problem precisely. The homogeneous preferences of consumers should be noted to have a good product design. The researcher can reveal those attributes which should and should not be included in the product design.

Important Attributes

It has been observed that the consumers cannot tell specific attributes required for a product because they are unaware of the product line and product specifications. Consumers at least can describe the product attributes in terms of product functions, product effects and benefits. The marketing manager and the production engineer should translate these attributes into ingredients, design characteristics and manufacturing procedures. It requires that the product research should be conducted jointly by the research-experts and the technical staff. The researcher may use depth interviewing and projective methods of word association, story telling and sentence completion to reveal the feelings and thoughts of the consumers.

The marketer has to define the relative importance of the attributes. It is revealed that brand preference is used for analysing attributes toward attributes of the alternative brands. The product research can reveal the specific operational techniques which can be used to measure product attributes. This can be done by the scaling technique which can predict purchase behaviour, different fundamental uses, and can provide the basis for ordering the relative importance of required attributes. Usage segmentation has been reliably used for prediction of brand popularity. Product attributes suggest the ideal level of each attribute for the product. The consumers can reveal the attributes within each use context. There have been *(i)* concept testing and *(ii)* preference testing for the product specification in the product research.

(i) Concept Testing: Concept testing has been used to determine potential customers' idea behind the product and the product attributes. Alternative products have been described and consumers have been asked to select the preferred product. It is operational research consisting of a sample of prospective consumers. A structured as well as unstructured questionnaire may be used for concept testing. It was observed by the researchers that the concept testing has been concentrated on questions dealing with the consumers' reaction to various product designs. The procedure involves answering questions dealing with many segments, the characteristics and the reactions to many concepts. It is possible to determine the competitive setting for the product by using multidimensional scaling techniques in large well designed samples.

(ii) Preference Testing: Paired comparison tests can be used for consumer preferences. The important features of the product may minimise the influence of external factors such as the brand name and packaging. The monadic test method is also used for testing preferences, under which test items are used under normal conditions and are evaluated using a questionnaire and rating instrument. The findings are also evaluated on a comparative basis to reveal the small differences. The consumer preferences are measured by using rating scales, rank orders and linking statements. The differences are given the percentage of the product attribute. This percentage can be compared with the products of the company as well as those of the competitors. It will predict how far a new product may be placed in the market. Seven points testing techniques have been used to measure preferences. The quartile range and dispersion are used for measuring the larger market segment. The factor analysis may evaluate product attributes. For example, without specifying the brand, the consumers can be asked to rate different types of tea. This rating would give an unbiased report about the product. Several attributes such as freshness, comfort, flavour etc. may be tested. Similarity as well as dissimilarity can be measured using such techniques.

Product Testing

After developing product specifications and designing the specific attributes, the next step involved in product research is to test the product under practical conditions. The product testing may involve paired comparison placement tests and experimental design.

(i) Paired Comparison Placement: Paired comparison placement is difficult to implement. This test involves two variations of the same product. Consumers are asked to select one variation of their liking. In case several different product variations are to be tested, a number of paired comparisons are made. Each variation is tested against the other. Although there may be only two different products at one time, the researcher can use different pairs at different times. It should be noted that different product designs should not be used at one time because this will give a misleading result.

The paired comparison tests suffer from certain drawbacks. They do not provide enough opportunity for comparing alternatives. Since the test does not permit multiple choices, it cannot be said with certainty that only two choices are more suitable. The consumers select only one choice and the selected choice may not be a true representative of the market universe. It may also cause biased results because of ignorance of the consumers towards the choice. Staggered comparison tests are used to modify the paired comparison whereby one product is tested at one time. The second product is tested after a gap or period, say, of one week or month. The products are undisclosed to the customers. However, it has been revealed that consumers are inconsistent in their preference over a number of trial uses. So, the behaviour in preference tests is mainly probabilistic rather than deterministic. It will create a greater instability when the differences are slight. It is said that the greater the difference between the test units, the less important the order bias.

The non-directive comparison method is used to avoid the drawbacks of the paired comparison and of staggered techniques. It attempts to duplicate actual market conditions in the test situation without going for the sales test. The consumers may be tested in different ways. For example, they may be given a pair of products in the same fashion without being told the differences between them. The respondents are not in a position to guess the differences. They are asked to use them without any indication whether they will be interviewed or not. They should think the product as free samples rather than product test. The interviewer, after lapse of a period, will call on and will a non-directive interview with the respondents about their experiences. The respondents have to reply to several questions pertaining to the two packets of the product. Their differences are required to be revealed. The non-directive interview will reveal a lesser degree of product differences. The non-directive method points out the possibility of product differences which are very important to the management. The minor differences may be very crucial.

(ii) Experimental Design: Experimental design has been commonly used for product research. Latin Square designs are used to eliminate the influence on sales of two important variables. Time period and advertisement may be used fruitfully for testing the influence of the advertisement. Over a period of time, factorial designs have also been used for undertaking a product experiment.

Test Marketing

Under product research, test marketing is used to test on a small basis the commercial viability of the marketing plan for a new or modified product or package. It is designed to provide a reasonable estimate of the sales and profit potentials in the new product, and to help the management identify and correct any problems with the marketing plans and product before final introduction in the market. Test marketing is used to find out the possibility of success of the product.

Test marketing is an expensive and time consuming activity. It gives some time advantage. It is required when new plant investments have to be made. Test marketing is imperative to discern the uniqueness of the product with which customers are not well acquainted. A new product therefore requires test marketing. Where costs and products failure are low, test marketing may be dispensed with. Prior testing reveals consistent and clear product superiority. A product may be benefited by the marketing organisation and distribution network. It should be kept in mind that competitors are very sensitive to the test marketing, and they may adopt a lethal strategy to defeat the purpose of the test marketing.

The extent and nature of test marketing depends upon the management and the proposed national marketing strategies. Provisions for testing the alternatives should be built in the test marketing. It involves controlled experiments whereby selected marketing variables are tested to determine their impacts upon the profit and sale. The test marketing may be successful only when two pairs of matched marketing, that is, one for the experimental group and the other for the control group are selected, including similar brands, media patterns, population, income and so on. The test markets should be normal so far as historical development, competitive advertising, industry and geographical regions are concerned. The market should neither be too small to provide meaningful conclusions nor too big to become expensive. National sales estimate, sales in units, market share, characteristics of consumers, frequency of purchases, use of the product, profitability, effectiveness of the advertising, effectiveness of marketing programme and so on.

Advertising Research

Advertising has been considered a very significant part of marketing. It involves a great deal of expenditure. So, advertising research has been given an important role in marketing research. Basic marketing research techniques also apply to advertising research, with certain adaptations. Advertising research agencies have been devoting their energies in this area for long. Advertising research is of three types: (1) setting advertising objectives, (2) copy testing and (3) media selection.

1. Setting Advertising Objectives

The marketing researcher may want to see the return in terms of sales or profits with the use of advertising research. This is a difficult measure because the sales and profits are outcomes of several factors which may be controlled as well as uncontrolled variables, apart from the advertising measures. However, there are several techniques which can reveal the impact of advertising on profits and sales. The marketing specifies the target segments in terms of geography, product characteristics and optimum sale of the product at a competitive price. Advertising objectives are measurable in terms of output, sales and profits. This is indirectly related to consumer behaviour. The use of attitude maintenance or measure of advertising effectiveness has become very important. Product benefits serve as the basis for market segmentation. Different brands possess the desired attributes. Attitudinal change objective is established. The attitudes of target audiences towards products and the attempt to determine the effect of advertising on these attitudes are decided under this research. Marketers have to measure attitudes towards their product's salient features as well as towards those of competing brands. Specific attitudinal changes must be effected in order to obtain sales. The objectives of advertising can be stated in terms of changing consumer attitudes with the selected product characteristics. Researches on attitude change have given mixed results. They have given an understanding of the process by which attitudes change. The use of attitudes as the focus of the advertising effort have great appeal because of their link with behaviour. Many advertising effectiveness measures recognise the importance of behaviour.

The research objectives assume that average consumers have reasonably stable sets of attitudes. With this assumption the researcher measures and compares one brand with another brand. The objective of advertising centres on attempting to alter the attitudinal set for the specific brand. The images of ones own brand are compared with those of competitors. Research techniques including perceptual mapping are used to collect information pertaining to behaviour which surrounds the purchase and use of the product. The objective is to weed out appropriate produce from inappropriate products. The purpose is also to know whether the product is or is not satisfactory. Activity and attitude researches, also known as the lifestyle, psychographics and opinion researches are being used to describe and predict the purchase behaviour of certain products. The attitude research is mainly related to product class, brands within the product class, lifestyle variables, demographics, media usage and so on. It portrays consumer behaviour. AIO (Activities, Interests and Opinion) are attitude measurements.

2. Copy Testing

Copy here refers to the entire advertisement including the verbal message, pictures, colours, etc. whether appearing in print, over the radio, television or some other media. It should not be confused with print media or the text of an advertisement only. Copy testing research aims to evaluate alternative methods for advertisers to present the messages. Copy testing research is divided into two major divisions: *(i)* those tests which are made before the copy is released on a full-run basis, and *(ii)* those tests which are applied after the copy is run. Technically these tests are known respectively as copy tests and advertising effectiveness. Copy testing has a limited scope, i.e., it comes after decisions have been made regarding target segments and product benefits. The advertising effectiveness represents an effort to improve the effectiveness of advertising. The basic difference between before and after tests is the purpose of the test. If the objective is to make an improvement as in the advertising copy prior to the full-run release it is known as before test, and if it aims to improve the advertising copy after a full run release, it is referred to as after test, although the distribution is not always clear because sometimes release takes place through several media. If the purpose is to determine which copy is to be released, it is before test. The fundamental objective behind the test research is to find out how advertising accomplishes its effect. Generally the results are measured to evaluate advertising effectiveness. The objectives of the advertising are taken into account for advertising researches or tests. Measures dealing with recognition, recall, comprehension and attitude changes are the typical measures used to judge advertising effectiveness.

Before Tests

The before tests are done by accepting the consumer as jury, rating scales, portfolio tests, psychological tests, laboratories testing, inquiries, simulated sales tests and day after recall tests.

(i) Consumer Jury: A group of consumers who represent potential buyers of the product are asked to vote on the alternatives of the advertisement. The copy may be made up in dummy form. The consumers who are the respondents are asked to rank the alternatives according to their preference, interest and influence. The rating is done on the basis of which advertisement is disliked the least. A television programme may be used to expose the variation in terms of liked, disliked and indifferent. The television may include the programme analyser whereby two buttons are given. When the respondent finds the programme interesting, he can push one button and when the programme is uninteresting, he can push the other button. If he is indifferent towards the programme, he does not push any button. The recording machine can summarise the data.

(ii) Rating Scales: Rating scales require the establishment of measures for effective copy and numerical weights. The weights indicate the measures or standard's worth. The advertisement is rated in accordance with the scale values and the numerical score. The total of the individual standard scores gives the numerical rating which is carried out by the advertising agency. Rating scales have been used to measure the attitude change resulting from exposure to the advertisement. The differential effect on readers' attitude to print advertisement can be recorded. Differential measurement is obtained by asking respondents to rate a number of statements on the extent to which they like. Tests are also done to measure the effectiveness of various types of scales.

(iii) Portfolio Tests: Mixed advertisements are tested and controlled. Sometimes, the advertisements are placed in dummy form. The respondents are given the dummy forms or folios and asked to go through them. The respondents are asked to recall the advertisement and record their attitudes. Additional questions may be asked about the advertisement and the extent of their belief recorded. The portfolio test provides a measure of selective exposure, selective perception and selective retention. It is used to test the merits of two or more alternative advertisements. Experimental design may be used to examine the pre-test efficiency of the advertisement. The control folio is compared with the given portfolio. Besides its advantages, there are many disadvantages such as that it requires memory factor, recall and recognition. Only large differences in the advertisement may produce significant differences because of the strong respondent interest in the product and brand. This test may not be effective if the test involves a strong emotional approach and personal understanding. Abnormal conditions cannot be tested properly. They can be worked only on radio and television, and it is very difficult to effect on other media. A before-after experimental design can be worked on a theatre type of test. This test has limited utility.

(iv) Psychological Tests: The individual mind displays certain reactions to an advertisement. There may be a wide variety of such reactions such as self pity, security, nostalgia, fear etc. After testing, the advertisement can be rated. A psychological test involves a large number of research techniques including word association, sentence completion, and interviewing in depth. The underlying objective behind the test is to find out what respondents see in various advertisements and how they review them. Such tests are administered by the experts.

(v) Laboratory Testing: Laboratory measurements of the respondent's psychological responses to the advertisement are used with the objective of measuring responses to stimuli. It has been observed that galvanic skin response like the lie detector has been used for measuring emotional changes with the help of an electronic device. The advertisement effectiveness is judged on the basis of "arousal" registered with the help of the machine. But it is not a very dependable measure because arousal does not necessarily mean a favourable reaction.

The recording of eye movement is another electronic device to measure the effectiveness of the advertisement. The eye camera records the horizontal and vertical movement of the eye ball. It reveals what part of the advertisement produces the initial reaction, what part is interesting and what is confusing. But interpretation is very difficult because it is not feasible to correlate eye action with the thinking of the readers. It is not very scientific.

Pupil dilation is another test whereby the respondents receive an interesting or pleasant stimulus. The pupil contracts when the respondents receive an uninteresting or unpleasant stimulus. With the comparison of changes with the base line, i.e., neutral stimuli, the effectiveness can be measured. The pupilometer measures emotional response to a stimulus. The techistoscope permits researchers to control the time an advertisement is exposed to. The perception and comprehension can be understood under rigid conditions. The beliefs and values can be determined to yield a more desirable attitude.

(vi) Inquiries: Inquiries can produce the direct result of the advertisement's worth. It may provide data for estimating sales. The inquiry if directed to the advertisements objective can reveal the degree of its effectiveness. Inquiry tests may be used in different ways. For example, the same offer may be placed in different pieces of copy and in different issues to record the effectiveness of the advertisement before the real advertisement. The same copy can be placed in different journals or newspapers. The adjusted returns will indicate the best copy. The long-term effect cannot be measured; only the immediate effect is measured. Only local media can be tested. Small differences may not be detected.

(vii) Simulated Sales Tests: Simulated sales tests are exposed to an alternative piece of copy through point of purchase displays or direct mail. The copy to be tested is made up in the form of store display material. Product sales are measured in each store before and after the introduction of the display pieces. The changes in sales between the two periods for the two groups, compared with the biggest sales increase, is presumed to have the best copy. Simulated sales tests are simpler and less expensive.

After Tests

The after test is the measure of advertising effectiveness. Since the results of an advertisement are confounded by the frequencies of several factors, it becomes difficult to measure the effectiveness of a particular advertisement. Therefore, after tests are designed in a number of ways. These are based mainly on the respondents' memory which has certain limitations. The respondents can remember only a part of the advertisement. Therefore, the repeated exposure of the advertisement is required. The performance of a given advertising should be measured by repeated exposure.

Recognition tests take qualified readers of a given issue of a magazine and ask them what they have seen and read. They are asked what part of the advertisement has been read. The respondents may not give the true picture of the advertisement because they may confuse the advertisement.

3. Media Selection

The advertiser selects appropriate media for the advertisement from the larger number of alternative media available. He must have the market segments in mind which he has to reach. They decide the frequency of the message exposure to effect a change in behaviour to increase sales. A specific selection is made in terms of media and issues. The media selection affects such things as the recall of the advertising messages, competitive advertising strategy, target population, media vehicles etc. because these have a greater impact on the advertising effectiveness. The respondents selected for viewing the advertising media should be prospective buyers. An important step in making media comparisons is to differentiate between prospective and non-prospective buyers. The effectiveness of the advertising message can be evaluated on the basis of vehicle distribution, vehicle exposure, advertising perception, advertising exposure, sales response and so on.

1. Print Media: Media research is concerned with measuring the size of vehicle audiences. In the case of print media, one or more major editorial reports may form the basis of analysis. The Audit Bureau of Circulation (ABC) reports about the utility of particular print media. The number of readers is the basis for providing information about the print media. Probability of exposure index to determine audience size, accumulation and duplication of specific media are used. The estimate of the size of readers for a given publication will prove how far the print media are popular. However, it may be a biased report because many non-readers may reply positively for the sake of displaying status. So a periodical study of such data may avoid bias in response.

2. Radio and Television: Radio and television have distinctive features over print media such as magazines and newspapers. Radio and television have no proof that they have been received. It is difficult to exclude advertising from the main messages of radio and television. The researcher can apply any of the four methods of evaluating the advertising effectiveness, viz., coincidental method, roster recall, the audiometer and diary method.

(i) Coincidental Method: The coincidental method is based on sampling of homes having telephones to inquire what radio and television programmes have been listened to or viewed. The researcher may ask what programmes on which channel, the members of the family are listening or viewing. He may ask the name of the sponsor or product advertised. It is based on the assumption that calls are spread evenly throughout the programme. This method has the advantages of speed and economy. But this method is limited to those people who have a telephone. The total size of the audience cannot be accurately estimated. It may not provide continuous information. No one can provide information about the total audience of a programme. The telephone may be attended by the respondents only during suitable hours but the programme can be released at different hours. The telephone coincidental method may not be literally followed.

(ii) Roster Recall: Roster recall is a personal interview which is held shortly after the particular time period of the advertisement. A list or roster is used to aid respondents in recalling what programmes have been listed and viewed. Since the interview is held after certain hours of the advertisement, the memory comes into block. The information may be inflated or deflated as a result of status. The less popular advertisement may be discriminated against. This method cannot provide any continuous information about the nature of the audience. It is not possible to estimate how many persons have viewed the program.

(iii) The Audiometer: The audiometer is the machine which records the programme; it is fitted with a television set. A continuous record of the use of the set is possible by decoding the tape. The audiometer can provide the number of the total audience, average audience and share of the audience. The measure of the cumulative audience can be obtained as the audiometer remains the same. Data can be classified according to the region, city, age of the male head, income and number of children. It relies on mechanical observation which may not always be correct.

(iv) Diary Method: The respondents are given a specially designed diary for recording the programmes heard or viewed. The interviewer may cooperate by helping to record or hear to record the programme, or viewing it at the time that it occurs. The data are obtained on individual viewing programme. Continuous panel operation can provide useful duplication data pertaining to radio and television programmes as well as to magazines and newspapers. Accumulation of data is possible, and they can therefore be predicted at any time. The American Research Bureau (ARB) has often been using the diary method.

Market and Sales Analysis Research

Marketing research has been used for setting marketing policies, planning marketing operations, controlling marketing operations and sales units. Market and sales analysis research include the identification and measurement of all variables àffecting sales. Specifically, measurements of the market potential, sales forecasting, sales territory evaluation and sales performance are included under market and sales analysis research. Market and sales analysis research are very important tools of management. This is invaluable to the management in pointing to the need for changes in the design of sales territories, the size and dispersion of the field force, preparation of sales expense budget and setting the guiding norms of activity or efficiency. Marketing research has been concentrating on the development of market potentials and market share analysis. Similarly sales research deals with sales analysis, short and long range forecasting and establishment of sales quotas. Sales forecasting is used for predicting sales of a particular product for a given period of time. Sales analysis includes analysis of the company's sales by territories, by type and size of customers, by product and other criteria. This section deals with (1) Market Analysis, (2) Sales Forecasting and (3) Sales Analysis.

1. Market Analysis

Market analysis is undertaken to reveal a set of geographical sales potentials, that is the maximum possible sales opportunities for all sellers of a product or service in a specific area. While estimating the market potential, the data of substitution and conditions of substitution are evaluated. Market potentials are confused with the sales forecast, whereas market potentials refer to total sales possibilities, and sales forecast refers to possible units of sale of a product by a seller.

Method: The market potentials can be developed by defining sales territories, allocation effort, sales quota, data collection and interpretation.

(i) Defining Sales Territories: Sales territories should be defined for estimating market potentials. The workload of the sales force, turnover, their overall performance and efficiency of the individual sales representative are defined. The workload is decided on the basis of a number of variables such as number and size of accounts, average order size, location, travel time and non-selling activities. The workload is also defined in terms of the number of clients and cell frequencies, designing sales territories and so on. The firm should try to eliminate extreme cases and insufficient potential.

(ii) Allocation Effort: Design of sales territories is an important function for developing the market potential. The next process is to allocate resources to each territory over a period of time. This requires knowledge about the relative worth of each territory and response of prospective buyers. The allocation of resources is done by the principle of incremental return for each unit of resources across all sales territories. The sales force, advertising and non-advertising promotional efforts should be allocated after consideration of potentials. The marginal return is considered the basis for the allocation of funds to a particular area. Advertising expenditure can be allocated in terms of the potential of the area. Although the potential is the focus for attention of individual worth of the market, no firm can rely completely on it for resource allocation because the potential does not reveal the competitive structure of the market and the firm's ability to exploit the market. The marketer may need some useful data for ascertaining the market potential, viz., the number of brands in the market and the brand share of each market, the trend of each market's brand amount of money spent by advertising agencies, the price structure and distribution form.

The marketing manager estimates the responsiveness of each market on the given advertising and sales effort, besides deciding the potential and competitive structure of the market. The manager allocates the funds to a market to the extent it is profitable. It requires exact measurements of the sales effort. The allocation of funds to different markets and returns thereon can decide the order of the use of funds.

(iii) Sales Quotas: After deciding the market potentials and resource allocation, the next step is to decide sales quotas. It is important to take an appropriate market decision. Sales quotas consider post sales performance and possibilities of sales increase as a result of sales effort and competitors' reactions. Quotas are decided for each territory and for each sales representative. Market potential does not mean that the sales quota is higher because the competitors may have shared a total or a higher percentage of the market. Sales quotas as discussed above are decided to fix sales goals and for measuring the efficiency of sales representatives. The sales representative's effectiveness is the basic determinant of sales return. Therefore, it is necessary to take into account the market potential, competitors' efforts, sales quotas and other factors which influence the sales of the area of the representative. The experience of the sales representative, the motivational effort of the sales representative and company efforts have a significant impact on the achievement of the sales quotas.

(iv) Measuring Market Potential: The market potential has been exploited for the purpose of determining the sales quotas and achieving the sales returns. Therefore, measuring of the market potential is an essential factor for the successful achievement of the market goal. This can be done by collecting (a) direct data and (b) corollary data.

(a) Direct Data: Direct data are data on the actual product to estimate potentials. The total sales of a product are considered for estimating the market potential. Sales take account of the characteristics of the individual markets and post sales efforts. The total industry sales are broken down into the firm's sales and the territory's sales. Sales are expressed as a percentage of total sales of the industry. Thus, the share of one firm in a territory can be estimated easily. The firm's total share in the industry's sales will be a summing up of the shares of all the territories. Comparison of potentials of each area will provide an insight to the weak areas where the manager has to exert to increase sales. The potential return is taken into account for allocating resources. There is no certainty that the sales efforts in difficult areas will automatically improve the situation. The behaviour of competitors is also taken into account to decide the degree of the sales efforts in such areas. The government records may be relied upon to find out the extent to which the marketer can achieve. Trade associations and other institutions can supply suitable information pertaining to sales. There are different agencies which can supply data pertaining to the sales of several industries. They can supply data according to region, product and brand. However, there are several industries for which sales data are not available. There may also be several limitations to such data. They may be ambiguous, unclassified, and duplicated whereas there is a need for breaking down the total market data into homogeneous parts to analyse quantitative marketing data in relation to available published data. The Government of India is preparing and publishing data pertaining to agriculture, forestry and fisheries, mining, construction, manufacturing, transportation, electricity, communication, trade, finance, banks and insurance.

(b) Corollary Data: The corollary data method can use single or multiple factors. It is based on the idea that a given series of data are related. The second series of data, similarly, can be used to indicate distribution of data.

The single factor indexes are simple corollary data. The use of the sales of one product may indicate the market potential of another product. The best example is demand, where complementary demand is derived from the total demand data. The number of consumers of petrol can be calculated from the number of scooters and cars in the area. From the using corollary data, the researcher should know that the two series are actually related. There may be a number of corollary data. Population and income may be used to decide market potentials. For example, if there is twice the population in an area as compared to other areas, the market potential of the former area will be twice that of the second area. Data pertaining to disposable income are available in government publications such as the Reserve Bank of India — Annual Reports, Statistical Abstract of India. These data may be used to assess the market potential of the area. Similarly a product meant for industrial workers may be evaluated by the data of industrial workers. There may be several single corollary data which can be used for the estimation of market potentials. It is necessary to compare two series of data over a period of time to establish the relationship between them. On the other hand, if total industry sales are available, the use of direct data method may be useful. This method indicates the data of past sales. It does not give the actual potential or what it will be in future. If there does not exist a close relationship between the index series and the company's sales, the index series may give a wrong impression.

It should be noted that market potential indexes are not developed from a single series only. Sometimes, a combination of several factors may be determinants of market potentials. The indexes of market potentials based on multiple factor indexes are being prepared by expert agencies and publishers. Special multiple factor indexes are designed to measure the relative potentials of different markets for a product only. It takes into account several factors which influence the sales of a given product when these indexes are prepared for some specific products. They are special multiple factor indexes and can predict market potentials of those products. Such indexes measure market potentials accurately. However this method suffers from certain drawbacks. Persons preparing the indexes may use their personal judgement. There cannot be a limited number of factors. Unlimited multiple factors cannot be used for calculating the indexes of market potentials. If absolute data are available for indexes, it is better to use the absolute data, i.e., direct data instead of indexes prepared from the data.

Multiple regression analysis is used to eliminate subjective aspects of the multiple factors. If the dependent variable cannot be established, it is not possible to obtain the regression equation. It is possible to study the relationship between sales and explanatory variables using regression analysis. The macro-level analysis is used to estimate sales potentials.

The general multiple factor indexes are prepared on the basis of income, retail sales and population. It differs from special indexes in the sense that the former is designed for use with many products while the latter is related with one specific product. It makes indexes to measure the real market potential, instead of the measure of past sales distribution. Comparisons of different general indexes reveal significant results pertaining to market potentials. The multiple factor indexes provide a unique and effective way of projecting data. It is easy to determine market potentials with the help of general multiple factor indexes.

2. Sales Forecasting

Sales forecasting is used to predict sales of a particular product, company and other units during a particular period. It is an important tool of decision-making for production and inventory scheduling, planning, manpower requirements, advertising, sales force expenditure and so on. It is used for the derivation of the strategy. Many companies can undertake accurate planning with this help. The problem of uncertainty about planning is removed by the alternative forecasts. There are several variables whose relationships can contribute greatly to the improved forecasts. Computers can be used for forecasting purposes. Sales forecasting is a complex subject which uses a large number of concepts and techniques. General economic indicators, industry data, plans for new products and anticipated action, price and promotion plans are several important variables for sales forecasting. There may be subjective methods and objective methods of sales forecasting.

1. Subjective Methods: Subjective methods include judgements or opinions of experts. A large number of data inputs from the organisational level, sales representatives and sales supervisors are used for forecasting purposes. The process of sales forecast can vary from firm to firm and within a firm from time to time. Experts like sales supervisors, product managers, company economists and marketing experts use the general economic climate, reactions of competitors and other variables. The sales forecast may be discussed with the sales representatives and incorporate changes to forward it to higher level management where the forecast is reviewed and sales forecast is finalised. Short-term forecasts may be added up to draw long-range forecasts. Sales representatives can do a better job of forecasting than the objective method. They can adjust their plans to the dynamics of the market requirements because they are well aware of the market positions. The executives can make an independent forecast of sales because they have reliable factual data and the ability to make mature judgement. The sales forecasts of the sales force can be reconciled to arrive at the final sales forecasts. They may discuss together and consider new ideas to modify the sales forecast. There is possibility of disagreement among the various estimates, then the chief executive can make his final decision.

The subjective method has the advantages of simplicity and uses expert views and opinions. However, the opinions may be too optimistic or too pessimistic. The subjective method is to be influenced by expertise error and contagion error. The former error is on account of the personal bases of the expert. This can be minimised on a trial basis to determine the relative magnitude. This error can be corrected with more information pertaining to the error, The contagion error is the tendency of individuals to be biased by factors. This error can be minimised by supplementary information of a general nature.

2. Objective Methods: Objective methods are statistical methods of forecasting. These methods may vary from simple to too complicated. A computer can be used to forecast sophisticated data. Only the most common techniques are discussed here:

(i) Trend Analysis: The trend analysis assumes that the current level of sale will continue in future. This is the simple predictive model which can be relied upon for a short period under stable conditions. All extrapolation techniques assume that past positions will continue. They are identified and measured. This method is useful to forecast a recurring type of data. The trend analysis is supported by long-term trend, cyclical variations, seasonal variations and irregular fluctuations. They can separate cyclical, seasonal and irregular influences from the trend.

(ii) Regression Analysis: The company's sales and economic factors can be correlated to forecast the sale. The income and education influence the sales. For example, when income increases, a person may like to purchase a car. The degree of relationship can be established with the use of correlation and regression techniques. The forecasting of general economic factors are done by the experts of the area. The marketer thus uses expert estimates of several individual experts. This enables the company to make better forecasts of sales. It may provide a lead lag relationship between the socio-economic series and company sales. Regression analysis is more useful and scientific than that of trend analysis or time-series, because in the former case the factors influencing sales are also forecast and their impact on sales are computed, whereas the latter analyses the sale data only. The expert forecast is undertaken by the specialised people leaving enough time for top executives to decide their other commitments.

(iii) Survey Method: This method is based on the survey done for a time. The survey is undertaken for getting information from the consumers. The researchers can ask the consumers several important questions and base their forecasts on the data collected. The survey method is more expensive and time consuming. The information may be biased if the consumers guess that the information is being collected for research purposes.

3. Sales Analysis

Sales analysis means actual analysis of sale-results according to the product, customer, order size and territory. The objective of sales analysis is to find out the areas of strengths and weaknesses. The maximum and lowest volume of sales in accordance with the product, territory, customers and order size can be revealed by sales analysis.

(i) Sales analysis by product: The products may be overcrowded unless strong action is taken. There may be such products which do not give an adequate return. On the other hand, there may be some products which give a higher return but are starved of investment. They are technically known as weak products and strong products. They are treated with disinvestment and depth investment respectively.

The firm should classify products by general groups such as industrial and consumer. It might classify separately each product fluctuations by colour, size etc. The detailed breakdown of product features may show weak and strong spots to be corrected. The product analysis may reveal market share trends, the effect of volume on product, contribution margins, profitability and so on. The purpose of analysis is to assist management in its product detection decisions. The standard cost accounting and market data of each product may give suitable suggestions. Product analysis will be very useful if combined with area analysis.

(ii) Sales analysis by territory: The sales analysis is carried out with the basic sales record which reveals the customer's name, location, products sold, quantity of each item sold, price per unit, total sale per product and so on. The order size, type of business user or wholesaler are computed to find out weak and strong territories. It may reveal geographical control units. The rural, semi-urban and urban areas will have a differing amount of sales which the marketing manager can decide accordingly. Comparison between potentials and results reveals the control-area in a particular territory. The territorial sales may be compared with the total sales to reveal the differences therein. Territories giving sales below potential may be given special attention to improve the sales volume. Reasons for the shortfall can be analysed and corrected accordingly.

(iii) Sales analysis by customer: The sales volume per customer can be a basis for motivation and incentives to improve sales. It has been revealed that a small percentage of customers accounts for a large percentage of sales. They can be motivated to purchase more units of the product. Inquiries can be made about their feelings and attitudes towards the product. The cost accounting is used to determine the useful number of customers. The smaller size customers can be dropped because they fetch profitable orders. More concentration on larger accounts may increase sales. The product, area and customer analysis of sales pinpoint the weak spots which require prompt attention. Remedial action can be taken to remove the weakness.

(iv) Sales analysis by order-size: The order-size analysis may point out good sales volume. It may be classified on the basis of originality. Cost accounting may indicate the cost of securing and handling an order. The loss-recurring order may be dropped. Analysis of sales by order size combined with product analysis, territory analysis and customer analysis will reveal exact spots of correction. The corrective action may consist of training of the sales representative of the area and dropping certain products, customers and orders.

(v) Distribution cost analysis: This is the technique for the determination of the costs of performing specific marketing activities and determining the costs and profits. It is used in contribution accounting to determine the profitability of products and market segments. Marketing and production variables are also analysed in relation to volume of sales. The direct costs and indirect costs are separately analysed. The direct costs in marketing include credit costs, shipping and merchandising costs. The indirect costs or overhead costs are similarly analysed to determine the profitability of a sale. The comparison of cost and return by customer and by product will direct the market manager to correct the weak situations.

4. MARKETING RESEARCH IN INDIA

Marketing research in India has been started very late. It was totally unknown upto 1960 when Hindustan Thompson Associates Limited published the Thompson Urban Market Index and Thompson Rural Market Index, although statistics and information useful for marketing research have been available since the latter part of the nineteenth century when the census in India started with the prime motive of revenue collection by the British.

The present Thompson Urban Market Index covers 20,000 population in different markets. There are a large number of market indexes useful to marketers of different commodities. These indexes pertain to households, literacy, employment in different industries, consumption goods produced and sold particularly television, radio, telephones and cars. Also, bank deposits, chemists and druggists, electricity consumption and entertainment facilities. These statistics are available for each market and are compared with the economic indicators. There are about 884 towns which are covered by such researches.

It is a unique form of marketing research. It can be depended on for the marketing decisions. The effectiveness of advertising expenditure can be checked by such researches. These are useful for planners and economists, media researchers, advertisers and trade associations. But it is not in depth research of consumer behaviours and other researches. Greater Mumbai is the largest market in India. It is taken as a base for comparison.

Thompson Rural Market Index is useful for the agricultural sectors. It has revealed inter-district disparities in market potential. Almost all districts have been covered by this research. This index gives information pertaining to literate males, illiterate females, cultivators, agricultural and non-agricultural workers' holdings, cropped area, irrigated area, area under food crops and non-food crops, rainfall and soil, and livestock. Midnapur district has been considered as the base index of 100. All other markets are measured in comparison to this market. Markets have been classified into five categories A, B, C, D and E. Index numbers between 70 and 100 are A class, between 50 and 70 are B Class, between 40 and 50 are C class, between 25 and 50 are D class and below 25 are E class. The indexes have been divided for varieties of purposes, viz., descending orders, shares in state and zone, rural economic indicators and so on.

Marketing Research Agencies

There are a large number of research agencies in India which are engaged in marketing research. There are the Indian market research Bureau, Market Motivation Studies, Market Research and Data Processing consultants, Market Research and Advertising Services, Marketing Advertising Associates P. Ltd., Indian Institute of Public Opinion, Marketing Services, and several other advertising companies and marketing research bureau.

Government Agencies

Government agencies are engaged in collecting data pertaining to population, occupation, crop patterns, irrigation, education, health, livestock hospitals, marketing units etc. The Gazeteers of India publish very useful information pertaining to agriculture, industries, banking and finance, communication, economic trends, general administration, law, order and justice, education, medical and public health and social services. This information and data regarding districts and villages are also prepared.

The district credit plan is another source of useful marketing research. This plan is prepared by the lead bank of the district. It includes district profiles, and depth study of blocks and resources.

5. FUTURE OF MARKETING RESEARCH IN INDIA

Marketing research in India has wide scope. It has to be used for farmers, small businessmen, price pattern and consumer needs.

1. Marketing Research for Farmers

Agriculture is the pivot of the Indian Economy. Farmers require prediction of certain variables for proper discharge of their duties. If the farmers are ignorant of the latest technology, they cannot produce adequate amount of goods. But Indian farmers are mostly ignorant of these developments although the Government of India has appointed several commissions to examine the problems prevailing in agriculture. The Royal commission on Agriculture, Imperial council of Agricultural Research and the Famine Enquiry Commission have been several commissions to find out the problems and solutions of the agricultural sector. The farmers are given some information pertaining to their activities. The agriculturists need knowledge of the structure of agricultural markets, characteristics of agricultural products, marketing agencies, finance, marketing channels, market changes, malpractices of markets, storage facilities, transportation, agricultural prices and methods of sale.

The agricultural markets are generally wholesale and terminal markets. Agricultural products are typical products regarding weight volume and perishability. The marketing of agricultural products is also very typical. The open action, quoting of prices, private sale etc. are the various methods of marketing. There are village purchasers, itinerant purchasers, "adatyas" etc. to purchase agricultural products and sell them in the usual agricultural markets. There are different sources of agricultural finance, e.g., cooperative societies, banks, merchants etc. There are several marketing channels through which agricultural producers are sold. There are various market charges which are paid by the farmers. The agricultural market may be regulated or irregulated. In an unregulated market, the farmers are exploited heavily because they have to pay different charges to the marketer. Manipulation of weights, deductions, deceptive bargaining, unscrupulous brokers and credit sales are several problems to which the farmers are exposed during the course of their marketing activities. The marketer indulges in unethical practices of adulteration of several products. In the absence of adequate and suitable storage facilities, the farmers are unable to get remunerative prices for their products. Since the transportation facilities are inadequate the produce does not come to the cities and government authorised mundies. The lack of standardised quality renders the agriculturists unremunerative, because the farmers are compelled to sell at a lower price in the name of low quality of the produce. Recently, the government has arranged publication and announcement of approved agricultural prices. Akashvani, All India Ratio, Doordarshan, Television and other institutions are announcing the agricultural prices. They try to forecast the prices of agricultural produce. Farmers are benefited by such announcements and advertisements. Since the communication and transportation facilities are not widespread in rural areas, the farmers are not adequately benefited by such announcements and publication. There is need of in depth researches of agricultural marketing.

The agricultural production is forecast on the basis of various factors such as crop patterns and economic factors. If the area under cultivation increases, the agricultural produce can increase. In India the area under wheat cultivation is declining as a result of increase of the area under cash-crops. The cropping pattern is influenced by the soil, climate, weather, rainfall and technological improvements. Improved irrigation facilities have enhanced agricultural produce like sugarcane, tobacco etc.

Price factors also influence the cropping pattern, and insurance against risks is taking another turn to increase crop production. Fertilisers and other agricultural inputs have added to the agricultural production. The green revolution has achieved a break-through in agriculture. It has increased agricultural production. The socio-economic and cultural conditions have improved in the light of the developing trend of agricultural production. The new patterns of motivation, attitudes and behaviour have influenced the consumers. These are the reasons why rural markets now require transistors, furniture, clocks, television, cosmetics and other modern varieties of consumption goods. Use of modern inputs into agriculture such as irrigation facilities, fertilisers and high yielding varieties of seeds have changed the rural market.

Researches into agricultural marketing and rural markets will reveal the emerging dimension of the market. Marketing information on rural areas is needed. The researches will reveal how far increasing investment is needed in distribution, advertising and marketing while intelligence will expand the marketing opportunities in rural areas. Through marketing research businessmen will know how to develop marketing techniques to promote their sales.

The future for marketing research in rural areas will be very bright. If a publicity company enters the rural areas, it can penetrate new markets. All the producers are trying to enter the rural market because the market potential is very high there. The expected competition in future requires that the marketers should enter there through proper researches. The marketing researches can reveal more problems and their solutions. Marketing revenues in rural areas can be successfully revealed by appropriate researches. Scientific marketing management for rural areas is very essential to meet the growing needs of consumption and production in rural areas, which is possible only with marketing research.

2. Marketing Research for Businessmen

Businessmen, particularly small businessmen, are suffering from a number of problems. They do not have marketing research facilities. Only very big business houses have a research department. The research facilities are also possible on account of available published data.

Small businessmen have low investment capacity and depend mainly on the local market for the sale of their products. They have to face a number of other problems such as finance, production and marketing. The researches on the problems of the small businessmen are negligible. There are some financial institutions such as Industrial Finance Corporation, State Financial Corporations, Commercial Banks and other institutions which conduct general research into the problems of business and trade. The small business houses suffer from marketing problems. Their produces are unstandardised and of varying quality. Therefore, the business houses face several problems. It is considered that marketing research is very essential for businessmen.

3. Researches for Price Pattern

The price pattern has been influencing the market situation. Agricultural goods cannot be produced beyond a certain limit because of the vagaries of the monsoon. The price policy pertaining to various products can be studied to forecast the market situations. Price fluctuations influence the production. The monopolistic situation may harass the consumers. Therefore, the marketer needs to research prices of inputs as well as outputs.

Essential commodities prices influence the total price of good articles which are stable, while other prices may remain almost constant.

The Indian market is governed by the price factors. Free competition prices have no existence in the Indian situation. Price regulation is essential to constraint the inflationary tendency. For maintaining the prices constant, the inputs of various produce should be subsidised. for example, irrigation equipment, fertilisers and seeds should be supplied at subsidised rates to the agriculturists. Similarly the cotton textile industry should be supplied cotton at lower prices. The deal pricing encourages production and investment. The government tries to hold agricultural prices at a constant level to benefit consumers and provide incentives to the producers. The buffer stocks developed by the government have been successfully containing the price level. The Marketing Research Bureau in India performs research on consumer behaviour and supplying information to various industries and business firms. The National Sample survey, the National Council of Agriculture and Economic Research and the Census Commissioner of India are conducting useful research on consumer behaviour and on expenditure pattern.

It has been revealed by such research that the consumer behaviour has been influenced by different factors such as rural and urban areas, the age of the head of the family, the size of the house, family education, household pattern and so on. The census in Indian provides very useful data pertaining to physiography, geology, minerals, forests, soils, rainfall, demographic structure and trends, laid utilisation, cropping pattern, agricultural inputs, industrial statistics, employment statistics and socio-economic characteristics.

Motivational researches have to find out the "why" and "how" of consumer preferences. The marketing research programme has to take into account the changing consumer behaviour. In India marketing research is generally undertaken by the advertising agencies. They have to find out the behaviour pattern of the consumers. There is need of both quantitative and qualitative researches. Advance research techniques will have to be applied to marketing researches in India.

4. Researches on Consumer Bahaviour

The researches on consumer behaviour include basic needs, as well as psychological and sociological needs. The basic needs have to be satisfied before going on to other needs of life. The researches may reveal whether the consumer satisfies the basic needs or not. What is the extent of satisfaction of the basic needs? These will pave the base for arriving at other decisions. The psychological needs follow the basic needs. They may be physiological, pleasure satisfaction, security, ownership and self-esteem. The consumers desiring to satisfy psychological needs may require different commodities and services for their satisfaction. The sociological needs follow the psychological needs. This may include love for family, social acceptance. The needs are prime movers of the consumers' behaviour.

The consumers need different types of satisfaction. Therefore the marketer has to find out the needs level of the consumer.

The researches in India have shown that the consumers' behaviour have been influenced not only by the hierarchy of needs but also by advertising, displays, personal talks, attitudes and opinions. It is a well established fact that the buying activity is influenced by awareness, knowledge, liking, preference, conviction and desires. The personal aspirations, temperament, cultural and organisational influences have a profound effect on consumer-behaviour. The understanding and goodwill of the organisation also influence the purchasing pattern of customers.

❖ ❖ ❖